INGENIOUS MACHINISTS

To Maureen,
fellow historian

Best regards,
Tony

Pawtucket Bridge and Falls (anon., c. 1810), Rhode Island Historical Society.
D.B. (Anonymous). [Pawtucket Bridge and Falls with Slater Mill]. Pawtucket, RI ca. 1810. Watercolor and ink on paper. Painting. RHi X5 22.

Two Inventive Lives from the American Industrial Revolution

ANTHONY J. CONNORS

excelsior editions

Published by
STATE UNIVERSITY OF NEW YORK PRESS
Albany

Printed in the United States of America

EXCELSIOR EDITIONS
is an imprint of State University of New York Press

For information, contact
State University of New York Press
www.sunypress.edu

Production, Laurie Searl
Marketing, Kate R. Seburyamo

Library of Congress Cataloging-in-Publication Data

Connors, Anthony J.
Ingenious machinists : two inventive lives from the American industrial revolution / Anthony J. Connors.
pages cm. — (Excelsior editions)
Includes bibliographical references and index.
ISBN 978-1-4384-5401-6 (hardcover : alk. paper)
ISBN 978-1-4384-5402-3 (pbk. : alk. paper)
E-ISBN 978-1-4384-5403-0 (ebook)
1. Wilkinson, David, 1771–1852. 2. Moody, Paul. 3. Machinists—United States—Biography. 4. Inventors—United States—Biography. 5. Industrial revolution—United States. I. Title.
HD8039.M22U695 2014
677'.02850922—dc23
[B] 2014002126

10 9 8 7 6 5 4 3 2 1

To Sharon

and

to the memory of my parents

Contents

Illustrations

Acknowledgments

This book started as a doctoral dissertation, under the guidance of Professor Drew McCoy, whose gentle criticism and clear vision greatly influenced the outcome. Clark University history professors Janette Greenwood and Amy Richter helped sharpen my writing and encouraged me to consider the social implications of this story. I also benefited greatly from the contributions of my fellow Clark history graduate students Russ McClintock, Carol Cullen, Lisa Connelly Cook, and Terry Delaney. The New England Regional Fellowship Consortium provided financial assistance and the opportunity to explore the valuable research collections at the Massachusetts Historical Society, the Harvard Business School's Baker Library, and the Rhode Island Historical Society.

It was eight years between dissertation and book, as there always seemed to be something else to work on. When I began to prepare it for publication, many people (some who had helped the first time) provided historical guidance and documents, including Gray Fitzsimons and Martha Mayo (Lowell), Andrian Paquette (Slater Mill), Brad Utter (Cohoes), David C. Mountain (Newbury), and the late Betty Johnson (Pawtucket). For illustrations I'd like to thank Jack Herlihy (Lowell National Park), Melanie Nichols (Lowell Historical Society), J. D. Kay and Dana Signe Monroe (Rhode Island Historical Society), Kelly Cobble (Adams National Park), and the staffs of the Smithsonian Institution Archives, Pawtucket Public Library, and the New York State Library. Audrey Connors and John Devlin helped prepare the illustrations. Beth Luey offered timely editorial advice, and Professor James Conrad shared his expertise on Samuel Slater. The anonymous SUNY Press readers not only knew the field of industrial history, but offered their critical comments in very productive ways. Everyone I dealt with at SUNY Press was professional and helpful. I would like to thank acquisitions editors Amanda Lanne, Rafael Chaiken, and Jessica Kirschner, production editor Laurie Searl, promotions manager Kate Seburyamo, and copyeditor Alan V. Hewat for making the process very smooth.

Brown University professor Pat Malone knows the industrial history of Pawtucket, Lowell, and Waltham as well as anyone, and as I prepared the book he generously shared his extensive knowledge of the field as well as a superb pen and ink drawing of the Wilkinson and Slater mills by his late father. I would like to thank Dave Ingram, an expert in early iron production, for his general wisdom and friendship. Although not involved in this book, Professor Bob Allison of Suffolk University played an important role in my early graduate work, and provided several confidence-building publishing opportunities.

My family has been a constant source of encouragement. My brother Ned is an avid listener and well-informed critic. I treasure the love and humor of John, Jennifer, Allison, Jenny, and Tim. My wife Sharon has kept me happy and balanced, and to her I owe a special debt of love and gratitude.

Introduction

Machinists in the Early American Republic

> There is not a working boy of average ability in the New England States . . . who has not an idea of some mechanical invention or improvement in manufactures, by which, in good times, he hopes to better his position, or rise to fortune and social distinction.
>
> —Scottish inventor James Nasmyth, 1854

Their contemporaries called them "ingenious machinists." More than a clever near-rhyme, the term suggests the degree to which Americans of the late eighteenth and early nineteenth centuries admired technological innovation and revered the men who could bring practical betterment to their lives by forging nails and tools, building clocks and other intricate machinery, and constructing water-powered mills. In a country of people known for mechanical ability they stood out from the ordinary mechanic, a broad term that might describe a bricklayer, a carpenter, even a shoemaker. Machinists had special aptitudes—ways of visualizing mechanical processes in three-dimensional space—that suited them to the design and construction of complex and precise moving machinery, such as lathes, spinning frames, power looms, and steam engines. Some used their distinctive talents to invent; others built machines in textile manufactories or small machine shops, or traveled around the countryside repairing equipment. Some became entrepreneurs and factory owners, while others chose to leave the business issues (and the financial risks) to businessmen.

In general, the initial phase of the American cotton manufacturing boom—from roughly 1790 to the 1830s—was advantageous for textile machinists. Their skills were in high demand, and those who were successful made good salaries or wages, moved geographically to maximize their value, settled down when the conditions were right, bought homes or lived in corporate housing that suited their status, joined churches and self-improvement organizations, and sent their children to good schools. In short, machinists were presented the opportunity to do interesting and important work that was consistent with the ideals of American independence as well as the emerging values of middle-class refinement.

Most of these men are unknown today, the details of their contributions lost to history, and the relatively few whose lives were recorded are often remembered in fragments and faint clues. Although literate, and rarely from the poorest rank, these men did not typically leave autobiographies, nor were their letters usually saved. Many of them were nonverbal thinkers known by their works rather than by their words. This problem is captured by an early-twentieth-century observer: "It is very difficult to trace [an innovation] in its early stages and the origin of its invention. The inventors themselves were too busy and too unaccustomed to the use of the pen to commemorate the fruits of their genius, and the writers of the day were unconscious of the great revolution in the industry that was silently proceeding."[1]

Two particularly inventive machinists, Paul Moody of Newbury, Massachusetts, and David Wilkinson of Pawtucket, Rhode Island, and Cohoes, New York, achieved degrees of wealth and recognition far beyond the expectations of ordinary mechanics, and left enough of a record to permit a relatively full picture of their lives. Born in the 1770s, both men responded to similar opportunities in the industrially expansive postrevolutionary era. Although less than a hundred miles apart geographically, they participated in two very different business and technology spheres, the large-scale Waltham-Lowell corporate system in which Paul Moody was the principal engineer, and the smaller-scale Rhode Island system in which David Wilkinson played the roles of pioneer machine and tool maker, manufacturer, investor, and mill village entrepreneur. Their different responses to the extraordinary opportunities of the early Industrial Revolution, especially when considered together, reveal a great deal about the economic and social life of the new nation in the late eighteenth and early nineteenth centuries.

What can the lives of two nearly forgotten machinists tell us about the larger story of American political economy in the early national period? This was an era rich in debate over issues of war and home industries, the diffusion of critical technological information from abroad, and the social and political consequences of industrialization and the rise of corporations. Wilkinson and Moody operated within a distinctively republican political culture, and their careers intersected one of its fundamental challenges: how to create and maintain "an economic and social order that would encourage the shaping of a virtuous citizenry."[2] Because textile manufacturing was the first large-scale industrial development in the new nation, textile machinists such as Wilkinson and Moody were part of a national debate over the relationship between manufacturing and republicanism. That debate evolved in several discrete stages. Briefly stated, Americans experimented with domestic manufactures in the Revolutionary era as part of the effort to free themselves from dependency on British goods. After winning political independence, the United States continued to struggle under British economic domination, and support for domestic manufactures increased, especially during the embargo of Thomas Jefferson's second term and the War of 1812, an era that saw not only increased clamor for economic independence, but also the willingness of a few wealthy merchants to risk their wealth by investing in domestic manufacturing. At the same time there was an influx of machines, models, designs, and ideas from Europe—a remarkable transfer of technology that enabled further development of domestic manufactures. Finally, despite fears that large-scale manufacturing was antithetical to the moral and economic values of the American people, the success of manufacturing led to an acceptance of industrialization as compatible with American ideals. Although the nation remained largely agrarian, it became increasingly apparent that an agricultural economy could not provide full employment, and that machine-filled factories would help put otherwise unemployable people to work to maintain their own—and the nation's—virtue. Men such as Moody and Wilkinson, who could design, construct, improve, and repair textile machinery, were agents of this great economic transformation, as well as its beneficiaries.[3]

Although Americans had been noted early on for their mechanical talents and ingenuity, the machines described in these pages did not spring to the minds of Yankee inventors out of the blue. All of the basic components of textile production by hand were well known to colonial Americans. Loose cotton or wool was passed back and forth through closely spaced wires embedded into wooden paddles (cards) in a process known as carding. The carded fiber was then joined into longer strands and twisted into yarn on the spinning wheel, typically a single spindle with a foot treadle to spin the wheel while leaving both hands free to handle the yarn. The sturdy yarn was then strung in parallel lines on a hand loom to form the "warp," and other yarn (called "weft" and often of a different fiber) was sent by hand between the warp yarns by means of a shuttle, and woven cloth was produced. It took time and dexterous hands at every stage of the process.

Important innovations in textile spinning and weaving had begun in Great Britain in the early eighteenth century and developed at an accelerating pace throughout the century. John Kay's "flying shuttle" loom of 1733, by which the shuttle was propelled back and forth through the warp threads by means of hand-operated cords, essentially doubled the output of the weaver. Now the bottleneck became spinning, performed on the traditional single-spindle wheel until about 1760 when several independent inventors, particularly James Hargreaves, devised what became known as the "spinning jenny," capable of driving multiple spindles from a single wheel. Carding—the process of aligning the fibers of loose cotton into long strands in preparation for spinning—also improved dramatically as hand carding was replaced by hand-cranked rotating cylinders, most notably by Lewis Paul. Next was the process of continuous spinning, which involved sets of rollers that stretched and twisted the carded cotton into yarn strong enough for weaving. The initial experimentation was done by John Wyatt and Lewis Paul in the 1730s, but Richard Arkwright was able to exploit the entire collection of carding and spinning innovations, which he organized into a coordinated system and patented in 1769. Most importantly, Arkwright's spinning frame could be adapted to be driven by an external force, and was so often propelled by the energy of a waterwheel that it became known as the "water frame."[4]

With all the processes involved in cotton preparation—the carding of the fibers, the stretching and twisting of the yarn, and the winding of finished yarn onto bobbins—working relatively synchronously and no longer dependent on manual force, weaving once again became the slowest stage of the process. In 1785, Reverend Edmund Cartwright, who by all accounts had never closely examined a handloom, invented the power loom. Improved by William Horrocks and Robert Miller, among others, the power loom became entrenched in British factories by about 1810, despite occasional violent riots by displaced handloom weavers.[5] The phenomenal output of the power loom cemented Britain's position as the preeminent textile manufacturer in the world.

To ensure its industrial supremacy, the British government placed restrictions on the export of machines, plans, or machinists outside the country, and backed the laws with stiff penalties. While this slowed the transfer of technology, it failed to stop it, and in fact the restrictions may have acted as a challenge both to the British inventors who saw better opportunities overseas, and to American machinists eager to try their hand at promising new technologies. The United States government and various states sponsored innovation—as well as espionage—and over time a wide range of machines and designs, some already outdated, some at the state of the art, made their way across the Atlantic into the hands and minds of risk-taking entrepreneurs and enterprising machinists.[6]

The story of British inventors is interesting, with dramatic successes and setbacks, machine-breaking riots and inventors dying in poverty, and an appalling record of exploited workers and grim industrial slums. But this story is about what the Americans—specifically David Wilkinson and Paul Moody—made of the opportunities to utilize British patents, to draw on tradition and family networks, to invent when necessary, to improve upon their own or others' innovations, and, in the process, to enhance their wealth and status in this exhilarating early phase of the American Industrial Revolution.

There have been a number of first-rate histories of New England cotton manufacture in the early years of industrialization, fewer of the Cohoes-Troy area. Most have concentrated either on the elite owners and financiers or on the mill "operatives"—especially the mill girls and immigrants who tended the production machinery. Machinists were the men in the middle, who helped propel the technology revolution forward and in turn benefited significantly from the growth of manufacturing. Their achievements have often been cited, and their influence traced throughout the eastern United States. Still, the men themselves have not been presented in depth—the particular opportunities and challenges they faced, the background that prepared them, and the consequences of their achievements, not only for the businesses they represented but for the dramatic changes in their own lives.

By no means was New England the only center of American industrialization. Valuable studies of Pennsylvania by Anthony Wallace, Philip Scranton, and Cynthia Shelton, for example, make it clear that the industrial impetus was widespread.[7] New England is the focus here because it was the first to develop powered spinning and weaving, as well as native machinists and machine shops. More to the point, these two pioneer machinists—Moody and Wilkinson—lived and worked in New England and eastern New York state, and the stories of their lives are grounded in the rivers and people and technological opportunities of that region. The village of Cohoes, New York, plays an important part because its industrial water power structure was based on the model that Paul Moody had helped develop at Lowell, and one of its early and influential developers was David Wilkinson, who greatly advanced the transfer of textile machinery and machine tool technology to the area.

Most histories of the textile industry, especially those written in the twentieth century, depict the rise of American manufacturing with an eye toward its eventual decline, perhaps rightly so, given how industrialization failed to live up to its early social promise, and in many areas was unable to sustain its economic success. Yet in many ways the early phase of this transformation brought comparatively good wages and working conditions, along with cheaper products for American consumers, while meeting the republican goals of national economic independence and the maintenance of the moral basis for work. While aware of the eventual decline, my focus is on the early stages when terms such as "utopian" were not entirely amiss, when the new industrial order was not yet rigidly fixed, when everything seemed possible—especially for talented machinists.

Paul Moody and David Wilkinson were well known in their time, but lack popular recognition today. References to them in the historical record are ample but scattered, and this is the first attempt to bring together all that can be known about their lives and their significant contributions. Given the "firsts" in American industrial history—water-powered cotton yarn spinning at Pawtucket in 1790, and water-powered weaving at Waltham in 1814—it seems appropriate to delve into the lives of the two machinists who were instrumental in those seminal events, and who continued to participate in so many of the technological advances of the period. Wilkinson's involvement in Samuel Slater's introduction of mechanized spinning in 1790 is particularly pertinent, because it allows us to examine the mythology surrounding technological advances, which were in fact less the product of lone heroic inventors and more the result of collaboration and emulation.

Wilkinson and Moody shared many traits—primarily great mechanical inventiveness—but their stories take remarkably different turns, largely because Moody was a company man and Wilkinson more of a risk taker. By choosing to work for a large corporation, Moody came to recognize both its security and its limitations, and his experience demonstrates how corporations became not only a comfortable and stimulating place to work, but more generally an environment where technological change occurred and where workers increasingly found employment. Men like Moody chose to work there because corporations offered the tools, encouragement, and funding for innovation, as well as a degree of economic protection. David Wilkinson, on the other hand, often worked alone or in small partnerships, and as he became increasingly entrepreneurial he experienced both the highs and lows of the new and risky economic order. Through these two careers we can see the opportunities, benefits, dangers, and challenges of this early stage of industrial and corporate capitalism in the United States. It is by no means the whole story, but it forms an important part of the larger picture of this great social and economic transformation, as shown by the lives of two key figures who helped shape it.

Finally, while there are elements of business and labor and industrial history in this account, this is fundamentally a *story*—or two interwoven stories—about men who learned, worked, invented, married and had children, relocated to follow opportunities, bettered their conditions, wrestled with social and religious issues, and played fundamental roles in a set of changes that transformed social, economic, and work life in America in the late eighteenth and early nineteenth centuries. It is in the form of a dual biography, with alternating, thematically related chapters that move the narrative forward chronologically while developing the overall context of industrial development. The two contrasting biographies—each man responding very differently to the opportunities of the textile revolution—impart more about this period than their individual experiences could do. I have found these men to be too interesting, and their experiences too rich about life and work in the early republic, to pass up the opportunity to tell their stories.

1

Industrial Glimmerings

Massachusetts before 1790

> I say that America will not make manufactures enough for her own consumption these thousand years.
>
> —John Adams to Benjamin Franklin, 1780

> The time is not distant when this Country will abound with mechanics & manufacturers who will receive their bread from their employers.
>
> —Gouverneur Morris, 1787

Samuel Slater established the first successful water-powered cotton spinning mill in America. Slater was an English textile factory superintendent who had gained a thorough knowledge of Arkwright machinery, emigrated to America in 1789, and teamed up with Moses Brown to establish his factory on the Blackstone River at Pawtucket, Rhode Island, in 1790. His notable achievement has obscured important indications of a vibrant—if still experimental and often unprofitable—textile industry elsewhere in America at the close of the eighteenth century. Another notable industrial endeavor before 1800 was Alexander Hamilton's manufacturing enterprise at Paterson, New Jersey, begun in 1791, and most famous for its dramatic collapse, due to poor management, inadequate facilities for workers, dumping of shares by the speculation-minded investors, and the financial improprieties of its director.[1] And it may be this well-known domestic failure and the Englishman Slater's success that have led to the general impression that before 1790 America was not ready for large-scale manufacturing, and that whatever meager success was achieved must be attributable to British contributions. Industrial innovation in other villages and towns in America, however, makes it clear that powered textile manufacture had been developing for some time, and had reached the size and scale at which the term *factory* is appropriate. Furthermore, although British machinery designs as well as skilled British immigrant workers were often involved, the bulk of the factory and machine building—the work force that kept the mills and machinery running—was distinctly American.

~

The colony and state of Massachusetts had long been a promoter of local textile manufacture. This encouragement ranged from financial aid to coercion, as in 1656 when the general court ordered all families to engage in home spinning to redress the scarcity of cloth. An early spinning school was established in Boston about 1718 to provide work for the poor, but likely for profit as well. As early as 1726, to help satisfy the need for duck (a heavy cloth for sails and work clothes), the General Court awarded a bounty to a Boston linen manufacturer. In the early 1750s, the Society for Encouraging Industry and the Employment of the Poor was formed, with philanthropic motives mixed with the desire to secure bargain labor. When the society petitioned the General Court to erect a building for linen manufacture, it was approved provided that the owners furnished training in spinning and weaving.

The building was used intermittently for various types of textile production, including a spinning school organized by William Molineux. In a petition to the colonial legislature in 1770, Molineux claimed that he had "learned" more than three hundred women and children to spin. Soon he had warping and twisting machines and at least ten looms in operation. This was probably the closest thing to a textile factory in America before the Revolution. Little is known about the equipment or the actual operation of the enterprise. What is important is that it was a sort of factory, it had government aid, and its ostensible aim was to give work to the poor. This description will be echoed in late-eighteenth-century attempts at industrialization in Massachusetts, although profit will become a more obvious goal.[2]

The other colony and state that notably promoted textile manufactures was Pennsylvania. In March 1775, the *Pennsylvania Gazette* reported on a meeting of subscribers to "a fund for establishing an American Manufactory of woollens, linens, and cottons." The organization behind this plan was the United Company of Philadelphia for Promoting American Manufactures. One of its members was Tench Coxe, a tireless promoter of manufacturing and later Alexander Hamilton's assistant secretary of the treasury. Another was Dr. Benjamin Rush whose speech at the inauguration of the society stressed the combination of economic, scientific, and philanthropic advantages to manufacturing.[3]

The manufacturing established by the United Company did not utilize the latest machinery. In Philadelphia, a manufactory was typically intended for poor relief on the British model, and between 1775 and 1790 the United Company employed more than four hundred women who spun yarn in their homes. In this variation on the classic "putting out" system, the yarn was purchased by the manufactory owners to be woven into cloth within the factory. By 1789, spinning jennies were in use in the company's Market Street factory, but a year later—reminiscent of the mob action of threatened hand workers in Britain—it was destroyed by arson.[4]

Philadelphia's textile industry would expand significantly, but not until after the War of 1812. To take one prominent example, Rockdale—so carefully documented by Anthony F. C. Wallace—began development in 1825. For a number of reasons the Philadelphia-area experience was different from that of New England. Since a major aim of manufactories in Philadelphia was to provide work for the poor, they concentrated on labor-intensive operations rather than labor-saving machinery. As a major immigration port (unlike Boston), a steady supply of English and Irish hand spinners and weavers was available, making the traditional putting-out system economically feasible (for the entrepreneurs, if not for the workers). Finally, because of the abundance of skilled mule spinners and handloom weavers, Philadelphia became a center for the production of fine goods, which early spinning and weaving machines did poorly. In short, the availability of water-powered textile machinery did not revolutionize work in Philadelphia as soon or as rapidly as it did in New England.[5]

This by no means suggests that the Pennsylvania-Delaware area was somehow incapable of supporting mechanical innovation. Oliver Evans, a brilliant and multifaceted inventor well known for his experiments with high-pressure steam engines and his creation of the first automated flour mill in 1787, got his start in manufacturing during the Revolution. Cards for combing wool (wooden paddles covered with leather embedded with small bent wires) were typically made by hand, but in 1777, Evans designed a hand-cranked machine that would precisely cut and bend the wire teeth, and another to insert the wires into the card. After his appeal to the Delaware legislature for $500 was turned down, Evans found a Wilmington textile manufacturer who contracted to implement his design. The machine made five hundred wire teeth per minute, and a later improvement brought the number to three thousand.[6] The fact that there existed a machine manufacturer in 1770s America capable of fabricating Evans's invention says much about the state of industrial development during this period. While America remained in the thrall of British mercantilism and was still industrially primitive, there were many signs of capacity and ingenuity as well as actual practical work already going on.

From time to time the federal government actively encouraged cotton and woolen manufactures, as attested by President Washington's high-profile tours of textile factories in 1789. Another strategy was to send recruiters to England and Ireland in search of knowledgeable machinists or models of the latest textile equipment. One such recruiter was Thomas Atwood Digges of Maryland, who spent the Revolutionary War years in England, and was accused by Benjamin Franklin and others of espionage. George Washington came to his defense, pointing out that Digges's more recent work had been invaluable: "Since the War, abundant evidence might be adduced of his activity and zeal (with considerable risque) in sending artizans and machines of public utility to this Country."[7]

Although older style carding machines and spinning jennies were occasionally imported, the holy grail of industrial espionage in this period was the Arkwright spinning frame and associated machinery, and as early as 1787 the U.S. Congress began secret attempts to procure it. Some of the impetus for American action may stem from the fact that by 1785, Richard Arkwright was so upset at Parliament's invalidation of his patent rights (by refusing to support his claim of patent infringements) that he threatened to "publish descriptions and copper plates of all the parts, that it might be known to foreign nations as well as our own." Now the American position became more public, when William Pollard, a merchant in Philadelphia, secured a model of an Arkwright roving and spinning machine in 1788 or 1789, made improvements (since it did not function), and applied for a U.S. patent in 1790. Although this put the United States government in the position of officially condoning the patenting of stolen intellectual property, Pollard was awarded the patent in December 1791.[8]

Prior to 1790, however, the federal government did not play a significant role in industrial development, although it is likely that Washington's visits helped change public sentiment. The most influential national figure was Tench Coxe, the moving force behind the Pennsylvania Society for the Encouragement of Manufactures and Useful Arts and later assistant secretary of the treasury, where he produced the primary draft of the famous Report on Manufactures (1791) and played a major role in the creation of the Society for Establishing Useful Manufactures.[9] Coxe also acted for personal gain, as when he used his own funds to send an agent, one Andrew Mitchell from western Pennsylvania, to England to acquire models or plans of Arkwright machinery. Mitchell managed to buy the models and drawings, but was caught by British authorities, fined, and forced to leave the country empty-handed. Coxe may have been more successful indirectly, as some of his promotional material appears to have been an important factor in Samuel Slater's decision to emigrate to America in 1789.

Unlike many Americans in the late eighteenth century, Tench Coxe had no problem reconciling the need for manufacturing with agriculture. He recognized early on that America needed industry to lessen its dependence on Europe, and that in a labor-starved nation, machinery would be an essential component of the economy. But Coxe had many detractors (John Adams described him as a "wily, winding, subtle and insidious character") and the American effort was desultory at best prior to Hamilton's Report on Manufactures in 1791.[10] Private initiative, enterprising British mechanics willing to emigrate, and state bonuses and tax relief would be far more important factors than federal aid or encouragement, and nowhere was this more true than in the state of Massachusetts.

~

After the Revolution, Massachusetts was a leader in legislative inducements for textile machinery. In October 1786, a joint House and Senate committee was appointed "to view any new invented machines that are making [*sic*] within this Commonwealth for the purpose of manufacturing sheep's and cotton wool, and report what measures are proper for the Legislature to take to encourage the same."[11] Earlier that year, two brothers, Robert and Alexander Barr, had emigrated from Scotland to East Bridgewater where, as employees of foundry and firearms manufacturer Hugh Orr, they built carding, spinning, and roving machines, based on British (probably Hargreaves) designs. The Massachusetts legislature, "as a reward for their ingenuity in forming those machines and their public spirit in making them known to the commonwealth," awarded them a £200 cash bounty and six tickets in the state land lottery. This was a coup for Massachusetts, which had managed to evade British export laws and boosted the state's chances of producing a viable textile industry. The machines were put on exhibition as "State's Models" for interested parties to examine.[12] Another British émigré, Thomas Somers, had settled in Baltimore in 1785, where he perceived that there were opportunities in America for those with knowledge of British textile machinery. After returning to England to obtain models of relevant machines, he settled in Massachusetts and petitioned the General Court in February 1787 to help him recover from the loss of half his property at sea and tide him over until he could engage in the textile business. Somers soon produced an Arkwright spinning frame in Orr's workshop in March 1787, and was awarded £20—whether as encouragement before he built the machine or reward afterward is unclear.[13] This state involvement was a critical spur to industry, much of it directed to enticing European machinists familiar with latest British textile machinery to emigrate. It also signaled to local machinists that, with the right skills and experience, there might be economic rewards.

The first mechanized cotton spinning manufactory in New England was established in Beverly, along the Massachusetts coast north of Boston. John, Andrew, and George Cabot—brothers who had made a fortune in shipping and distilleries, as well as privateering during the Revolution—organized the Beverly Cotton Manufactory in 1787. They constructed a small brick mill on Bass River the following year with several spinning jennies and carding machines built by James Leonard and the same Thomas Somers who had built the state models in Bridgewater. Weaving, performed on hand looms, was done in the same building, suggesting an early form of the integrated factory—one that comprised all the production stages, from raw cotton to finished cloth—although the machinery was powered by horses rather than water.[14]

While profit was the obvious motive, the investors phrased their incorporation petition to emphasize the public good: not only would the factory's output reduce the dependence on foreign imports, but it would employ women and children who might otherwise be a burden to society. Forty people, in fact, were employed in 1790. The petition also spoke of financial sacrifice and risk, with careful positioning to induce the court to grant the owners certain immunities or aid in return for their public-spirited pioneering. The Beverly manufactory had already benefited from state aid by securing the services of machinists Leonard and Somers, at least one of whom had received a bonus from the Massachusetts legislature. According to the Salem *Mercury,* however, it was George Cabot who had essentially saved these artisans from returning in disappointment to Britain:

> With such talents [Leonard and Somers] supposed that the risk and expense of coming to this country would be amply recompensed by the encouragement such valuable manufactures deserve. But they made various applications with no other effect than loss of time and money. Such difficulties, co-operating with the want of energy and system in our governments, reduced them to the disagreeable necessity of resolving to leave a country so unpromising to manufactures, when the Hon. George Cabot generously patronized them, and influenced a number of gentlemen in Beverly to associate for the purpose of establishing these much wanted industries. These gentlemen merit the thanks of their fellow citizens.[15]

Politics were undoubtedly at work as the *Mercury* hewed the Federalist line in chastising the state for insufficient assistance to manufacturing. How Cabot came in contact with the Bridgewater artisans is unknown. Their "disagreeable" state is questionable, however, since—as will become evident later—there was a great deal of interest in their carding and spinning machines, especially from Rhode Islanders who were setting up their own cotton manufacturing.

The Beverly factory received a great deal of national attention as well, highlighted by George Washington's tour of the facility in 1789. A good description of the works can be found in Washington's diary:

> In this Manufactory, they have the New Invented Spinning and Carding Machines. One of the first supplies the work, and four of the latter, one of which spins eighty-four threads at a time by one person. The Cotton is prepared for these Machines by being first (lightly) drawn to a thread on the common wheel. There is also another Machine for

> doubling and twisting the threads for particular cloths. This also does many at a time. For winding the Cotton from the spindles and preparing it for the Warp, there is a Reel which expedites the work greatly. A number of looms (15 or 16) were at work with Spring shuttles, which do more than double work. In short, the whole seemed perfect and the Cotton stuffs which they turned out excellent of their kind. Warp & filling are both now of cotton.[16]

The whole was not as perfect as it seemed, however. Even before Washington's visit, the company had been forced to petition the Massachusetts legislature for £500 to help defray unexpectedly high startup costs. In fact, the president's visit was likely devised as part of the lobbying effort for government subsidy. George Cabot, the most prominent of the investors, was personally acquainted with Washington and Alexander Hamilton. Again in 1790, the investors asked for relief, assuring the state that "the manufacture, having been once established, will be sufficiently lucrative to support and extend itself, and will afford not only a supply for domestic consumption, but a staple for exportation." There may have been a note of desperation in their appeal, for they used as inducements the fact that the raw cotton they imported was traded for codfish, thus providing that local industry with much needed encouragement.[17]

The most serious financial problem was the cost of building and maintaining the machines. The carding machine alone had cost £1,100, and by 1790 an equivalent machine could be purchased for as little as £200. This is an indication of the risk that pioneer entrepreneurs faced, as well as the rapid reduction in price that results from technological advances and increased demand. "Our machinery has been bad and dear," lamented George Cabot in 1791, "it is now perfectly well made and cheap."[18] The Beverly Manufactory was also plagued by the loss of trained workers who were lured to other start-up enterprises for higher wages. Moses Brown of Providence wrote to the owners of a textile manufactory in Worcester: "The beaverly people appeared highly offended at your taking the Woman from them, and say they will not again employ her if she returns." Probably more painful was the defection of the English machinist James Leonard to Brown's company in 1789. Despite Moses Brown's positive description of cooperative relationships among the various New England cotton manufactories during this early period, the Beverly owners were furious over the theft of their trained employees. "You are not ignorant," complained George Cabot to Massachusetts congressman Benjamin Goodhue,

> that the Worcester people got their machinery made by a man whom we had taught at great expense, and that their carding engine did not consequently cost an eighth part as much as ours; they also took away the second spinner we had instructed. This woman, after hav-

> ing destroyed our materials and enjoyed our support in learning to spin, was bribed to desert us as soon as she could be useful to us. The Rhode Island undertakers [Almy & Brown] have, to a degree, treated us in the same manner; and we have not yet been able to stop this evil which has cost us so much money.[19]

In their 1790 petition to the House Committee for the Encouragement of Arts, Agriculture, and Manufactures, the Beverly owners presented themselves as public-spirited men who had assumed great risks for the benefit of the fledgling nation. "The proprietors having already hazarded, some their whole fortunes, and others very large sums," they pleaded, "are obliged to declare, without aid from this honorable court, no further advancement can be made, and, mortifying as it is, they feel themselves in the necessity of relinquishing a design highly beneficial to the public and undertaken by them from the purest motives." The legislature agreed.[20]

Yet the following year, despite an appropriation of £1,000 ($4,500), George Cabot confided to his friend Alexander Hamilton that the investors were currently $10,000 in debt and making no headway since the price they could charge for the finished cloth was now lower than the net cost of producing it. Cabot explained that "a want in skill in constructing the machinery and in dexterity in using it, added to our want of a general knowledge of the business we had undertaken, have proved the principal impediments to its success." While this early attempt at mechanized cotton manufacture managed to stay operational for more than twenty years, it was not profitable. The original owners appear to have been whittled down to John Cabot and Joshua Fisher by 1798, at which point they sold the factory for $2,630.29.[21]

The unprofitability of the Beverly Cotton Manufactory is easy to explain in retrospect: insufficient capitalization, the high cost of equipment, few trained mechanics, and competition for workers in a tight labor market. As the investors themselves admitted, having made their fortunes in shipping, they lacked knowledge of the new industry they had undertaken. Even the rudimentary, reliable, well-understood principle of water power was not exploited. Perhaps Beverly, like most seacoast towns, had no river with sufficient falls to power the mill. Or the owners could have been using a British model: many small factories in England in the 1770–1790 period used horse-powered capstans to drive the carding machines and did spinning by hand. It also appears that, despite the experimentation done in Bridgewater, the Beverly mill used hand-operated jennies, not Arkwright water frames as anticipated.[22] Yet the Beverly investors were trying something entirely new in America, and had few business rules to guide them. The fact that they had paid £1,100 for a carding machine in 1786, and could have purchased one (presumably better) for only £200 in 1790, is strong evidence that they were just a few years ahead of their time. The next manufacturing experiments would take advantage of improved machinery and water power—and learn specific lessons from Beverly's failure.

~

As 1790 approached, all manufacturing roads appeared to lead to Providence. Yet a few brief examples will help to bolster the role of Massachusetts in the development of decentralized textile production and machine manufacture. A duck cloth factory was established in Haverhill in 1789. George Washington visited there after touring the Beverly factory, and deemed the setup "ingenious." The president seemed particularly impressed with the looms, which were "differently constructed from those of the common kind, and upon an improved plan." Just what was different is unknown—the point is they were considered innovative. Also in 1789, the Worcester Cotton Manufactory was established on Mill River. The investors included famed printer and American Antiquarian Society founder Isaiah Thomas, and Levi Lincoln, who would later serve as United States Attorney General. The *Massachusetts Spy* declared that the corduroy produced in the mill was preferable to British imports—but we must bear in mind that the *Spy* was owned by Isaiah Thomas. As noted earlier, the Worcester factory had the advantage of a trained machinist from Beverly, which reduced their machine costs considerably. By 1791, however, seventeen of the eighteen original investors had sold their interests, and in early 1792 an appeal to the state legislature for a £600 loan resulted in a ten-year tax abatement, but no money. The enterprise appears to have survived at least until 1799, but within a short time the factory building was sold, moved, and converted to a store.[23]

The typical carding machine of this era was a revolving cylinder with removable covers. The card clothing—the leather strips pierced by bent wire staples that performed the actual carding of cotton or wool—was attached to both the cylinder and the covers. The machinist who produced the Worcester factory's card clothing was Pliny Earle, from the town of Leicester, five miles west of Worcester along the old Post Road. Earle (1762–1832) began making hand cards in 1785 in the employ of Edmund Snow. The following year Earle went into business for himself, and was hired to build the card clothing for the Worcester Cotton Manufactory. Moses Brown may have heard about Earle through the Worcester factory connection, but a more likely link is the fact that they were both Quakers, as were a significant number of the mechanics working with Brown during this period.[24] In November 1789—before Samuel Slater came to Rhode Island—Brown contracted with Earle to make the card clothing for the Almy & Brown carding machines.

In an example of early machine specialization, there were several card clothing makers to whom the Providence manufacturer could turn. As Brown's letter to Earle reveals, "We have conferred with our Card Makers in Town about doing the Jobb, who appear desirous to do it, and are willing to take their pay, all excepting the cost of the wire in our way, but, it being our object to have it well done, and thinking we could rely upon thy performance, have preferred thy doing it." Perhaps to make it clear to Earle that he had further competition, the Brown & Almy letter continues, "We have also had it in contemplation to write to Boston, but, being desirous of having it done soon, and that being likely to protract the time of having it done, we waved [*sic*] that also."[25]

Two additional important facts can be gleaned from this letter. One is that Earle had made progress in building machine tools to aid in the fabrication of the card clothing: "Thou hast thy machinery now prepared, which was not when thou did that for the company at Worcester." The other is that Moses Brown was well acquainted with the owners of the Worcester Cotton Manufactory. In advising Earle to go to Worcester to see if he could observe any needed improvements to the cards there, Brown informed him that "Stowell, who superintends the business there, will chearfully give thee any information respecting the working of theirs, no doubt, upon thy own account and upon ours also, as we are upon friendly terms with him, having divers times been mutually helpful to each other."[26] Given how the Beverly owners felt about Moses Brown, we can only wonder how open the Worcester investors might have been.

According to one nineteenth-century account, the first of Earle's card-clothing installed at Slater's Pawtucket factory did not meet expectations. In an early example of the traveling repairman, Earle journeyed to Pawtucket to examine the cards himself and found that the pitch of the teeth was incorrect, causing the cotton to clog the machine. He quickly remedied the situation—whether by hand or by machine is not noted—and the carding process proceeded smoothly from this time on.[27]

Pliny Earle built a machine business, survived the downturn after the War of 1812, and passed on a company that was still successfully making up-to-date carding machines at the end of the nineteenth century. He and his family provide an instructive example of the upward mobility of a mechanically gifted man of the early republic. Two of his sons were educated at the Leicester Academy and went on to distinguished national careers. Thomas Earle (1796–1849) worked in his father's business until the economic slump of 1816, then moved to Philadelphia where he became a lawyer, newspaper editor, and advocate of immediate emancipation, and was selected (although not ultimately chosen) to be James G. Birney's running mate for the Liberty Party in 1840. Pliny Earle Jr. (1809–1892) earned a medical degree from the University of Pennsylvania, became a pioneer in the treatment of the insane, and was cofounder of the American Medical Association.[28]

A failed textile factory in Worcester and a small machine shop in nearby Leicester—for all practical purposes relegated to the dustbin of industrial history—may be more significant than initially appears. First, they indicate a more extended geographical dimension of pre-1790 mechanized textile development. Bridgewater, Beverly, and Worcester-Leicester form a triangle that covers most of eastern and central Massachusetts. More significantly, all three locations will figure in the success of Moses Brown and Samuel Slater at Pawtucket. Several letters from Almy & Brown indicate that they were keenly aware of machinery, labor, and general business issues in both the Beverly and Worcester factories; a machinist from Leicester made their card clothing; and their initial Arkwright machines were procured from Bridgewater.

The realization of America's first successful cotton spinning mill at Pawtucket, Rhode Island, is properly ascribed to Samuel Slater, and even the briefest biography highlights the fact that he emigrated from England with a thorough understanding of Arkwright machinery in 1789. While his achievement is remarkable, too great an emphasis on Slater obscures the technical experimentation going on in New England before Slater's arrival, the lessons learned from earlier textile factories in Massachusetts, and the general state of industrial development in southern New England in the late eighteenth century. Moreover, the Slater-centric view devalues the contribution of David Wilkinson and other local artisans who actually built the equipment. Wilkinson was a talented machinist who seized the opportunities offered by the evolution of the textile industry and in turn contributed to its further development. His story forms an indispensable part of the early industrial history of America.

2

Revolutionary Technology

Rhode Island, 1775–1790

> The Wilkinsons were at one time the leading mechanicians and manufacturers in New England, and were regarded as authority on all questions related to mechanics. The descendants are numerous, and are generally considered the inheritors of superior intellects.
>
> —*Scientific American,* July 26, 1862

One day in April 1776—about the time that Oliver Evans was experimenting with card manufacture in Delaware—five-year-old David Wilkinson sat on a workbench in his father's blacksmith shop in Smithfield, Rhode Island. David watched intently as a man named Eleazer Smith built a machine to make the small wire staples used in wool hand cards.[1] Independently, Smith seems to have been thinking along the same lines as Evans, for "after Smith had finished the machine, so as to make a perfect card tooth, he told the people in the shop that he could make a machine to make the tooth, prick the leather, and set the tooth, at one operation." The boy's experience made a lasting impression. "Seventy years afterwards," David remembered, "I could make a likeness of nearly every piece of that machine,—so durable are the first impressions of the mind of youth." One might rather say that such was the particular mind of David Wilkinson and such were the industrial conditions in revolutionary America that new machines were being conceived and mechanically minded boys were caught up in the possibilities.[2]

The trade of machinist had unknown potential at the time, for it would have been impossible to predict the ways in which traditional iron making would develop and merge with the nascent textile industry—but even in its current state it was exciting. While farming continued to be the dominant occupation in colonial America, there had always been work that required mechanical skill, such as millwright and gunsmith, watchmaker and coppersmith. Sometimes these men specialized; more often they were farmers who simply made and repaired the things they needed. In a cash- and labor-starved economy, practical men made what they could not buy.

Among these farmer-mechanics was a type marked not only by mechanical ability but also by a special quality of inventiveness—a quality that in many ways defined who they were. Practically anyone could be a small-scale farmer, but only an exceptional few could construct a waterwheel or fabricate wire. Despite the Jeffersonian idealization of agriculture as the only virtuous occupation, these men saw no contradiction in their profession. Mechanical work was as necessary as farming, and making use of fire and water and iron ore was as natural as any other occupation. In fact, many European observers considered mechanical aptitude to be an intrinsic part of the American character. As one historian put it, "The stereotypical American was the Yankee who could not look at Niagara Falls without calculating the number of wheels it could turn, or, more modestly, could not permit any New England river to fall more than eight feet at any point without being made to propel some piece of machinery."[3] Not until the coming of the factories in the late eighteenth century was there a dichotomy between mechanization and more "natural" work, and even then it appears that the machinists themselves felt no such disharmony. Even Thomas Jefferson—perhaps the most prominent promoter of the virtuous yeoman farmer myth—installed patented Oliver Evans inventions in his flour mill and made use of the latest nail-making machinery at his Monticello nailery.[4]

Mechanization was therefore, like farming, in the natural order of things. Furthermore, machine making had a social and cultural significance: just as it defined the men who had the particular talent, it became part of the definition of American, not only in the way visitors viewed them but in the way Americans saw themselves. The particularly inventive mechanics used their talents and ingenuity freely, and were rewarded for it—if not directly with riches (for colonial America was largely a barter economy) then with social standing and high regard in the community. No wonder, then, that a boy such as David Wilkinson would aspire to technological prominence, in the footsteps of his father and cousins.

The industrial conditions in late colonial New England were not so primitive as typically portrayed. While well behind Great Britain in textile development, America by 1770 was the third largest iron producer in the world, and Rhode Island was one of the centers of technical expertise.[5] As Peter J. Coleman has noted, Rhode Island's greatest industrial assets were

> the mechanical aptitude and ingenuity of a large and traditionally opportunistic artisan class. . . . Cottage spinners and weavers, saw- and

> grist-millers, tanners, coopers, ironworkers, shoemakers, candle-makers, charcoal burners, and all manner of workers in wood had by 1800 come to constitute that reservoir of skill and experience essential to the successful launching of large scale industrial experimentation.[6]

Iron making was vitally important in the formation of the textile industry, for the precision parts—gears, shafts, spindles, rollers—were made of metal. Equally important, the local craftsmen who would be called upon to fabricate and modify these new machine parts were those who had engaged in previous industrial ventures with the new textile entrepreneurs. And no group of artisans more clearly represents this phenomenon than the Wilkinsons, a family of industrious and industrializing Quaker iron manufacturers, all descended from Lawrance Wilkinson, who had emigrated to Providence from England in 1645.[7] These Wilkinsons were hard-working, temperate, willing to experiment, technically gifted despite minimal formal education, and from families whose economic status would best be described as middling yet who enjoyed relatively high status in their communities.

David Wilkinson's family played at least as important a part in his development as did the Revolution and its opportunities for technological innovation and economic gain. His father and two of his older cousins stand out as important ironworkers, textile innovators, tool makers, and—to a degree remarkable for the era—entrepreneurs. A summary of the careers of these three Wilkinson relatives up to the time of the Revolution will help to place David in the context of Rhode Island industrial development and suggests how factors such as family, religion, the colonial economy, and independence contributed to his growth.

~

The first of the Wilkinsons to gain industrial prominence was Israel, a farmer-blacksmith whose accomplishments demonstrate both the auspicious industrial conditions in late colonial Rhode Island and the growing involvement of Rhode Island's leading merchants in the colony's industrial development. Born in Smithfield in 1711, Israel and his wife Mary Aldrich raised eight children in the red farmhouse he built on the 172-acre family homestead on the road that followed the river between Worcester and Providence.[8]

Israel enters the historical record in the early 1750s as the "ingenious mechanic" who provided the technical expertise for the spermaceti candle works owned by Rhode Island's famous Brown family, who by 1760, as Nicholas Brown and Company, were the leading spermaceti candle manufacturer in the American colonies.[9] Early candle manufactories were not particularly sophisticated, yet did require large iron screw presses for squeezing the oil out of the crystalline spermaceti. And Israel Wilkinson was one of the few men who could make them.[10]

Israel's involvement with the spermaceti works began as early as 1753, and probably arose from a combination of his iron-working experience and his family connections with the Browns: two of Israel's nephews were captains of merchant ships owned by Obadiah Brown and Company. David Wilkinson remembered how "old Israel," along with an Englishman named Benjamin Crabb, made cast iron screws seven inches in diameter and weighing five hundred pounds for the candle works, and there is a possibility that Israel learned to cut screws "in the same manner as the English plan, brought over by Mr. Crabb." After setting up the Browns' candle works, Israel began making screws in his shop in Smithfield. According to Israel's great-grandson, "screws for pressing spermaceti oil, and clothier's screws, paper and cider mill screws were manufactured here, and so far as we know, they were the first made in New England."[11]

A clear indication of the value placed on Israel's knowledge of spermaceti candle technology is his agreement with Obadiah Brown by which Israel was "under a tye for the sum (£500) t'was thought best he should have which we accordingly gave him, for which he barred himself from erecting or repairing, etc. any spermaceti works without our consent."[12] Since their success had begun to draw competitors into the field, the Browns—much like English authorities with regard to textile technology—sought to keep their secrets from potential rivals. In effect, Israel was paid a retainer fee for his silence. Yet in 1763 he offered to return it with interest if the Browns would free him from the obligation. He had received an offer from two Quaker businessmen to build a spermaceti works in Philadelphia. This is both an example of the Quaker business network in which the Wilkinsons participated, and a tribute to Israel Wilkinson's far-reaching reputation as a skilled technician.

The Browns had no intention of freeing Israel from his obligation, concerned that he would build several spermaceti works in Philadelphia and more in New York on his return home. But they also feared that the wily Wilkinson would find another way around the restriction since, as rival candlemaker J. R. Rivera and Company warned them, "by tying the old gentleman and [leaving] his son (who works with his Father's ingenuity) at Liberty is really doing of nothing." In fact, Rivera revealed, that is exactly what had happened with another Newport spermaceti works: "They applied to the old gentleman who readily told them he could not on any account assist them, but hinted that he was under no obligation not to teach his son anything he knew and the consequence was that his son undertook and the Father directed."[13]

Israel declined the Philadelphia offer, apparently because he was occupied with a "furnace that is now going and in which my concern and engagement are such that I cannot attend on any account."[14] Although the Browns managed to control the situation, it is important to note that this "mechanic" was able to command a sizable retainer fee from the most powerful entrepreneurs in Providence and at the same time find clever ways to maintain his freedom of initiative—even if it meant the actual or threatened circumvention of a binding agreement.

~

The business enterprise that Israel gave as the excuse for declining the Philadelphia offer was likely the Unity or Amity Furnace on the Blackstone River in the village of Manville. Whatever the specific furnace, Israel and his brother-in-law John Rogers were engaged in iron making at some point before 1765 on a scale well beyond that of the blacksmith's forge. A blast furnace was a much more extensive enterprise than a common forge, and typically involved a twenty to forty-foot stone chimney, a sand-covered work floor where molten iron was tapped into rough molds called "sows" and "pigs," water-powered bellows, and extensive charcoal-making pits. An integrated facility might include a finery for reheating and hammering the pigs into more refined wrought iron bars, and perhaps a separate building for casting iron utensils such as kettles and pots. Unlike a forge, which could be operated by a single artisan and shut down after a day's work, a furnace employed a dozen or more men, and a "blast" might last for weeks or even months.[15]

This experience made Wilkinson and Rogers likely partners for the Browns when they established the Hope Furnace in 1765 in the town of Scituate, about ten miles southwest of Providence, to capitalize on an ore bed that had been discovered in nearby Cranston.[16] This powerful partnership brought together the most prominent merchants in Providence (the Brown brothers), two men with iron-making expertise (Wilkinson and Rogers), and a former governor of Rhode Island who would later sign the Declaration of Independence (Israel's nephew Stephen Hopkins).

Hope Furnace was an extensive enterprise with water-powered bellows and a labor force of seventy-five workers at its peak. The associated ore bed in Cranston was technologically interesting, employing a "large steam engine, which raised the water seventy-two feet from the bottom of the ore pit."[17] (This steam engine will play an important role in David Wilkinson's technological development.) Although the original plan to manufacture hollow ware for the Browns' Caribbean trade failed, Hope Furnace was a profitable producer of pig iron and during the Revolutionary War turned out cast-iron cannons. Wilkinson family lore has it that Israel and his brother-in-law were not rewarded commensurate with their contributions to Hope Furnace.[18] Perhaps once the furnace was up and running Israel's participation was no longer needed. This may indicate the limits of Wilkinson's ability to compete on equal terms with the powerful entrepreneurs: he was able to manipulate the Browns when they needed him, but powerless when his skills were no longer in demand.

Although Israel was not associated with Hope Furnace during the years when it produced cannon for the Revolutionary War effort, he was involved in cannon making and at least once traveled to Boston "for the purpose of extracting the 'core' of the cannon after casting, a difficulty the workmen could not overcome there." While making weapons was contrary to Israel's Quaker religion, it is possible that he did so as a means of demonstrating his patriotism while avoiding direct engagement in the war. The family biographer certainly considered him a patriot: "If he did not fire the cannon—he cast them, and if he did not use carnal weapons, he put no obstacles in the way of others using whatever was necessary to utterly destroy oppression and tyranny."[19] In any event, little more is known about Israel between this wartime activity and his death in 1784.

Hope Furnace and the spermaceti candle works are significant examples of what Peter J. Coleman has called the transformation of Rhode Island from a maritime economy to a burgeoning industrial economy in the late eighteenth century.[20] These commercial endeavors have particular relevance to our story because they establish a connection between the Wilkinsons and Moses Brown a quarter-century before the Wilkinsons' collaboration with Samuel Slater in the 1790s. Hope Furnace also establishes a relationship between the Browns of Providence and the Cabots of Beverly. In 1780 and again in 1781, the Cabot brothers purchased cannon from Hope Furnace to outfit their privateers. Despite continual demands for payment, the Cabots refused to settle the debt for three years. Thus, the two families demonstrate a history of adversarial business relations nearly a decade before their pioneering ventures in textile manufacturing.[21] Finally, this early industrialization in Rhode Island—and the Wilkinsons' involvement in it—sets the stage for a connection between ironworking and the development of a class of machinists who would specialize in the increasingly important manufacture of textile machinery.

~

Jeremiah Wilkinson (1741–1831), a second cousin of David's father, grew up working at the forge established by his grandfather in the town of Cumberland, just north of Providence. An accomplished ironsmith, Jeremiah also worked in silver and gold, crafting spoons and other pieces from melted coins, but his main concern in the years before the Revolution was the manufacture of the hand cards used to prepare wool or cotton fibers for spinning into yarn. Because there were no wool carding mills at the time, carding was done at home and there was a great need for hand cards—for currying horses as well as for carding wool. The process of manufacturing cards was slow and tedious: small wires had to be cut and bent, the leather card base punched with hundreds of holes, into which the wires were inserted. Jeremiah devised a way to mechanize production, inventing a machine that cut and bent the wires in the same movement, and another that, with the pull of a lever, punched all the holes for a card. When English wire became scarce, he drew his own wire by horse power—possibly the first drawn wire in America. From this wire he also made needles and pins, the value of which are attested to by his wife's claim that she was able to purchase a spinning wheel in exchange for three of her husband's darning needles.[22]

Jeremiah's major contribution to industrial history is in the manufacture of nails. Since the earliest days of the colonies, nails had been fashioned individually from slender shafts of wrought iron, called nailrod, which were heated in a forge, hammered to a point, then cut and headed. In the eighteenth century, mechanics of various sorts often found it more convenient to buy imported British nails. As British imports diminished in the mid-1770s, however, Americans were forced to revert to the slow process of forging wrought nails by hand.

According to David Wilkinson, Eleazer Smith told David's father in 1776 that Jeremiah had made nails, not by heating and hammering nailrod, but out of cold iron. Jeremiah had run out of the tacks he used to secure strips of leather to hand cards, and finding an old door lock on the floor, cut four thin pointed pieces with shears and headed them in a vise. Not only did this meet Jeremiah's need for his card-making business, but it became a business in itself. "The making of tacks proved quite lucrative," wrote Reverend Israel Wilkinson. "They were put up in papers and sold in Providence, Boston and other places." Within a year another Wilkinson—David's father Oziel—was producing his own nails by flattening iron plates with his water-powered trip hammer and cutting the points with shears, while his son sat on an improvised pinch press and headed the nails. "This was," David remembered, "the commencement, in the world, of making nails from cold iron."[23]

The fact that much of this activity occurs in the 1775–76 period is no coincidence. A scarcity of imported nails opened the door for innovation in domestic nail making; a war with Great Britain provided the opportunity for inventive men to lend their talents to the revolutionary cause; and a disrupted economy gave rise to (or extended) a barter system in which those who could provide technical tools, products, and services had an economic advantage. The war and the rise of industrialization reinforced each other. Early industrialization (cannon making, for example) made it possible to wage war, and the prosecution of the war spurred further production of tools, cloth, and other manufactured goods for which Americans had previously been dependent on Great Britain.[24]

Yet despite opportunities, it was clearly a time of hardship. A snapshot of the Jeremiah Wilkinson family in 1776—the year in which Jeremiah had achieved some success with his nail and card-making business, and young David had become enamored of tool making—suggests a difficult period. First, the war had come home to the Wilkinsons. In 1776, Jeremiah's brother Benjamin received a promotion from ensign to lieutenant in the local militia, and was a member of the Committee of Safety—the kind of military involvement that shook Quaker communities to their foundations. We can assume that the Quaker meeting warned Benjamin; we know for a fact that when two of his younger brothers, Stephen (21) and Jeptha (19), were discovered to be training as soldiers, they were disowned by the Quakers. Going to war was not an option for Jeremiah: his wife had died in 1774, and he was the single parent of five children, aged two to eight.

Yet war was an option for other Quakers (General Nathaniel Greene of Rhode Island is a prime example of the "fighting Quakers" of the period). There appears to have been a generational split between younger Quakers who were caught up in the spirit of the Revolution and older Quakers who were philosophically opposed to war—and also had wealth to protect. Some, such as Israel Wilkinson, compromised by supporting the war effort materially (manufacturing cannon) without actually fighting. It might even be argued that, while incompatible with Quaker religion, war might be compatible with the commercial interest of Quakers who were in demand for their products or services in wartime.[25]

Whatever the reasons that some of the Wilkinsons chose to support the war, the Cumberland Society of Friends strongly disagreed and took even harsher action against the family. At the same time that the Friends were dismissing the Wilkinson brothers, they also disowned their twenty-nine-year-old sister Patience, who had borne a child out of wedlock. Against this background of war and social problems, twenty-four-year-old Jemima, who had been influenced by the great English evangelist George Whitefield when he toured the colonies in 1770, was dismissed for having attended meetings at the local New Light Baptist church.[26] By late 1776, the war, her brothers' and sister's ouster, and her own dismissal by the Quakers brought on a crisis for Jemima. In October she awoke from a fever claiming that she had died during the night and that a Spirit reanimated her body "to warn a lost and guilty, perishing dying World, to flee from the wrath which is to come." Now known as the Public Universal Friend, she began to preach her own brand of evangelical religion in Cumberland and neighboring towns. Her poor father, obviously worried about her mental health, accompanied her on her travels, and for this he too was dismissed from the Society of Friends.[27]

Jemima became a well-known religious leader throughout southern New England and Pennsylvania. By the late 1780s, she had given up proselytizing and directed her efforts toward settling her congregation where they could "shun the company and conversation of the wicked world." Under her leadership they created a settlement near Seneca Lake in the wilds of western New York state. With houses, a sawmill, and a gristmill, the 260-person settlement was the largest in western New York in 1790.[28] This formation of a virtuous new society was, in its own way, consistent with the utopian principles of the Revolution, and played an important social and economic role in the westward expansion of the new nation. Like her more industrial-minded brother and cousins, Jemima exhibited her own pioneering spirit in the turbulent and expansive context of the Revolution and early republic.

Jeremiah outlived his famous sister and achieved his own small measure of renown, including a mention in *Scientific American* and having his original nail-cutting shears presented to the Rhode Island Historical Society. His son Gardner was an inventor and went into business with his brothers. It should be noted that these pioneering blacksmiths were farmers as well, and in addition to his industrial pursuits Jeremiah was known for his beautiful cherry orchards—considered by many the finest in Rhode Island.[29]

~

David's father, Oziel Wilkinson (1744–1815), to a greater extent than his successful cousins, launched an industrial dynasty. At least four of his sons were trained as blacksmiths, and all appear to have joined their father's trade very willingly, as the vignette of five-year-old David watching Eleazer Smith suggests. The term *blacksmith,* with its association of crude and sweaty work with clumsy tools, conveys the wrong image. In fact, Oziel and his sons made products and employed methods that were decidedly more sophisticated than those of the stereotypical village blacksmith. As we have seen, they were innovative, entrepreneurial, and well connected to businessmen such as the Browns as well as to other Wilkinsons and the wider Quaker community.

Oziel's father had also been a blacksmith, with a shop in Smithfield on Mussey's Brook, which empties into the Blackstone River, and had used a water-powered trip hammer to do the heavy work of pounding metal. With little formal education, Oziel learned the trade in his father's shop, and built a reputation in the greater Providence area as a first-rate mechanic. The Smithfield workshop was a focal point for technical innovation in the area, in the words of the family biographer "a school of invention, and although some of the machines were unshapely things, still they were the Genesis of greater improvements." Eleazer Smith's work on the machine to make card teeth is only one example. Another is Oziel's extension of his cousin Jeremiah's nail-making innovations, to which he added a machine for heading nails of various sizes—a notable improvement over heading nails one at a time in a vise, and particularly welcome in the late 1770s when nails were no longer imported from England. While the war opened opportunities for this sort of manufacture, it also posed risks. As early as 1775, Oziel had decided to move his operation from the small brook in Smithfield to the powerful Pawtucket Falls on the Blackstone River. But the British possession of Newport and the constant threat to the Providence area dissuaded him, and it was not until peace was restored in 1783 that he moved his operation to Pawtucket, at that time a village of North Providence. It should be noted that as an elder in the Society of Friends, Oziel did not engage in any military activity during the war. But, like Israel and Jeremiah, he did contribute by means of his workshop.[30]

The new Wilkinson shop in Pawtucket was primarily an anchor forge, supplying anchors and chains for large ships built in Providence and Boston. About 1786, Oziel bought from Israel Wilkinson's son the equipment Israel had used to make molds for casting iron screws and began making screw presses. This proved to be a profitable business, with customers in Taunton, New Bedford, and elsewhere. According to family history, the other Wilkinsons were not envious of Oziel's success with this acquired technology but rather "contributed their patronage and co-operation." This demonstrates the value of the family associations and the larger Quaker network in which the Wilkinsons operated, as well as the sort of technology sharing that is an essential part of successful industrial development.[31]

Oziel's prominence in the iron industry positioned him to expand into other technical businesses, such as steel making, flour milling, and textile manufacturing. These endeavors properly belong to a later period, between 1790 and 1815. What concerns us more here is Oziel's influence on his son David's early development. David took to his father's business readily, and the combination of his native intelligence, early experience in metalworking, and connections with men who were experimenting in the budding field of textile tool development were of decisive importance. Together they contributed to his prominence at the point when Samuel Slater arrived in Rhode Island, as well as to his success in tool and machine manufacturing later in his career.

~

David Wilkinson was born in 1771 in Smithfield, the fourth of Oziel and Lydia Wilkinson's ten children. He was very much at home in his father's workshop, where he was put to work as early as age six. "I think in 1777," he later wrote, "my father made a small pinch press, with different sized impressions, placed on an oak log, with a stirrup for the foot, and sat me astraddle on the log, to heading nails, which were cut with common shears."[32] David had little formal education, none past the age of nine. His last day of school can be dated precisely, due to a detail noted by his friend George Taft:

> He told me that he graduated and took his degree on the dark day; a day memorable in the history of New England. It occurred in the year 1780. He was then attending a female school. The good woman was very much alarmed and dismissed her school. He was then nine years old, and went to school no more.[33]

The "dark day" was Friday, May 19, 1780, when the sun's light was completely obscured to the point that many thought Judgment Day was at hand. It is now believed that the sky was darkened by smoke and ash from forest fires raging in Ontario, Canada. We can imagine the bewildered boy and his terrified teacher—in fact the whole community of people devoted to biblical prophecy and signs of revelation; but we cannot determine whether the fear and uncertainty of this event caused him or his parents to decide against further schooling. We know nothing else of David's formal education other than its dramatic finish.[34]

David was schooled in the workshop. Reverend Taft later remarked that "[h]is education did not consist in an accumulation of learned rubbish, nor did it make a dazzling show; it was pre-eminently useful and practical." By the age of fifteen he was doing a man's work, still under his father's guidance but increasingly on his own. "My father had once seen old Israel Wilkinson mould one screw," David recollected,

> and, after he had bought these old tools of young Israel, as he was called, and at a time when he wanted some moulding done, he took me—then about fifteen years old—into his chaise and carried me to Hope Furnace . . . to mould a paper mill screw, as they had no moulder at their furnace who would undertake to mould one. I had never seen a furnace in operation, or seen a thing moulded, in my life. I moulded three or four screws before I left for home. I stayed there about a month. The screws weighed about five hundred pounds each.[35]

Although the war ended in 1783, British economic policies and the inability of the American Continental government to tax and provide an adequate money supply had resulted in a postwar depression. One response to this adversity was innovation, particularly in the field of textile production, where British hegemony notably hurt the American economy. With experience in metalworking and tool making, as well as the benefit of technology that had been transferred across the Atlantic, American entrepreneurs and mechanics began to experiment with the manufacture of cotton yarn. In 1784 or 1785, David heard that John Reynolds, a Quaker woolen manufacturer in East Greenwich (about fifteen miles south of Providence), was producing yarn on a jenny—a machine less sophisticated than the Arkwright machines then in vogue (and protected) in Britain, but one that promised a start toward practical textile technology. David soon began forging and grinding spindles for the machine. "I made a small machine to grind with, which had a roller of wood to roll on the stone, which turned the spindle against the stone, and so ground the steel spindles perfectly." Thus, young David Wilkinson was not only making parts for spinning machinery but creating tools to make the parts. The method he described closely resembles the process of centerless grinding, and if so, he was—at the age of fourteen—among the first to put it into practice.[36]

David had become an active participant in a much broader effort—particularly by Friends—to introduce successful textile manufacturing in the United States. Quaker businessmen such as Moses Brown had suffered disproportionately during the postwar depression, because their strict ethical codes prevented them from engaging in the West Indian or slave trades (both of which Moses' non-Quaker brother John did), or from delaying or reneging on payments to creditors. Under these circumstances, Brown was convinced that the only way to remedy the debt and trade problems with Britain was to develop an American textile industry. In 1788, he sent fellow Friend John Bailey, a well-known clockmaker, to examine the model equipment commissioned by the state of Massachusetts at Colonel Orr's workshop in Bridgewater, then personally visited Bridgewater as well as the manufactories at Beverly, Worcester, and Hartford. He also drew on the Quaker network, many of whom had engaged in technical trades such as iron, clockmaking, or carding, and thus for whom textile manufacturing would be a natural choice for the investment of their capital and labor.[37]

Daniel Anthony—for whom Eleazer Smith had made cards in Oziel's workshop as young David looked on—was still in the textile business in 1788, in a partnership with Andrew Dexter, a former importer of British goods, and Lewis Peck of Providence to produce "home-spun cloth." Their original plan was to spin cotton and linen yarn by hand (probably using jennies) then weave jean cloth from a combination of these two yarns. (Linen yarn could withstand the strain placed on the warp threads in a loom. Cotton yarn was considerably weaker and, particularly when spun by jennies, could only be used for the weft, or filling, threads.) The plan changed when the partners learned that Hugh Orr had models of British spinning and carding equipment in his Bridgewater shop. Anthony and the East Greenwich wool manufacturer John Reynolds traveled to Bridgewater to examine the state model Arkwright spinning frame. According to Anthony's son William, they made drawings of the model, although by David Wilkinson's account they also returned with "some parts of a machine, called the Arkwright Water Frame, which was commenced by a European, in the employ of Colonel Orr . . . and given up, or the few parts thrown by." The European is presumably Thomas Somers, who we know moved on to the Beverly Cotton Manufactory. The state of the machine parts suggests they were junk, yet Wilkinson goes on to say that Anthony "soon had one [Arkwright frame] under way in Providence, which was made and finished in Pawtucket, and put in operation there," by Anthony and his four sons. Wilkinson assisted "in finishing and keeping in order their machine."[38] Either the state's model from Bridgewater was in relatively good shape, or Anthony and Wilkinson had become adequately skilled in textile machinery, or were sufficiently intuitive, to construct a working Arkwright frame from a collection of parts.

While Anthony was experimenting with the Arkwright frame, his partners engaged yet another Quaker mechanic, Joshua Lindley, to build a carding machine. Oziel Wilkinson did the ironwork along with brass founder Daniel Jackson. "The card was put in operation in the Market House chamber, in Providence," David Wilkinson wrote, "and was turned by a colored man, named Prince Hopkins, who had lost one leg, and I think one arm, in Sullivan's expedition at Newport, a few years before." The lack of integration in the production line is evident from Wilkinson's report that "the cotton was taken from the card, in rolls about eighteen inches long, and carried one mile from town to Moses Brown's, where it was made into roping [roving], by a young woman in Mr. Brown's employ, named Amey Lawrence."[39] Still, despite an awkward arrangement, the Rhode Island textile pioneers were producing cotton yarn by means of carding machines and jennies, as well as weaving cloth by hand on flying shuttle looms, all the while hoping for the breakthrough that would come with the successful implementation of the Arkwright system.[40]

The Arkwright frame actually worked, although not to everyone's satisfaction. Wilkinson blamed the state of the cotton—in this pre–cotton gin era, the cotton was delivered with seeds, which had to be removed by hand, resulting in its "bad condition." He also admitted, vaguely, that the machinery was "imperfect," and that after producing "some few tons of yarn [they] laid the machinery by." Moses Brown's version—recorded in 1791 and probably more accurate in this respect than Wilkinson's long look back—mentions the jenny and the carding machine based on the Bridgewater models, both of which worked adequately after "great alterations," as well as a hand-operated Arkwright frame, which was tried in East Greenwich without success. Brown purchased all of this machinery, and "attempted to set [the Arkwright frame] to Work by water and Made a Little yarn, so as to answer for Warps, but being so Imperfect, both as to Quality and Quantity of the yarn that their use was Suspended until I could procure a person who had Wrought or seen them wrought in Europe."[41]

At this point Moses Brown—who now owned almost all of the experimental machines in Rhode Island, including two twenty-four-spindle Arkwright frames, Lindley's carding machine, and twenty-eight- and sixty-eight-spindle jennies from Dexter and Peck—began advertising for an individual with Arkwright system experience, which resulted in Samuel Slater's coming to Rhode Island.[42] It is important to summarize at this point that before Slater's arrival, Arkwright machinery had been built in Rhode Island, by local mechanics, and was made to operate well enough to produce some amount of yarn that could "answer for warps." But a single spinning frame does not constitute a factory, and—as the earlier example of the mile ride between the carding and roving stages suggests—what was most lacking was a factory *system,* something Slater understood better than anyone in America.

~

Samuel Slater's story is well known, and only a brief summary is necessary here to close this initial phase of textile experimentation in New England. Slater (1768–1835) was raised in a relatively affluent family in Derbyshire, England.

Figure 2.1
This 48-spindle spinning frame was put into operation in December 1790 at Samuel Slater's original mill in Pawtucket. It was donated to the Smithsonian by the Rhode Island Society for the Encouragement of Domestic Industry. *Courtesy of the Smithsonian Institution Archives, image #91-3686.*

He was apprenticed to Jedediah Strutt, a textile mill owner and former partner of the famous Richard Arkwright. Strutt's factory at Belper turned that tiny village into the second most populous town in Derbyshire. Samuel was no ordinary apprentice and received training in factory management as well as in technical matters. He excelled at both, and by the age of twenty-one was a supervisor with a thorough knowledge of the most up-to-date Arkwright-style textile factory.

Exactly what prompted Slater to emigrate is not clear. He was not an inventor, so neither the hostility of displaced hand workers nor the vagaries of the patent system would have driven him from England. Furthermore, what he contemplated was illegal; he faced fines, imprisonment, and loss of citizenship. With his excellent prospects, what would have motivated him to take such a risk? One strong possibility is that by 1789 he feared the overexpansion of the cotton textile business in Britain. Strutt seems to have told young Samuel early in his apprenticeship that business might never be as good as it currently was, "but I have no doubt it will always be a fair business, if it be well managed."[43]

According to Slater's friend and biographer George S. White, "Mr. Slater told me that he contemplated trying America for some time; and that his object was, to get a general knowledge of the business, in order to come to this country and introduce the manufacture of cotton, on the Arkwright improvement, and that he remained after the time of his indenture with that special object in view." Slater certainly knew of the opportunities in America, having read in a 1787 news article that a man named John Hague, originally from Slater's home county of Derbyshire, had received £100 from the Pennsylvania Society for the Encouragement of Manufacture and the Useful Arts for the construction of a water-powered carding machine. This—and undoubtedly other reports of rewards in America or concerns about the future of the textile industry in England—finally convinced Slater to elude detection by dressing as a farm laborer and to board ship for the United States.[44]

His first job upon arrival in 1789 was with the New York Manufacturing Society, where, he wrote, "we have but one card, two machines, two spinning jennies, which I think are not worth using." He was soon informed that Rhode Island entrepreneur Moses Brown was experimenting with carding and spinning equipment, and was looking for a "manager of cotton spinning" with Arkwright machinery. Slater came to Rhode Island, evaluated the models that Brown had collected, worked with local machinists and mechanics to build new machines based on designs he knew well from his factory experience in England, and in partnership with Brown and Brown's son-in-law William Almy and nephew Smith Brown, set up a mechanized spinning mill at the falls of the Blackstone River in Pawtucket. The venture was a success far beyond expectations.[45]

Little wonder, then, that in the vast majority of references to the introduction of cotton manufacturing in America, Samuel Slater gets all the credit. Part of the reason is the tendency to simplify a complex story by concentrating on a main character. As Robert B. Gordon and Patrick M. Malone explain, "The sum of the incremental improvements in technique made by many individuals becomes identified with one person in the historical record through the social reconstruction of invention in the patent system or through efforts to simplify and organize history."[46] Of course, Slater does indeed deserve much of the credit, but by ignoring the contributions of so many machinists and mechanics and underestimating the technological progress that had been made in America prior to 1790, we miss the sequence of steps from nonfunctioning models to successful water-powered machinery.[47]

Much of the mythology about Slater derives from an early biography, written in 1836 by George S. White.[48] While a gold mine of letters and facts about early textile manufacturing, White's appraisal of Slater borders on the worshipful, as in this passage:

> Samuel Slater, *without the aid of any one who had ever seen such machinery, did actually, from his personal knowledge and skill,* put in motion the whole series of Arkwright's patents; and that he put them in such perfect operation, as to produce as good yarn, and cotton cloth of various descriptions, equal to any article of the kind produced in England at that time.

Picking up White's reverent tone, the *North American Review* offered this description of Slater's challenge: "With his own hands he commenced making machinery, working with indefatigable industry, night and day."[49] This idealization of Slater's contribution both diminishes the efforts of local mechanics and suggests that the mechanization of textile production at this point was more primitive than it actually was. Other sources, such as the reminiscences of firsthand participants David Wilkinson and William Anthony, indicate the degree to which Slater relied on local mechanics to put his—or rather Arkwright's—ideas into operation.[50]

On Slater's arrival, he was brought by Moses Brown to Oziel Wilkinson's home, where he lived for a time, and met Oziel's fifteen-year-old daughter Hannah, whom he married the following year. He was set up in the Pawtucket shop of carpenter-millwright Sylvanus Brown who fabricated all the wood components, while Oziel and his sons Abraham, Isaac, and David furnished the iron and brass parts. Together they built, according to David's youngest brother Smith Wilkinson, "a water frame of 24 spindles, two carding machines, and the drawing and roping frames necessary to prepare for the spinning, and soon after added a frame of 48 spindles." Smith, it should be noted, went to work in Slater's first mill, tending the "breaker," or first carding machine, at the age of ten.[51]

Most of the machinery appears to have been made with relatively little difficulty: within three months, Oziel had fabricated all the metal parts for the roving, drawing, and spinning frames, a feat largely attributable to all the trial and error work that had gone on before Slater's arrival. The carding machine, however, took much longer to complete and furnishes us with a final example of Slater's dependence on American mechanics. After the Arkwright frames were finished, the system was "still imperfect for want of Other Mashines such as Cards of a Different Construction from those Already Made and remadeover," as Moses Brown phrased it. Even with Slater's reworking, the cotton would bunch up inside the carding cylinders. Part of this machine—the card clothing which consisted of sets of bent wire bristles—had been contracted out to Pliny Earle, the well-established card maker from Leicester, Massachusetts. Although outside the closed group of mechanics secretly working in Pawtucket, Earle was

Figure 2.2

Englishman Samuel Slater (1768–1835), with partners Almy & Brown and technical assistance from the Wilkinsons, created the first successful water-powered spinning factory in America.

Courtesy of the Rhode Island Historical Society. Samuel Slater. Rhode Island. n.d. Ink on paper—steel engraving. Print. RHi X3 1069.

nevertheless a member of the Quaker network. In consultation with Slater he determined that an alteration in the angle of the wire bristles would resolve the problem, and the last remaining technical difficulty was surmounted.[52]

~

This phase of the story might be visually depicted by two contrasting portraits. One is the classic view of Samuel Slater working feverishly and alone in a shuttered shop with a pile of unusable machine parts discarded by the side and a new Arkwright frame emerging by dint of his prodigious memory and skilled hands. The other shows Slater still at the center, but surrounded on one side by the warm and supportive Wilkinson family and on the other by an array of talented and experienced local mechanics in the process of transforming those experimental machines into the Arkwright-design mill, with Moses Brown in the background orchestrating the funds and obtaining resources from the network to keep the process moving forward. This more historically and socially accurate second portrait gives Slater his central position, but places a more proper emphasis on the supporting cast of Oziel and David Wilkinson, Sylvanus Brown, Pliny Earle, Daniel and Richard Anthony, Daniel Jackson, John Field, William Tefft, and certainly others.[53] This was a joint effort with a long history, dating back to the achievements of Israel and Jeremiah Wilkinson. These new textile experimenters of 1786–1790 were at the leading edge of a new industry, and perhaps they were aware of its significance. Why else would Oziel send his ten-year-old son Smith to work in a cotton mill rather than his own iron workshop? Conscious or not of the impending transformation, these craftsmen were, thanks to Moses Brown's vision, deliberately working to develop a new and desperately needed industry. On a more basic and individual level they were also engaging in technological experimentation to further their own economic ends—which was simply a continuation of what artisans such as the Wilkinsons had been doing for generations.

Figure 2.3

Moses Brown (1738–1836), the leading entrepreneur behind the introduction of mechanized cotton spinning in America, induced Samuel Slater to settle in Pawtucket.

Courtesy of the Rhode Island Historical Society. Martin John Head. Moses Brown. Providence RI c. 1856. Painting. RHi X5 75.

3

The Progress of a Textile Machinist

Paul Moody, 1794–1814

> Never shall I forget the awe with which I entered [the woolen factory]. The huge drums that carried the bands on the lower floor, coupled with the novel noise and hum increased this awe; but when I reached the second floor where picking, carding, spinning and weaving were in progress my amazement became complete.
>
> —Sarah Emery, describing Byfield factory in 1794

Young David Wilkinson had already learned the rudiments of the iron trade from his father when Paul Moody was born on May 23, 1779, in Byfield Parish, in the town of Newbury, Massachusetts. His father was known as Captain Paul Moody, having commanded a company of men from Newbury in Colonel Timothy Pickering's regiment during the Revolutionary War. Captain Moody was "a man of much influence in the parish and town," not only for his military rank, but for his grist mill. He married Mary Jewett of Lyme, Connecticut, on October 25, 1762.[1]

Depending on the source, the younger Paul Moody was either the ninth of eleven children or the tenth of twelve, the discrepancy probably attributable to the inconsistency with which infant deaths were recorded in the eighteenth century. In any event, Paul grew up with at least four older brothers (Samuel, Nathan, Enoch, and Sewall) and two older sisters (Mehitable and Deborah). He also had two younger brothers, William (1781) and David (1783). Paul was baptized on July 4, 1779.[2] Whether his parents intentionally chose the newly meaningful day for his christening is unknown.

The Moodys appear to have been of middling status, owning their own farm as well as an important mill site that adjoined their property at the falls of the Parker River. Both Paul Moody senior and his father had been millers as well as farmers. Millers had a special status in any village or town, often granted a monopoly by the local officials to maintain the grist mill and provide a vital service to the farmers in the vicinity. The mill also provided income, further enhancing the family's status. The Moody family home, still standing today, was large, with generous high-ceilinged rooms and interesting Georgian interior details. It was one of the more refined homes in Newbury.[3]

In many respects, the Moodys were similar to many other independent farming families in late-eighteenth-century New England. Yet there was also something special about them, perhaps due to their lineage. Paul senior was a fifth-generation descendent of William Moody, who had emigrated from Ipswich, England, to Ipswich, Massachusetts, in 1634, later becoming one of the first settlers of nearby Newbury. Many of William's descendants had distinguished themselves as ministers or teachers, and education seems to have been a distinctive aspect of the family history: in the first six generations of the family in America, nine graduated from Harvard College and six from Dartmouth. Paul's older brothers Nathan and Samuel were two of the Dartmouth graduates. The Moodys were also associated with Dummer Academy, a school "intermediate between the common school and college," the first such preparatory school in Massachusetts.[4] When the school opened in Byfield in 1763, Paul's great-great-uncle Samuel Moody was its principal, and he remained in that position until 1790. By all accounts Samuel was an odd man, although probably less eccentric than his father, the Reverend Joseph Moody, well known throughout New England as "Handkerchief Moody" for his lifelong custom of hiding his face from public view. In his youth, he had accidently killed a friend, and chose this means of atoning for it. Reverend Moody's peculiarity provided the basis for Nathaniel Hawthorne's short story "The Minister's Black Veil."[5]

Dummer Academy (now The Governor's Academy) was free to all boys from Byfield. The school records for the eighteenth century do not specify dates of attendance or whether students completed their studies, but all of Paul's older brothers are listed under the first headmaster, and Paul and David are recorded under the second, Isaac Smith, who presided from 1790 to 1809. The family histories report that Paul left school at the age of twelve; if he was at Dummer no earlier than 1790, then he could have been there only a year or two (he was eleven in 1790). This suggests that his earlier education was at the local common school.[6] According to the family history, when Paul left school he decided not to be a farmer and resolved to be no longer financially dependent on his family. What sort of pressure he might have been under to carry on the family farm we can only surmise. His two Dartmouth-educated brothers moved to Hallowell, Maine, where Nathan became a teacher and Samuel a merchant. Enoch took up farming, a few miles away in Newburyport. Sewall and William remained in Byfield parish and also became farmers. But at the time Paul was making his momentous decision, Sewall was seventeen and William only ten; thus it is possible that the stewardship of the family farm was yet to be decided.

Family histories and early reminiscences provide clues to how Paul considered his future. As a child, Paul was "more inclined to mechanical pursuits than to books, and somewhat disposed to have his own way," wrote family biographer Charles Moody. But youthful willfulness and an interest in mechanical things—including the playthings that he insisted on taking to bed with him—provide weak proof of a burgeoning mechanical genius. "He long afterwards described to his sister," Charles Moody wrote, "the favorite and well-known spot, on their father's farm, where he lay and resolved these thoughts in his mind."[7] But what specifically the thoughts and aspirations might have been is not recorded. We have to look to what Paul did, rather than what he might have been thinking.

What Paul Moody did was to take an interest in textile machinery. Given his later career, this of course is significant, and we have to ask whether this was prescience or simply chance. His mechanical aptitude, so patently obvious later, was probably evident by the time he was twelve. Just as important, there were models for him to follow. Men who understood such things as mills, waterwheels, and fulling (wool-cleansing) machinery were vitally important to the small towns of New England. These were men of standing, with power over the elements. Higher education may have been the more customary route to status in the community, but we should not discount the economic and social possibilities of the miller, the fuller, or the men who could build and maintain the mills and equipment.[8]

Although Paul's personal declaration of independence suggests that it was counter to his family's wishes, he may in fact have been following an alternative family tradition. Since his father and grandfather had been mill owners, it is likely that a career involving mills or mill machinery would have appealed to him. Aside from his rejection of farming, and the suggestion that higher education would not be his path to independence, we simply have no record of his precise intentions.

There is a tendency in nineteenth-century biography to attribute success to destiny. According to the Moody family biography, written in 1847, Paul's decision to follow a path different from his brothers is a matter of fate: Paul succeeded as a machinist and therefore must have been destined for a career in machine making. But destiny had less to do with it than the simple fact that in 1794 the British textile revolution came to Byfield, where Captain Paul Moody owned the land surrounding the falls of the Parker River.

The falls near the center of Byfield parish had been an important factor in the economic life of the town of Newbury throughout its history. Called

Quascacunquen or Quascycung ("the falls") by the Native Americans, it still retained a certain quality of mystery during Paul Moody's youth. Legend had it that the falls was a witches' meeting place, a myth popularized in John Greenleaf Whittier's "The Witch of Wenham":

> For Tituba, my Indian, saith
> At Quasycung she took
> The Black Man's godless sacrament
> And signed his dreadful book.[9]

Salem was less than twenty miles away from Byfield, and the pall of the witch trials still lingered in the 1790s. We are fortunate that Newbury native Sarah Smith Emery, a contemporary of Paul Moody, left a clear-eyed reminiscence of her town. "Though the days of Salem witchcraft were ended and old women were no longer hung as witches," she wrote, "in every community there was one or more believed to possess the 'evil eye,' and in every house could be seen horse shoes above the doors, and other charms against their machinations." Such beliefs often have a more immediate basis, and young Sally's real fear was tramps. "In my more youthful days the roads were infested by tramps. Ugly looking men and women, begging their way from one place to another. The meeting of such people on my way to and from school was one of the terrors of my childhood." But there was a witch in Byfield too, an old woman by the name of Tuggie Noyes, whom Sally remembered faintly—"a dim recollection of stealing behind my mother to peep at the witch, as she bargained for some tobacco that my father had raised." As a boy, Sarah's husband David Emery tested whether Tuggie Noyes was a witch by dropping a sixpence in her path, a measure known to stop a true witch. When "she passed over it with a curtsy and good day," he no longer believed she was a witch.[10]

Even more important than its contribution to the folklore of the town, the falls proved since the earliest European settlement to be a dependable source of water power. In 1636, just a year after Newbury was founded, Richard Dummer and John Spencer built the first mill—a sawmill initially, but by 1638 a gristmill. Most relevant to textile history is the establishment of a fulling mill in Byfield in 1643. During the colonial era, the woolen yarn was spun on hand spinning wheels and the cloth woven on hand looms. Fulling—the process of cleaning and shrinking woven woolen cloth—was required to improve the texture and appearance of the cloth.[11]

Fulling was one of the earliest stages of cloth manufacture to be mechanized. It was a rudimentary process: the cloth was soaked in a wooden vat of soapy water; a pair of rollers, driven by the mill's waterwheel, raised the cloth partially out of the water; finally, a set of large wooden mallets, driven by cams off the waterwheel, pounded the cloth, further concentrating and strengthening the wool fibers. The cleaned cloth was then hung on "tenterhooks" to dry. The fuller often dyed the cloth as well, unless it was dyed "in the wool"—that is, by the household wool spinner while the wool was still loose fleece.[12] Sarah Smith Emery described the fulling mill of her childhood:

> In September . . . the weaving of woolen cloth was begun, in order that it should be returned from the mill where it was fulled, colored and pressed in time to be made up before Thanksgiving. This mill was in Byfield, at the Falls . . . and was owned and run by Mr. Benjamin Pearson. The winter's stocking yarn was also carded and spun, and the lengthening evenings began to be enlivened by the busy click of knitting needles.[13]

In those days, when Sally Smith was a child and Paul Moody in his early teens, home textile production was a central part of everyday life in Newbury, and the fulling mill at the falls was the hub of the network.

The Moody family did not own the fulling mill, but were the proprietors of the gristmill, another node in the network of the local economy. As prominent and influential citizens, they were engaged in all the political and religious issues of the town. There is no record of the political leanings of the Moodys in Paul's early years, but the area was predominantly Federalist. They probably agreed with the Byfield minister, Reverend Elijah Parish, who believed "the accession of the Democratic party to power to be a great national calamity, and that Mr. Jefferson was utterly unfit to be President." Dr. Parish "especially denounced what he deemed the antiscriptural sentiments of the President."[14] This opinion became much more widespread during Jefferson's 1807 Embargo, which devastated the New England economy.

In ecclesiastical matters, however, the Moodys did not see eye to eye with Reverend Parish. When the young Mr. Parish was called to the Byfield church in 1787, Paul's father was one of the signers of a petition to rescind the offer, partly because the salary of eighty-five pounds and fifteen cords of wood per year was excessive, but primarily because, as one of the dissenters bluntly put it, "I know not but [Parish's doctrines] will sink all into Hell who die in the belief of them, and would it be thought wisdom in me to walk in a path which I fear might at last land me in Hell?" At the heart of the controversy was Parish's insistence that children of "halfway covenant" parents (those members who could not claim to have had a religious experience) could not be baptized in the church. This was a daring innovation in a church whose majority were halfway covenant members, and it drove the Moodys and about thirty other families to form an independent society. The separation lasted about ten years, at which point, Sarah Emery tells us, "the talent and fame, coupled with the genial humor of the celebrated Dr. Parish, drew the seceders back to the old church."[15] This experience, covering most of Paul Moody's youth, will echo later in his purposeful change of religious affiliation when he moves to the new factory town of Lowell.

~

In contrast to the introduction of mechanized cotton spinning in Rhode Island, the industrial story in Paul Moody's Byfield begins with wool. Briefly noted in our earlier discussion of textile development in Rhode Island was John Reynolds's wool-weaving operation in East Greenwich, where Scottish weavers James McKerris and Joseph Alexander had immigrated in 1788, bringing with them an understanding of the flying shuttle loom, which was employed in Providence for Moses Brown's early effort in textile manufacture. A similar but more consequential event occurred in Massachusetts shortly thereafter. Two weavers from Yorkshire, brothers Arthur and John Scholfield, arrived in Boston in May 1793, with the intention of establishing a woolen cloth manufactory in the United States. They set up a small woolen-weaving operation in a rented house in Charlestown, using a forty-spindle jenny and a hand loom that they built from memory. Their operation so impressed Reverend Jedidiah Morse—minister of the First Congregational Church in Charlestown, as well as a noted geographer, historian, and father of inventor Samuel F. B. Morse—that he put the Scholfield brothers in touch with William Bartlet, a wealthy Newburyport merchant. Late in 1793, the Scholfields moved their equipment to Newburyport and began building a carding machine which was operated by hand in a local stable.[16] All the essential components—carding engine, spinning jenny, and loom—were now present, except for the water power to drive the carding machines.

Newburyport was rich with investment funds but lacked a source of water power sufficient to drive textile machinery. The Newburyport Woolen Company was incorporated on January 29, 1794. The venture was highly capitalized at $300,000, and one of the shareholders was Moses Brown (of Newburyport) who had been a correspondent of his more famous namesake from Providence and had been an investor in the Beverly Cotton Manufactory. The critical water power was supplied by Captain Paul Moody.[17]

The Moody farm included a dam on the Parker River, where the family operated a grist mill and leased land and water privileges to Thomas Thompson for a snuff mill and Daniel Plummer for a chocolate mill. When approached by the Newburyport investors, Moody accepted "four hundred and fifty pounds lawful money" for six acres, including the dam, the gristmill, and permission for the renters to stay until their leases expired, allowing "a reasonable time to remove said snuff mill of said Thompson and the chocolate mill of the said Plummer off the premises."[18]

Why would Captain Moody sell the land and mills that had been in the family since 1710? He was fifty-two years old at the time, apparently in good health and able to work (inferred from the fact that he lived to be eighty years of age), and had seven sons ranging in age from twelve to twenty-eight. Perhaps it was the kind of offer he could not pass up, one that provided more money than he could possibly earn from working and leasing the mills. He probably knew some of the investors, although he did not become an investor himself. If he were caught up in the excitement and believed in the potential of this new technology and business venture, it would be logical to think that he would have struck a deal that would have ongoing revenue potential. Instead, he sold for a one-time payment of £450, and was apparently satisfied.[19]

Late in 1794, a marvelous three-story factory building was constructed, measuring one hundred feet long by forty feet wide. (For comparison, Samuel Slater's 1793 mill was only 43 by 29 feet.)[20] "The erection of this mill created a great sensation throughout the whole region," wrote Newbury native Sarah Emery, who was seven years old that year. "People visited it from far and near. Ten cents was charged as an admittance fee. That first winter sleighing parties came from all the adjacent towns, and as distant as Hampstead and Derry, in New Hampshire." Rather than distrust this early technology, Americans appeared to be enthralled by it. Nor was this fascination with mechanization something new: even in the seventeenth century, people wanted to see the iron-works at Saugus, Massachusetts, annoying the agent who had to take time from his work to show visitors around, to the point where the practice was forbidden in 1652. We have no record of the initial reaction of young Paul, but there is every reason to think that he was as captivated as his neighbors, one of whom later wrote: "Never shall I forget the awe with which I entered . . . the vast and imposing edifice. The huge drums that carried the bands on the lower floor, coupled with the novel noise and hum increased this awe; but when I reached the second floor where picking, carding, spinning and weaving were in progress my amazement became complete."[21] Paul's wonder and excitement may have been even keener, since this splendid structure was right next to his home.

Aside from the curiosity and entertainment aspect, this new factory affected the parish of Byfield in several important ways. It had brought foreigners to the neighborhood—besides the two Scholfield brothers there was another Yorkshire weaver, John Shaw, plus John Scholfield's wife and six children, as well as British machine makers James Standring, Samuel Guppy, and John Armstrong, who built the carding engines for the factory. It had also brought factory jobs, presumably some of which went to local people, although Sarah Emery remembered that "most of the operatives were English." She also noted that "most of the operatives were males, a few young girls being employed in splicing rolls." However, there is no direct evidence that the factory owners intended to furnish "employment for the honest industrious poor" as the Beverly Cotton

Manufactory and many other early textile mills had claimed. Whether the poor tramps that Sarah feared so much found jobs at the factory is unknown.[22]

~

Fifteen-year-old Paul Moody was captivated by everything about the new mill, especially the process of weaving. The weavers themselves were an exotic sort. As British technology historian Harold Catling writes, "This was a time of unprecedented prosperity for weavers [in England]. They wore topboots and ruffed shirts and would parade the streets of the town with a £5 note stuck carelessly in their hat bands." While it is unlikely that weavers went to this extreme in America, it suggests that they enjoyed high status while they were in demand. But what fascinated Paul was what they did—how they controlled the loom, with its spring-loaded flying shuttle, and produced fine woven cloth.[23]

Determined to master the loom, Paul was rebuffed each time he asked one of the weavers to teach him. There may have been a bit of British snobbery at work here: no rude American boy could learn the fine art of weaving. Paul eventually got the weaver's attention by incapacitating his loom, blocking its operation in such a subtle way that upon discovering the obstruction the weaver exclaimed, "Paul Moody is the only one who could have done it." This, apparently, was a reference to the boy's mechanical aptitude rather than any propensity for troublemaking. Paul had made his point, and soon another weaver agreed to teach him. By the age of sixteen, Paul Moody was adept at operating the woolen loom—an experience, he later said, that proved invaluable for building power looms at Waltham.[24]

Paul's career as a weaver lasted about a year. Another change came to the Byfield factory that drew him onto a more technical path. Jacob Perkins, aptly described as "probably the most ingenious and versatile mechanic and inventor in America" in this period, set up his recently invented nail-making machinery in the woolen manufactory. Perkins (1766–1849) possessed a wide range of technical skills: he became a goldsmith's apprentice at age thirteen, invented a method of plating silver shoe buckles, and about 1790 built a machine that would cut and head nails in one operation, which he patented in 1795. He appears to have juggled several occupations at once, as suggested by an advertisement in November 1793 for "two or three stout active Lads 14 to 16 years old . . . wanted as Apprentices to the Buckle-making Business," at the same time he was actively engaged in nail making.[25]

The most likely explanation for Perkins to choose Byfield is that the Newburyport native knew some of the investors in the factory and through them could gain access to a dependable source of water power. He apparently also knew Guppy and Armstrong, the carding machine makers, for an advertisement in the *Newburyport Impartial Herald* in late 1795 announced that "Messrs Guppy & Armstrong and Jacob Perkins, inventor" have three machines in operation at Byfield and are producing nails "much superior and twenty per cent cheaper than imported nails."[26]

The nail machines fit nicely with the mill's other powered equipment. A visitor in 1796 wrote: "The bands pass over a Cylinder moved by the water works, and communicate with the Nail machines, and pass also through the floor and move the Carding Machines above. In the nail manufactory we first came to the machine for cutting the plates, which did the work very expeditiously. There were four machines for the brads, and then a hammer for heading the nails. The whole was done in a masterly manner."[27]

Young Moody was impressed with Perkins, an inventive man in his late twenties, well known throughout the region. The entire community, Sarah Emery recalled, "justly took pride in their gifted townsman." Soon Paul was working for Perkins in the nailery, a wise move both financially and technically. Despite its high capitalization and latest technology, the woolen factory was not profitable. Although the mill produced and delivered a good supply of broadcloths and flannels to the Newburyport store of William Bartlet, the principal investor, sales of the cloth were disappointing. Timothy Dwight's view in 1796 was that "while population is so thin, and labor so high, as in this country, there is reason to fear that extensive manufactories (of woolens) will rarely be profitable."[28] The directors sought various financial remedies, including the previously noted admission fee. The company also resorted to public auctions of cloth, appeals to the state legislature for aid (not granted), and loans to pay the workmen. In 1798, it was agreed to continue operation only "if laborers could be procured for one-eighth less than the year preceding." The following year the Scholfields sold their interest in the mill and sought their fortunes in Connecticut. By 1804, Bartlet had bought all the outstanding shares and sold the manufactory to an Englishman named John Lees who, with drawing and spinning frames smuggled from England, converted the operation to the manufacture of cotton cloth. Lees was successful at manufacturing bed-ticking, sheeting, and gingham for about ten years, but encountered financial difficulties during the next decade and was forced to sell the property in 1824.[29]

Although the woolen manufactory was not a commercial success, it had several positive and noteworthy consequences. One is that the subsequent cotton factory was successful well into the nineteenth century. The manufactory also brought about "quite a revolution in the domestic manufactures of the neighborhood," Sarah Emery wrote.

> The introduction of cotton opened a new channel of industry. The weaving was still performed by hand; as the business increased, this loom power was not sufficient to supply the demand for cloths. Their goods consisted of heavy tickings and a lighter cloth of blue and white striped or checked, suitable for men's and boys' summer wear, aprons, &c. The tickings were woven by men on the looms at the factory, but

> much of the lighter stuffs were taken into families and woven on the common house loom. The yarns were spun and dyed at the factory; these could be purchased there, and in lieu of the hitherto universal linen and tow, cotton began to be mixed with flax or woven alone. Quite fine cotton fabrics were woven; bleached they looked very nice.

Wool and flax had been the primary raw materials for home textile production, but now cotton introduced a new occupation to the neighborhood. Again according to Sarah Emery, the cotton "came just as it had been gathered in the field, and many of the females in the neighborhood of the factory were employed to separate the seed from the cotton. For years one rarely entered a farm house in the vicinity without finding one or more of the inmates busy picking cotton." Thus, the mill economy blended with and slowly transformed the local economy, and even changed clothing fashion, apparently much to the satisfaction of all concerned.[30]

The second significant consequence of the Byfield factory was the development and diffusion of textile machinery knowledge. In the words of one nineteenth-century observer, "It was the training-shop for specialists in wool, in all the varied departments of manufacture, dyeing, carding, spinning, weaving, and finishing, the normal school in textile and mechanical manufacture." Moody was not the only local boy to benefit: Paul's younger brother David was trained there, along with John and Samuel Dummer, Jacob Kent, and Eben Pearson—all recognized for their technical skill.[31] And they learned from an acknowledged master, for it was said that "no more frequent recommendation of a carding machine was made than that it came from Arthur Scholfield's Workshop, and evidently it was believed that none higher could be made." There is at least one indication that Paul felt a special connection with the place where he had learned his trade. In 1826, at which point he was the superintendent of a major machine shop in Lowell, he personally acquired half the shares of the old Byfield factory.[32]

~

In the spring of 1796, a year before the Scholfields left, Jacob Perkins moved his nailery to the town of Amesbury and took Paul Moody with him. In the purely geographical sense it was not a momentous move, for Amesbury is only five miles north of Byfield. But in other respects Amesbury was another world and the new location would have profound personal and professional consequences for young Moody. Despite its small size—with a population of 1,757 in 1800 it was less than half the size of Newbury—Amesbury was much more industrialized than the surrounding towns. The Powow River, with a vertical drop of seventy-five feet in the space of a quarter mile, provided sufficient water power for machinery, and as early as 1710, the iron works and shipyards made for a busy place. Furthermore, within the town borders the Powow converged with the Merrimack, a navigable and heavily trafficked river that provided access to raw materials and markets, especially by way of the bustling commercial town of Newburyport at the mouth of the river. In addition to these industrial and commercial advantages, Perkins was drawn to Amesbury by the availability of a mill privilege that happened to be owned by three of the directors of the Byfield factory. Perkins bought the old corn mill in November 1795, and by early spring of the following year moved his nail machinery to the new location.[33]

Amesbury also appeared distant from Newbury because of their separation by the wide Merrimack River, which, until the construction of Timothy Palmer's "chain bridge" in 1792, could be crossed only by ferry—the means that George Washington used when he briefly visited Amesbury on his 1789 tour of New England. Amesbury people had a different orientation on their side of the river, so close to New Hampshire both in distance and spirit that the townspeople would vote in 1816 on the question of separating from Massachusetts to join the Granite State. "This was no fanciful movement," wrote Amesbury's historian, "but there was a strong feeling that the river should be the boundary between the states. It was occasioned in part by the fact that taxes were then lighter in New Hampshire and, in all probability, would continue to be so." The measure to separate from Massachusetts was defeated.[34]

Paul was surely excited about moving to Amesbury, although he was leaving the comfort of Newbury, where the Moodys were one of the best-known families. At the age of nineteen, he was striking out on his own. This new environment would play a big part in his maturation, for in Amesbury he would meet his lifelong friend and business partner Ezra Worthen, as well as his future wife. On July 13, 1800, at the age of twenty-one, Paul Moody married twenty-year-old Susan Morrill, daughter of Jonathan Morrill, a Revolutionary War veteran and later the first postmaster of Amesbury.[35]

Little is known about the kind of work Paul performed in Perkins's new nail factory or how successful the business was. An advertisement in the Newburyport *Herald* of August 4, 1801, reports that the nail factory was for sale, including Perkins's patent rights. It was sold in 1804 to Salem entrepreneur William Gray Jr. and his associates, who had purchased other land nearby and erected a rolling and slitting mill. Neither Moody nor Perkins is named among the eleven associates, which strongly suggests that Perkins at least was no longer associated with the enterprise after 1804. A further indication that Perkins left the nail-making business in 1804 is his invention that year of a process for hardening steel plates without damaging the engraved surfaces. He was engaged in this business no later than March 1805, at which point he declared in the Newburyport *Herald*: "The Patentee of the Stereotype Plates for the impression of Bank Bills informs the Public that he has constantly on hand ready made plates (the name of the Bank and Town excepted), and will be happy to supply Banks on the shortest notice."[36]

Just after midnight on December 24, 1805, the factory was destroyed by a fire that also consumed a grist mill, two blacksmith shops, and three hundred cords of wood. In March 1806, new owners, led by George Dodge, appealed to the state legislature to have Perkins's patent renewed for at least seven years. When their application was denied, they sold the property to new owners, who rebuilt the mill as an ironworks until that too was destroyed by fire in 1811. Jacob Perkins's biographers maintain that when the factory was rebuilt soon after the 1811 fire, Paul Moody and Jacob Kent were still employed, but there are no records to corroborate that claim.[37] All we can say is that Moody was gainfully employed during this period, mostly if not exclusively at the Amesbury Nail Factory.

There is evidence indicating that the Paul Moody family—which by 1812 included David (born 1803), Mary (1807), and William (1812)—lived in a house close by the factory. In 1819, well after the family left Amesbury, Paul sold this land, "together with a dwelling house and other buildings," to the Amesbury Nail Factory for $1,650. The deed indicates that this plot adjoined the land of Capt. Jonathan Morrill, Paul's father-in-law, which suggests that this property was given or sold to them by Susan's father. The size of the parcel was "fifty three rods and an half," or about a third of an acre—a fair sized house lot.[38]

During Paul Moody's early years in Amesbury, another man had been acquiring textile technology skills in ways that parallel Moody's development. Ezra Worthen (1781–1824) was apprenticed as a shipbuilder, his father's trade, until 1804 when two English machinists, Richard Gookins and James Standring, moved to Amesbury from Byfield, where they had been employed in the Newburyport Woolen Manufactory, and set up a carding machine manufacturing business. Worthen began working for them in 1804, using his boat-building skills to make the wooden parts of the carding machines and wooden patterns for the fabrication of the metal parts. At some point he left the employ of the English machinists and joined with Amesbury native Samuel Kendrick in the business of buying Gookins & Standring's machines and selling them throughout Massachusetts, Rhode Island, New Hampshire, and Maine. Later still, the partners formed Worthen & Kendrick, to make carding machines themselves, and they hired Paul Moody as "their agent, in selling and setting up the machines."[39]

Although recently employed in a nail factory, Moody had a deep understanding of textile machinery. He had woolen experience at Byfield, and before he left an Englishman named John Lee had introduced cotton manufacture there, so it is likely that he had been exposed to up-to-date machinery. This suggests that although he worked for Perkins in the nailery, Paul had a hand in the textile machinery building or repair as well. This is plausible, given that the nail machines were driven by the same waterwheel and power bands as the textile machines were, with just a floor separating the two departments. Moody had evidently gained enough experience to be entrusted with the responsibility of installing carding machines throughout Massachusetts and New Hampshire for Worthen & Kendrick.[40] Moody had become an active participant in the sweeping economic and technological changes affecting the northeastern states and providing significant new opportunities for men with his background and talents.

~

In November 1810, Ezra Worthen bought one-twelfth interest in the "middle sawmill privilege" on the Powow River. (There were three privileges—land with rights to the water power—in a short space along the river, giving the name "The Mills" to this area of Amesbury.) It is likely that he set up his shop there, and was apparently successful. By early 1812, when he first became involved in woolen manufacture, he had amassed the considerable sum of five thousand dollars. Moody and Worthen were now thinking more ambitiously, very much in line with the upbeat assessment of a Massachusetts House of Representatives report in 1810 claiming that "Industry and enterprize mark the character of our citizens, and are ever certain of reaping their rich rewards." And nowhere was this more evident than in the explosive growth of machine carding in this period. By 1810, there were more than seven hundred carding mills in New England and, according to Treasury Secretary Albert Gallatin, "in the Eastern and Middle States, carding machines worked by water are everywhere established, and they are rapidly expanding southwardly and westwardly." Machine carding actually produced more regular and even yarn than hand carding, and the machines were relatively easy to operate and required only moderate water power—all factors that fueled the spectacular expansion of small carding mills. Moody's training in the 1790s had dovetailed nicely with the growth spurt in the carding machine industry in the early nineteenth century.[41]

Between February and June 1812, Worthen bought all but one-twelfth of the shares of the mill privilege, and on June 17 sold one-third of the total shares to Paul Moody. When the final sale of shares had been completed, there were four investors in a new partnership: Worthen owned one-third, Moody one-third, and Thomas Boardman and Samuel Wigglesworth one-sixth each. The business was textile manufacturing, for which they built a two-story brick factory, fifty by thirty-two feet, with basement and attic. On February 13, 1813, the partners officially incorporated as a joint stock company, called the Amesbury Wool and Cotton Factory, with a capitalization of $46,000. Most accounts indicate that the factory produced "satinet" (a popular cloth woven of cotton warp and wool filling), and the company name does suggest that they produced both wool and cotton. But William Bagnall, who interviewed one of the former employees while researching his classic *The Textile Industries of the United States,* disagreed. His authority was James Squires, "a venerable member of the Society of Friends in Amesbury, still living at the age of nearly ninety-four years [in

1884] and whose memory is very distinct concerning the early history of the mill. He says that 'the old factory should not be called a satinet factory, for all-wool cloth—broadcloth—was made there.' "[42]

Regardless of what they made, the factory was profitable, as the War of 1812 had eliminated foreign competition. The company also had advantageous contracts with the United States government to produce cloth for army clothing, although with the postwar glut of foreign cloth the business suffered along with the textile business in general. Before the end of the war, however, Moody had sold his shares in the company. Ezra Worthen stayed at the Amesbury factory until 1822 when, through his friendship with Moody, he was offered the position of superintendent of the new Merrimack Manufacturing Company in East Chelmsford (later Lowell), Massachusetts. The lives of Paul Moody and Ezra Worthen would intertwine, both personally and professionally, until Worthen's untimely death in 1824.[43]

Some observers may have considered 1814 to be an unusual time for Moody to sell his shares in a profitable business. It was wartime and, while clearly disruptive, the war was also responsible for the excellent markets for domestically produced textile goods. It is unlikely that Moody foresaw that the peace of 1815 would result in the wholesale dumping of British cloth on the American market and the consequent depression of the American textile industry. His motivation was an exceptional opportunity, which had come as a direct result of the good impression he had made on his former employer, Jacob Perkins.

Amid the fervor for textile manufacturing enterprises during the War of 1812, Boston businessman Francis Cabot Lowell, in coalition with several family members and business partners, founded the Boston Manufacturing Company, on the Charles River in Waltham, Massachusetts. While the story of BMC properly belongs to a later chapter, it is important to note that Lowell's plan was ambitious, no less than the introduction of power loom weaving in the United States. He desperately needed a skilled machinist to build and repair the full range of textile equipment—carding engines, roving machines, spinning frames—and, more importantly, to aid in the design and manage the construction of the power looms. And since this would be a huge undertaking, the machinist would have to be able to supervise the work of other machinists and mechanics—in effect to build and superintend a machine shop. Lowell, originally from Newburyport, went to the man who best fit the job description in all of New England, Jacob Perkins. But Perkins, whose entire career demonstrates an interest in invention rather than attention to the business side of any venture, was headed in another direction, and about to move to Philadelphia to promote his method of engraving counterfeit-proof bank notes. His recommendation to Lowell was to hire Paul Moody.

So it was that in October 1813, at the age of thirty-four, with nearly twenty years' experience in the burgeoning field of textile machinery, Moody became superintendent of the Boston Manufacturing Company in Waltham.

This required relocating some forty miles away; Paul moved in November 1813 and his family joined him early the following year. He had worked at times farther away from home, in central New Hampshire and Maine, but this move to Waltham was more than a business trip, and it was the first move away from home for his wife and three children, aged two to eleven. Americans in the early nineteenth century had become increasingly willing to move for economic opportunity, and they had also deepened their belief that machinery could solve economic problems—what Brooke Hindle has described as "a kind of folk understanding of the ways of technology and a bubbling up of enthusiasm for mechanization"—which Moody's career epitomizes.[44] Despite the apparent security of his recent venture in Amesbury, this opportunity was simply too good to pass up. To use a modern sports metaphor, Paul Moody had been invited to move from Triple-A to the Major Leagues.

A brief comparison of the careers of Paul Moody and David Wilkinson to this point serves to highlight their very different backgrounds and responses to the economic opportunities of the postrevolutionary era. Paul Moody had progressed from a boy with no background in mechanics (save perhaps a familiarity with the family grist mill) to wool weaver, to nail maker, to carding machine repairman, and then to small-scale textile businessman. His progression was quite different from that of David Wilkinson, who had been schooled in his father's iron business and naturally transitioned to textile machinery as the iron and textile businesses became more integrated. Moody's early experience was in the woolen industry, at the first incorporated woolen mill in Massachusetts; Wilkinson's was in cotton, at the first successful spinning factory in America. Moody learned a great deal from immigrants, such as the Scholfields and the British carding machine builders who worked at the Byfield factory, although the influence of Jacob Perkins was of singular importance. Wilkinson, on the other hand, learned from locals—his father and cousins, Eleazer Smith, the Anthonys, Sylvanus Brown, and many others, including, to some degree, Englishman Samuel Slater. Finally, in rejecting both the family's agricultural heritage and the path of higher education (which his older brothers took), Moody made an explicit break with tradition, while Wilkinson followed his father and cousins on a path that coincided with, and helped create, the new industrial order.

4

Oziel's Son

David Wilkinson, 1790–1815

> Mr. Wilkinson's ingenuity had then actually contrived a machine of such masterly power . . . that it has to this day proved the most effective tool placed within the control of mankind for shaping refractory metals and for accomplishing the triumph of mind over matter.
>
> —Zachariah Allen, 1861

David Wilkinson continued to follow his father's lead in the expansive period after Samuel Slater's successful introduction of water-powered cotton spinning in 1790. Of the four sons that Oziel brought into his metalworking business (Smith, the youngest, worked in Slater's mill), David most resembled him in inventive thinking. And when he invested outside his area of expertise, it was with companies in which his father had an interest. Being "Oziel's son" in no way suggests that David was dependent on his father, nor was it the least hindrance to his development. On the contrary, Oziel was a good model, and David very skillfully adapted the model to the opportunities of the evolving industrial revolution. To a remarkable degree, he worked within this framework until 1815, a year of important changes in the Wilkinson family, as well as the point at which the power loom, which Paul Moody had already begun working on at Waltham, became the next big idea in the textile industry. This new and consequential development would mark an important crossroads in David's career.

Slater's commercial success sparked phenomenal industrial growth between 1790 and 1815. Investors throughout the northeast had contracted "cotton mill fever," building new factories at an accelerating pace. A Connecticut newspaper reported in 1811 that within a thirty mile radius of Providence there had been "an increase of 36 mills and 31,454 spindles in less than two years! Are not the people running *cotton-mill mad?*" In 1812–14 alone, sixty-two mills were established in New England.[1] Thus, the experience of the Wilkinsons was part of a widespread phenomenon that proved a boon to metal workers and machinists, as men like Oziel and his sons became more directly involved in the construction of equipment for cotton factories. To the Wilkinsons there was no "madness" in this trend. If American self-sufficiency required more machinery, then these metal workers and machinists could be patriotic simply by expanding their traditional business, and in the process exploit a remarkable opportunity for financial gain.

Revolution is too strong a term to apply to what was clearly an evolution in the methods of factory production. Yet there was a radical aspect to this transition, for it was not simply a matter of producing more textile machine parts, such as gears and spindles, but the introduction of more sophisticated metals shops and more complex tool making. Few Americans could claim to have played a more important part in these developments than the Wilkinsons.

Metalworking was the Wilkinsons' traditional business, and its connections to the manufacture of textile machines and parts both predated Slater's arrival and were furthered by his success. Oziel and his sons worked together in this business, but Oziel gradually became more interested in cotton manufacture, and David's brothers gravitated in the same general direction. It was David who transformed his father's blacksmithing operation into one of the earliest independent machine shops in America. During this same period he also experimented with steam engines and developed one of the most important machine tools for manufacturing. These were considerably more than sidelights to his iron business—so important to industrialization in America that, with the possible exception of Oliver Evans, it would be hard to find a man who was more broadly involved in the industrial revolution at this stage than David Wilkinson. Everything he did—iron products, machine tools, steam engines, textile machines—was related and relevant to the industrial development of the new nation.[2]

~

In 1790, nineteen-year-old David was unmarried, living at home and, along with his older twin brothers Abraham and Isaac, working in his father's anchor shop in Pawtucket Village. His exceptional strength suited him to work at the forge. His friend George Taft, referring to David's lack of formal education, called him "physically educated—every muscle was developed, every nerve braced up, and his whole frame energized by manual labor."[3] In addition to his strength and zest for hard work, he was full of curiosity and practical ideas. While all the brothers acted independently to some degree, they remained within the framework of the expanded metal shop. Daniel—six years younger than David—joined his older brothers in the shop and later became foreman. Abraham and Isaac formed their own firm, the A. & I. Wilkinson Company, in 1790, with furnaces in Pawtucket, Providence, and Fall River. Smith, the youngest, worked for Slater in 1790 feeding raw cotton into the breaker, but probably learned something of the family trade in the anchor shop as well.[4]

Much of what the Wilkinsons produced was heavy iron—huge anchors and five-hundred-pound screws for oil presses, along with nails, shovels, and farm tools. Before the end of the century the Wilkinsons' Pawtucket Cannon Foundry advertised cannon "bored from solid iron, neatly finished, and well proved." The cannon were "bored out by water power," according to Oziel's grandson Edward, and in an innovative way: "They were bored by making the drill or borer stationary, and having the cannon revolve and press up against the drill." Bored cannons were much safer than those cast in molds, which had a tendency to explode.[5]

Throughout the 1790s, the Wilkinsons began to make more refined parts through more sophisticated means. Oziel mastered the difficult process of adding carbon to wrought iron to produce steel. In 1791, Moses Brown reported to John Dexter (who was collecting information for Alexander Hamilton's Report on Manufactures) that "the Manufactory of Iron into Blistered steel Equal in Quality to English has been begun within about 12 Mo. in this Neighbourhood and is Carried only by Oziel Wilkinson."[6] A Providence newspaper notice placed by Oziel in 1790 described "a Steel Manufactory, where he has for Sale for Cash or Bar-iron, Steel in the Blister or drawn into Bars." The advertisement added that Oziel "also makes Paper-Mill, Clothiers and Printers' Screws, Machines for cutting cold Nails by Water or Hand, Irons for Carding-Machines and Spinning-jennies, Mill-Irons, Anchors &c."[7] There was little in the way of iron products that the Wilkinsons could not make.

That same year, David remembered, Oziel "built a small air furnace, or reverberatory, for casting iron, in which were cast the first wing-gudgeons known in America, to our knowledge, for Samuel Slater's old factory." A reverberatory furnace had a roof over the hearth to reflect the heat from a coal fire onto the pig iron on the hearth, and while this was a common means of making wrought iron in England in the late eighteenth century, it was not common in America until the 1830s. A wing gudgeon is a metal cylinder with (usually) four projecting "wings" that fit into the corresponding slits in the end of a shaft. The wings keep the cylinder from slipping its connection to the shaft, while the other end of the cylinder (the journal) rides in a bearing. Its purpose in Slater's mill was to connect the wooden power shaft of the waterwheel to a bearing.[8]

Fabricating iron parts for Slater was only one part of the Wilkinsons' connection with the young Englishman. Slater stayed with the family in Pawtucket during his first year in Rhode Island, and fell in love with David's sister

Hannah, who was fifteen when Slater arrived in early 1790. As Quakers, Oziel and Lydia Wilkinson disapproved of Hannah's marrying outside the Society of Friends. They considered sending her away to school, to which the determined suitor allegedly responded, "You may send her where you please, but I will follow her to the ends of the earth." Regardless of Slater's actual words, the parents relented and the couple married on October 2, 1791. To some degree independent of this courtship is Slater's socially and technologically nurturing relationship with the Wilkinsons. "In Oziel Wilkinson's family, he found a father and mother, who were kind to him as their own son," Slater's friend George White wrote. "He found consolation in that family, he found a *home*."[9]

There were important economic connections as well. When Almy, Brown & Slater began operations in 1790, their makeshift "factory" was in the fulling mill of Ezekiel Carpenter at the southwesterly end of the Pawtucket bridge over the Blackstone River. The success of the mechanized spinning process encouraged them to build a mill expressly suited to their purpose, and in 1793 they constructed a new factory a few hundred yards upstream. Originally quite small, only twenty-nine by forty-three feet, it is the building now preserved—with later extensions—as the "old mill" at the Slater Mill Historic Site. The land for the new mill was purchased from the Jenks family in November 1791 by Moses Brown (three-fourths) and Oziel Wilkinson (one-fourth) for "three hundred and fifty Spanish milled dollars."[10] Oziel's position as a successful businessman in Pawtucket, and his affiliation with Moses Brown and the Quaker network, thus helped Slater at a critical time of business expansion.

The new mill was a yarn-spinning factory, not a manufacturer of cloth. While Almy, Brown & Slater had employed as many as twenty-three weavers in 1791, they rarely operated the weaving shop at full capacity and soon found it more profitable to make the yarn available at retail stores to be "put out" to hand weavers. Children provided the bulk of the work in the mill, tending the carding and spinning machines, with only a few adults required to supervise. It is clear that deeply religious men such as Oziel Wilkinson had few qualms about child labor, as he demonstrated by putting his ten-year-old son Smith to work feeding cotton into Slater's breaker. Smith Wilkinson himself never complained about his own childhood labor, and years later defended the practice on moral grounds: "The usual working hours, being twelve, exclusive of meals, six days in the week, the workmen and children being thus employed, have no time to spend in idleness or vicious amusements." When Smith wrote these words in 1835, he was agent and principal owner of a mill in Pomfret, Connecticut, and may have seen his apprenticeship as a fortunate first step toward a successful textile manufacturing career, and certainly would not have considered himself idle or vicious at the age of ten. His use of child labor at Pomfret, however, compromises his objectivity.[11]

Yet many clergymen and philanthropists, including Moses Brown, defended the system.[12] One reason is that in the same year that the new mill was established, Slater instituted a Sunday school, taught first by him then by students from Rhode Island College (later Brown University). Here Slater was following the example of his former mentor, Jedidiah Strutt, who had established such a school in his Belper (England) mill village in 1782. Unlike present day religion-only Sunday school, Slater's filled a public education role by teaching reading, writing, and arithmetic—with plenty of Christian instruction mixed in. This was just one of many instances in which capitalism and Christianity converged to serve common social and economic goals. "Hundreds of families . . . originally from places where the general poverty had precluded schools and public worship, brought up illiterate and without religious instruction, and disorderly and vicious in consequence of their lack of regular employment, have been transplanted to these new creations of skill and enterprise," wrote Slater's friend George White, an Episcopal minister; "and by the ameliorating effects of study, industry, and instruction, have been reclaimed, civilised, Christianised." Oziel Wilkinson who, along with Moses Brown's son Obadiah, helped Slater establish the school, would have concurred. Most children, however, might have agreed with Hannah Josephson who remarked that "[c]hildren from five to ten years old, who worked in the mills fourteen hours a day six days a week, were strangely inappreciative of the boon of Sunday school on the seventh day."[13]

Oziel's good works and influence extended far beyond the Society of Friends. During the period of David's young adulthood, his father was a member of the Providence Society for Abolishing the Slave-Trade and was on its standing committee in 1790 and 1791. He also held elected and appointed offices in the town of North Providence, including Town Council member and surveyor of highways. For a nominal charge he leased land to the town for a pound and acted as pound keeper, and he donated land on Church Hill for a village common—now known as Wilkinson Park. Oziel was, in short, not only a model for David's business practice, but for moral and civic responsibility as well.[14]

Oziel and his family took great pride in the achievement of Slater, and firmly believed cotton manufacture was good for the nation. His grandson, Edward Wilkinson, recollected his grandmother (Oziel's wife Lydia) having told him "that she wove cotton shirting on a hand loom, from some of the first yarn spun by Mr. Slater, on his water frame. . . . She made shirts from the same cloth for her husband, and he took great satisfaction in wearing them and talking about them. He also took a specimen of the cloth and exhibited it on Cheapside, in Providence. It attracted a great deal of attention, and every one seemed to be very much pleased to think that we could now manufacture yarn and cloth for ourselves, and no longer be dependent on England for a supply."[15]

As part of an industrial revolution that encompassed these developments in iron and textile manufacture, a transportation revolution was also in progress at the end of the eighteenth century. "Internal improvements" became a rallying cry for many who believed that the new nation required a more developed infrastructure to survive economically. Corporations were formed to build toll roads, bridges, and canals—at times with a sort of mania far beyond the means of generating adequate dividends. Most in fact were financial failures, although the transportation network they provided was a major contributor to the economic expansion of the new nation. The Wilkinsons played an important role in this expansion, not only by forging iron parts, but also by their active participation in the building of canals, bridges, and roads. "In, or about 1794," David wrote, "Col. Noami Baldwin came from Boston to Pawtucket, after machinery for a canal he was going to make, north from Boston. We made the patterns and cast his wheels, racks, &c., and he took them to Charlestown and finished the locks." His nearly accurate reference was to Loammi Baldwin, chief engineer of the Middlesex Canal, which was begun in 1793. When it was completed in 1803 the canal connected the Merrimack River near present-day Lowell to the Charles River at Boston. Its length (26 miles) and number of locks (20) made it an engineering marvel of its day. "It being the first canal in the country," David said, "a good deal of curiosity was excited among the people."[16]

In the first example of what became a pattern in David's life, he traveled away from his home base to learn more of what was happening in industrial development outside Rhode Island. "I was there and saw the operation," he said of watching Baldwin and his workers finish the Charlestown locks. There he got ideas and made contacts. "A Mr. Mills, who built the South Boston bridge, came to me for the machinery for the bridge," David recalled. "I fixed the patterns, and went to Raynham [Massachusetts], got the castings, and carried them to Boston for the first new bridge." The Wilkinsons' Pawtucket shop also cast the iron for the draw of the Charles River Bridge. These were major internal improvement projects, involving durable and precise wheels and gears, and it says much about the reputation of the Wilkinsons that they were entrusted with such important contracts. Undoubtedly, Oziel was in charge of the business, but it was David who traveled to the construction sites, met with the engineers, and saw their iron products in action. This is very much in line with what industrial historians tell us about technology transfer during this period: it was a tactile and visual process communicated by interaction with working machinery and skilled artisans.[17] This is precisely what David Wilkinson was doing by the age of twenty-four, and in this important respect he took on a leadership role within the family.

The Wilkinsons continued to provide equipment, tools, and labor for transportation projects into the next century. Oziel's grandson Edward Wilkinson later recalled that "in 1804, the Norfolk and Bristol Turnpike, running from Pawtucket to Boston, was commenced. Oziel Wilkinson had charge of building 13 miles of said Turnpike. Daniel Wilkinson had charge of the hands." This was of course a perfect project for a man who made shovels, and indeed "all the shovels used by them were manufactured at Oziel Wilkinson's works." There is a suggestion of the makeup of the work crew in Edward's description of how the shovels were made. "The method of making them was, by rolling the plates of proper thickness; trimmed by hand shears, and made into proper shape by swedging. Round pointed shovels were first made here and used on the Turnpike, and were called Irish Spades."[18]

~

While all this heavy iron work was going on, David was constantly thinking about more sophisticated and efficient manufacturing methods, and in particular about tool making. He had been fascinated with tools since as a boy he watched Eleazer Smith make a machine to manufacture card teeth. Now David would begin building machines to make other machines, which made large-scale industrial enterprises feasible.[19]

It began with the huge screws that the company produced using the hand tools and methods of "Old Israel" Wilkinson. In David's view the screws were "imperfect," so "I told my father I wanted to make a machine to cut screws on centers." This was in 1794, when Oziel built a rolling and slitting mill—a mill for rolling iron into thin plates, which were then slit to produce long thin rods of iron for making nails or wire. It is possible that at this point the screw-making operation was managed by David and his brother Daniel; in any case, it is clear that the Wilkinsons were all working together in this expanded business and that much of the innovation is attributable to David. By all accounts it was a profitable line of business, supplying industrial screws for oil presses, iron hoops for whale oil barrels, as well as shovels and other metal implements. David and his two older brothers even put their own oil presses to use in an oil mill that produced linseed oil from flaxseed imported from North Carolina.[20]

What is most important about this screw-making process is that the "imperfect" results impelled David to devise a new tool—one that would have profound implications for the machine tool business in America. What he had in mind was a machine that rotated a piece of metal and cut threads into it in proportion to the screw to be replicated. On the power shaft of the waterwheel of Oziel's new rolling and slitting mill, David remembered, "I put my new screw machine in operation, which was on the principle of the gauge or sliding lathe now in every workshop almost throughout the world. . . . I cut screws of all dimensions by this machine, and did them perfectly." The perfection of the machine he attributed to "that most faithful agent *gravity,* making the joint, and that almighty perfect number *three,* which is harmony itself. I was young when I learned that principle. I had never seen my grandmother put a chip under a three legged milking stool; but she always had to put a chip under a four legged table, to keep it steady." He seems to have relied equally on science (that faithful agent gravity) and religion (that almighty perfect number three), but perhaps the anecdote of his grandmother's three-legged stool tips more toward the practical than the spiritual. The three bearing points under the slide rest were, in fact, the key to the tool's precision, and an inexpensive way of achieving it.[21]

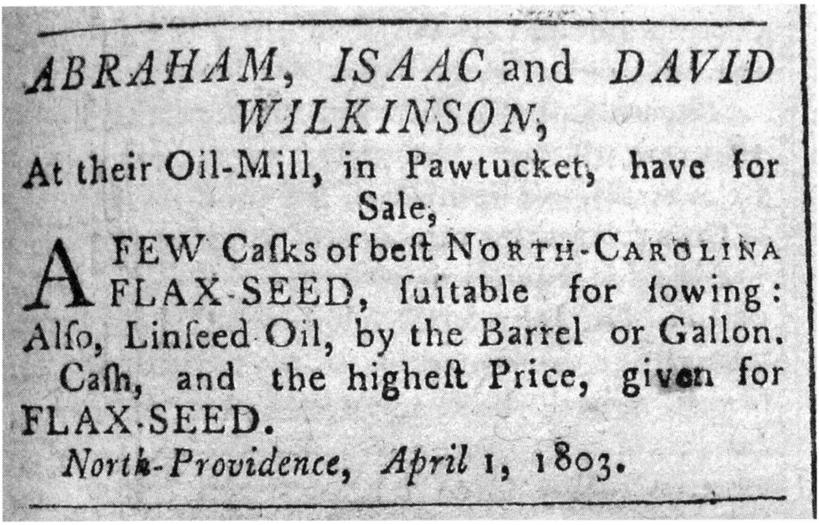

ABRAHAM, ISAAC and *DAVID WILKINSON*,
At their Oil-Mill, in Pawtucket, have for Sale,
A FEW Caſks of beſt NORTH-CAROLINA FLAX-SEED, ſuitable for ſowing: Alſo, Linſeed Oil, by the Barrel or Gallon.
Caſh, and the higheſt Price, given for FLAX-SEED.
North-Providence, April 1, 1803.

Figure 4.1
This advertisement from the *Providence Gazette* shows that the Wilkinson brothers were using their own screw presses to produce linseed oil from flax seed. *Courtesy of the Slater Mill Historic Site.*

It is important to note that David did not claim to have invented a lathe—he specifically calls it a screw machine, but on the lathe principle. A lathe is a machine for turning metal—rounding or shaping it, or cutting threads—in which the metal stock to be shaped is held and spun precisely on center while a cutting tool (a hardened chisel, attached to the base of the machine) is placed against it. It is similar in principle to the more familiar rotating grinding stone, except that with the lathe the piece to be shaped is spinning and the cutting tool is fixed. What David had built was a powered machine with a turning reference screw (the "lead screw") that guided a cutting tool along the rotating stock and replicated the pattern of the screw threads. It is not clear if the machine had a set of "change gears," which would have varied the speed of rotation of the lead screw relative to the lateral movement of the cutting tool, thereby permitting the production of screws of a different pitch than the original. But the patent drawing does show a clever attachment capable of cutting the threads into a nut that would exactly fit the screw being made.[22]

The importance of this innovation cannot be overstated. David's screw-cutting lathe produced accurate threads for screws or bolts, which was essential for the greater precision demanded by increasingly sophisticated textile machinery. But at the time David was not convinced that he had achieved a technological

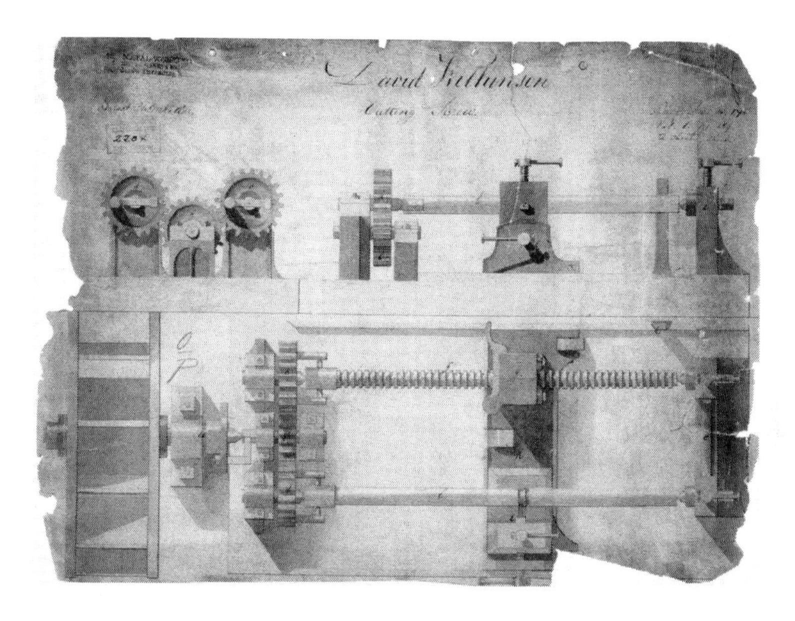

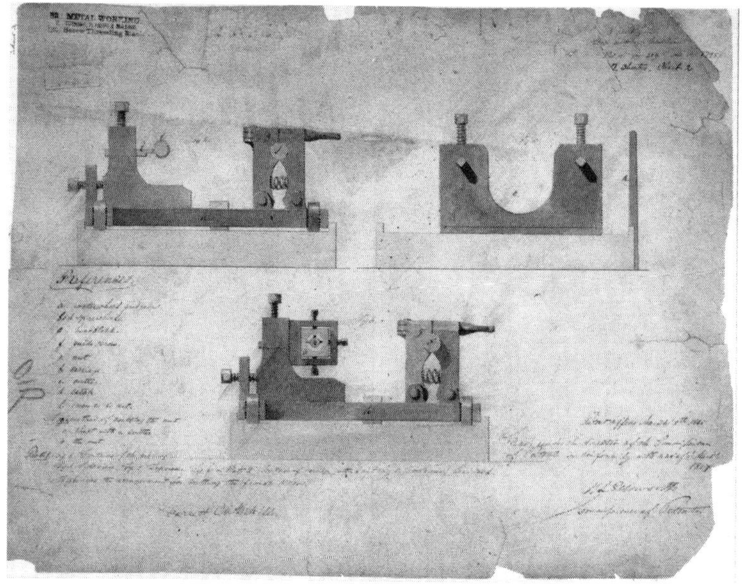

Figure 4.2 and 4.3

David Wilkinson patented his water-powered screw cutting machine, made "on the principle of the gauge or sliding lathe," in 1798. It was the basis of a more general-purpose lathe that he developed in the early 1800s.
Courtesy of the National Archives and Records Administration.

breakthrough. He would patent his invention only if he could be certain that no one else had built a similar machine. To that end, he made a small model and "started off to make inquiries." These were extended trips to places where screws were manufactured, locally as well as in New York and Philadelphia. David's wandering is interesting—he was young and single and apparently had the time and money to be away for some time to do this research, which is fortunate, given the poor means of travel in the late eighteenth century. While in New York he heard of a screw maker in Canaan, Connecticut. "I went on board a sloop, old Captain Wicks, of Long Island, master, bound for Albany. In five days I landed at Fishkill, and went ashore, and walked some thirty miles to Canaan."

In his visits to screw manufacturers, all he observed was the old method of "welding an iron guide on the end of his tap, and forcing it through a socket, with an iron bar, by hand, which was the old imperfection that troubled me always." With no apparent impediments to a patent application, he went to Philadelphia in 1797, while congress was in session, to make his case for a patent, assisted by Rhode Island Senator Joseph Tillinghast. Upon his return to Pawtucket he was told that he had missed a visit from one of the few men who would have been astute enough to see the value of his lathe—someone we have already encountered in another context. As David later related, "on my return home, my father informed me that Jacob Perkins had been there and wanted to see my machine, and that when he saw it, he laughed out, and remarked that he could do his engraving on cast steel, for Bank Note plates, with that machine—that he could make a hair stroke with that, for it would never tremble—that he could put an oval under the end of the rut, and, with an eccentric, make all his oval figures. I suppose Mr. Perkins afterwards derived great benefit from the thing."[23] It was a very small world of New England machine and tool makers. Perkins, who had only recently established his Amesbury nail factory with Paul Moody, was now involved in bank note engraving, and somehow he heard about David Wilkinson's new tool that would be equal to the more sophisticated requirements of his new endeavor. This is the first of several indirect but significant links between Moody and Wilkinson.

David's patent for a screw-cutting lathe with slide rest was awarded December 14, 1798. Given the importance of the lathe to the machine tool industry, there is much contention over who actually invented it. Credit is often given to the English machinist Henry Maudslay (1771–1831), but in fact the basic elements of this tool existed before Maudslay's and Wilkinson's time; Leonardo da Vinci made a drawing of a screw-cutting machine as far back as 1500, and by the seventeenth century such machines were being used for clock making, although not on an industrial scale. Like most inventions, the lathe was developed over time, so while David Wilkinson may not have been the single inventor of the screw-cutting lathe, he appears to have come up with a similar idea and made it into a practical industrial tool. And the application of the principles of this tool had far-reaching implications for the nascent machine tool industry.[24]

Wilkinson made extensive use of his screw-making machine, but his goal was to evolve it into a more generally useful lathe and to apply it to the fabrication of textile machine parts. Oziel and his sons had been making parts for Slater's mills since 1790, but when David suggested the use of such a tool he was dissuaded. As he explained it, "Whilst I was at work on Slater's machinery, the owners were unwilling that I should make a slide lathe on the principle of my screw machine, which was made for large turning; it was too heavy for cotton machinery." When Samuel Slater's brother John came from England to America in 1803, he was asked to bring with him a machinist who had made a slide lathe. "John came, and brought a Mr. John Blackburn, who made a slide lathe which was on the principle of the old fluting machine [that is, different from David's]. They worked this lathe some few weeks, and then threw it out of doors, and then afterwards did their work by the old hand tool, as before."[25]

It may seem odd that Slater would pass up the chance for a technological breakthrough. However, he was not a machinist, and was often cautious about new technology. Slater did introduce the innovative spinning mule in America, in 1803 when his brother John arrived from England, but that was an *English* invention, so there may have been a bit of chauvinism in Slater's rejection of David's invention. Supporting the idea of British bias is the advice from Samuel Ogden, a master machinist who had emigrated from England to help build a factory at Hope Furnace, about 1806. "[Ogden] was a man of great experience and good abilities," David remembered. "He advised me as a friend to abandon my new machine, for said he, 'you can *ner* do it, for we have tried it out and out at *ome,* and given it up; and don't you think we should have been doing it at *ome,* if it could have been done?' "[26]

The negative response to the practical application of his invention did not deter David, for he was soon presented with an opportunity that did not involve Slater. In 1805, the Wilkinsons teamed up with James Rhodes and his brothers, of Warwick, Rhode Island, to buy land along the Quinebaug River in Pomfret, Connecticut, for a Slater-style cotton factory. Of the sixteen total shares, Oziel, his sons, and two sons-in-law held eleven, of which David owned one and one-third. The driving force behind this venture was David's youngest brother, Smith, who had been a child laborer in Slater's first mill at the age of ten in 1790. Now only twenty-five, Smith had become a seasoned textile mill manager.[27]

To David, this was more than an investment opportunity. In addition to providing machinery from his Pawtucket shop, he brought a team of workers from Rhode Island to build and install equipment, using a furnace in Stafford, Connecticut (in which he was likely part owner), to cast iron parts for the carding machines. More important on a personal level, he asked the principal owners for permission to "build a gauge lathe, like my big one," and they consented. David continues, "I then went to work, and made my patterns in Sylvanus

Brown's shop in Pawtucket." In a curious and still largely unexplained incident, just before David was to deliver the wooden patterns for casting, Brown "took it into his head to put them into the stove, and burn them up." David commented no further on why Brown, with whom the Wilkinsons had worked closely since before Slater's arrival, would burn his lathe patterns, although there is some evidence that Brown believed he had some claim to a lathe invention. David simply states that he remade the patterns, had them cast, built the lathe, "and it worked to a charm."[28]

The new lathe was a more generalized version of his screw machine, adapted and refined for shaping the precision parts of textile machinery. Like the earlier tool, it had a lead screw which accurately moved a carriage that held the cutting tool, and apparently had change gears for greater versatility. The prominent Rhode Island industrialist Zachariah Allen, writing in 1861, described the impact of Wilkinson's "original improvement of the slide engine for turning iron."

> By means of this engine, the steel chisel is held with the firm untrembling grip to cut off large chips of iron as readily as those of wood are pared off by a chisel held by the hand on a turning [wood] lathe. The effectiveness of this engine led to the subsequent adaptation of steel chisels to plane the flat surfaces of huge masses of iron. Mr. Wilkinson's ingenuity had then actually contrived a machine of such masterly power for putting refractory [hard to work] metals in desired forms, that it has to this day proved the most effective tool placed within the control of mankind for shaping refractory metals and for accomplishing the triumph of mind over matter.

There was nothing like it in America in 1805, yet Wilkinson did not apply for a patent.[29]

David's lathe was put to work in two contrasting ways. The first was the direct use by the Wilkinsons in making textile machinery. The company he formed with his brother Daniel—called David Wilkinson & Company—was very successful in this regard, not only at the Pomfret mill managed by his brother Smith, but throughout the eastern United States. "We built machinery to go to almost every part of the country—to Pomfret and Killingly, Connecticut; to Hartford, Vermont; to Waltham . . . and other places in Massachusetts; for Wall & Wells, Trenton, New Jersey; for Union and Gray, on the Patapsco; for the Warren factories, on the Gunpowder, near Baltimore; to Tarboro' and Martinburgh, North Carolina; to two factories in Georgia; to Louisiana; to Pittsburgh; to Delaware; to Virginia, and other places." It is clear from David's reminiscences that he considered his lathe invention to be the single most important factor in the success of his textile machinery business.[30]

The second consequence of David's lathe improvements was, from his point of view, less satisfactory. Richard Anthony, one of his machine-building colleagues in the early years of textile experimentation as well as a family friend who "was intimate with Abrm and Isaac Wilkinson and used to visit and play with them in Pawtucket," showed an interest in the lathe. David wrote that Anthony, "who was building a factory, in Coventry, with his brother William, paid me ten dollars for the use of my lathe patterns, to cast after. And this is all I ever received for so valuable an invention." This is not quite true, since David sold the lathe to an English mechanic who, "after using one of my slide lathes awhile, he bought one, and returned to England with it; remarking that with that lathe in England, he could do better than at any business he could get into in this country."[31]

Perhaps David sold his lathe patterns so cheaply because the Anthonys were friends. But his failure to renew the patent on the screw-cutting lathe and to protect his general purpose lathe is a mystery. The family biographer wrote that "his head was full of other projects, and he gave but little attention to securing the pecuniary advantages his discovery would naturally give him." Looking back at the age of seventy-five, David's excuse was that it was simply a matter of timing.

> It was unfortunate for me patenting my machine, when the machine making and manufacturing business in this country was only in its infancy. The patent would run out before it could be brought into very extensive use. It certainly did run out without my deriving that benefit from the invention, I was so justly entitled to. One solitary ten dollar note is surely but small recompense for an improvement that is worth all the other tools in use, in any workshop in the world, for finishing brass and iron work. . . . I was always too much engaged in various businesses to look after and make a profit from my inventions.

Then, with a characteristic resignation that softened the bitterness, he added: "Other people, I hope, gained something by them."[32]

Perhaps it was timing. But the fact remains that in 1812, when the fourteen-year patent for his screw-cutting lathe expired, David did not renew it. This failure may be fundamentally related to David's transition from inventor and machine shop owner to investor and entrepreneur, a change that resulted in a loss of focus on the basics of his early success. This subject will be explored later in the context of his business expansion in the 1820s. But no one would argue with the fact that during this period of David's early adulthood, he was an extremely busy man.

~

One of the many technologies that interested David Wilkinson was steam power. As noted earlier, David first saw a steam engine in 1792 or 1793 when he visited the Cranston Ore Bed. This Newcomen-type engine had been built about 1780 by Moses Brown's brother Joseph and was now being maintained by Elijah Ormsbee. The atmospheric steam engine was certainly not new—it had been developed by Thomas Newcomen in 1712—but very few existed in America. When American ingenuity was finally applied to steam power it would be driven by the need to solve the problem of transportation, and only secondarily to produce industrial power by means of the stationary steam engine.[33]

Twenty-two-year-old David Wilkinson learned the principles of steam power from Ormsbee. This engine was primitive by English standards, because, as David explained, "the news of the cap on the cylinder by Boulton & Watt had not yet come to this country when that engine was built."[34] During their conversation, Ormsbee related that "he had been reading of a boat being put in operation by steam, at the city of Philadelphia," a likely reference to an experiment by famed steamboat pioneer John Fitch. This was hardly breaking news: Fitch's demonstration in Philadelphia had taken place in 1787, and by 1791 both Fitch and James Rumsey had received patents for their competing steamboat inventions. But by 1792, as the two Rhode Island mechanics talked, nothing of the sort had been seen in New England.

As David casually described it, "if I would go home with him and build the engine, he would build a steamboat." Ormsbee borrowed a boat from John Brown (another of Moses' brothers) and David made the patterns for the engine, then cast and bored the cylinder. He also devised a paddle system. "I told [Ormsbee] of two plans of paddles, one I called the flutter wheel and the other, the goose foot paddle. We made the goose foot, to open and shut with hinges, as the driving power could be much cheaper applied than the paddle wheel." Elijah's twelve-year-old nephew John H. Ormsbee (later Captain), who steered the boat, explained that the paddles "were moved forward and aft, no wheels being used, but upright paddles, which did not lift out of the water, but when moved forward they closed, and when moved aft they expanded—their whole width being about eighteen to twenty-four inches wide."[35]

The most informative account of the experiment is that of Captain Ormsbee. "Elijah Ormsbee got the loan of a long boat belonging . . . to the ship *Abigail,* then lying in Providence.

> This boat he took to a retired place about three and a half miles from Providence known as Winsor's Cove. A copper still, of from one hundred to two hundred gallons capacity, owned by Col. Ephraim Bowen, used by him in his distillery in the south part of the town for the distilling of herbs, was loaned him by Col. Bowen. . . . The cove was selected for its little exposure to travellers [*sic*] by land or water, that he might not be disturbed at his work, and in case of his want of success, he would not be subject to the derision of the community. He succeeded in getting his machinery in operation, and on a pleasant evening in autumn, he left Winsor's Cove in the first boat

> propelled by steam that ever floated on the waters of Narragansett bay and Providence River, and arrived in safety at the lower wharf. The next day they left in the boat for Pawtucket, to show the friends in that village the success that had attended the enterprise. At Pawtucket the boat remained a day or two, and then returned to Providence.[36]

What a wonder this ungainly boat must have appeared, with its goose foot paddles, bulky iron engine, and copper still boiler. But it made relatively good speed, "from three to four miles per hour in smooth water," Captain Ormsbee estimated, "and if wheels had been substituted for paddles, would probably have increased her speed to five or six miles per hour." It appears that David was not on the first evening's voyage, but he was on board the next day when Ormsbee "went in his steamboat to Pawtucket, to show her to his friends, and the two ingenious mechanics exhibited her between the two bridges."[37]

Yet nothing came of this wonderful experiment. "After our frolic was over," David said, "being short of funds, we hauled the boat up and gave it over." Apparently, Ormsbee sought funds for a larger steamboat, but was unable to raise the capital. Several nineteenth-century chroniclers of the history of Pawtucket could not get over the might-have-been quality of this event. Reverend Massena Goodrich, in his Centennial Address, said: "It is fair to claim that, had the Pawtucket been a longer stream, so that stream had been as important for it as for the Hudson, or had some discerning capitalist been ready to afford the pecuniary aid needful for testing and perfecting the invention, the chaplet that adorns the head of Fulton might have been woven for the brows of Wilkinson and Ormsbee. And the Pawtucket River and Narragansett Bay would have had an additional claim to fame."[38]

This is fit hyperbole for a centennial celebration, yet there are two developments that demonstrate how Wilkinson's experiment with steam power was no mere "frolic." The first is his further connection with Robert Fulton and the development of the steamboat. Sometime around 1796, David was in New York, "and saw some work commenced at Fulton's Works, for steamboat shafts, and saw a small steamboat in North River, built by Col. John Stevens, of Hoboken. I went over to his place, and saw his boring mill. I thought he was ahead of Fulton as an inventor." If we skip ahead almost twenty years, David is in Trenton, New Jersey, attending the Winter 1814–15 session of the state legislature at which a dispute between Fulton and Aaron Ogden would be decided. Ogden, the governor of New Jersey, opposed Fulton's monopoly of steam ferry service between New York and New Jersey, and also claimed to own the late John Fitch's patents. David apparently was there because the quarrel between Fulton and Ogden included a contested paddle wheel design. "I had the curiosity to attend," he wrote, "as I always thought it singular that the idea of the paddle-wheel should strike two persons so, at the same time, at such a distance apart; yet I knew so simple a thing could happen." David knew something about paddle wheels from the time of his steamboat experiment when, "after we had got the boat nearly done, Charles Robbins made a pair of paddle wheels, and attached them to a small skiff, and run about with a crank, by hand power."[39]

David wrote nothing more about the trial, at which Ogden's challenge to Fulton's monopoly was defeated. But he did relate that he shared a coach ride from Trenton to Jersey City in a heavy snow storm with Fulton and his attorneys. Due to ice, the ferries to New York were not running, so Fulton and the lawyers "took a boat, with four oarsmen, and got over by crossing the cakes of floating ice, and launching the boat several times." When the boat returned, Wilkinson was able to cross over. Shortly after he returned home he learned of Fulton's death. One of the attorneys had fallen through the ice on their crossing, and in pulling him to safety Fulton was soaked and exhausted. He died of pneumonia and consumption on February 23, 1815, at the age of fifty.[40]

The final connection between David Wilkinson and Robert Fulton links two pieces of a puzzle that spanned nearly five decades. It starts with David's recollection that, at the time of his steamboat experiment, "a young man called on me, and wished to see the boat, and remained a day or two examining all the works. He told me his name was Daniel French, from Connecticut. I never knew where he came from, nor where he went." Many years later, about 1840, while David was traveling by railroad from Utica to Albany, New York, he struck up a conversation with "an aged gentleman" who had been in the state legislature and was well informed on the subject of steam power. They were both of the opinion that "more credit had been given to Fulton than was his due," David adding that he "never thought Fulton an inventor, but simply a busy collector of other people's inventions." The old gentleman replied, "I always said so, and he would never have succeeded had it not been for Daniel French." David asked what he meant. "Why a Yankee," said he, "that Fulton kept locked up for six months, making drafts for him." David was astounded. "The name of Daniel French burst upon my ears for the first time [in] forty-nine years, and almost explained some mysteries."[41]

What had occurred was a monumental transfer of technology. John Fitch had demonstrated a steamboat in Philadelphia in 1787. Five years later, Elijah Ormsbee read about it and mentioned it to David Wilkinson. Wilkinson and Ormsbee built and successfully exhibited their own steamboat, which a young mechanic named Daniel French examined in detail. French then went on to influence Robert Fulton, the first great steamboat entrepreneur. David Wilkinson had been an important, though generally unacknowledged, agent in this transfer.[42]

~

David never again applied himself to steam power for transportation after his "frolic." But steam engines continued to fascinate him, and this interest was maintained by combining what he had learned with what he knew best—the application of steam power to machine manufacture. In Great Britain, stationary steam engines were used mostly for pumping water from mines (which earned it the nickname "miner's friend"). Not only did America lack deep mines at the beginning of the nineteenth century, it also had such an abundant supply of cheap water power that steam was considered too expensive. Steam visionaries like Oliver Evans saw the matter differently. "Water-falls are not at our command in all places, and are liable to be obstructed by frost, drought, and many other accidents," he wrote in 1805.

> Wind is inconstant and unsteady: animal power, expensive, tedious in the operation, and unprofitable, as well as subject to innumerable accidents. On neither of these can we rely with certainty. But steam at once presents us with a faithful servant, at command in all places, in all seasons; whose power is unlimited; for whom no task is too great nor yet too small; quick as lightning in operation; docile as the elephant led by a silken thread, ready, at our command, to rend asunder the strongest works made by the art of man.[43]

When Oziel Wilkinson began building a new three and one-half story stone textile mill in 1810, he had available to him the same inexpensive power of the Blackstone River as the adjacent 1793 Slater mill. In 1812, Oziel conveyed a quarter interest in the new mill to David, and one-eighth each to David's brother Daniel and brother-in-law Hezekiah Howe. When the three younger partners set up the machinery, they installed as a supplementary source of power a steam engine that they had built. This was the first textile mill to be powered by steam in Rhode Island, and among the earliest in America.[44] Within a few years, two Rhode Island factories—the Providence Woollen Manufacturing Company and the Providence Dyeing, Bleaching, and Calendering Company—installed Oliver Evans steam engines. Apparently, David Wilkinson did not commercialize his innovation, which seems remarkable, given that the Evans engine bought by the Providence Dyeing, Bleaching, and Calendering Company reportedly cost seventeen thousand dollars.[45]

While there is no direct explanation for David's failure to exploit the potential of the stationary steam engine, the likely answer is that the market barely existed at this point. Steam engines could be disassembled and shipped without greatly affecting cost, so well-capitalized reputable makers from afar (such as Philadelphia) could compete with local companies. Had Wilkinson invested heavily in steam engine manufacture, few local enterprises would have been interested. The steam engines of the period were huge and prone to failure, and devoured expensive wood fuel, when cheap water power was still available in Rhode Island. In fact, with improvements in dam construction and more efficient water turbines, total horsepower from water was still on the increase at the beginning of the twentieth century.[46] Because David could make his own engine, in his spare time, steam power was more affordable for him than it would have been for potential customers in the area. Considering how busy he was making textile machinery, he was wise not to enter the nascent and risky business of steam engine manufacture.

~

Making machinery was indeed David Wilkinson's forte, and the workshop he built in the new mill between 1810 and 1812 was to become another first in industrial history. Prior to this time, a machine shop was typically an integral part of a cotton or woolen factory, built during construction and functional before the factory began operations. David's shop was, according to industrial historian William Bagnall, the "earliest and for some years the only independent machine-shop for the construction of textile machinery" in America. This was not a matter of David's deciding one day to set up a revolutionary machine shop. What most likely occurred was a decision to share space in his father's new factory building and to continue his ongoing anchor, screw, and tool business there. Making textile machinery was just one activity in a busy iron foundry. But the success of his lathe and the increased opportunities for textile machine making turned the forge into a machine shop.[47]

The machine shop took up the entire first floor of the mill building. It was a noisy place, with the constant rumble of the waterwheel in the basement and the clatter of the iron gears and shafts that transmitted power to the upper floors. The shop's main power shaft ran the eighty-foot length of the building, with secondary shafts that powered the lathe, screw- and gear-cutting machines, grinders, and drills, as well as woodworking equipment. There would have been files and chisels, as much of the work was still done by hand. There was probably a forge in the basement, producing the iron that David and Daniel Wilkinson, assisted by various apprentices, would fabricate into precision parts for the textile industry.[48]

This concept of an independent machine shop is fundamental to the progress of the Industrial Revolution and of course dovetails with the development of the lathe as a precision tool for making the machines demanded by the expanding textile industry. As Rhode Island lost its lead in the cotton textile business to large, integrated mills such as Waltham and Lowell in the 1820s and beyond, it developed and maintained leadership in the machine tool business. This success can be traced, at least in part, to the Wilkinsons in general, and to David in particular. More immediately, David was well positioned for the next big technological requirement in the textile industry—the power loom—which with his lathe and independent shop, he could exploit more readily than shops that were attached too directly with a particular factory, that used more old-fashioned methods of production, or that simply could not make machinery

Figure 4.4
The Wilkinson Mill (left) was erected in 1810 adjacent to Slater's 1793 factory. David set up his machine shop in the basement, and also experimented with worsted wool manufacture.
Drawing by P. D. Malone courtesy of Patrick M. Malone.

to the more precise tolerances delivered by his lathe. "It is not too much to say," wrote J. T. Lincoln, "that the machine age became possible only with the perfecting of the slide lathe."[49]

While the particulars of David's interests and business concentrations varied from his father's, the pattern was similar. David had taken over from Oziel the role of technology pioneer and tool maker in the widening web of Wilkinson family business enterprises, while Oziel had become a textile magnate. Oziel's investments were not on the order of Slater's, yet by 1815 he was principal owner of the Wilkinson Mill adjacent to Slater's original mill, and had financial interest in the Yellow Mill (1793), the White Mill (1799), Pomfret Factory (1806), and the "Stone Mill" addition to the White Mill (1813).[50]

David appears to have initially steered clear of outside investments. When Samuel Slater built a new mill in 1799 in Rehoboth, on the Massachusetts side of the Blackstone River, his partners were his father-in-law Oziel Wilkinson and Oziel's other sons-in-law Timothy Greene and William Wilkinson. (David's sister Marcy Wilkinson married William Wilkinson, adding a bit of confusion to the family genealogy.) Oziel had partnered with Moses Brown and Thomas Arnold to buy this land at the opposite end of their Pawtucket dam in order to control the entire water power at that point. The mill they built was similar to the 1793 mill across the river, except for the color, by which it became known as the White Mill. This enterprise, Slater's first out of the controlling hands of Almy and Brown, was known as Samuel Slater & Company. Despite the shared ownership, Slater possessed all the textile business expertise: "The business was wholly under the control and management of Mr. Slater," William Bagnall wrote; "neither of his partners in either factory having any practical knowledge of cotton spinning." Oziel and William Wilkinson were blacksmiths and Timothy Greene was a tanner. All the partners were linked through their in-law relationship to Oziel.[51]

Perhaps David was too occupied with projects related to his recently patented screw lathe to participate in the White Mill partnership. But in 1805, when his youngest brother Smith spearheaded the effort to build a factory at Pomfret, Connecticut, David was ready. This was even more of a family affair than the 1799 factory. The shareholders were Oziel Wilkinson, his five sons and two sons-in-law, and three Rhodes brothers from Warwick. Of the sixteen total shares, David split four with his twin brothers Abraham and Isaac. Smith, who had grown up in the textile business, was the only family member to live in the mill village, and took on the role of agent. David had been allowed to use his lathe to build machinery for this factory, so his major interest in Pomfret was as a customer for his machine shop in Pawtucket. He also got his first taste of investing in businesses in which he was only tangentially involved.

The thousand-acre property, encompassing parts of Pomfret, Killingly, and Thompson along the Quinebaug River, had been known as Cargill's Mills, which included a sawmill, grist mill, blacksmith's shop, and an abandoned gin distillery. Smith Wilkinson, who by 1835 owned the controlling interest in the mill, explained the economic and moral purposes for the large land purchase. "A leading object of this company in buying so much land, was to prevent the introduction of taverns and grog shops, with their usually corrupting, demoralizing tendency. Another object was, to give the men employ on the lands, while the children were employed in the factory. The company very early exerted their influence in establishing schools, and introducing public worship on the sabbath." It appears that Wilkinson's labor system and religious orientation were modeled on the Slater factory system in Rhode Island. This was the rule in the development of eastern Connecticut's industry. As one mill agent wrote, "There is not a mill village on the Quinebaug that does not owe its existence to Rhode Island manufacturers or Rhode Island capital."[52]

In 1810, when Slater sold his shares in the White Mill, David bought a one-twelfth interest. This enterprise, whose name was changed to Wilkinson, Greene & Company, was still a family business, with Oziel retaining his original quarter interest. Again there is no evidence of David's playing a direct role in the management of the company, even though the White Mill was a few minutes' walk from his workshop at the opposite end of the Pawtucket Bridge. It was at this time that David was setting up the machine shop in the new stone mill he shared with Oziel, so it makes sense that the White Mill interest was purely a business investment. Once again, he had followed his father's lead and invested in a family-owned business related to textile production.[53]

David's penultimate investment during this pre-1815 period was somewhat unusual. In 1813, he built the four-story Pawtucket Hotel at the corner of Main and Mill streets, just steps from the Old Slater Mill and the Wilkinson Mill. The need for a hotel in Pawtucket Village is apparent: a growing town required rooms for travelers—especially since the main road to Boston (the construction of which the Wilkinsons had managed) passed right by this location. The factory-building frenzy during the War of 1812 was also a likely factor: with productive mills on both sides of the river, Pawtucket was quickly becoming a business center. As a successful local businessman, David was attuned to the economic and social needs of the community, and simply made a shrewd move to invest outside his normal area of expertise. And while far from his own business experience, catering to travelers may have been familiar to his wife Martha, whose father, Jeremiah Sayles, owned the Sayles Tavern. Another likely reason for this investment is the space it provided on the first floor for a retail store that sold products from his workshop: kettles, nails, latches, shovels, as well as chisels, saws, axes, and other hand tools.[54]

A hotel was also a tavern, a place of conviviality and business meetings, as well as a source of the alcohol that promoted brawls and other dangerous or immoral behavior. David's ownership of a liquor-serving establishment is in direct contrast to his family's factory in Connecticut, whose mill village was intentionally devoid of taverns. Perhaps David, as a remote investor in Pomfret Factory, did not share his brother Smith's views on the evils of drink. In any event, this was before the development of a temperance society in the area, which first met, ironically, at the Pawtucket Hotel in 1826.[55]

David returned to Connecticut for his final investment in this period. With several Rhode Island and local businessmen, including his brother Smith, he became a partner in the Killingly Manufacturing Company, which converted an old gristmill on the Five Mile River to a cotton manufactory. Listed among the investors was Henry Howe of Pawtucket, but this was more likely Hezekiah Howe, who was born in Killingly and moved to Pawtucket after marrying David's youngest sister Lydia in 1809. Hezekiah was also the brother of Betsey Howe, Smith Wilkinson's wife. David and Hezekiah would remain close friends and business partners for the rest of their lives.[56]

We have seen David Wilkinson grow from a talented young ironmaster in 1790 to a successful tool and machine maker, inventor, investor, and prominent businessman by 1815. He had taken his father's position as leader in the traditional family business. Beyond simply maintaining the iron business, he expanded it to take advantage of the opportunities created by the textile revolution. He turned his father's anchor forge into a machine shop and his own screw-making machinery into a general purpose lathe. For the most part, he invested only in companies in which his father held shares. In some ways he held back as his father and brothers entered new spheres. Oziel became the first president of the Manufacturers Bank, which was originally established in Pawtucket but later moved to Providence. Abraham, two years David's senior, went into politics and was elected to the Rhode Island Legislature and "frequently returned by his constituency." Young Smith was in control of all aspects of an entire mill village, very much in the style of Samuel Slater. David stayed primarily with his core competency—machines and tools—at least for the moment.[57]

In his memoir, David reveals absolutely nothing of his personal life during this period of young adulthood to early middle age. We know from other sources that he married Martha Sayles of North Providence. Like David, Martha could trace her ancestry back to the earliest European settlers of Rhode Island, in her case to the state's founder Roger Williams. They had four children, all born while the couple lived in Pawtucket. The first, Joanna, was born in October 1802. Albert Sayles arrived in December 1804. Then, after six years with no further children, at least according to the record, Martha gave birth twice in 1811: to John Lawrence in January and Ardelia in December.[58]

The Wilkinsons lived on Pleasant Street, near the intersection with Main. David's brother Abraham's house was the first on Pleasant, David's was three houses to the south, two houses farther was Slater's, and just beyond was St. Paul's church. Although the evidence is indirect, we can assume the family was financially secure. The companies in which he had invested, such as Pomfret Factory and the White Mill, were profitable, and he had sufficient funds to invest in Killingly in 1814.[59] It appears that his machine shop was profitable, since one of the reasons he gave for not exploiting his screw lathe patent is that he was too occupied with other business matters at the time. We have also seen that he could afford to take time off periodically to pursue his technical interests. Insofar as financial condition is an indicator of the Wilkinson's pursuit of happiness, it appears that the family was doing well.

This sparseness of social detail necessarily limits a full portrait of David Wilkinson during this period. In the business and technological aspects, however, and particularly the inventive facet of his life, the picture is clear. At this stage David had become the embodiment of the ingenious machinist of the Industrial Revolution, intimately involved in all the key aspects of that development: ironwork; precision instruments and the creation of machines to make machines; steam power (both experimental and applied); and textile machinery of increasing power and sophistication. And, like other technology leaders of the period, he had also experienced a taste of capitalistic investment in textile manufacturing.

In all these respects, David was his father's son, with a zest for hard work, astonishing inventiveness, and—at this stage—cautious entrepreneurship. There are early indications that the success of his investments began to lure him away from his core expertise; but if so, this trajectory would be deflected by the textile business downturn at the end of the War of 1812. As 1815 approached,

Figure 4.5
The only known portrait of David Wilkinson shows him in his late forties. The formal dark coat and high white collar befit his status as a leading entrepreneur in Rhode Island. The original painting was apparently commissioned by his Masonic Lodge around 1820.
Courtesy of the Elizabeth J. Johnson Pawtucket History Research Center.

Figure 4.6

Martha Sayles Wilkinson (1776–1852) was about 45 when she sat for this portrait. She and David were married for over 50 years and had four children. Martha was the great-great-great-granddaughter of Roger Williams, the founder of Rhode Island.

Courtesy of the Slater Mill Historical Site Archives.

David of course could not foresee that he was on the verge of a new era—new not only because the war would end and the textile industry would be sorely challenged, but also because it would bring great personal loss. This new phase would lead to great economic and technological opportunities, in particular the crucial challenge associated with the introduction of the power loom in America. This was the same challenge facing Paul Moody as he left his entrepreneurial position in Amesbury to join the new corporation in Waltham that had been specifically formed to exploit the power loom.

5

Company Man

Paul Moody at Waltham, 1813–1823

> America, in 1813, had machine tools of a kind, and men who could use them to build intricate machines. Even if, as a Massachusetts manufacturer of the time said, these machines were slightly constructed and had to be nursed with all the attention required by rickety children, the very existence of these machines was prophetic.
>
> —George S. Gibb

As Paul Moody began the next phase of his career in 1813, the positive aspects of his new job with the Boston Manufacturing Company were obvious: a high-level position in his area of technical expertise with good pay and increased responsibility. There were troubling aspects as well. The job itself would be daunting: building a mill of great size and scope, supervising a large number of mechanics, and perfecting a power loom that had yet to be put into successful operation anywhere in America. He would no longer be part owner of a small-scale but profitable factory, among friends and family. Instead, he would be a salaried worker for a large but untried corporation with elite Boston owners whom he did not know. There was no assurance that, in the economic uncertainty of war, the new company would have a better chance of success than his entrepreneurial venture at Amesbury.

In this period of economic and political turmoil, there was considerable debate about America's industrial future. The traditional source of the New England Federalist elite's power—the international shipping interests of Boston, Salem, and Newburyport—were in financial straits due to the disruption in

European trade, yet few were ready to hazard their fortunes in manufacturing. Francis Cabot Lowell, one of the few willing to take the risk, had been considered mad by his Cabot uncles, whose bitter experience at the Beverly cotton factory had convinced them that manufacturing was a foolish investment.[1] Yet the war and the embargo that preceded it, however devastating to New England's economy, had presented an opportunity to producers of native alternatives to imported goods. Men like Paul Moody already knew this, and ignored conservative mercantile leaders who opined that manufacturing was an evil to be avoided. Nor did Lowell heed his fellow merchants, for his aim was more than a safe haven for his capital in a time of restricted mercantile activity. He also had in mind the exploitation of an innovative idea: the manufacture of cotton cloth by water-powered looms in a highly capitalized corporation.[2]

The War of 1812 was a watershed event in the debate over American industrialization, largely because it crystallized the various long-running arguments regarding the nation's need for economic independence while maintaining the "republican virtue" that Americans had traditionally associated with agriculture. Nowhere is this more clear than in the case of Thomas Jefferson, whose admonition to steer clear of large-scale industrialization had become the catch phrase of American anti-industrial sentiment after the Revolution. "For the general operations of manufacture," he wrote in *Notes on Virginia,* "let our workshops remain in Europe." But by 1816 he had changed his opinion: Americans needed to be economically independent. "We must now place the manufacturer by the side of the agriculturist. . . . He, therefore, who is now against domestic manufacture, must be for reducing us either to dependence on that foreign nation, or to be clothed in skins, and to live like wild beasts in dens and caverns. I am not one of these; experience has taught me that manufactures are now as necessary to our independence as to our comfort."[3]

Like many critics of industrialization, Jefferson's fear was not manufacturing itself, but the squalor and crime that plagued European industrial centers. If European social problems—most dramatically the blighted example of Manchester, England—were imported along with its technology, the moral basis of republicanism would be undermined. Industrialists shared this concern, and often confronted it directly. "God forbid," wrote Rhode Island cotton manufacturer Zachariah Allen, "that there ever may arise a counterpart of Manchester in the New World."[4] Allen had seen Manchester first hand, and firmly believed that such degradation could be avoided. Not only could America learn from Britain's mistakes, but, given the nation's abundance of rural settings, there was no need to concentrate industrial development in cities. As the American Society for the Encouragement of Domestic Manufactures put it in 1817: "Our factories will not require to be situated near mines of coal, to be worked by fire or steam, but rather on chosen sites, by the fall of waters and the running stream, the seats of health and cheerfulness, where good instruction will secure the morals of the young, and good regulations will promote, in all, order, cleanliness, and the exercise of the civil duties."[5] In this utopian and bucolic view, factories were as natural as waterfalls, and industrialization could be perfectly congruent with the virtuous and orderly aims of republicanism.

Some critics refused to buy this idea of the machine in the garden, to use Leo Marx's phrase. A writer in the *Connecticut Courant* expressed the view that American village life was already idyllic and could only be ruined by factories. "Who that has seen the happy state of society throughout our villages," he asked, "can wish it to be exchanged for the dissipated and effeminate manners and habits, which extensive establishments of manufactures, never fail to bring in their trains?" Pro-manufacturing views dominated, however, partially because embargo and war underscored the need for economic independence, and also because industrial promoters were successful in deflecting the potent and widely held argument that manufacturing would necessarily lead to crime-ridden cities by insisting that factories would be nestled in remote natural settings. One proponent went so far as to argue that America's potential mill locations were God-given: "Unless business of this kind is carried on, certain great *natural powers* of the country will remain inactive and useless. Our numerous mill seats . . . would be given by Providence in vain."[6]

Furthermore, as Drew McCoy has noted, after the war Jeffersonians came to believe that British mercantilism was the culprit rather than manufacturing itself. Great Britain's exploitation of the poor to manufacture luxury goods for export to America was evil, but America's uncorrupted government, freer trading policies, and relative lack of urban poor would guard against a replay of Europe's industrial experience. Critics of industrialization, it appears, had come around to the position espoused by Alexander Hamilton in the 1790s, although they remained more skeptical than Hamilton had been regarding emulation of the British manufacturing juggernaut and showed more concern for the social consequences of such progress. The days of idealizing Jefferson's industrious, frugal, surplus-exporting farmer as the sole repository of republican virtue were over. The War of 1812 taught Americans that the United States could not rely on European markets to absorb the nation's agricultural surplus and that a balance of farmers and manufacturing workers could actually enhance the republican vision by providing domestic markets for agriculture.[7]

Yet how could workers be safely shifted from agriculture to manufacturing when, as everyone agreed, labor was in such short supply? As one opponent put it, "we can more profitably employ our citizens in cultivating the land, in preparing timber for market, in making pot and pearl-ashes, than in weaving cloth, or in making locks and hinges. We have neither the hands nor the capital requisite to the establishment of such existing manufactories as would enable us to supply ourselves cheaper than we could purchase from Great-Britain."[8] But, the counterargument ran, if labor were scarce, all the more reason to bring labor-saving machines into production, requiring only light supervisory attention by those unfit for agricultural labor. In other words, the labor scarcity was actually an asset because it led to the development of labor-saving machinery, did not detract from agriculture, and employed the otherwise unemployable—and not incidentally limited the opportunity for vice and public disorder. As social order emerged as one of the essential components of the republican ideal, the metaphor of the machine seemed to fit: efficiency, dependability, and conformity could work for society and business as well.[9]

In this transition of republicanism to accommodate industry and the development of labor-saving devices, Paul Moody had become a model of civic virtue—if in fact he ever thought about his work in such abstract terms. More practically, his own experience bore little resemblance to the picture painted by anti-industrialists. Not only had he never seen Manchester, but his working life in a small factory in the agricultural setting of Byfield had perhaps more closely resembled the machine in the garden ideal. Moreover, the factories he knew had created jobs and were locally popular. Later, at Amesbury, he worked in small factories in a mixed agricultural-industrial-commercial setting, with no concentration of exploited workers or urban blight.

This is not to deny the negative effects of industrialization for many workers. It is, in general, true that as factories came to dominate American work life, the skills and autonomy of artisans were being supplanted by more rigid job classifications. Yet we must be careful neither to overstate the simple pleasure of preindustrial labor nor to understate the positive aspects of factory opportunities among, for example, underemployed New England farm women. The point is that Moody and other machinists had little experience with the negatives that so troubled the anti-industrialists.[10]

The idealized view of farming conflicted with the reality of the rocky and relatively unproductive soil in Moody's native Massachusetts, and many who saw their future in agriculture chose to move west for better opportunities. The state's economy was already diversified by 1812, including fishing, shipping, and artisanal trades such as shoes, candles, and other handcrafts, sometimes in proto-factory settings. Thus, the agriculture versus manufacturing dichotomy was not so strict, and starting a new type of business enterprise was not necessarily viewed as a dramatic break with the past. The editors of the Boston-based *North American Review* noted the following advantages to further development: "distance from other manufacturing countries—abundance of water privileges in some districts, of coal in others—ample supplies of the raw materials—remarkable skill in the use and invention of machinery—the proximity of almost every part of the country to navigable waters—and a country not overstocked with population."[11]

It must also be kept in mind that, despite the drama of "cotton fever," the Industrial Revolution may not have appeared so revolutionary while it was occurring. It was a more evolutionary shift, still based on traditional work and social structure. And many factory owners—through mill village architecture, concern for the working/living environment, and their own appeals to republican idealism—attempted to prove that the change was not radical. In fact, the kind of factories that had existed in the 1770s—hand weavers operating company-owned equipment in one large building, providing jobs for the poor in the spirit of public good—were not greatly different from the quasi public-oriented corporate manufactories of 1815.[12]

In essence, there was no reason for Paul Moody or men like him to question the value, to themselves or to America, of factories and labor-saving machinery. The national need for a balanced economy now *required* labor-saving machinery, and New England leapt into the forefront. It was men like Moody about whom Horace Mann wrote when he noted that "the people of Massachusetts, to a greater extent than those of any other State in the Union, are a mechanical people."[13] Moody was doing what inventive men would be doing anyway, only now, in the postrevolutionary atmosphere of upward mobility, they acted with considerably greater opportunity for economic and social reward. For a man to do what he had proved he was adept at, on a grander scale, working on unprecedented technical challenges, this was the epitome of opportunity. At the same time he could be a model republican citizen as well.

The distinguishing features of the Boston Manufacturing Company factory at Waltham were its size, the integration of all manufacturing processes, its corporate organization, and the introduction of the power loom. No one in America had dared to dream on this scale, except at Alexander Hamilton's industrial village at Paterson, New Jersey, which began operations in 1794 but due to mismanagement and poor timing ceased production within three years.[14] While it was not entirely novel to perform all phases of cotton cloth manufacture in a single factory, from baled cotton entering the building to finished cloth exiting—this was done at Beverly, for example—all previous endeavors had made use of handlooms. The most successful early factory, Samuel Slater's mill at Pawtucket, used Arkwright water-powered carding and spinning, but weaving was "put out" to hand weavers. Paul Moody's own Amesbury factory employed the latest in carding technology, but spinning was done on hand jennies and weaving on handlooms. This mode of production was standard even for up-to-date mills in America. But by the early 1800s, advances in spinning had outstripped the capacity of hand weavers, as captured by a nineteenth-century historian: "The jenny and the drawing frame being fairly at work, the cry was now, 'What is to become of the yarn! There will not be enough hands to weave it.' "[15]

Only in Great Britain was weaving performed by water-powered machinery. The power loom had been invented in 1785 by Reverend Edmund Cartwright, although its introduction had been greeted with economic failures and riotous mobs of hand weavers who (correctly) saw their future employment jeopardized. Despite a lag in commercial adoption of the innovation, power weaving begin to catch on in Britain about 1810, and by 1813 there were an estimated 2,400 of these looms in operation.[16] They were in use at several factories in England and Scotland visited by Francis Cabot Lowell in 1811–12 and he quickly saw the utility of this labor-saving machine in America, where yarn from mechanized spinning factories greatly exceeded the capacity of hand loom weavers. In the often repeated and essentially accurate story, the Harvard-trained mathematician Lowell gained a sufficient understanding of the components and movements of the power looms he saw in Britain, and upon his return to America he built a working model.

Most accounts correctly credit Paul Moody for his role in turning Lowell's idea into a working loom suitable for production. Lowell began his experimentation with a model of the loom late in 1812 in a loft he rented in Broad Street, Boston, assisted by his business partner and brother-in-law Patrick Tracy Jackson. Lowell and Jackson were no ordinary businessmen, but the two Americans knew their limits when it came to building complicated machinery. They began to search for an associate with practical experience, not only to make the power loom workable, but to build the factory itself. They chose the best-known mechanical man in New England, Jacob Perkins. Perkins declined but suggested his former apprentice, Paul Moody.[17]

While Moody was not the primary choice of Lowell, Jackson, and their fellow investors, his recommendation from Perkins allayed some of their concerns. It is possible that Newburyport natives Lowell and Jackson knew of the Moodys from nearby Byfield. Jackson was a graduate of Dummer Academy, and may have attended at the same time as Paul's brother William who was about Jackson's age. In any event, Nathan Appleton, one of the original directors of the company, said that Moody's "skill as a mechanic was well known." Given his technical aptitude and experience building textile machinery, the recommendation from his revered mentor, and specific training in the art of weaving, Moody was as well positioned as anyone in America to do the job—even though it was on an unprecedented scale. Whatever risk the founders had assumed in choosing their new machinist, it was amply rewarded. As George Gibb aptly summarized, "Even though [Moody] was Lowell's second choice, he immediately proved to be as powerful and significant a figure in the Boston Manufacturing Company as Francis Lowell himself."[18]

On November 1, 1813, Moody began his new job in Waltham. A company accounting entry for November 22 by P. T. Jackson for $4.94 "for one half Moody & my expenses to Mendon," indicates than Moody was on the payroll and already engaged in machine-making issues.[19] The task before him was monumental, for in addition to his role as Lowell's assistant loom builder, his contract stipulated that he was "to oversee the building of the Dam, Mills, Houses, &c, and the making of all the Utensils, machinery & whatever else the company shall see fit to direct to complete their establishment—and also when established, he is to take charge of the conduct of the workmen & of every part of the business of the manufactory." He was, in short, "Superintendent of the works of the Company." While this technical role did not include hiring or supervision of the female employees, his responsibilities did extend to the revenue-producing side of the business, for in addition to building and repairing machinery for the Boston Manufacturing Company he would manufacture machinery to sell to other cotton mills. There was a great deal of flexibility in this aspect of the business. Given the growing number of machine makers in New England at this point, Moody could buy machinery that he could not or chose not to build himself; and as his machine shop grew more sophisticated, he could make copies of purchased machinery—a common practice of the time—for use in the BMC mill or for resale.[20]

Moody set to work right away, beginning with the construction of a machine shop in the factory basement that also housed the waterwheel, and hiring a staff of mechanics and machinists. Perhaps surprisingly, machinists were readily available for hire, as evidenced by P. T. Jackson's comment that "I have had so many applicants for employment that I can't remember all that passes between me & them." Not counting the numerous day laborers, there were twenty-nine men under Moody's supervision by 1817.[21]

The early machine shop was really a basement workshop, and the men who worked there in 1813–14 were carpenters, blacksmiths, wheelwrights, and masons (more machinists were hired as mill construction neared completion and purchased machinery began to arrive). With this team of mechanics Moody began the initial task of erecting the mill building and putting into place the system by which the power from the waterwheel would be transmitted throughout the factory. This waterwheel, not incidentally, was designed by Moody's mentor Jacob Perkins. Apparently when Perkins declined Lowell's offer to supervise the Waltham machine shop, he did agree to install one of his newly patented waterwheel improvements for the first mill.[22]

The four-story mill that Moody and his crew erected was ninety by forty feet—not much bigger than a typical New England mill of the time. It was built of brick on a granite foundation, with brick chimneys at the gable ends and an octagonal bell cupola in the center. This building and the two mills that followed a few years later were not only solid and practical, but unexpectedly graceful. Carding was performed on the first floor, spinning on the second, and weaving on the third and fourth. Picking (breaking apart the baled cotton stock) was done in a separate building due to the potential for fire.[23]

While power loom experiments probably took place in the basement shop, there is no evidence that other machines were built there in the first year. This is supported by a December 1813 order for carding and spinning machines from Luther Metcalf & Company of Medway, a small town twenty miles southwest of Waltham. This substantial order of machinery, not fully delivered until January 1815, included ten carding machines and a number of throstle (spinning) frames and mules, plus associated machine accessories. According to the Boston *Gazette*, the Metcalf spinning equipment was based on "new and exceedingly improved construction [which] requires much less power, less space, and the cotton comes out much more equal. . . . The most respectable and satisfactory references can be adduced of their giving complete satisfaction."[24] Given this availability of apparently reliable spinning equipment, it seems that the BMC plan was to build only the power loom and to buy all other equipment from companies already specializing in these machines. Regardless of the original intention, the decision was important, not just for the success of the Waltham model, but to drive Moody and his machinists to become familiar with and improve upon the most up-to-date textile machines available.[25]

Most of the labor during the preproduction phase at Waltham was by hand—as indicated by the fact that the tool that appears most often in early orders is the common file. (At the same time, David Wilkinson was using a powered lathe in his machine shop at Pawtucket.) Then, in June 1814, the company ordered a roller lathe, a fluting lathe, and a cutting engine (also a lathe) from an Easton, Massachusetts, foundry owned by General Shepard Leach. By the latter part of 1814 there are no more such orders, which suggests that Moody's machine shop had begun to make its own tools.[26]

By that time, Moody and the construction crew had completed the mill building, and now he could concentrate his efforts on machinery. With the arrival of the Metcalf carding and spinning machines in December, along with the stretcher and drawing frames ordered elsewhere, his task now shifted to the installation and repair of the production equipment and the perfection of the power loom.[27] The pressure to make power loom weaving practical was intense, for the notable accomplishment of mill construction and integration of purchased spinning equipment would be worthless without the machine that was the main reason for starting the Boston Manufacturing Company in the first place.

The power loom was not a conceptual breakthrough, in that its three main actions mechanically reproduced those of the handloom: forcing the shuttle through the warp threads; alternately separating the two sets of warp threads; and beating the filling yarn against the weft edge or "fell" of the cloth. The challenge was to duplicate what a human weaver could do by feel—avoiding excessive pressure that would snap threads—in a machine. Early adoption of the power loom in Great Britain had shown a significant boost in productivity compared to hand looms, since one person tending two power looms could produce an estimated seven times the yardage of a handloom weaver.[28]

Lowell and Jackson had been experimenting with the model loom since 1812, more than a year before Moody's participation. By the start of 1814, with Moody's machinist skills applied to the full-size loom, they were ready for a trial run. On January 30, Jackson wrote to Lowell, "I have got our Loom up & yesterday wove several yards *by Water*. The Loom is excellent, tho' still susceptible for improvement. Our shuttle caught it twice . . . owing to our not fixing the stop motion properly . . . & to the unequal motion of the [water] wheel, which owing to the ice or some other cause performs one part of its revolution about twice as fast as the other." These difficulties clearly had the chief machinist worried. "Moody began to be quite afraid of its success," Jackson wrote. "I offered to weave for him gratis if he would find yarn . . . he says he would gladly take me up if he was not afraid that his attention would be too much taken off from his [machine] patterns which he begins next week."[29]

Moody's anxiety was justified, for no one had yet produced a production-quality power loom in America. As late as November 1814, the owners of Poignand Plant & Company, a cotton manufacturer in Lancaster, Massachusetts, had received word of a power loom, but declined even to inspect it because "most if not all of the attempts to make looms go by water have failed & we think with such present means as we possess it would not be provident to embark on an undertaking of that kind till we have such indubitable evidence that there can be no doubt of its practicability."[30] The BMC directors were anxious as well. With the prospect of an end to the war and British dumping of cheap cloth on the American market, the stockholders began to wonder if they had missed their opportunity.

Until late 1814, only the small team of Lowell, Jackson, and Moody had seen the loom in action, but now Lowell agreed to demonstrate it before other BMC principals. Nathan Appleton recalled: "I well recollect the state of admiration and satisfaction with which we sat by the hour, watching the beautiful movement of this new and wonderful machine, destined as it evidently was, to change the character of all textile industry."[31] In fact, it did change the American textile industry, even though the loom was neither completely new nor solely developed by the BMC in the United States. The fact remains that Lowell, Jackson, and Moody had indeed constructed and made practical a machine that with little intervention took bobbins of filling yarn and shuttled them between alternating rows of warp yarn to produce long rolls of sturdy, uniform, unbleached cloth.

This coarse cloth, described by Appleton as "heavy sheeting of No. 14 yarn, 37 inches wide, 44 picks to the inch, and weighing something less than three yards to the pound," first came off the looms in the spring of 1815. Sales through Isaac Bowers's shop on Cornhill in Boston were disappointing—only $297.84 from May to September. Once Appleton's partner Ward & Company began selling on commission, sales soared to a year-end total of nearly $3,000. Within two years sales had increased to about $35,000, and by 1822 to $345,000. Total company assets for this period increased from $39,000 in 1814 to $771,000 in 1823. The Boston Manufacturing Company's spinning and weaving operation at Waltham was an unqualified success.[32]

~

Moody's position in the corporation was one that had little precedent and, because of its range, is difficult to categorize simply. On one level, he was the practical machinist who could turn Lowell's ideas and calculations into efficient reality—a special assistant to the chief architect or designer. His background as a weaver added to his unique qualifications for this role. On another level, he was a hired manager, the clerk-of-the-works for a major construction project, which involved both the oversight of the factory construction and the fabrication or acquisition of the machinery for the mill. If this was not entirely new to Moody, it was certainly well beyond any scale he had previously attempted—in fact there is no evidence that he had ever constructed any of the mill buildings in his previous associations.[33] Moreover, the management of employees in a large department of a corporation was not only new to Moody—it was simply *new* in America. The breadth of this role, only part of which he was specifically prepared for, makes his success remarkable.

One of the new challenges was his relationship with the leaders of the corporation. Moody was both a high-level manager and a hands-on machinist, perhaps not an unusual role in a small mill or machine shop, but somewhat anomalous in the new corporate structure. He was not an officer of the corporation nor, at the outset, a stockholder. His initial salary was $1,500 per year, which is impossible to compare to his previous job since we do not know his compensation at Amesbury. Nathan Appleton's biographer considered Moody's salary "meager"—perhaps as "industrial architect" his compensation should have been closer to that of Patrick Tracy Jackson, who as treasurer received $3,000. Moody was also provided a single-family house, for $100 per year, which at 7 percent of his salary was a bargain. When we consider that the company paid $1,000 for the Waltham mill site, the water privilege, and sixty-seven acres of land, Moody's salary looks generous. And compared to machine shop employees, he was well paid: on average, BMC machinists earned $8.72 per week, or about $450 per year. Department superintendents made between $520 and $625 per year. The most highly compensated machine operators at any cotton factory—the mule spinners—still earned less than Moody, at about $1,050 per year.[34]

Perhaps earning half the salary of the top paid professional and 50 percent more than the highest skilled workers in the factory was about right. Yet Moody's managerial and technical contributions, without which BMC might not have prospered, seem to warrant a compensation package equivalent to Jackson's, which was clearly not the case. This second-tier status was certainly related to Moody's being outside the inner circle, all of whom were members of the Boston-Salem-Newburyport merchant elite. This group of investors (usually referred to as the Boston Associates) made no secret that their top managers were "gentlemen selected for their offices not on account of any mechanical knowledge or experience in manufacturing . . . but for their executive ability, their knowledge of human nature, their ability to control large numbers of operatives, and their social standing." By contrast, at least as late as 1817, Moody was referred to in a company document as "Paul Moody . . . Artisan."[35] As we have seen, Paul was not from humble origins. His family had long maintained a solid middling economic status, and his brothers' college degrees attest to an elite educational, if not economic, status. Still, Paul himself had only modest formal schooling, and even the college-educated Moodys could not hold a candle to the Lowells, Jacksons, and Appletons in matters of class.

Yet there was a special relationship between Moody and Francis Cabot Lowell—the machinist and the privileged businessman—and it had little to do with status and much to do with a manner of thinking. Like David Wilkinson, Moody was a visual thinker who rarely articulated his designs, improvements, or ideas in writing.[36] This does not mean that he lacked a philosophical framework within which to make technology decisions. Opinions on such matters were rarely expressed by the very men who lived their lives within the machinist's context, for they tended not to use words for what they felt most fundamentally. Their understanding of their world was visual and nonverbal; like the "inventive mechanicians" described by the nineteenth-century scientist Sir Francis Galton, "they invent their machines as they walk, and see them in height, breadth, and depth as real objects, and they can also see them in action."[37]

As Anthony Wallace suggests in his study of the industrial village of Rockdale, Pennsylvania, the visual and tactile work of practical machine makers was indeed intellectual, but did not use the symbolic language of mathematics or philosophy to communicate ideas to others. Rather, these men used models and experiments to further their purposes. It is true that Francis Cabot Lowell's ability to calculate precise movements and timings and gear ratios was critical to the success of the loom. Yet in ways that more resemble the style of a machinist, Lowell seems not to have thought in paradigms, but rather pursued his goal through models and experiments. One indication of this is his tinkering with a scale model of the power loom for a full year before an actual loom was built. During the development of the loom, Lowell and Moody researched (or bought) whatever was available at the time, used the ideas or parts that suited them, and continually experimented until the loom behaved as they believed it could.[38]

This is especially true of the first three years at Waltham, a period in which, aside from the power loom, it was more important to purchase, improve, and integrate existing machinery. This does not suggest that Moody was a mere copier of other men's inventions. Rather, it means that Moody operated in a way that is consistent with Brooke Hindle's idea of emulation, which was true of most of the "inventive" men of the era, including David Wilkinson. While Moody clearly did invent, in the context of his entire career invention was the exception. As the great nineteenth-century industrial historian William Bagnall put it, Moody bent his genius to "the improvement of special adjustments and to the invention of new machines for particular processes."[39] This remains the most accurate way to view Moody's lifelong contributions: not wholesale invention, but small, critical improvements, with occasional inventions where gaps existed in the new industrial processes.

This may also explain why Lowell and Moody had no articulated philosophy or paradigm for their power loom, which was in the strict sense not an invention so much as a collection of adaptations and improvements. Beyond the fact that Lowell had purloined the idea and design from Britain, there were already prototype power looms in the United States, and the BMC directors were well aware of these developments. Before the Waltham loom was operational, Jackson wrote to Lowell, who was traveling in the South: "See if Stimpson has got a patent for his loom. As you return, go to Paterson, New Jersey. If Stowell is there, he can show you all worth seeing. See the looms in Baltimore if you can." In fact, BMC did buy a loom from E. Stowell in March 1814 for $100, and one from J. Stimpson in December 1814 for $200.[40]

These precedents are absent from most accounts of the Waltham story. Typical is the version by F. C. Lowell's nephew John A. Lowell, who explained that

> [n]ot even books and designs, much less models, could be procured [by Moody]. The structure of the machinery, the materials to be used in the construction, the very tools of the machine shop, the arrangement of the mill, and the size of its various apartments—all these were to be, as it were, re-invented.[41]

Accounts such as this and by Nathan Appleton and others who were directly involved were careful never to call into question the unalloyed inventive genius of Lowell and Moody. Yet we know that mills similar to those at Waltham (absent the power loom) had been built in America and that a wide range of textile machinery was available for purchase. If we understand the real manner of technological innovation as adaptive, experimental, emulative, and cumulative, the Waltham story fits a more accurate pattern. And the lack of inventive purity hardly detracts from Lowell and Moody's accomplishment, since their collection of improvements was significant enough to launch a wildly successful new means of production in the United States.

To the list of characteristics of successful innovation must be added the important concept of collaboration. The history of invention is littered with the failures of lone inventors. It is doubtful that Lowell would have succeeded without Moody; and Moody, who had no patents to his credit before his association with Lowell, blossomed as an inventor and innovator in its aftermath. Their shared style of visual and tactile communication created one of the great technical partnerships of the early industrial revolution. Thus, Moody's position in the corporate hierarchy was enhanced by a mutual high regard between Lowell and himself. Despite their differences in education and class they spoke the same "language." Moody may have been shut out of the top echelon, working for men who would remain his betters, yet his short happy relationship with Lowell must have eased his fit into the new structure. He was treated with respect throughout the company, and as his value to the corporation became increasing evident, the directors generously demonstrated their appreciation.

~

At the time Paul Moody and his family moved to Waltham, it was primarily a farming community best known for the "Great Road" that ran through the lower part of town. Connecting Boston to points west, it was also known as the Boston Post Road—now Main Street and Route 20—and its many taverns provided cheer or a night's rest to travelers. It was at one of these establishments, the Old Stratton Tavern, that John Adams stopped for breakfast on his way to New York City to take the oath of office as president. Prior to 1813, Waltham had been relatively homogeneous—that is, English—with a single meeting house. The establishment of the Boston Manufacturing Company brought profound changes to this quiet agricultural town.[42]

Waltham was not entirely unknown, for the Boston elite had discovered it as a fine location to build their country estates. The best known of these was Christopher Gore, who was a one-term governor of Massachusetts (1809–10) and United States senator from 1812–16. The Gores built an exquisite estate on forty acres, later extended to four hundred acres, and moved there permanently after the senator retired in 1816.[43] But even with its traditional farms and new retreats for the Beacon Hill elite, Waltham was not entirely devoid of manufacturing. Industrialists tend to discredit or ignore the industrial assets they appropriate. This was especially true in the early nineteenth century, perhaps because the situating of an industrial factory in a pristine natural setting might appear more positive if it could be matched to the machine-in-the-garden ideal. In truth, Waltham already had significant industry before the Boston Associates chose its factory site.

By 1812, there were twenty-three mills along the Charles River's eighty-mile length, several of them in Waltham. In addition, Waltham's many brooks afforded power for grist, saw, and fulling mills. Thomas Rider had established a mill on Chester Brook before 1700, which later under Moses Mead produced rakes, hoe and axe handles, mortars, pestles, and rolling pins, and was well known in Waltham and beyond. In 1788, John Boies built a dam and paper mill on the north side of the Charles River, just east of the current Moody Street bridge. In 1794, the aforementioned Christopher Gore built a competing mill on the Charles at the eastern end of town; and in 1802 one of Boies's employees, Nathan Upham, built a third paper mill. The Gore mill failed, and was sold in 1810 to Wiswall, Holland, and Coverley, the new owners of a cotton mill who used Gore's factory as their fulling mill. This enterprise became incorporated in 1812 as the Waltham Cotton and Woolen Manufacturing Company.[44]

With cotton mill fever sweeping New England and the abundance of water power on the Charles River, it is no surprise that Waltham was busily industrializing during this period. The Waltham Cotton and Woolen company prospered during the war and by 1815 had two thousand spindles in the cotton factory and 380 in the woolen mill, employing more than two hundred workers, mostly women and children. Reverend Samuel Ripley wrote in 1815 that the company had built "four dwelling houses, a large store and warehouse, dye house, grist mill, mechanick's house, woolen factory, weaver's, and school house." Setting a precedent for the BMC, this school was distinct from the four other school districts in town and was known as the "factory school." Thus, the BMC borrowed much from its industrial predecessors. Due to competition, harsh economic conditions, and outright hostility from the BMC, the Waltham Cotton and Woolen company remained in business only until 1819, when the BMC bought it and all the land on the north side of the river between the two factories, and built the Waltham Bleachery and Dye Works.[45]

The Moodys' new home town had grown substantially from a population of 903 in 1800 to about 1,250 in 1815, but it was still smaller than Amesbury had been in 1800 (population 1,757). The best land—"tolerably fertile," according to Reverend Ripley—lay in the northern part of town. The area of greatest population growth was in the flat land known as "Waltham plain," along the post road and the river. No admirer of manufacturing in general, Ripley spoke favorably of the Waltham Cotton and Woolen company. "Unlike most manufacturing establishments, this is free from the disorder and immorality which, in general, are found to exist, and by many are supposed to be almost their necessary evil." He attributed this to the company's orientation toward families, who were able to maintain order, and to the character of the superintendent, who in this case was also an owner.[46]

Nor was Waltham completely devoid of cultural institutions. Before 1815 there was a "Social Library" with three hundred volumes (although there was no local newspaper until 1833). Reverend Ripley estimated that there were 120 dwelling houses, mostly wood, and seven "excellent houses" of brick. He noted as well a malt house, several retailers' shops, and "English and W.I. [West Indian] goods stores." These stores undoubtedly benefited from the influx of BMC employees. Unlike the typical cotton manufactory of the period, Boston Manufacturing paid its workers in cash rather than in company-store credits, so the employees were free to spend their money in the town shops.[47]

Before building tenements to house the female factory workers, the BMC purchased four houses to rent to favored employees. One, a "brick house on the road" (presumably the Post Road), was rented to Paul Moody. Then, in 1815, the company began building employee housing, most of it in two rows directly across from the factory office, a two-story hip-roofed brick building with a center chimney, separated from the mill yard by a white picket fence, and from the street by a board fence, with an entrance gate through which all workers and visitors passed. Although the reality of mill life was less idyllic than the bucolic image suggested by contemporary paintings of the stately brick buildings perfectly placed within a setting of river, trees, and animals, the BMC complex was nevertheless an impressive sight, especially after the second four-story mill was added in 1819. One-story cottages and two-story houses alternated in the neat row opposite the entrance. One of the old houses bought by the company was torn down and replaced by the "new House building for P. Moody" in early 1817. So within three years of resettling in Waltham, the Moodys—Paul, Susan, and their four children—had a fine new home in the fastest-growing section of town.[48]

They also drew family and friends from their former home towns. Paul's younger brother David began working for the Boston Manufacturing Company as early as May 1814, and probably moved to Waltham sometime before February 1815, when P. T. Jackson was authorized "to hire Mr. David Moody to serve the company as Agent, for one year."[49] After that year, Jackson became the company agent, and David Moody disappears from the account books. Susan's brother, Jonathan Morrill, worked for the company between 1818 and 1821. Experienced as a bookkeeper—probably for Worthen and Moody's factory in Amesbury—he served the BMC as an agent of sorts, since he was one of four men (including Paul Moody) authorized in 1820 to "order out & expel from

Figure 5.1
This diorama shows the Boston Manufacturing Company complex at Waltham as it would have looked about 1825.
Courtesy of Lowell National Historical Park.

the Building & Lands of the Company any persons whom they shall think fit." Finally, Moody's friend John Dummer came to Waltham from Byfield in 1815. Paul's son David later recalled that "[m]y father knowing him to be such a kind of workman as he wanted, made him foreman of the water-wheel and pattern work, &c." Although described as "extremely odd," Dummer had a special relationship with Paul, and was at least sociable enough to become engaged to a BMC machine operative in 1817 (although they did not marry until thirteen years later).[50] Through the company, Moody was able to draw familiar people to Waltham, improving both his work and personal life.

The town clearly benefited from BMC investment. In addition to the new housing, the company improved existing streets and laid out new ones, and planted several thousand shade trees along the way. Visitors came to view the new factory and its wonderful machines that wove cloth with only minor supervision from their female "operatives." (Even South Carolina congressman John C. Calhoun paid a visit in 1818 and declared his approval, while attributing some of the success to his support for Lowell's pro-manufacturing tariff proposal in 1816.) But the curious also came to see the social experiment that produced a bustling section of town without the anticipated moral decay and with relatively satisfied workers. One reason for worker contentment was the higher than normal wages paid to skilled male workers as well as to the single women who primarily staffed the factory. (The adult males were mechanics, overseers, and various common laborers, with only a few children employed as bobbin boys and pickers. This was in marked contrast to the more typical practice, as at Pawtucket, of hiring entire families, which resulted in a large percentage of child laborers.) Moreover, the machine operators did not typically remain on the job long enough to build up resentment. The young women had short-term goals, such as saving for a dowry or helping relieve family debts, and they stayed on average less than four years. Thus, as labor historian Howard Gitelman notes, the BMC had accomplished "a grand American *coup*: it engaged in manufacturing without creating at the same time a dependent and debased laboring class."[51]

All this was done at some cost to the company: the boarding houses brought in less than banking interest rates, and because the work force was temporary the cost of training was high. In addition, the BMC contributed liberally to the local Congregational church and maintained the grammar school that had been established by the Waltham Cotton & Woolen Factory. While these can be seen as practical business decisions, as well as a way to deflect the criticism that factories were incompatible with virtue, Lowell and his partners must be credited for their successful blending of profitability and benevolence.[52]

This places Paul Moody in Waltham during the idyllic years when the republican experiment was generally alive and well. As a senior manager, Moody was not only an influential person within the corporation, but in the town as well. While he had enjoyed a certain social standing in Amesbury as part owner of a successful small business, he now found himself a leader in the transformation of Waltham. Because a successful manufacturing company meant jobs and general prosperity, voters in town tended to support the corporation's positions. The religious center shifted to "the plain" where the BMC specifically aimed to provide a moral setting for the mill girls. Without explicitly forcing the citizens of Waltham to bend to its wishes, Boston Manufacturing's largesse—to the fire department, schools, library, and church, as well as general beautification—made the company a difficult target for those who opposed it.

Moody's position in the company may have given him a special perspective on these unfolding changes. Although a senior manager, he was not, and perhaps never wanted to be, at the top of the organization. Yet he was positioned well above the carpenters, bricklayers, and machinists under his management, and even the well-paid male mule spinners. This distinction—a short but unbridgeable distance from the top and a comfortable distance from the bottom—had both professional and social dimensions. Aside from Jackson, Moody was the only BMC manager or stockholder who resided in Waltham.[53] While there is no extant evidence of his influence in town matters, except for his role in an important religious dispute, it seems safe to assume that he derived some social benefit from his position as a leading representative of the company whose economic power was unmatched in the area.

He could take great pride in all he surveyed from his home and his factory buildings. He occupied one of the best properties, a fine new brick single-family home, just outside the main gate of the factory complex he was responsible for building. There he and his family would be seen and admired. In at least one important respect, however, the Moodys kept their distance: their children were sent to private school at Bradford Academy, at that time a small coeducational boarding school.[54] Paul and his wife may have entertained doubts that the system they were building was sufficiently sophisticated or moral at this point. Perhaps they were simply exercising a class consciousness of their own, not of the elite but sufficiently elevated to keep their children from mixing with factory boys and girls (however morally upright). The Moodys now had social status, as well as the money to act accordingly.

The previously noted church controversy raises the question of whether Moody's corporate and social status were in conflict. The population of Waltham grew by 60 percent between 1810 and 1820, mostly because of the influx of workers drawn to the steady employment and cash wages, and company benefits such as a savings bank, library, and safe, reasonably priced housing.[55] Perhaps nowhere was the company's interest in town matters more evident than in religious affairs, where Paul Moody assumed a degree of leadership that reflected both his personal concerns and those of the corporation.

Although Waltham had been a one-church town throughout its early history, it was not entirely the coming of the Boston Manufacturing Company that changed it. Conflict had been occurring for other reasons, such as the arrival of the Methodists, who held the first non-Congregational service in Waltham in 1794. Another cause was dissention within the church resulting from the appointment in 1809 of Samuel Ripley as pastor, combined with the tension between Federalists and Republicans during the period of Jefferson's Embargo and the War of 1812. Like most New England clergy at the time, Ripley was a Federalist. On July 23, 1812, on the first fast day proclaimed by President Madison, Ripley delivered a sermon highly critical of Madison and his administration's policies, which in Ripley's opinion were destroying New England's economy. The war, Ripley declared, was the product of "ignorance, error, immorality & party spirit." Two prominent members of the congregation walked out, and the troubles began. In October 1813, fifty-five members left the church to form the Second Religious Society. This lasted until 1814, when Samuel's father, Rev. Ezra Ripley of Concord, organized a truce.[56]

On the surface, this was classic tension between Federalists and Republicans, but deeper divisions included Ripley's liberal theology (the newer congregants from the mills were more orthodox), his family's snobbery (his wife had no sympathy for "the feelings and occupations of ordinary and vulgar minds"), and the fact that war was actually a boon to the manufacturing interests because it stemmed the flow of competing textile imports. Even after the war ended, tensions remained. As Ripley's wife Sarah wrote to her brother in 1819, "the parish are making a rout, finding fault loud with their minister for keeping school, building too large a house, marrying a learned lady, &c." A town meeting petition was drawn up to remove Ripley on the charge that he devoted more time to his school than to ministering to the needs of his parishioners. Paul Moody was one of the eight signers of the petition. Just as his father had done in Newbury, Paul had taken on a leading role in a religious schism.[57]

Ripley was exonerated at town meeting by a three to one margin, but the dissenters would have no more of him or his church. In April 1820, Moody was one of a seven-member committee to represent the Second Religious Society, which incorporated two months later and built a church near the factory. More than one-half of the 122 members were engaged in manufacturing or trade, and fifty were mill employees. The farmers and artisans who had controlled the town before the BMC was established suspiciously regarded the new arrivals as temporary residents who had no permanent interest in the town, and opposed them in town meetings and church. They may have been right about the short tenure of individual mill girls, but they badly misjudged the staying power and influence of the Boston Manufacturing Company.[58]

While church splits commonly occur for reasons of geography or theology, the hand of the BMC can clearly be seen in this case. When the new church was built, the company subsidized twenty of the eighty pews and purchased a silver communion service, whereas it had earlier declined to help the First Parish when it appealed for money for an extension to the church. Between the time that the Second Religious Society was formed and the completion of its church building, services were held in the factory schoolhouse. The BMC simply wanted a church that was close to its employees (both geographically and theologically) and over which it could exercise some control.[59]

It is unclear whether Moody was on company time while he participated in this split from the established church and the formation of the new society. He could have played an active role in these matters independent of the corporation's will and interest, yet his stance was probably influenced by the company (although it seems unlikely that he was following orders). He was a high-level manager and a prosperous stockholder in a corporation that had brought jobs, roads, and schools—and now a church—to Waltham. For a company man this was perfect congruence: what was good for the Boston Manufacturing Company was good for Paul Moody.

This suggests that Moody was fully in step with F. C. Lowell's industrial plan in all its economic, social, and technical dimensions. As he grew wealthier, with stock and dividends, and as other textile companies failed or struggled in the postwar depression, he must have become a believer in size, heavy capitalization, and the mobilization of all available resources for economic success. Given what we know of Paul over his lifetime (more apparent from his later years in the town of Lowell), it is likely that he believed that manufacturing should and could provide jobs and safe, moral living conditions, and that industrialization was good for the country as a whole, serving the cause of independence by lessening British economic domination. The results of Lowell's plan certainly proved personally satisfying for Moody, conferring wealth and status on him and his family, while providing diverse and challenging work. While machine tenders or "operatives" generally suffered from the division of labor that accompanied industrialization, the manager of a growing machine shop still had tremendous variety in his job. In fact, Lowell's technologically progressive blueprint could not have been more in line with Paul's own objectives, providing as it did a giant step in the direction that he had been following all his life through natural bent and as a response to opportunity.

The Boston Manufacturing Company's success is usually attributed to the introduction of the power loom. Other important factors, however, included continued domestic demand for the sturdy, inexpensive cloth that the BMC produced; the F. C. Lowell–inspired tariff of 1816 which was moderate except for the twenty-five cents per yard minimum value it placed on cheap Indian cloth, which made BMC's low-priced goods competitive; and the high capitalization of the company, allowing it to reduce prices and even expand during hard economic times.[60]

One particularly relevant example of the difficult postwar period is Nathan Appleton's description of a visit that he and F. C. Lowell paid to David Wilkinson in June 1816. "We proceeded to Pawtucket," Appleton wrote. "We called on Mr. Wilkinson, the maker of machinery. He took us into his establishment—a large one; all was silent, not a wheel in motion, not a man to be seen. He informed us that there was not a spindle running in Pawtucket, except a few in Slater's old mill, making yarns. All was dead and still." Lowell in essence tried to encourage the Rhode Island manufacturers by promoting the superiority of the Waltham power loom, but "they were incredulous—it might be so, but they were not disposed to believe it."[61]

There is a certain smugness in Appleton's recollection: his Waltham factory was a success, and if only those poor Rhode Islanders had recognized the superiority of the Waltham power loom they too could have shared in the prosperity. But the Rhode Islanders—seemingly down and out—were poised to rebound. As we shall see, David Wilkinson and others were already experimenting with power looms of their own. Furthermore, as Rhode Island industrialist Zachariah Allen noted later, when Lowell and Appleton visited Pawtucket to "sneer at" David Wilkinson about the downturn in the Rhode Island textile industry, Wilkinson's slide lathe "was before the gentlemen in his Machine shop without attracting their notice." Appleton, in other words, learned nothing of value about the textile business while a power tool of inestimable worth in textile machine making was right under his nose.[62]

Still, the Boston Manufacturing Company had the power loom in production and, as yet, no one else in America did. In addition to their de facto advantage, Lowell and Jackson jointly held patent ownership. The patent, dated February 23, 1815, no longer exists so it is impossible to know its exact features, or what was specifically patentable. The Waltham loom was based on Lowell's observations of Robert Miller's English wiper loom, so called because the shuttles were driven by eccentric wheels or wipers. (A wiper is essentially a cam, which rotates off-center, to convert a rotary motion into a back-and-forth motion, as in a sewing machine, for example.) Lowell's adaptation undoubtedly benefited from close inspection of the Stowell and Stimpson looms purchased by the BMC in 1814. Despite his obvious contribution for more than a year, Moody was not a co-patentee, perhaps reflecting his later entry into the process.[63]

Oddly enough, the Waltham loom was technologically out of date from the beginning, for it was based on a design that had been superseded in Britain by a superior model that Lowell had not seen during his visit. William Horrocks had patented a power loom in England in 1803 (with improvements in 1805 and 1813) that was different in several respects from the loom Lowell had examined, most importantly in that it was made of iron (Waltham's were mostly of wood), and was simpler in design, cheaper, and capable of higher speeds.[64] As we will see, it was the Rhode Island machinists—among them David Wilkinson—who would exploit this technological alternative.

The Boston Manufacturing Company patent, based on the collaboration of so many men, was used to great financial advantage before other practical power looms came into use in America in 1817. While Moody did not share in the official credit for the Waltham power loom, his collaboration with Lowell and the opportunities presented to him during this period spurred him to patent his own inventions and improvements in one of the most remarkable displays of inventiveness in American business history.

Patent protection was an important part of the BMC's business strategy, not only in their resolve to take infringers to court, but also in their insistence on company ownership of any inventions by their employees. When Allan Pollack came to work in Paul Moody's machine shop, his contract stipulated that "[s]hould I be fortunate enough to make or suggest any improvement for which it might be thought proper to obtain a patent, such patent or patents are to be the property of the company." This was common practice for dealing with the threat that unscrupulous machinists posed to the company, although it did not guarantee the safety of the company's technology secrets. Patents were easily obtained during this period—usually involving a formal description and a thirty-dollar fee—and inventors were left to defend their patent rights in the courts. The BMC used patent litigation frequently to protect the corporation financially during the early years. Lowell and Jackson's original patent, and subsequent patents by Moody, were used in two ways: by selling patented machinery to textile factories and by selling the patent rights to other machine manufacturers. For example, anyone could build and use the Waltham power loom by paying a license fee of $15 per loom, a policy that contributed $3,555 of the $8,354 that the company received for patent sales between 1817 and 1823. Similarly, a loom built in BMC's shop could be purchased for $125. Machine sales for that same period netted a profit of $33,190.[65] Paul Moody's machine shop not only outfitted the largest, most successful factory complex in America, but had also become a very profitable business in itself.

Given the BMC's effective use of patents, much of the company's early success can be attributed to Moody's blossoming as an inventor. Although he had no patentable inventions before joining the BMC, he obtained nine patents between 1816 and 1821. Because it was company policy that all inventions belonged to the corporation, conventional wisdom might suggest that working under these constraints would tend to stifle creativity, and that an independent machinist—because he owned his intellectual property—would be more inventive. Yet it is clear from Moody's prolific output that rather than being constrained he was inspired by the opportunities presented to him by the corporation.

An example of this is an anecdote told by Nathan Appleton about a visit that Lowell and Moody paid to Silas Shepard, a machine maker in Taunton, to discuss the possible purchase of a number of yarn-winding machines for which Shepard and John Thorp held the patent rights. Because he planned to buy many winders, Lowell asked Shepard for a discount.

> Mr. Shepard refused, saying "you must have them, you cannot do without them, as you know, Mr. Moody." Mr. Moody replied, "I am just thinking that I can spin the cops [cones of filling yarn] direct upon the bobbin." "You be hanged," said Mr. Shepard. "Well, I accept your offer." "No," said Mr. Lowell, "it is too late."[66]

This story was corroborated by Samuel Batchelder, a more detached observer, who said that Appleton's version was "in substance the same as Mr. Moody related it to me." But Batchelder added an important coda: Moody was simply trying to help Lowell get a bargain, and actually had no idea how he might invent a way to spin yarn directly on shuttle bobbins and thus eliminate the need for Shepard's winders. On the ride back to Waltham, "Mr. Lowell told Mr. Moody that he had suggested the plan of spinning the filling on the bobbin, and now he must accomplish it." Moody applied himself to the task by inventing a machine that spun the soft filling yarn directly onto bobbins that could be used in the loom shuttles. This so-called filling frame, after several improvements, was patented by Moody on February 19, 1821.[67]

Industrial historian Patrick M. Malone has studied the phenomenon of "shop floor incremental change"—the idea that most technical advances are small and incremental rather than breakthroughs and that "shop floor" group work, as Paul Moody would have experienced with his large department of machinists, is often the spur to improvement, sometimes resulting in patentable change. Furthermore, as the Shepard anecdote demonstrates, the corporation provided opportunities that *required* Moody's inventiveness. Rather than being antagonistic to creativity, companies such as the BMC, which valued technological innovation as a vital business advantage, could foster an environment of innovation. They demonstrated this by their vigorous protection of patent infringements in the courts, as well as their generous compensation to their inventors, which was an effective recompense for the loss of control over their intellectual property.[68]

Paul Moody thrived under these conditions. As Patrick Tracy Jackson testified in 1821, Moody had come out from under Lowell's wing:

> [I]n 1815 Mr. Moody invented and made a machine for warping [organizing yarns in preparation for weaving]. The next year he made important and useful improvements in the English Dressing machine for sizing yarn. . . . He was not assisted in making them by Mr. Lowell or myself. In 1815 we were informed by Mr. Thomas Faulkner that machines were used in England for roving Cotton, called Bobbin & Fly frames, which he thought better for the purpose than the stretcher we then used. Mr. Moody (with the consent of Mr. Lowell & myself) built one as nearly like those used in England as he could, from the information given him by Mr. Faulkner and what we could

> obtain from other sources. This frame was put in operation in the summer of 1816.[69]

As the reference to English machinist Thomas Faulkner suggests, Moody was copying as much as inventing, which should keep us mindful that at this stage the American textile industry was still technologically inferior to that of Great Britain, although gaining quickly in the ability to make useful incremental improvements and occasional original contributions to machine technology. The distinction between copying and inventing is not only blurred, but is also in a sense irrelevant: Moody was doing exactly what the corporation wanted him to do, which was to give them the technological edge the business required. And the work was exactly what Moody wanted to do, which was to use his inventive mind and skilled hands to make and improve textile machinery. His particular genius was to address the bottlenecks in the processes of yarn and cloth production—warping, dressing, stop motion—that cost the company time and money. His goals and those of the company were perfectly aligned.[70]

The first of Moody's patents during this period of remarkable creativity was the warper (March 9, 1816), a machine that took several hundred warp yarns from a rack of bobbins, laid them side by side, and wound them onto a roller that would then be placed onto the loom. A break in any one of the threads meant stopping and rewinding the warper to locate and piece together the broken strand. This took a vigilant eye on the part of the operator, and limited the speed at which the warper could be run. Moody, once again with the help of Jacob Perkins, fitted his warper with a "stop motion" device which, by means of a drop wire that fell when its associated yarn had broken, stopped the machine almost immediately. Moody's achievement was recognized early on: in his classic 1840 comparative study of cotton manufacture in Great Britain and the United States, James Montgomery considered the Waltham stop-motion warper an important improvement over British models. "The warping machines used in Great Britain require the utmost attention on the part of the attendant to notice instantly when a thread breaks; as should her eye be diverted from her work but one moment, the end of a broken thread might wind round the beam so far as to require five minutes or more to find it and put the machine in motion again." This benefited the BMC not only in the reduction of time lost to thread repair, but also allowed them to use less skilled operators to mind the warpers. Moody's labor-saving innovations were just what the BMC management required to protect their profit margins by allowing their machines to be operated by inexpensive unskilled female workers rather than men.[71]

Between 1816 and early 1818, Moody made improvements to a dressing machine that had been patented in England in 1804. Dressing is the process by which the warp yarns are prepared with a starch solution called "size" or "sizing" in order to strengthen them for the demands of machine weaving. (Sizing was a strange concoction of vinegar, yeast, potato starch, tallow, and sulfate of copper.) In handloom weaving, two to three feet of warp yarn strands would be dressed with sizing, allowed to dry, then woven. If this procedure were applied to power weaving, the loom would be stopped at least twice per hour, resulting in a substantial loss of efficiency. The Waltham dresser was a significant labor-saving improvement, because the reduced time required for sizing allowed an operator to tend more than one loom at a time. Moody clearly stated in his own dressing frame patent application of January 17, 1818, that his machine "resembles in many particulars one intended for the same object, said to have been invented in England by Thomas Johnson and for which he obtained a patent." Copying British patents was an accepted practice, so long as there were no U.S. patent implications (few inventions in this period were expressly patented in both countries). "I have never seen a machine made according to the said Johnson's patent," Moody further explained, "but I have seen the specification and drawings accompanying his patent, from which I constructed a machine resembling [his]." While this appears to be an exercise in simple copying, it is important to note that Moody's dresser was a great improvement over the original. James Montgomery said that it was "much more simple, more easily attended and kept in order, besides requiring less power and oil" than any dresser he had seen in England or Scotland, and cost about half as much to build.[72]

One of the improvements that Moody made to the dressing frame was by accident. In the story he related to Samuel Batchelder, Moody had been using wooden rollers to move the warp yarns into the sizing vat, and the wet, glue-like sizing caused the wood to swell and deform. The machinists tried covering the rollers with pewter, but were having difficulty casting the pewter. Moody had discussed the problem with his brother, David, who had left Waltham when his BMC contract ran out and was now superintendent of the Boston Iron Works. Visiting David in Boston, Paul brought up the matter and asked his brother if soapstone might be suitable. Paul was referring to the mold for the pewter coating, but his brother assumed he meant the material for the rollers. "Well, I should think soap-stone would make a very good roller," his brother replied. With no acknowledgment of the misinterpretation, Paul went back to Waltham and made his rollers of soapstone, which suited the purpose perfectly. The anecdote (probably accurate given the general reliability of Batchelder's accounts) demonstrates the collaborative—and occasionally accidental—nature of technical innovation. It also provides a rare glimpse into Paul's relationship with his mechanically minded brother David.[73]

Moody's remaining six patents between 1819 and 1821 were all related to the filling frame (discussed above) and the double speeder. Despite the patent date of the double speeder, the evidence that F. C. Lowell worked on it indicates it was begun before his death in August 1817. This machine, essentially a "roving frame" that stretches the carded cotton (called roving at this stage) and imparts a slight twist for strength, required that the bobbin, on which the result-

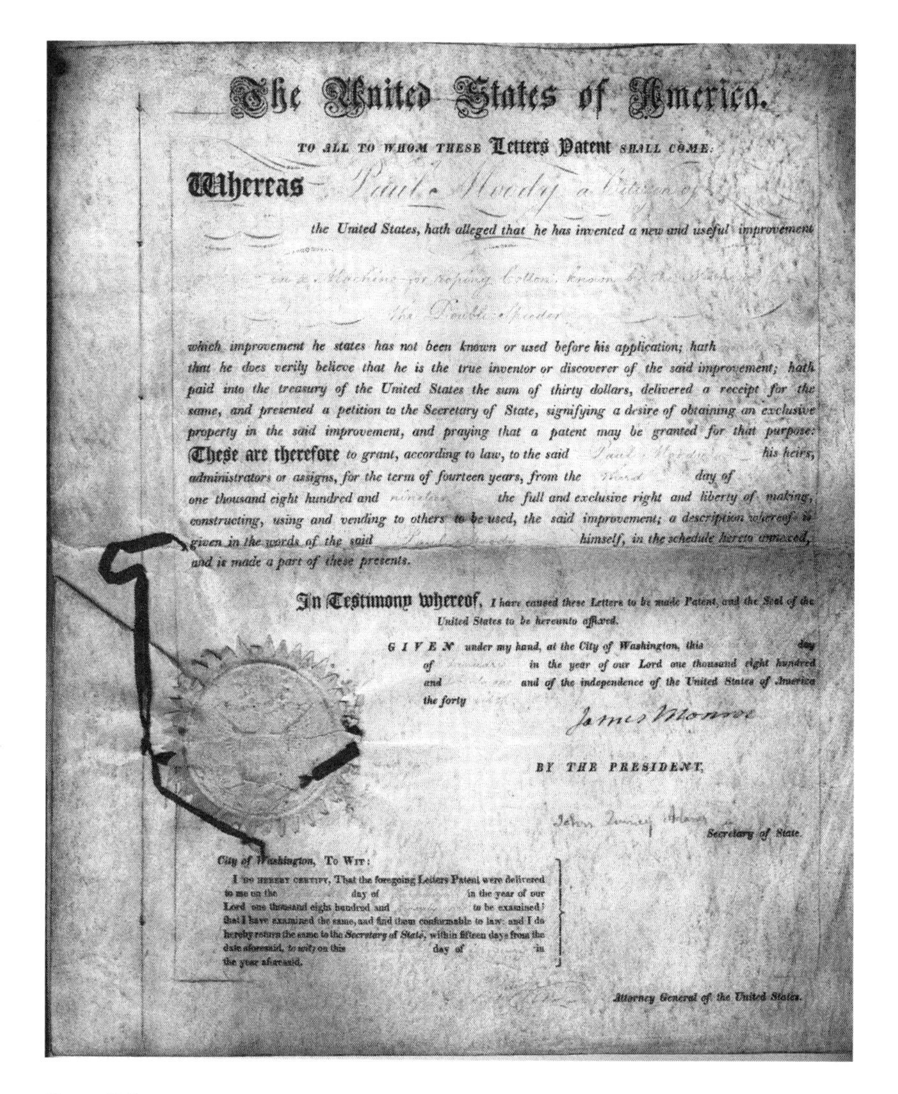

The United States of America.

TO ALL TO WHOM THESE Letters Patent SHALL COME:

Whereas Paul Moody a Citizen of

the United States, hath alleged that he has invented a new and useful improvement

in a Machine for roping Cotton, known by the name of

the Double Speeder

which improvement he states has not been known or used before his application; hath that he does verily believe that he is the true inventor or discoverer of the said improvement; hath paid into the treasury of the United States the sum of thirty dollars, delivered a receipt for the same, and presented a petition to the Secretary of State, signifying a desire of obtaining an exclusive property in the said improvement, and praying that a patent may be granted for that purpose: These are therefore to grant, according to law, to the said Paul Moody his heirs, administrators or assigns, for the term of fourteen years, from the third day of one thousand eight hundred and nineteen the full and exclusive right and liberty of making, constructing, using and vending to others to be used, the said improvement; a description whereof is given in the words of the said Paul Moody himself, in the schedule hereto annexed, and is made a part of these presents.

In Testimony whereof, I have caused these Letters to be made Patent, and the Seal of the United States to be hereunto affixed.

GIVEN under my hand, at the City of Washington, this day of in the year of our Lord one thousand eight hundred and and of the independence of the United States of America the forty

James Monroe

BY THE PRESIDENT,

John Quincy Adams

Secretary of State.

City of Washington, To Wit:

I do hereby certify, That the foregoing Letters Patent were delivered to me on the day of in the year of our Lord one thousand eight hundred and to be examined; that I have examined the same, and find them conformable to law: and I do hereby return the same to the Secretary of State, within fifteen days from the date aforesaid, to wit, on this day of in the year aforesaid.

Attorney General of the United States.

Figure 5.2

Although the ink has faded, this official letter documents Paul Moody's double speeder patent of 1819. It was signed by President James Monroe and Secretary of State John Quincy Adams.

Courtesy of the National Park Service, Adams National Historical Park.

ing yarn would be wound, turn at a variable speed to keep the surface of the wound yarn uniform even as the circumference of the wound yarn increased. That is, the winding of the roving on the bobbin had to remain at the same speed at which the roving was coming off the rollers of the drawing machine, otherwise the roving would stretch or break. (Anyone who has wound string on a spool knows that it takes more string for each succeeding revolution around the spool. The only way to keep the feed constant is to reduce the speed of the spool proportionally.)[74] Lowell put his Harvard mathematics degree to good use in making the precise calculations for the variable velocity of the bobbins, and Moody built the machine to Lowell's specifications. The famed mathematician Nathaniel Bowditch, testifying in a case that raised the question whether a mathematical calculation could be patented, considered Lowell's computations so intricate that it was amazing that anyone other than Bowditch himself could have devised them.[75] Moody patented the double speeder April 3, 1819, and added several patented improvements in 1820 and 1821.

It was during this great period of inventive activity that the celebrated champion of American manufactures, Speaker of the House Henry Clay, visited Waltham and extolled the combination of talent and capital that had resulted in the success of the Boston Manufacturing Company. One of the most important components of that success, he reported in a speech to the House of Representatives in April 1820, was "a machinist of most inventive genius."[76]

Moody and Lowell collaborated on one further useful device, although it was apparently never patented. Moody had been struggling with the problem of irregular waterwheel speed, which made weaving uneven, and he visited Lowell at his home in Boston to discuss the matter. Lowell explained that he had seen a speed governor in England (possibly James Watt's fly ball governor for steam engines) but could not remember the details—simply that it consisted of balls on the ends of two arms connected by pivots to a rotating shaft; as the shaft speed increased, centrifugal force spread the arms, which raised a connecting link that in turn adjusted the gate that controlled water volume. Lowell suggested a governor be ordered from England. Instead, on his drive back to Waltham, Moody figured out a design in his head, and the next morning his men started building the device. It worked, and was in use at Waltham into the 1830s.[77] This demonstrates a different aspect of Moody's versatility: there was no specification to copy, simply a verbal description, which he translated into an operational device—apparently even to the surprise of Lowell. It is also another example of how Lowell and Moody communicated and collaborated. Although Moody had wrestled with the uneven waterwheel speed problem, it is unlikely that he would have conceived the idea of a governor unless Lowell had suggested it.

~

Given Paul Moody's extraordinary talent for producing patents during this period, the important question that arises is whether he would have found it more personally satisfying and lucrative to have been an independent inventor rather than a corporate machinist whose patents belonged to his employer. Perhaps Moody felt that way at first; any inventor obviously takes great pride in seeing his patent approved, and he might have added up the sales of patented machinery or the royalties paid to the BMC for permission to use his patents and considered how that financial reward could have been his. In addition, inventors were held in high regard in the culture—a phenomenon that Brooke Hindle calls "the inventor as hero"—partially because of the tendency to oversimplify the process of invention by associating it with a single person: a Franklin, a Fulton, a Morse, or a Colt. Furthermore, it is apparent from Jackson's previously cited testimony that Moody could only work on projects "with the consent of Mr. Lowell & myself," rather than when the entrepreneurial or technological spirit moved him. "Mr. Lowell & myself had, during his lifetime, the immediate direction of the business of the company," Jackson explained, "and Mr. Moody made no alterations or improvements in any part of the works without consulting one or both of us, explaining the alteration he wished to make, and obtaining our consent thereto."[78]

As mentioned earlier, the process for obtaining a patent was relatively easy and inexpensive before the reorganization of the Patent Office in 1836, and it was left to the courts to decide the validity of a patent. Legal defense could be an expensive process, as illustrated by a vast array of inventive losers in American history. Steamboat pioneer John Fitch is one notable example, but there are many in the specific area of textile machinery. Most of the important British technology trailblazers, such as James Hargreaves (spinning jenny), Samuel Crompton (spinning mule), and John Kay (fly shuttle loom) died in poverty. Closer to home, John Thorp—a gifted Massachusetts-born machine maker whose revolutionary ring spinning frame, patented in 1828, eventually replaced Moody's filling frame, and who was Silas Shepard's partner in the patented bobbin winder that Moody and Lowell haggled over at Taunton—received so little in royalties from his nine patents that he spent his later years as a machine operator and died in near total obscurity. Even Oliver Evans, who was financially successful, spent a bitter old age bemoaning the infringements on his patents and the lack of legal protection. As Francis Cabot Lowell's uncle complained to Nathan Appleton in 1816, "You know our Countrymen are ingenius in defrauding Patentees, and there are few, very few, Patentees, especially where resort is had to Law suits, who have received any profit from their patents. Whitney, the Inventor of the invaluable Cotton-gin, actually gained a loss."[79]

Moody's patents faced similar problems. In an early infringement case, Jonathan Fisk and Ephrain and Jacob Stevens, three BMC machinists who had been employed to make patterns or gears for Moody's dresser, left the company and began making textile machinery in violation of BMC patents. The company sued, and the case was heard from October 1820 to May 1821 in the First Circuit Court. It was a victory for the BMC, although the court awarded only $2,000 of the $6,000 claim for damages. It would be the only successful defense of a Moody patent.[80]

In October 1820, Moody was forced to defend his double speeder patent of April 3, 1819, and because of a problem with the drafting of the patent the decision went against the BMC. Moody quickly revised the patent and reregistered it on January 19, 1821, but in that intervening period his ex-employee Jonathan Fisk had taken out *six* double speeder patents. The BMC sued Fisk, and the parties convened in Boston District Court November 6, 1821, for a special hearing with Judge Joseph Story presiding. When another litigant, Ebenezer Wild, challenged Moody's patents on both the double speeder and the filling frame, Moody and the BMC withdrew. Nor did they contest three double speeder infringements in Rhode Island the following year.[81]

In this rough and tumble atmosphere of patent challenge and defense, untrustworthy fellow workers could and did copy machinery just as the BMC copied British models. And just as the British could not hold back the flood of ideas and machinists leaving their country, so American patent holders had difficulty controlling the diffusion of their ideas and improvements. Equally damaging to patent holders was the fact that in a time of rapid technological change, inventions were superseded by perfectly legal means. Moody's double speeder was rendered obsolete by Aza Arnold's differential gear, which he patented in 1823. Despite a "notable prejudice" on the part of BMC directors against Arnold's breakthrough, and toward Rhode Island innovation in general, even Moody admitted that it was a superior way to achieve compound motion. Arnold was by no means the only threat. While Moody was working on Lowell's power loom, for example, David Wilkinson and William Gilmore busied themselves on a competing design, an indication that men just as talented as Paul Moody were also in the game.[82]

So, while it is possible that Paul Moody could have made more money exploiting his own patents, it is much more likely that he would have met the same fate as most independent inventors. Given the lack of stringent control in the patent application process, and the constant threat of patent theft, he would have been forced to defend any infringements by means of the courts, which was not only an expensive proposition, but one for which Moody appears to have been temperamentally unsuited. He had, as several contemporaries noted, a retiring personality; at one of the double speeder infringement trials, Moody was so nervous on the witness stand that his attorney feared he would harm the company's case, and only Daniel Webster's careful leading got him through it.[83] It appears that Moody was by nature a man who would thrive in a corporate culture, where security and protection far outweighed any ceiling on his career advancement.

Incorporation had become increasingly popular in the late eighteenth century for public works projects such as turnpikes, bridges, and canals, and was now emerging as an advantageous organizational model for private companies as well. While there were only three state charters granted to manufacturing corporations in Massachusetts before 1800, and fifteen before 1810, there were

133 granted in the 1810–19 decade. This was the threshold of what would evolve to our present condition, in which partnerships and proprietorships still outnumber corporations, but corporations account for 90 percent of total sales and receipts. Even at this early stage we find corporations variously in league and at odds with state governments over issues of subsidies, monopolies, control of labor, and concepts of "public good." Although it was not until 1829 that Massachusetts granted limited liability to members of a corporation, which shielded individuals from the responsibility of the corporation's debts, state incorporation did lend to businesses a sort of legitimacy (real or perceived) and enhanced their ability to attract investors—a critical consideration given the capitalization needs of large-scale manufacturing establishments. State incorporation could also bring valuable benefits such as land and water rights, and the power of eminent domain.[84]

In this second decade of the nineteenth century, few could have predicted the long-term consequences of the corporate model. Still, Moody must have recognized the benefits of incorporation, since his own Amesbury Wool and Cotton Factory had been granted a state charter in 1813.[85] One difference here is that at Amesbury he was one of the joint stock owners, while at Waltham he did not initially own any of the company shares. Nor could some of the personal benefits and disadvantages of corporate employment yet be apparent to him, since he had not attempted to patent anything that needed protection. Nor would he have yet worried about his inability to personally exploit an idea because it belonged to the corporation. These important considerations of corporate life and rules would come later. At Waltham he would no longer be directly entrepreneurial, as he had been at Amesbury, yet he could still be inventive—a significant motivator for a man of Moody's inclination.

As it turned out, corporate employment worked out very well for Paul Moody. Initially, his only financial compensation was his salary, along with the intangible rewards of respect and encouragement that his position in the corporation offered. But in short order he became very wealthy. His path to wealth was not his salary (which in fact was never raised while he was at Waltham), but rather the use of an unusual stock purchase plan. At $1,000 per share, BMC stock was not widely distributed: there were only twelve shareholders in the first subscription of 1813, all of whom were family or close business associates of Lowell and Jackson. Yet in the summer of 1814, when Boston merchant Uriah Cotting decided to give up two of his five shares, Paul Moody was allowed to purchase them, and was "granted the same privileges he would have possessed had he been an original subscriber."[86] Then in the second subscription, in October 1815, the directors voted to keep the holdings closely controlled, and Moody was the only nonfounding member allowed to purchase stock. He was certainly out of his league in this elite group, and his six shares would have cost him about four times his annual salary, but in 1817 the directors made a special provision that allowed him to delay payment for as long as necessary and to have his dividends credited toward his unpaid balance. "Whereas it is the wish of the company to have Mr. Paul Moody largely interested in the stock," wrote the directors, "he shall not be obliged to pay for the seventeen shares he owns in the stock of said company . . . any faster than he conveniently can pay for the same, and that the assessment on the same shall be charged to him by the Treasurer, in the company's books, as they may become due, and all dividends which are or may be made on said shares shall be retained by said Company and credited to him on account of such assessments as they may become due." In an arrangement similar to modern forms of executive compensation, Moody had become a shareholder without putting up any cash.[87]

Like any stockholder, Moody was required to pay interest on unpaid assessments on his shares. But on at least one occasion the company awarded him a special bonus to cover his interest payment. On September 22, 1818, the directors, "wishing to express their acknowledgement of the services rendered by Paul Moody the year past, exhibited in the improvements made by him in the machinery, do hereby authorize & direct the Treasurer to credit to Mr. Moody in his account with the sum of nine hundred ninety five dollars 86 cents being the amount of interest charged to him on his stock."[88]

While this bonus was unusual, high dividends were not. The BMC paid a 17 percent dividend to shareholders in 1817, and for the 1817–1824 period the average yearly dividend was an astonishing 19.25 percent. In the third and final subscription round in May 1817, Moody was offered seventeen additional shares, again with the same privilege of applying dividend income toward his payments.[89] He was now making considerably more in dividend income than he was in salary, and even though this money went toward his stock ownership rather than into his pocket, he was rapidly building a fortune for his future.

In 1819, the Moodys augmented their financial position with the sale of their Amesbury property to Paul's former employer, the Amesbury Nail Factory.[90] Why they would wait five years to dispose of their former home can only be surmised. It seems unlikely that they had an immediate need for the $1,650, although it could have been for assessments or interest on stock. Perhaps the Panic of 1819 convinced them that their small-company days were truly over and that their future was much more secure in a company such as the BMC, with its abundance of uncommitted capital to ride out the toughest of economic downturns. Whatever the specific reason, Paul and Susan had decided that things were going too well in Waltham to ever move back to Amesbury.

~

All was not perfect in Waltham, however. As the 1820s began, the BMC faced problems, especially in the form of a strike by its usually compliant work force in 1821. One of the few records of the event is a letter by Isaac E. Markham, one of Moody's machinists, to his brother. "Tho they have ever treated *me* well but still they are determined their word shall be law & shall be obeyed," he wrote in May. "A few weeks since they cut down every unmarried mans wages (except mine) that they employ & without giving them the least notice until the day came for payment[.] the same trick was played off on the girls but they as one revolted & the works stopped 2 days in consequence." How the matter was settled is unknown: the BMC employee records for March to August 1821 are missing, and there is no mention of the strike in the directors' or stockholders' records. Despite Harriet Martineau's later observation that the workers she saw at Waltham enjoyed good conditions and fair pay, it was no lark working in a clamorous, lint-filled factory for twelve hours a day, six days a week.[91] While Waltham conditions were considerably better than those in Britain or the child labor system in Rhode Island, the BMC mill girls and day laborers were certainly not enjoying the variety, independence, and intellectual challenge that characterized Moody's employment.

Another problem confronting the BMC was that the Charles River lacked the power to efficiently and reliably propel all the machinery for the three mills. While business was booming, and the Boston Associates considered entering the uncrowded field of calico printing, it became clear that further expansion in Waltham was unfeasible. Moody played a key role in the evaluation of potential mill sites in 1821. After inspecting the thirty-foot drop of the Merrimack River at East Chelmsford, about twenty miles north of Waltham, Moody reported favorably to Jackson, who set in motion a plan to buy all the land and water rights in the vicinity.[92]

As plans for the new industrial complex began to take shape, Moody could foresee that his life and work at Waltham would be coming to an end. He had succeeded beyond all expectations, yet he did face occasional professional and personal difficulties in the early 1820s. Most of the legal attempts to protect his patents, eight in all, were either lost or settled out of court. The BMC never publicly stated its reasons for withdrawing from active patent defense, although it is probable that in an environment of constant infringement, out-of-court settlements were less expensive, and that the BMC had moved beyond its early phase of tariff and patent protection as critical business success factors. Perhaps the reticent Moody welcomed the end of court appearances, yet he might have fretted that his period of great inventiveness was over.[93]

As he immersed himself in the work required to expand the company's manufacturing to the new location, Moody could compare from a comfortable vantage point his current circumstances with his situation back in 1813 when he made the decision to move to Waltham. None of the uncertainty of that time remained. The company had survived war and depression, he had been richly rewarded for his technical contributions, and it was unlikely that the Boston Associates would fail in their upcoming expansion. While there was little chance of his climbing any higher in the corporation, he could certainly expect to do what he had already been doing on a grander scale.

Once again, he would have to uproot his family. As the year 1823 came to a close, David was twenty, Mary nearly seventeen, William eleven, Susan was celebrating her eighth birthday on New Years Eve, and Hannah was an infant.[94] Paul's father had died just after Christmas the previous year, and if distance from home and family had been a concern, he could comfort himself that the new location would be an hour's ride closer to Byfield and Amesbury, and closer still to his children's private school at Bradford. He could also look forward to working with the man who would be superintendent of the new corporation, his old friend Ezra Worthen.

Moody was preparing to leave the town where he had become a leading citizen. He was active in church affairs. He occupied a respectable brick house, although he rented rather than owned it (nor would he buy a house in Lowell). Perhaps company-owned property had just the right blend of status and low rent. He certainly could have afforded a fine house: with twenty-three shares of BMC stock, which in an average year yielded over $4,000 in dividends, he was indeed prosperous. At forty-three, he was, next to company treasurer P. T. Jackson, the most important employee of the preeminent cotton factory in the United States.

Even with this rise in social standing, he could not count himself in the same class as his fellow shareholders. Perhaps he had no such aspirations. By the comfortably middling standards of his own family, he had done exceptionally well, certainly materially better than his college-educated brothers. His mechanically talented brother David had, with Paul's influence, gained valuable experience as the BMC agent in 1814 before landing the job of superintendent of the Boston Iron Works. But another brother, according to a nineteenth-century historian by the name of Perley Poore, "spent much time and money in visionary mechanical projects, in which much mechanical skill was exhibited, but little judgment, all tending to show that the family had mechanical proclivities."[95] What it more accurately shows is that given the alternative paths of advanced education on the one hand, and losing money in visionary technology schemes on the other, Paul's course eventuated in protected corporate employment, motivating technical challenges, great respect, and significant wealth. He could not have known when he begged to be taught weaving that it would lead to this. But as he looked back over the decisions and chance events of thirty years, he doubtless saw that his particular path suited him exceptionally well.

6

Toward Wilkinsonville

David Wilkinson, 1815–1828

> An American in this ardent climate gets up early some morning and buys a river; and advertises for twelve or fifteen hundred Irishmen; digs a new channel for it, brings it to his mills, and has a head of twenty-four feet of water; then to give him a appetite for his breakfast, he raises a house; then carves out within doors, a quarter township into streets and building lots, tavern, school and the Methodist meeting-house.
>
> —Ralph Waldo Emerson

As in Massachusetts, the combination of the Embargo and the War of 1812 proved a great benefit for Rhode Island industrialists. While the merchants of Providence and Newport suffered for scarcity of British goods to import, manufacturers took advantage of the lack of foreign competition to expand their textile operations. David Wilkinson had already been well established in business before the war, producing a wide variety of tools and machines at his Pawtucket factory. Wartime expansion of American industry increased demand for his products, especially textile machinery. While profits or patriotism spurred new entries into manufacturing, the Wilkinsons essentially carried on their generations-long trade—and exploited every opportunity they spotted. Like Paul Moody, David was driven by a personal interest and exceptional skill in mechanics rather than by ideology, but it helped that his chosen field was consistent with the growing national faith in industrial development as a means of combating British economic domination. Manufacturing could be both good for the nation and personally rewarding.

David, along with his father and brothers, felt no need to question the community value of their work in this new era. They produced essential products and provided jobs, they built roads, they went to church, and they were active in town affairs.[1] Relative to their Pawtucket neighbors, the Wilkinsons had always been prosperous and prominent. Now, as the town began to expand rapidly, so did their wealth and their influence.

Yet a closer look raises questions about the kind of republican environment that leaders like the Wilkinsons were creating. As we have seen, Waltham was shaped by the combination of business imperatives and the humanistic vision of Francis Cabot Lowell and his Boston Manufacturing Company co-founders, including progressive innovations such as supervised housing, an impermanent work force of young women, cash wages, town beautification, and very little employment of children. But Samuel Slater's "Rhode Island System" of manufacturing was more traditionally English, based on family labor in small factories, with worker independence checked by means of store credits. Aside from the simple elegance of his mill buildings Slater added little to the Pawtucket townscape. Moreover, Slater's view of workers was based on the widely held belief that the uneducated poor had a natural tendency toward vice, laziness, and violence; working long hours in the factory would, if not cure them, at least prevent them from exercising their baser proclivities. Like Alexander Hamilton, whose *Report on Manufactures* expressed the opinion that "in general, women and children are rendered more useful, and the latter more early useful, by manufacturing establishments, than they would otherwise be," Slater hired mostly children to tend his factory machines.[2]

Nor was Slater alone in this regard. As late as 1820, two-thirds of Pawtucket's textile mill workers were children, and for most of the nineteenth century Rhode Island ranked highest among the Northern states in the incidence of child labor. Yet, until about 1830, few criticized the practice. David Wilkinson's brother Smith worked in the mills as a ten-year-old, and he later insisted that long hours in a factory kept children from "idle and vicious amusements." Even a reformer of Moses Brown's stature seems to have overlooked the moral issue of child labor. As late as the 1830s, Rhode Island mills employed more children under twelve than women, and twice as many women as men. While skilled labor, especially mechanics, was scarce and mobile, unskilled workers were often unable to move due to family considerations or by unpaid bills at the company store, in stark contrast to the Waltham factory, which avoided both child labor and payment in store credits.[3]

This approach to labor control in Rhode Island mills actually had some social and economic advantages when considered in context. From the business perspective, child labor matched the slow pace—relative to Waltham-style factories—of technology adoption. With a source of cheap unskilled labor and a dearth of skilled mechanics, it was more economical to use unskilled workers, simple machinery, and the "putting out" system of hand weaving than to upgrade to more expensive machinery requiring more skilled and expensive operation and maintenance. Furthermore, there was little social pressure to change. At least until the 1820s, manufacturers were generally held in high esteem for providing work for otherwise marginally employable people, under conditions and hours that were generally no worse than household or farm labor; plus the mill villages offered relatively inexpensive housing, stores, churches, and a social community that may not have been available in rural areas. Beneath this apparent benevolence, of course, was a strict system of social control, blacklisting of troublesome employees, and concerted opposition to any sort of legislative oversight or factory inspections that might have aided the health, safety, and economic condition of the workers at the expense of mill management.[4]

The industrialization of Pawtucket had a long history, beginning with its founding in 1671 as an ironworking village by Joseph Jenks Junior, whose father had been a blacksmith and tool maker at the Saugus Iron Works in the Massachusetts Bay Colony. Given his own ironworking heritage, David Wilkinson would have tolerated the grimy aspects of iron production, including the smoke from smelters, waste runoff into the river, and the noise—trip hammers, ringing anvils, the vibrations of the factory machinery by day, and at night the water coursing through flumes and trenches and over the falls. "Pawtucket," Brendan Gilbane summed up, "was never a quiet place." However disquieting the constant noise may have been to villagers closely packed in the industrial center, to David Wilkinson this was the sound of business.

The Blackstone River was the lifeblood of Pawtucket Village, not only for water power but for fishing and recreation as well. Its presence was not always benign. Summer droughts occasionally reduced the mighty river to a trickle; winter or spring storms raised the water level to the point at which backwater interfered with the rotation of the waterwheels. If that were all, the manufacturers and their neighbors could feel lucky, for in a severe storm the river became an uncontrollable torrent, as in February 1807, when fourteen buildings were destroyed. Among those buildings were the anchor and screw manufacturing shops of Oziel Wilkinson and his sons.[5]

While manufacturers steadily gained the upper hand in controlling the river for their own profit, the less fortunate of Pawtucket village claimed their traditional right to fish above the falls for the abundant eel, shad, salmon, bass, herring, and alewives, just as the Indians had done before white settlement. Originally the river split above the falls, and a stream known as Little River provided a bypass for fish to make their way upstream. In the early eighteenth century, Little River was filled in to support a bridge over the Blackstone, whereupon someone by the name of Sargent or Sergeant obtained permission to build a bypass trench, and, according to David Wilkinson's nephew Edward, "this arrangement gave a full supply of fish to the people above." The Wilkinsons appear to have supported the idea of a trench to aid fish migration, for in 1786 Oziel Wilkinson and other landowners along the trench petitioned to widen and deepen the ditch "in order to give a free and uninterrupted passage to the Fish," the result of which was later deemed to have been "verry Valuable particularly to the poorer inhabitants." Then in 1792, Oziel's son-in-law Samuel Slater and his partners Almy and Brown built a dam *above* Sargent's Trench, and once more fish spawning was blocked. Manufacturers along the trench—including David's brother Abraham and their father—protested, but for reasons of flood safety, not because of the fish. The state legislature agreed, but exempted the new dam of Moses Brown and his partners. Although the Flood of 1807 proved them right, the petitioners were no match for the political power of Moses Brown. As Gilbane concludes, "The loss of fish as a traditional source of food for the poor, the controversy over the danger of the dams, the disastrous flood of 1807, the bitter contest in the Sargent's Trench case represent only the more dramatic physical and social implications of that race to harness the power of the Blackstone."[6]

There is no record of David's position regarding the dams and the trench, but most likely he joined his father and brothers in the concern for the safety of their buildings at the falls. His sympathy for those who were not benefiting from the industrial exploitation of the river can only be surmised. He was, by all accounts, a good and fair-minded man who had lived in the village since he was twelve. On the other hand he was a leading manufacturer in town with an eye toward further expansion. A man in David's position—the owner of a successful factory producing both yarn and machinery, an investor in several other mills, and owner of a hotel in the village—could only feel satisfaction with his personal situation and with the overall direction of the industrialization of Pawtucket and the Blackstone River area.

The general trend toward increased manufacturing in the country also worked to his advantage, since he sold his machinery over a wide geographical area. Despite the postwar downturn in 1815, Rhode Island entrepreneurs remained optimistic about the prospects for making fortunes in mechanized textile production, and David Wilkinson was no exception. He became noticeably more entrepreneurial during this period, and there is a direct connection between what he began doing in 1815 (investing in textile mills in which he was only financially involved, with less emphasis on the machine and tool-making that had been his stock in trade since the 1780s) and the creation of his own textile mill village on the Blackstone River in Sutton, Massachusetts, in 1823. Many of the influential factors had to do with his family, in particular the extension of businesses in which his father, brothers, and brothers-in-law had become engaged. An important factor was the heady economic atmosphere of the postwar era, a decade in which manufacturing expansion seemed limitless, despite downturns in 1816, 1819, and 1825 that perhaps should have served as clear warnings. It was during this postwar period that he became truly an entrepreneur and investor, and much less an experimenter, inventor, and preeminent machine maker. He was on the road to Wilkinsonville.

~

The immediate postwar period was a poor time to ask how well David was doing. We know that when Francis Cabot Lowell and Nathan Appleton visited Wilkinson and other Rhode Island mill owners in June 1816, they reported, with some satisfaction, that business was at a near standstill. While we might suspect the Waltham entrepreneurs of exaggerating the economic devastation to their south, it was essentially true. One striking example is the Providence Woollen Manufacturing Company, which was organized in 1812 by a group of local cotton manufacturers, with experienced workers from the west of England. They built a stone mill with carding in the central portion of the first floor, spinning on the upper floors, and hand weaving in two wings. The shears for trimming the nap from the woven cloth were powered by an Oliver Evans steam engine—a very early use of steam power in manufacturing in America. This well-managed, technologically advanced company produced a first-rate product, but the flood of British goods after the war bankrupted the business with the staggering loss of $150,000 to shareholders. Only a few of the 169 Providence-area mills managed to stay in business after the peace of 1815. Furthermore, the Tariff of 1816, which F. C. Lowell managed to work to the advantage of the Boston Manufacturing Company's low-priced plain goods, did not adequately protect higher-priced cloths, such as the colorful ginghams that had been Rhode Island's specialty. Even Samuel Slater admitted there was nothing promising on the horizon. "The cotton business now appears gloomy and I fear will continue," he wrote in 1816. "Many establishments are stopped. And many have already done it of their own accord, and many are daily stopping from mere necessity, they being indebted to a much larger amount than everything they possessed would bring under the *hammer*."[7]

David Wilkinson faced this economic crisis from a position of deep personal loss. In January 1815, just as the war was ending, his oldest daughter Joanna died at the age of twelve. Then, in October, his father passed away. Oziel had been a good Quaker all his life, and was buried with his wife, Lydia Smith Wilkinson, at the Smithfield Friends meeting house, the grave marked by a plain slab of stone. There is nothing in the records to indicate whether his death, at age seventy-two, was sudden or expected, but in either case, coming in the same year as young Joanna's death, it was a severe blow to the family, and perhaps to David in particular. It would be difficult to overstate his father's influence on David's career, as well as on his sense of moral and civic responsibility. Of Oziel's five sons, David seems to have most resembled his father—in generosity of spirit, inventiveness, and focus on the iron business, as Oziel's tutoring of young David in nail making and paper mill screw manufacture attest. And now, after Oziel's death, David would turn his attention, cautiously at first, to the same kinds of textile investments that had occupied his father in his later years.[8]

Nathan Appleton's remark that "all was quiet" in David Wilkinson's factory in 1816 was not completely accurate. As previously noted, the Boston Manufacturing Company principals had overlooked David's lathe. Furthermore, they failed to see the underlying strength of the Rhode Island textile business, which through a process of winnowing and consolidation would bounce back from the economic effects of peace. Finally, while Lowell and Appleton justifiably concentrated on the enormous economic potential of the Waltham power loom, they ignored or downplayed the development of a competing loom that was already underway in Rhode Island and southeastern Massachusetts.[9]

By 1814, Rowland Hazard of South Kingstown had installed power looms built by Newport inventor Thomas R. Williams in his Peace Dale woolen mill, an indication that Rhode Island was not as sleepy as Appleton would have his audience believe, although a small woolen mill with a few specialized power looms was hardly considered a threat to, or model for, large-scale cotton manufacturing.[10] Better known to Appleton and Lowell, however, was the textile machine development in nearby Taunton, Massachusetts. We remember Silas Shepard as the manufacturer of the bobbin winding machine who had been outmaneuvered by Lowell and Moody (see chapter 5), but Shepard had also started experimenting with power looms in 1811 and patented one in 1812—before the establishment of F. C. Lowell's Boston Manufacturing Company.

Shepard's loom was mostly the work of his partner, the brilliant but unlucky inventor John Thorp. The loom that they began manufacturing in 1812 was heavy, slow, and awkward, but the partners installed at least fifteen in Shepard's Green Mill in Taunton. The results were disappointing, for many of the same reasons that all early attempts at power weaving failed: mildewed dressing (sizing), improperly rolled warp yarns, and poor "smash" protection of the warp in case the shuttle jammed.[11] The lack of commercial success of these looms should not detract from the boldness and ingenuity of Shepard and Thorp. Within four years they built and patented a new power loom, with vertical warp threads rather than the typical horizontal layout. Thirty were installed in the Green Mill, and at least as many shipped to Rhode Island manufacturers. Demand was so strong that Shepard licensed the manufacturing rights to a well-known Rhode Island machinist—David Wilkinson. This is not mere coincidence, for Thorp and Wilkinson knew each other well. David has been his mentor when the younger machinist worked for him at David Wilkinson & Company.[12]

There were other power looms in use in Rhode Island at this time. Thomas Williams moved to Pawtucket to work in Aza Arnold's mill in 1813, where he improved on the loom he had built for Hazard's Peace Dale woolen mill.

Williams later contracted with David Wilkinson to build his looms, which were installed in mills owned by David's brother Abraham and brother-in-law Timothy Greene. Elijah Ormsbee, David Wilkinson's partner in the steamboat experiment of 1792, built a loom in 1813 for a mill in Olneyville, Rhode Island. According to Zachariah Allen, the first fully powered integrated cotton mill was not at Waltham but at Henry Franklin's Union Factory near Providence. John Waterman, the mill manager, told Allen that "some power looms were put in operation in the year 1813, and operated there several years. One girl attended two looms and made into good cloth of No. 15 yarn 240 to 275 yards per week, at the wages of three dollars per week." Allen adds: "These looms [I] saw in actual operation at that time, and before the power looms at Mr. Appleton's Waltham mill were used in the autumn of the year 1814." However, it appears that a mechanic was required to be on duty at all times of operation, an indication of the unreliability of the machines, so while Allen is correct about the existence of functioning looms in Rhode Island prior to 1814, it is also clear that these looms had only marginal commercial success prior to the introduction of the Waltham loom.[13]

More critical to the commercialization of the power loom, and to David Wilkinson's role in its diffusion, is the development of the "Scotch" loom, so called because of its introduction in America by a Scotsman named William Gilmore. A machinist from Dumbarton, Gilmore (or Gilmour) arrived in Boston in September 1815 with a solid knowledge of the current state of British power loom and dressing machine technology. Within a short time, he was introduced to John Slater, the brother of Samuel Slater and his business partner in the large mill village known as Slatersville, in Smithfield, Rhode Island. This, in retrospect, was the perfect opportunity to combine Slater's successful business model with the latest in power loom innovation (at this point Slater's weaving operations were all by hand) to challenge the Waltham supremacy in large-scale cotton cloth production, or at the very least to develop a power loom that was not protected by BMC's expensive patent rights. But, according to the eminent industrial historian William Bagnall, John Slater "was overruled in the matter by his older and more conservative brother, Samuel, who considered it unwise to make any investment at that time when the prospects of the cotton manufacture were so discouraging."[14]

It now appears more likely that Samuel Slater was an avid proponent of power loom weaving, but could not convince his partners Almy and Brown to adopt an experimental technology during a difficult economic period. Slater asked his brother in late 1816, "Are you making any progress with water looms at Smithfield, I do think we ought to get some underway as soon as is practicable," but it was another two years before the Slatersville factory was producing cloth from Gilmore looms. During the months of uncertainty, Gilmore offered his services to Judge Daniel Lyman, principal owner of the Lyman Cotton Manufacturing Company in North Providence. Gilmore got off to a poor start, which lends some support to those who hesitated. As the judge's son, Henry B. Lyman, described it in 1861, "The warper worked badly, the dresser worse, and the loom would not run at all."[15]

There are two versions to the resolution of these problems. Henry Lyman claimed that "an intelligent though intemperate Englishman," who was also a hand weaver, was brought in. "After observing the miserable operation, he said the fault was not in the machinery, and he thought he could make it work. . . . Discouragement ceased; it was an experiment no longer. Manufacturers from all directions came to see the wonder. . . . To this day [1861] the same loom, with trivial alterations, is in use in all our mills." The other version, that of Pawtucket historian Massena Goodrich, credits David Wilkinson for the resolution of the problems with Gilmore's power loom. "Judge Lyman, of course, thinks of David Wilkinson when any difficulty arises, and Mr. W goes over to see the machine. He quickly discovers the trouble, suggests a means of removing it, and, in due time, the loom does its work." Other historians have picked up this thread, but it appears to have started with Goodrich, a booster of Pawtucket's role in the iron and textile revolution, and while much of Goodrich's view can be verified, it is unlikely that David Wilkinson single-handedly rescued Gilmore's loom at the Lyman Mill. He did play a significant role in the improvement and diffusion of the Scotch loom, but the process was subtle and incremental, and thus more typical of technological change.[16]

David's contribution was to recognize that Gilmore's power loom was superior in many ways to Lowell and Moody's loom and to acquire the rights to build and sell it. As Zachariah Allen recollected in 1861, "Nor was Mr. Wilkinson lacking in enterprise for modern improvements in machinery, as was verified by the fact that he speedily commenced making power looms with cranks which entirely superseded the Waltham loom by the perfection of their operation to this day." This Scotch loom was simpler in design and capable of weaving finer cloth than Moody's loom. It was also cheaper to build—about seventy dollars in 1817, compared to $125 to $300 for a Waltham loom.[17] And unlike at Waltham, royalties were not an issue, since neither Gilmore nor Judge Lyman sought a patent, perhaps because of the vagaries of the patent system, or simply because the public-spirited judge was more interested in improving textile efficiency throughout Rhode Island than keeping the benefit to himself. Lyman did charge for permission to use Gilmore's machine patterns, which he sold to David Wilkinson for a mere ten dollars. While it may appear that Wilkinson took advantage of Gilmore, it was actually part of Judge Lyman's plan to ensure widespread use of the power loom in Rhode Island. Moreover, the Scotsman was amply rewarded when a group of Southern New England cotton manufacturers contributed $1,500 to a fund that was presented to Gilmore in gratitude for making available a low-cost, efficient power loom as an alternative to the expensive Waltham loom. This loom (along with a similar design brought to Rhode Island by Englishman David Fales) rendered all previous experimental power looms obsolete. As veteran manufacturer Peleg Wilbur put it, "When Gilmore and Fales introduced their looms, all other inventions were thrown into the shade."[18]

Wilkinson was not the only machinist to take advantage of this offer. According to Judge Lyman's son, "manufacturers from all directions came to see the wonder. They obtained from Gilmore, for the sum of $10, the privilege to use his pattern for the warper, dresser and twelve looms." But David made the most of the opportunity by improving on Gilmore's original. As Job Manchester, another pioneer machinist and loom builder, recollected: "Those who have used the Gilmore looms are aware that the patterns built by him were quite too light, and otherwise faulty; but they were soon superceded by patterns got up by David Wilkinson & Company, of Pawtucket."[19]

The most important improvement to the Gilmore loom was Wilkinson's sturdy cast iron frame. In December 1817, he joined Samuel Slater and three other partners to form the Providence Iron Foundry, whose main purpose was to manufacture these frames for anyone who wanted to build Gilmore-style looms. Customers could buy loom castings to finish in their own shops, but most went to David Wilkinson & Company, where David and his partner Samuel Greene built and sold fully assembled "Power Looms, together with all the apparatus for weaving on the most improved plans." Making looms was a profitable business: his company sold more than one hundred of them to factories and machine shops as far away as Georgia, Louisiana, and Pittsburgh. David Wilkinson & Company also built the matching warper and dresser—at $650 a rather expensive set of machines, but apparently there was enough demand for a competing Pawtucket machine shop, Pitcher and Gay, to sell the same machines.[20] It is likely that the competition was friendly, since both Larned Pitcher and Ira Gay had formerly been apprentices in David's shop.

So, in addition to playing a part in the introduction of the power loom into the southern New England economy, as well as making a profit from it, David Wilkinson was instrumental in the successful diffusion of power loom technology elsewhere in America. He did this by making key improvements to the loom, selling his assembled looms throughout the eastern United States, and training the next generation of textile machinists who would start up their own shops—and make their own improvements—over the next decade. He also responded to this opportunity by taking the risk of forming a new company to make a critical machine part—notably an iron frame, an area of manufacture in which he was perhaps the best-known practitioner in the area. He did this in association with his kinsman Samuel Slater, another example, as James L. Conrad Jr. has pointed out, that Slater was not averse to investing in power loom technology after all.[21]

~

David Wilkinson's investment in the Providence Iron Foundry was a form of vertical integration: a new company made a component (iron loom frames) that his primary company could use to make an appealing new product (fully assembled power looms).[22] In doing so, he stuck to his iron-making roots while expanding still farther into the textile machine business. Although there was an element of risk in his investment, it was not particularly speculative, since the Gilmore loom had excellent potential and David was within his primary area of expertise. He also expanded his iron business in a more traditional way, partnering with his brother Daniel in the Pawtucket Nail Manufacturing Company in 1817. According to Daniel's son Edward Wilkinson, a man named Dwight Fisher started a nail manufactory in Pawtucket with two nail-making machines in 1816. He went out of business soon thereafter and the machines were sold to Crocker & Richmond of Taunton. "Early in 1817, David and Daniel Wilkinson becoming the proprietors of the Splitting and Rolling Mill, purchased these two machines and commenced the manufacture of nails, in connection with their other business. Soon after, they erected six or eight more

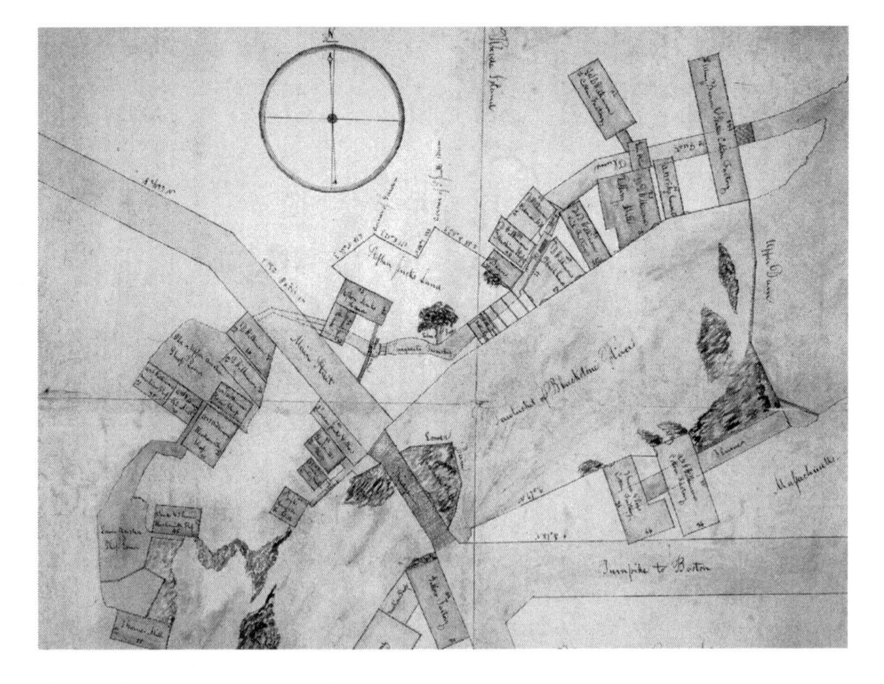

Figure 6.1
This 1823 map of Pawtucket Village illustrates the extent of David Wilkinson's enterprises: cotton factory, rolling mill, nail factory, calendering mill, bleach house, and machine shop.
Courtesy of the Slater Mill Historic Site.

machines, and the business was carried on until 1829. About 4000 pounds of nails were manufactured daily." They also produced iron hoops, stoves, kettles, and nail-making machinery. In a further example of vertical integration, the two brothers became partners in George S. Wardwell & Company, a Providence retailer of the products of their nail manufactory.[23]

Another product of David's shop was the fly ball governor, used to control the volume of water falling on a waterwheel and thus regulate the speed of the machinery. He began fabricating and selling waterwheel governors sometime before 1821, when the Blackstone Manufacturing Company wrote to ask for parts for the governor he had made for them. This device would have been similar to the one Paul Moody built at Waltham sometime before 1817. There is no evidence that Wilkinson had been directly influenced by Moody, but since Moody and Francis Cabot Lowell are usually credited with the transatlantic transfer of this important technology, some influence is likely.[24]

Yet these iron-related enterprises actually proved to be somewhat atypical of Wilkinson's financial ventures during this period. Like his father, David had made some investments in areas outside iron making. Building the Pawtucket Hotel in 1813 is an example of a business in which he neither worked directly nor had a managerial role. He continued this village business development in the 1820s with the construction of two Main Street commercial buildings, the Union Block and the Dorrance Building.[25] David's engagement in this sort of investment became more frequent after Oziel's death.

While his father was alive, David had invested in cotton factories with other family members (as detailed in chapter 4). These included the Pomfret Factory (1806) managed by his brother Smith; the White Mill (1799) that had originally been owned by Samuel Slater and several Wilkinson in-laws (excluding David), and which David bought into when Slater sold his shares in 1810; and the Killingly Manufacturing Company, another Connecticut textile mill started by his brother Smith and his Howe in-laws. David had no involvement in the management of these factories, although the investments were not entirely divorced from his own businesses since they represented potential sites for sale of his textile machinery. When Oziel's estate was settled late in 1815, his one-fourth interest in the White Mill was divided among his five sons, David receiving one-twentieth ownership in addition to his original one-twelfth. By late 1816, David had sold his inherited interest to Smith and the original one-twelfth to his twin brothers Abraham and Isaac. Perhaps his growing involvement with the Gilmore loom had brought about a need for cash to invest in this promising area. Whatever David's reasons for selling his interest in the White Mill, he was fortunate. In August 1825 both the White Mill and the adjoining Stone Mill burned in a fire, causing losses to Abraham and Isaac Wilkinson, owners of the Stone Mill, that far exceeded their insurance.[26]

One investment during this period was well ahead of the curve of textile development and a bit of a gamble. In 1819, David became involved in the manufacture of worsted wool yarn and cloth. Worsted is long-fibered and processed differently from ordinary wool. Instead of carding (which intermixes the curly woolen fibers), worsted yarn is "combed" into more parallel fibers, resulting in a lighter material that can then be processed using machinery appropriate for cotton manufacture. As noted earlier, the huge investment in the Providence Woollen Company in 1812 had ended in failure, and the "Merino mania" during the Embargo and War of 1812 had also subsided in the post-war dumping of woolen goods by the British, driving Providence entrepreneur John Waterman to convert his Merino Mills to cotton production.[27] Although Providence-area manufacturers remained distrustful of woolen manufacturing, David and his partners saw an opportunity for a new kind of fabric as well as a machine-making niche, and in 1819 they began the manufacture of worsted yarn and cloth. "The machinery was built in Pawtucket, by David Wilkinson & Co.," wrote David's nephew Edward. "An Englishman, by the name of William W. Wood, was employed to superintend the work. They manufactured Scotch plaids and vestings. A vest pattern was made expressly for, and presented to the Hon. Nehemiah R. Knight, which was made up, and Mr. Knight wore it to Washington the first time, to take his seat in Congress, as Senator from Rhode Island." David Wilkinson & Company now added to their list of advertised products "Cotton and Woolen Machinery of all kinds."[28]

This venture went well beyond the manufacture of new machinery. Mr. Wood and seven workers spun worsted yarn on a seventy-two-spindle spinning frame located in the Wilkinson mill, above the machine shop. They were in David's employ, so the risk was Wilkinson's. Since this operation was part of David's upstairs cotton factory, and not a separate business, little is known regarding this expansion into worsted manufacture, although it was apparently unsuccessful and abandoned after three or four years.[29]

Wilkinson continued in this expansive pattern throughout the postwar years. What was good for the textile industry was good for the Wilkinson enterprises, as evidenced by David's investment in 1819 in the *Manufacturers and Farmers Journal,* a twice-weekly newspaper that clearly stated in its first editorial in January 1820: "Our Journal will be devoted to the support of the *Manufacturing and American Policy*. It will be a medium of *Scientifick, Manufacturing and Mercantile Information,* and a faithful Reporter of the Passing News." David Wilkinson & Company often advertised their machinery and iron products in its pages.[30] The editors of the *Journal* portrayed themselves, along with Samuel Slater and David Wilkinson ("one of the greatest mechanics the world has ever produced"), as heroic defenders of the manufacturers who were "viewed with jealousy, distrust, and aversion by a portion of the business community and received no countenance or support from the current newspapers. . . . But the men who had thus embarked their property and their destiny in a new undertaking were not to be disheartened by trifles." For decades the Wilkinsons had been moderately well-known manufacturers during the era of merchant primacy in Rhode Island. Now that the industrialists were in the ascendancy, David was unmistakably among the most powerful businessmen in the state.[31]

Wilkinson's influence also extended beyond the region. At a pro-tariff conference in Harrisburg, Pennsylvania, in 1827, with nearly one hundred delegates from thirteen states "friendly to the encouragement and support of the domestic industry of the United States," David was one of four Rhode Island delegates, and was on three subcommittees (iron, glass, and a group to encourage states to prepare for a convention the following year). It is unknown what he contributed to the convention, although his thoughts on the iron industry would have been carefully heeded. In any event, he was now acting on a national stage with the likes of publisher Hezekiah Niles and political economist Mathew Carey. Plus, he had the opportunity to interact with two delegates associated with the Lowell mills, Abbott Lawrence and Ezekiel Webster, brother of the newly converted friend to protectionism, Daniel Webster.[32]

As an important business and civic leader, David had become a Mason in 1808, serving as the first treasurer of Pawtucket's Union Lodge No. 10. His friend George Taft explained that David was less concerned with Masonic ceremony than he was with the fundamental tenets of the organization. "He understood well the principles of the fraternity," Taft wrote. "He looked beyond the external trappings and regalia. He saw and felt their moral significance. Hence he stood firm, when some quailed and fled before the storm of the Morgan excitement." This last reference is to William Morgan, a disgruntled former Mason in New York state who was about to publish the secret rituals and oaths of the fraternity when he was abducted and presumably killed in 1826. Many of the sheriffs, judges, and jurors involved in this case were Masons, and were able to frustrate the investigation and trials, which engendered further resentment among the general population and propelled an isolated incident into a far-reaching social and political movement that swept New York, Pennsylvania, and New England.[33] Anti-masonry riled Pawtucket, especially when a polemical anti-masonic newspaper, the *Pawtucket Herald and Independent Inquirer,* began publication in September 1828. This caused family stress as well, since two of the leading anti-masons in Pawtucket were David's brothers Abraham and Isaac, who provided financial backing for the *Herald*. (His brother Smith was also active in anti-masonic politics in Connecticut.) While the Pawtucket anti-masons denied "any feelings of prejudice, ill-will or unkindness against the members of the Fraternity in our village, or within our acquaintance," they also made clear their firm opinion that Freemasonry was "unchristian, anti-republican, a hindrance to the cause of religion, and dangerous to our liberties"—hardly a means of promoting open dialogue. Abraham later testified that he had publicly quarreled with his nephew Samuel Green over the Morgan affair and received a death threat from another Mason. David appears to have stayed away from personal confrontations, and remained a loyal Mason, although it cost him the friendship of his twin brothers for the rest of their lives.[34]

David also remained a staunch Christian, but broke with the Quaker religion of his parents. As early as 1811, along with Abraham and Isaac and brother-in-law Samuel Slater, David had been among the petitioners for a lottery to expand the meeting house of the Catholic Baptist Society. This indicates less a leaning toward the Baptist religion than it does the diversification of religion in Pawtucket. Mill owners—whether Quaker, Baptist, or Episcopalian—did not allow their sectarian differences to interfere with their common interest in controlling the behavior of their employees. Their sense of civic responsibility may have been genuine, but they were also well aware that religious laborers would be more industrious. The textile manufacturers and their wives cooperated in the creation of the village Sunday school and general religious organizations such as the Female Beneficent Society, organized in 1809 with David's sister Hannah (Mrs. Samuel Slater) as treasurer and his youngest sister Lydia as one of the directors. David's brothers-in-law Timothy Greene and Samuel Slater were the first president and vice president of the Pawtucket Moral Society, established in 1815 to combat, among other evils, drinking, profanity, and Sabbath-breaking. Later, when the Pawtucket Bible Society was formed, Slater was elected president, and David Wilkinson and Timothy Greene were vice presidents.[35]

Yet there was something more to this religious investment than mill owner solidarity, as the sons of Oziel and Lydia Wilkinson began to abandon their Quaker heritage. Isaac became a Baptist in 1816. Smith, the agent and majority owner of several mills in Connecticut, joined the local Congregational church, most likely that of his wife's family. And in 1815, while Oziel was still alive, an Episcopal parish was organized in Pawtucket, with David and Daniel as vestrymen and among the group that petitioned the Rhode Island Assembly for incorporation, which was granted in February 1816. David subscribed for six pews in the new St. Paul's Church, and all five Wilkinson brothers donated land for the church in the middle of the village—ironically, overlooking Quaker Lane. It is difficult to ignore the influence of Wilkinson in-law Samuel Slater in this. He had been raised in the Church of England, and was now the most prominent member of Rhode Island's industrial elite. Not surprisingly, he was elected St. Paul's first senior warden.[36]

The issue of class is very much evident in these religious transformations. The establishment of an Episcopal church in Pawtucket was met with hostility by many of the townspeople and factory laborers who felt that it served the needs of the elite or of British immigrants rather than their own. The sale of pews not only brought market commerce directly into the church, but also underscored the gulf between the wealthy and the less privileged in town, and not just among Episcopalians: the Catholic Baptist Society also instituted this fund raising method in 1823. David's six pews at St. Paul's, which cost roughly $400 each plus a yearly assessment, clearly denoted his status among the congregation (Slater owned eight pews).[37] When a group of Pawtucket workers created their own Free Will Baptist church in 1820, mill owner Daniel Greene—the son of David's oldest sister Lucy—managed to wrest control of the organization and tone down the evangelical enthusiasm that the business leaders of the village found so troubling. One historian of religion in nineteenth-century Rhode Island has noted the divide between the "theology of taste" of the factory owners and the more enthusiastic religion of the workers. The owners were uncomfortable with emotional expressions of religious sentiment and preferred more genteel displays of faith. This seems to match David's personal style, and may partially account for his break with the family's Quaker heritage.[38]

The increasingly evident distinction between elite owners and factory workers placed Pawtucket's many artisans in the middle, looking hopefully upward to independent ownership as well as downward to the factory jobs that might await them if they were unsuccessful. Among these artisans, the master machinists saw that the key to upward mobility was to associate with the textile industry leaders, which meant adopting the attitudes and behavior of models such as David. That the Wilkinsons had become estranged from the lower-class artisans and workers may be evident in the fire at their rolling and slitting mill in the early morning hours of October 5, 1811, the origin of which was generally thought to be arson, especially when the nearby Slater mill was damaged by fire three nights later.[39] David was never targeted as pointedly as the richer, more ostentatious (and English) Slater, perhaps because the Wilkinsons had a long tradition of artisanship and civic involvement in the village and at least occasionally defended the rights of the poor, as in their opposition to dams that would block the passage of fish in the Blackstone River. But the sons of Oziel Wilkinson had clearly strayed from their artisan roots. As a factory owner with shares in associated companies, a high church vestryman, an investor in the *Manufacturers and Farmers Journal,* and a Mason, David had clearly established himself as a member of the Rhode Island manufacturing elite.

The earlier cooperation between mechanics and industrialists was evident in the formation of the Pawtucket Association of Mechanics and Manufacturers in 1810. Although led by the industrialists (David was one of the founders, and Slater was the first president) there was a general alignment of interest among the members. But in 1825, a group representing skilled mechanics formed the Pawtucket Mechanic Society. Owners were now split from skilled workers, who in turn kept their distance from machine operators—all indicative of the growing divergence along class lines.[40]

Yet even as mechanics and machinists began to lose some of their independence in big shops, those working for David Wilkinson overwhelmingly considered him not only a benevolent manager, but an exceptional teacher and mentor. He understood the concept of apprenticeship and encouraged the upward mobility of the young men in his shop. Jonathan Thayer Lincoln wrote that when he was a boy in the 1870s, "his grandfather often spoke with pride of having, as a young man, worked for David Wilkinson, 'making machinery for Sam Slater.' I had always thought that my grandfather's pride was in having some part, however small, in Slater's historic venture, but as the figure of David Wilkinson becomes clearer to me, I am inclined to believe that he, like so many other early American machinists, cherished throughout his life a loving loyalty to Wilkinson, the man." Lincoln went on to describe how Wilkinson often took these young machinists into his home, where they learned not only mechanics but moral character. It should also be noted that David cared about those who had influenced his own career—in this case, one of the nail-making pioneers in America. "I think about 1820," he wrote, "I went to Cumberland, with Samuel Greene, my nephew, and purchased of Jeremiah Wilkinson the old shears with which he cut the first four nails. He was, I think, ninety years of age at that time. The shears were a pair of tailor's shears, with bows straightened out, and the blades cut off half the length." David donated this historic artifact to the Rhode Island Historical Society.[41]

As noted earlier, John Thorp apprenticed in Wilkinson's machine shop before joining Silas Shepard at Taunton to build early power looms. Thorp would later patent an important ring-spinning invention, although he found neither fame nor fortune during his lifetime.[42] But many of Wilkinson's young protégées went on to distinguished careers. Sylvanus Brown, the Pawtucket carpenter who had inexplicably burned David's lathe patterns in 1798, entrusted to Wilkinson the training of his son James, who later made a crucial improvement to the slide lathe, allowing the height of the cutting tool to be adjusted while the machine was in motion. Another Wilkinson trainee was Alfred Jenks, who later moved to the Philadelphia area where in 1820 he established the Bridesburg Machine Works, one of the most important textile machine manufacturers outside of New England, and in 1830 set up a power loom for weaving checks at Manayunk. David also mentored David Fales and Alvin Jenks (Fales & Jenks, Central Falls, Rhode Island), Jonathan Thayer Lincoln (Kilburn, Lincoln & Co., Fall River, Massachusetts), Clark Tompkins (machine shop in Troy, New York), and Aza Arnold, whose differential speeder would supersede Paul Moody's Waltham speeder.[43] Already mentioned are the Pawtucket machine-making team of Pitcher & Gay, both of whom had been trained by Wilkinson. David may have increasingly moved away from his artisan roots, but for as long as he worked in his machine shop he was very generous to the next generation of machine makers, who spread the Wilkinson work ethic and technical expertise throughout the eastern United States.

Rhode Island had not fully emerged from the postwar economic doldrums by the time of the larger economic crisis that engulfed the nation in 1819. While overextended manufacturing investments were among the causes of the panic, the brunt of the effect was felt in the southern and western areas of the country. Rhode Island certainly had business failures—two out of five existing mills closed in 1819 or soon thereafter—but for the most part these failed mills were either undercapitalized, lacking in modern equipment, or poorly managed. In fact, mill construction continued as old ones failed, and overall spindle capacity in the state remained about the same. By 1820, a recovery was under way, partially due to the fact that rapid population growth in the United States meant more consumption of Rhode Island's cotton goods, but also because the British responded to American tariff protection by aiming at new Latin American markets, giving domestic producers a larger market share.[44]

Driven by the power loom, Rhode Island cloth production increased fourfold between 1820 and 1824, encouraging Rhode Island manufacturers to expand. There were still risks: prices for machine-made cloth dropped, cotton prices soared, and technological advances outpaced markets. These conditions would impel Pawtucket textile manufacturers to add an hour to the work day and lower wages by 20 percent, which resulted in the strike of May 1824—an event that further exacerbated the economic and social tensions in Pawtucket.[45]

In this mixed economic climate, David Wilkinson maintained a successful machine-making business, along with the production of nails and other iron wares, and continued to expand his interests. He patented a cotton-baling press on December 8, 1825. This machine appears to have been an outgrowth of his traditional iron business: the industrial screws that he made for paper or oil presses could be adapted for compressing cotton bales.[46]

Other aspects of his business expansion were more speculative. On September 5, 1823, he bought an interest in the Smithfield Cotton Manufacturing Company, then sold it on October 6. This was another family affair—brothers Abraham and Isaac were part owners (although they also sold their interests before year's end). In the summer of 1824, David, Daniel, and three other investors organized the Washington Bed Tick Company. A few months earlier, David had become part owner of the "Yellow Mill," which he now leased to his new company.[47] These transactions are perhaps the first clear-cut examples of David's investments as strictly business dealings with no direct connection to his core business interests. Certainly, we would have considered him a capitalist before this point, but now his ventures became much more speculative as he used his money, rather than his own specialized skills and experience, to make more money.

This flurry of financial activity was related to a huge project that David had been planning since before 1823—one that would require a great deal of capital. Up to this point, virtually all of his investments had been in conjunction with his father or brothers, but this one was on his own. He would create his own mill village on the Blackstone River in the town of Sutton, Massachusetts, about twenty-five miles upstream of Pawtucket. He may have chosen the upper reaches of the Blackstone Valley because the Blackstone River was familiar: various Wilkinsons had operated forges on this river for generations. Another reason is that the Blackstone Valley was industrializing rapidly in the 1820s, as the untapped potential of the 438-foot drop of "the hardest working river in America" generated a second wave of development after the cotton fever of the Embargo and war era. Finally, there were plans to build a canal from Worcester to Providence, promising to link the agricultural area of central Massachusetts to the markets and seaport of Providence. The canal was not a financial success, and ultimately lost out to the Boston and Worcester Railroad. Still, after it became operational in 1828, the canal did help open up the Blackstone Valley for Providence-oriented commerce, and David probably benefited from the expanded transportation facilities and population expansion in the valley near his new development in Sutton.[48]

The town of Sutton had been a mixed farming and manufacturing community since before the Revolution, with five companies making scythes and axes, and several water-powered trip hammer shops by 1793. There was further expansion in the 1810s and 1820s, when new water privileges were developed and existing ones enlarged. One of these small businesses was Asa Waters's 1815 cotton spinning mill, which was destroyed by fire in 1822. Wilkinson bought the site in 1823 and quickly built a stone factory to produce cotton thread and woven cloth, most likely using the Scotch looms he manufactured in Pawtucket. Over the next six years, he enlarged the main factory, built a hotel, a bank, and a few houses for employees. He also erected an Episcopal church, largely at his own expense, and paid the minister's salary out of his own pocket. While his holdings eventually consisted of three "estates"—Pleasant Falls, Centre Falls, and Lower Falls—the main factory was at the Centre Falls Estate, and the village around it became known as Wilkinsonville.[49]

If the American Revolution had unleashed the drive to pursue financial happiness and social prestige, and if manufacturing could now be seen as a means of furthering the cause of republican citizenship, then what could be more virtuously American than to own, manage, and profit from one's own eponymously named industrial village? For some time Wilkinson's developing entrepreneurship had taken him away from the tool and machine making upon which he built his reputation, toward more speculative ventures, but the ground-up development of a factory community was entirely new and marks a significant change in David's career and fortunes.

For reasons that will become clear later, David's memoir makes no mention of his motive for developing Wilkinsonville, although it is not difficult to imagine the sense of control, status, and satisfaction felt by an entrepreneur with his own "-ville"—even if it does seem uncharacteristically vain for a former Quaker.[50] David's ownership of mills and machine shops had always been in collaboration with his father, brothers, or brothers-in-law, and while there are no indications of friction with his partners, he appears to have felt the need to strike out on his own. There were several nearby models for this sort of paternalistic enterprise. Samuel Slater and his brother John created Slatersville in 1806. The North Providence mill village of Judge Daniel Lyman—the textile entrepreneur who had sponsored David Gilmore's loom—was known as Lymansville. Less than a half mile away, Zachariah Allen built his Allendale woolen mill and village in 1822. That same year, Job and Luke Jenckes (relatives of the Pawtucket Jenks family that David knew well) created their mill village of Jenckesville on the Blackstone River in what is now Woonsocket, Rhode Island.[51] Although the Pomfret, Connecticut, factory of David's youngest brother Smith did not carry the Wilkinson name, Smith's majority ownership and successful management of that mill would have been a model—and perhaps a spur—for David's venture.

Perhaps no spur was needed. A mill village was an entrepreneur's dream during this expansive period. The occasional advertisements for entire manufacturing villages in the *Manufacturers and Farmers Journal* in the 1820s not only extolled the advantages of the particular property for sale, but also the benefits to prospective owners who would "embrace the opportunity of becoming rich and useful members of the community." David's financial stake in the *Journal* suggests that his opinion was in line with this republican view of mill ownership. Of course, he already owned a combination cotton mill and machine shop in Pawtucket and dominated the field of machine making in Rhode Island, but the lure of further riches in cotton manufacturing and control over an unblemished mill village diverted much of his attention from iron work. He even let his 1798 screw lathe patent expire without capitalizing on it. As he later rued, "I was always too much engaged in various businesses to look after and make a profit out of my inventions."[52]

Although David was well established and very busy in Pawtucket, there are reasons why he may have wanted to start fresh in Wilkinsonville. There he would have a degree of control over the total environment and could put his own economic, religious, and social stamp on the village. Like Zachariah Allen's model village, with its neat row of three identical wooden duplex cottages, or Slatersville with its main street of stores, Congregational church, school, and one- and two-family workers' homes with garden plots, a neat and orderly Wilkinsonville could be an enlightened alternative to a Pawtucket that had grown messy, dirty, crowded, and unruly.[53]

Yet David Wilkinson never moved to the village he created and, like Slater, continued to consider Pawtucket his home. He had too many business interests in the Providence area, as well as family, church, and Masonic ties in Pawtucket. While absentee ownership and outside capital often spelled trouble for a factory village, it was not a problem at Sutton, largely because Wilkinson chose competent local managers to run the mill. The man who appears to have been his first agent, Deacon John Morse, had been Asa Waters's agent at the previous mill on this site, so he knew both the community and the business. His family's regard for the village owner can be seen in their naming their last son for David in 1825. Joshua Armsby Jr. was David's superintendent for a number of years. He also was well established in town with a large two-story house and a mixture of farming and mechanical interests. Morse and Armsby did not *have* to work for Wilkinson; but the coming of larger-scale industrialization to Sutton provided the opportunity for them to enhance their income and status by putting to use their mechanical and business skills in an environment that they found agreeable.

Given New England's chronic labor shortage during this period, factory owners went to some pains to attract working families. As at Slatersville and Allendale, the appealing appearance of Wilkinsonville was not only the working out of the republican vision of the owner, but also a very practical means to attract and retain a dependable work force. The neatness of the village belied what were still severe working conditions inside the mill: mind-numbing repetitive work for fourteen hours a day. Even by 1832, the sixty women and girls laboring at Wilkinsonville earned only forty cents per day. As with most mill villages created on the Slater model, the factory workers were predominantly women and children. Often it took an entire family's labor to maintain a minimum standard of living.[54]

Besides the factory itself, the requisite buildings for an attractive community included a church, a store, and tenements or cottages for employees. The worker housing at Wilkinsonville consisted of four simple but well-constructed two-and-a-half story gable-front houses, each probably accommodating two or more large families. In 1824, Wilkinson built a tavern. This constituted a variation from the model villages of Zachariah Allen, who prohibited liquor in Allendale, and of Smith Wilkinson, who proudly stated that he had "prevent[ed] the introduction of taverns and grog shops, with their usually corrupting, demoralizing tendency." Apparently the villagers thought the tavern was a good addition, for "they had a great raising and a dinner, the tables being spread in the barn. The Rev. Edmund Mills was there and asked the blessing." Sometime before mid-1825 David also built the two-and-a-half story Federal-style Wilkinsonville Hotel, and it was there on July 17, 1825, that the first Episcopal church services took place.[55]

Wilkinson's role in the establishment of St. John's Church demonstrates his increasing commitment to the Episcopal religion. He built a parsonage that year for Reverend Daniel LeBaron Goodwin, whose young wife Rebecca was the daughter of David's sister Marcy. Thus, although David did not reside in the village, other family members did—most prominently his brother-in-law Hezekiah Howe, who became the first treasurer of St. John's Church. David also donated the land and $1,000 toward the construction of the Greek Revival–style church, which was begun in June 1828. This generosity is tinged with the type of paternalism that was common among mill village owners and was often deeply resented by the villagers. While few of the inhabitants of the village were Episcopalian, Wilkinson chose the denomination of the village church. Only David, his son Albert, and one local man, Amasa Roberts, were able to give the responses at the first service. This is an interesting divergence from Zachariah Allen's course of action at Allendale. Although a devout Episcopalian himself, Allen allowed the community to choose the religious denomination for the Allendale church. They chose Free Will Baptist, and Allen supported their decision.[56]

The final community building erected by Wilkinson was for the Sutton Bank, established in 1828, with Hezekiah Howe as president. David also built a house for the cashier of the bank. This early Greek Revival house was more elegant than the vernacular architecture of the workers' houses, as befit the status of the man who was in charge of daily banking operations. The first cashier was his late brother Daniel's son, Edward, although this was a temporary measure until a permanent cashier was appointed in mid-October 1828.[57]

Like many New England banks of this era, the Sutton Bank was not intended for depositors but for creditors, to fund the development of the mill village.[58] A decade earlier, by virtue of their manufacturing prominence, the Wilkinsons had become involved in the development of banking in Pawtucket Village. David's father Oziel was elected president of the Manufacturers Bank when it was chartered in 1813, and his brother Abraham was one of the original shareholders. When the Pawtucket Bank was established on the Massachusetts side of the village the following year, David and his brother-in-law Hezekiah Howe became directors. David left a few years later to become a director of the Manufacturers Bank, presided over by Samuel Slater after Oziel's death in 1815. Abraham and Isaac invested in the Farmers and Mechanics Bank of Pawtucket when it was chartered in 1822. Abraham was elected president. Thus the Wilkinson network of kin and fellow manufacturers had substantial involvement in banking by the time David set up the Sutton Bank.

The creation of a credit bank was not unusual for the period. Many banks in New England were established by prominent men to provide funds for their manufacturing operations, to the point where one Rhode Island congressman complained in 1826 that "those who have sought after banks have, generally, been those who themselves were in want of capital." While this practice was decried by wealthy merchants who dominated the oldest regional banks and whose self-interest would naturally pit them against a policy that provided up-and-coming industrialists with easy access to credit, a moderate degree of insider lending was both safe and useful. At the Sutton Bank, however, the vast majority of the loans were awarded to the Wilkinson family members who were the major stockholders, a practice that invited danger.[59]

Throughout the 1820s, Wilkinson continued to expand, both at his mill village and in his Pawtucket-area investments. He formed the Pawtucket Calendering and Bleaching Company in partnership with Jabel Ingraham in 1824. The "calenders," machines that rolled and heated fabric to produce a glazed finish, were manufactured by David Wilkinson and Company. In nearby Rehoboth, Massachusetts, he built a new manufactory "of no inconsiderable dimensions" in 1826 to exploit the new interest in calico cloth. "It is to be worked by machinery altogether new," announced the *Pawtucket Chronicle*. "Mr. Wilkinson and others are the proprietors of the works, and a small village already appears rising around them, in the middle of a forest."[60] David was also a founder of the Pawtucket Calico Manufacturing Company in a village that became known as Ingrahamville, one mile downstream from Pawtucket village, and built its three-story brick factory in 1827. In 1828, he extended the west side of the stone factory at Wilkinsonville, increasing the length to 111 feet. And sometime during this period he started doing business with Henry Donaldson, a Rhode Island businessman who had moved to North Carolina to establish cotton manufacturing in the South.[61]

Amid all this investing, his loom-making business in Pawtucket continued to thrive as more Rhode Island mills adopted the power loom. He did sell some of his stock, including the half ownership of the Yellow Mill that he had previously leased to the other titleholders (July 1828), and his remaining interest in the company (January 1829). Whether his disinvestment was due to a sense of financial overextension is unknown. He had easy access to credit at the Sutton Bank in Wilkinsonville, as well as from the Manufacturers Bank in Pawtucket and Abraham and Isaac's Farmers and Mechanics Bank. His twin brothers had been using the bank for their own business expansion, such as the Fall River Iron Works, of which Abraham was elected president in 1826.[62] Most of this expansion by the Wilkinson brothers was based on credit from the banks they controlled, with their loans endorsed by other leading manufacturers.

One more very important investment must be noted, one that took David a surprising distance from home. In 1826, he joined a group of investors that included Canvass White, one of the chief engineers of the Erie Canal project, to incorporate the Cohoes Company, in the small village of Cohoes, situated at the confluence of the Mohawk and Hudson rivers near Troy, New York. With business interests in Rhode Island and the nearby portions of Massachusetts and Connecticut, what would attract Wilkinson to upstate New York? We know that he had traveled to New York to research screw-cutting methods and tools, and he had been on the North River (Hudson) to visit Colonel John Stevens's steamboat works in 1796. Another possible connection is through Job Wilkinson, the son of David's nail-making pioneer cousin Jeremiah from Cumberland. Job moved to Milton, near Saratoga Springs, where he manufactured carding machines, and in 1808 Job and Benjamin Peck petitioned the New York Legislature for $2,000 to start a cotton factory in Waterford, the town immediately across the Mohawk River from Cohoes.[63]

There had been some industrial development in Cohoes before David's involvement. In 1811, the Cohoes Manufacturing Company had been incorporated, with the goal of producing cotton and woolen goods and iron products. The company manufactured screws at first, and only after a fire destroyed the factory about 1816 was it rebuilt as a cotton mill. This sleepy village had tremendous industrial potential, in particular the transportation facilities of the Erie and Champlain canals (completed in the Cohoes area in 1823) and the immense water power of the Cohoes Falls on the Mohawk. The owners of the Cohoes Manufacturing Company had in fact planned a large industrial village made up of twenty-two factories, but lack of capital apparently prevented the execution of their ambitious plan.

Then, in 1826, Canvass White—who knew the area well from his Erie Canal engineering experience—joined with a group of investors to form the Cohoes Company. For reasons that are unrecorded but undoubtedly relate to his reputation as a man with expertise in all aspects of textile production, David Wilkinson was invited to become a director of the company. Whether he traveled to New York during this period is unknown; if so, he had little time to devote to the venture at Cohoes, since these were the prime years of his development of Wilkinsonville. In any event, very little progress was made during the 1820s. While this Cohoes venture was slow to develop, it later proved to be a fortuitous association for David Wilkinson.[64]

As we have seen, David maintained his base in Pawtucket and from there directed the operations of his increasingly widespread investments. While his social vision can be seen in the church, tavern, and mill housing at Wilkinsonville, he remained socially committed to his home town. In 1823, David and Martha Wilkinson, with Samuel and Hannah Slater, founded the Pawtucket Academy, a preparatory school. In 1825, David helped establish the Pawtucket Lyceum, a civic and educational institution that suggests the increasing cultural refinement of the village. In August 1828, David donated a small lot at the edge of Pawtucket village to the Catholic church. Earlier that year the *Pawtucket Chronicle* had opined that "the design of establishing a church in this vicinity is a good one. Irish Emigrants under judicious instruction, make useful citizens."[65] The Quaker Wilkinsons had certainly shown an ecumenical spirit with regard to religious diversity, becoming Baptists, Congregationalists, and Episcopalians—but Catholicism at that time would have been beyond the pale. Given the many testimonies of David's generosity and fair-mindedness, this donation might be seen as an example of his unbiased benevolence, but business considerations also played a part. After his Catholic workers convinced him they would settle in Pawtucket if there were a Catholic church there, David met with Bishop Fenwick of Boston and deeded the land for St. Mary's Church. Religion in America had become increasingly unregulated—a marketplace in which people chose the religion that best suited them. Like leaving the Quakers and becoming an Episcopalian, his gift of land to the Catholic church was a means of joining the club of wealthy and paternalistic mill owners who made these sort of donations as an investment in the morality of their increasingly Catholic workers.[66]

Pawtucket was indeed becoming a town of foreign workers whose values—and whose poor prospects for advancement—put them at odds with the "Village Aristocracy." This had become evident in 1815, when David, his father, and Samuel Slater had petitioned the town of North Providence for more police, because "from the Great increase of Inhabitants in the Town of North Providence . . . particularly that part called Pawtucket, it has often been found difficult to preserve order and due subordination therein." Oziel Wilkinson and Otis Tiffany were appointed to build or otherwise provide a prison "provided the same be done without any Expense to the Town." Oziel died soon thereafter, and no prison was built, but aside from a few isolated problems, the village remained relatively orderly until the 1820s.[67]

By the mid-1820s, Pawtucket had grown more rowdy and dangerous. Fighting, bordering on riot, was the most common problem—and apparently the most entertaining, as crowds would gather on the porch of the Pawtucket Hotel to watch the brawls. Worse was the increase in robberies. One victim was David's brother Abraham, who in 1828 was robbed of bills and checks worth more than $1,300. Two bank robberies within two days in 1829 showed how daring the criminal element had become. This was, as Pawtucket social historian Brendan Gilbane has pointed out, more than simply growing pains in the transition from a small village where privately funded night watches had been sufficient to a larger town in need of municipal police services. It was a direct outcome of long and monotonous hours in the mills, poor wages, crowded living conditions, and the persistent threat of unemployment. Perhaps understandably, given their philosophies and their success model of hard work and temperate living, men such as Slater and the Wilkinsons were at a loss to understand "that changing social conditions were breeding a different society, an industrialized society born out of that transplanted water frame which Slater had constructed in this very village."[68] Of course, we know now that all industrial towns would go through this ordeal; Pawtucket's early adoption of industrialization simply meant it would be in the vanguard of the attendant social problems, and it took the village leaders and their families by surprise.

Slater was the particular target of the Pawtucket have-nots. While he was lauded in the pro-manufacturing *Journal,* the Jacksonian *Pawtucket Chronicle* considered Slater's economic and social control tantamount to tyranny. "Every village, as well as every monarchy, has its tyrant," the editor wrote as the full extent of an economic crisis was becoming evident in August 1829.

> Wealth or talents constitutes some one to domineer over the multitude, and to keep down the poor and the indigent. We have seen more of this in manufacturing communities than any other—we have seen it in our own village—where one man occasionally rules those in his immediate power, as if the Almighty had created him better, or of different materials from his neighbors.[69]

The Wilkinsons, who had been hard-working, well-respected pioneers in this town, were now unavoidably associated with Slater in this "aristocracy." David was Slater's brother-in-law, a wealthy Episcopalian, an investor in business enterprises in five states, a banker, and the proprietor of his own mill village. His brothers and various brothers-in-law were engaged in politics, banking, and investments in textiles, metals, and shipbuilding. The Quaker relations that had sustained the early Wilkinson businesses had evolved into an extended network of Episcopalians, Baptists, and Congregationalists. And instead of going to Quaker merchants for capital to fund their ventures, they borrowed from banks whose directors were these same extended Wilkinson-Slater-Greene-Howe family members. Although now highly diversified, David had lost touch with the inventive iron working and machine making that built his reputation, and had become predominantly an investor and absentee factory owner. At fifty-eight, he looked to be at his entrepreneurial peak, but his financial position was less secure than it appeared. His substantial loans and overextended investments had left him vulnerable to any downturn in the textile industry.

7

Respectable Company Man About Town

Paul Moody at Lowell, 1823–1831

> And so a great plan was formulated; the neat, well-kept boarding house with pleasant, home-like habits and restrictions was established; the church, the library, and the lecture-room followed; and religion, culture, refinement lent their influences to the life of toil.
>
> —Frederick T. Greenhalge, Lowell Anniversary, 1886

After ten years at Waltham, innovating and adapting the integrated machinery that provided the Boston Manufacturing Company its technological edge, Paul Moody and his family made plans to move to the nascent industrial village at East Chelmsford. Mobility was nothing new for Moody: up into New Hampshire and Maine as a carding machine repairman, the short move to Amesbury, the longer family relocation to Waltham. The move to Chelmsford would be something relatively new—a corporate transfer, initiated, organized, and paid for by the company, for its own benefit. Moving the family would, as always, be a chore after ten years spent establishing a home in Waltham, but the company's handling of the details and the expenses, and a secure position waiting for him at the new location, removed much of the anxiety. David, now nearly twenty, would find good work opportunities in Chelmsford, and at least two of the other Moody children would be relatively unaffected by the relocation since they attended boarding school at Bradford Academy, which was only twenty miles from the new location. Paul and Susan would also be moving closer to their families in Newbury and Amesbury. Susan's brother Jonathan Morrill, who had spent several years working in Waltham before moving to a farm in

New Hampshire, had recently opened a store in East Chelmsford, so he and his family, along with another of Susan's brothers, would already be there.[1]

Certainly, the new job presented challenges, but it is unlikely that Paul experienced great concern. When he had accepted the opportunity at Waltham, success had been by no means guaranteed (remember that Francis Cabot Lowell's relatives considered him mad) but the Boston Manufacturing Company had been so profitable that few doubted the success of this extensive expansion. The sheer scale of the planned factory complex, the potential of the falls once channeled into power canals—everything about the new enterprise would dwarf the Waltham mills. Once the factories and canals were sited, Moody's primary responsibility would be the machine shop, a replica of the Waltham shop on a greatly enlarged scale. He would be doing what he knew well, with many of the same workers, and considerably more of them. The challenge was great, but not daunting. He had done everything the BMC could have expected at Waltham, and there was no reason for him or the company to think that things would be any different at Chelmsford. The corporate transfer of a senior executive—especially one that suited the social needs of the family—promised to work well for all concerned.

While this is not a history of the early development of East Chelmsford (which became incorporated as Lowell in 1826), establishing Moody's role requires a review of the founding of the industrial village. There is a bit of controversy—especially as some of the principals disagreed in the 1840s over what actually happened—but most versions place Moody in the inner circle of founders, and his rewards from the company suggest an important role. What is clear is that the BMC directors had decided to enter into the business of weaving and printing calico cloth, which was relatively new in America and would not compete with the company's current production of coarse shirtings and sheetings at Waltham. Having recognized the limits of the Charles River to provide enough water power for further extension of operations at Waltham, the directors began to search for a site with sufficient power for their new factories.

Most accounts relate that in the fall of 1821, Moody was visiting relatives in the Amesbury area and stopped by to see his old friend and former partner Ezra Worthen. Moody had been asked to inspect a site on the Spicket River in the town of Methuen (about twenty miles north of Waltham), but Worthen advised him look at East Chelmsford where the Merrimack River falls thirty feet and the volume of water would accommodate any need they might have, plus an existing transportation canal could be adapted for water power. Paul returned to Waltham by way of Chelmsford, and having ascertained that there was sufficient water power available, reported back to Patrick Tracy Jackson, drawing a chalk diagram on the floor to show the relationship of the canal to the Merrimack and Concord rivers.[2] Some versions add that Worthen knew that the owner of the water power at Chelmsford—the Proprietors of the Locks and Canals on Merrimack River—were in financial trouble and would consider selling their land and privileges. In any event, Appleton and Jackson, along with Kirk Boott, the recently appointed agent of the new enterprise, negotiated the deal with the canal company, and sometime in November a meeting took place at which Appleton, Jackson, Moody, Boott, and BMC directors Warren Dutton and John W. Boott, "perambulated the grounds" amid a light snow, and began planning their ambitious undertaking.[3]

There are other versions, but Reverend Theodore Edson, who moved to East Chelmsford in 1824 and knew all of the principals very well, related the founding story late in life with the sort of details that gave it the ring of truth. "Mr. Moody had two of his children, Mary and William, in Bradford Academy."

> Taking Mrs. Moody and his daughter Susan in a chaise, he drove to Bradford to see his children, with the expectation of meeting some of the leading Waltham proprietors in or near Bradford for the purpose of exploring. The day, however, was rainy, and the gentlemen did not come according to his expectations. The next day he took his family and went down to Amesbury, where he saw Mr. Worthen, who, having been given to understand the object of the excursion, said: "Why don't you go up to Pawtucket Falls? There is a power there worth ten times as much as you will find anywhere else."

Edson went on to describe how the Moodys and Worthen drove to the falls—with details of who rode in which chaise, and where they stopped for dinner—and that Moody reported his positive assessment when he returned to Waltham the following day.[4]

Whatever the details of Moody's and Worthen's roles, it is clear that the Boston Associates considered Moody an essential contributor, since they rewarded him with the opportunity to subscribe for one-tenth of the six hundred shares of the newly incorporated Merrimack Manufacturing Company "for his agency in the discovery" of the Chelmsford site. And in all versions, Ezra Worthen was offered the position of superintendent in charge of construction and setting up machinery, as well as ongoing factory operations once construction was completed. For this he received a salary equal to Moody's $1,500 per year, along with the privilege of subscribing for a small number of company shares, which could be paid for from dividends—similar to the deal that had worked so well for Moody at Waltham. Although Ezra had remained involved as senior partner and business manager of the Amesbury Wool and Cotton Factory—the company Paul had left in 1813 to join the BMC—he was fully aware how well his friend had done with the Boston Associates and decided to trade his independence for the security and financial potential of the big corporation.[5]

The BMC machine shop produced all the machinery for the first Merrimack Company factory, so Moody spent the bulk of 1822 and 1823 at Waltham. In the initial phase of construction at Chelmsford, however, Moody made significant contributions to the plans for placement of the factories and the optimal utilization of the water power. It was his recommendation, for example, to locate the new power canal where it would deliver the maximum head of water to the new factory. "Mr. Moody had a fancy for large wheels," Nathan Appleton recalled, so "it was decided to place the mills of the Merrimack Company where they would use the whole fall of thirty feet." Merrimack Company agent Kirk Boott noted in his diary for September 4, 1823, that he "went to the factory and found the great wheel moving round its course, majestically and with comparative silence. Moody declared that it was the 'best wheel in the world.' N. Appleton became quite enthusiastic." (Moody was not singing his own praises: the waterwheel was built by his protégé, John Dummer of Newburyport. Ezra Worthen's son William, later a noted civil engineer, wrote of Dummer: "As a millwright, he was the best I ever knew. . . . He built the first wheels at Lowell in 1822, and none of them, I think, were ever renewed.")[6] Moody and Dummer together worked on the various gates and speed governors that ensured constant power and consistent speed to the mills. Moody was also instrumental in the rebuilding of the Pawtucket Canal, which would be the main feeder to the other power canals, as well as its continued use as a transportation canal. The plan of a uniform sixty-feet wide and eight-feet deep channel had to be altered in the face of ledge and other obstructions, and Moody's practical experience helped Boott make the necessary compromises to complete the project on schedule.[7]

Moody was also responsible for the calculations of water power that would determine the total manufacturing capacity of the site. He advised Nathan Appleton that a canal system with a drop of thirty feet could power up to sixty factories the size of the second Waltham mill. That impressive estimate proved to be conservative, but easily supported the grand scheme the directors had developed for a huge industrial complex. Even though he was only occasionally on site at Chelmsford during the construction phase, Moody's dual roles as advisor to the directors on hydraulic power and superintendent of the Waltham machine shop were essential to the quick success of the Merrimack Manufacturing Company.[8]

In the spring of 1824, Moody relocated to Chelmsford. He was certainly aware well before then that the Waltham machine shop would be moved to the site of future growth. On August 9, 1823, the BMC agreed to sell all their patent rights, patterns, and all tools not currently in use to the Merrimack company for $75,000. At the same time, the directors voted that "the agreement now subsisting between the Boston Manufacturing Company and Paul Moody shall be given up and cancelled, and the said Moody be left at liberty to make a new agreement with the Merrimack Manufacturing Company." The BMC machine shop would continue to make machinery for their own use and for sale, and would still have the right to consult with Moody and "shall have the benefit of all inventions and improvements that may be made by said Moody at Chelmsford"—not surprising, given that essentially the same group of men controlled both companies. This, along with a letter from Jackson indicating that his duties as BMC treasurer no longer justified his $5,000 salary, indicate the degree to which Waltham was being deemphasized in favor of the bright new prospect at Pawtucket Falls.[9]

Moody signed the agreement on January 1, 1824, although it was not until May 1 that the Merrimack directors voted to "conclude the agreement with Paul Moody at $2500 per ann. & a house rent free." This salary increase represented a significant raise (67 percent), with the added advantage of no longer having to pay rent, as he had at Waltham. His title was Superintendent of the Merrimack Manufacturing Company machine shop, and he would also be responsible for the canals and various construction projects. His new boss was the high-powered Merrimack agent, Kirk Boott.[10]

Construction of a new house for the Moody family began late in 1823 and continued into the spring of 1824. It was a large federal-style house, two and a half stories, with an extensive two-story ell. In January 1824, the company books noted payments for lumber, a Rumford stove and a boiler, and labor costs for constructing brick chimneys and for lathing and plastering. The house must have been nearly completed by May when the company paid $20.50 for 8½ days of painting. It is possible that Paul moved to Chelmsford before the house was quite finished, as early as March 1824, since that is the point at which activity (as measured by number of machinists on the payroll) at the Waltham machine shop dropped abruptly, and about half the machinists were transferred to the new shop.[11]

The largest of the single-family company houses (with the notable exception of Kirk Boott's mansion), the Moody residence was a substantial and highly respectable dwelling for the family, with a total of fourteen rooms and ten fireplaces. There were refined touches, such as the ten-foot ceilings, the window seats flanking the fireplace in a front bedroom, the pocket shutters in the front windows, and the barrel vaulted ceiling and Palladian window in one of the large rooms on the third floor. A woman who grew up nearby remembered, "We had one nice house in our neighborhood, built on Worthen Street in 1823 and 1824, for Mr. Paul Moody, the agent for the Machine Shop. It had a beautiful lawn in front, sloped down to a handsome pond on Dutton Street." There was a barn in back, where they kept their horse and chaise, along with a cow and one or two pigs.[12]

Like most of the company buildings of this period, the Moody house was designed by Kirk Boott. While Boott's house was in the center of the village, close to the factory complex, Moody's was located in a relatively unpopulated area, a few hundred yards south of the company's main office. Benjamin Butler, at the 1876 semicentennial celebration, gave a panoramic description of Lowell as it looked from Christian Hill in 1828, and specifically noted Paul Moody's house, an indication both of its size and its distance from other buildings, a view corroborated by an 1832 map drawn just after Worthen street had been

Figure 7.1
Paul Moody's house still stands at 243 Worthen Street, little changed and protected from destruction not by Moody's residence there but because it was the home of Lowell engineer George Washington Whistler and the birthplace of his famous son James McNeil Whistler in 1834.
Courtesy of the Lowell National Historical Park.

cut between the house and the semicircular pond that had previously been the Moody's front yard.[13] The other buildings in the neighborhood were the well-made wooden tenements and brick row houses built about 1825 for company employees. It was typical to place supervisors' houses close to the tenements to maintain control over employees, but whether this is the case with Moody's house is unknown. An odd aspect of the placement is the proximity of the house to the Irish slum known as The Acre (the Moodys in fact would have a ringside seat to the erection of St. Patrick's Catholic Church in 1830–31). However, this location of the machine shop superintendent's house made perfect sense, because the Merrimack directors had decided to site the machine shop on a separate water power, cleverly constructed between two canals of different elevations. This site provided a certain independence from the Merrimack

Company, which made it less problematic to build machinery for other mills. The new shop was one short block from Moody's home.[14]

Moody made frequent trips to Chelmsford while the new machine shop was being erected—on one trip he brought weaving instructor Deborah Skinner from Waltham in his own chaise.[15] An additional reason to travel to the new development was his role as a founding shareholder of the Merrimack Company. His initial 10 percent stake diminished fairly quickly. He had the smallest share of stock (60 shares) compared to Appleton and Jackson (180 shares each) and the Boott brothers (90 shares each), but he was now—if only temporarily—among the privileged investors. Sixty shares at $1,000 per share represented a financial commitment that Moody was incapable of sustaining: over time, as these shares became fully assessed, he would have owed $60,000. It is therefore unlikely that the original stock subscription of December 1, 1821, was intended to last, and in fact only three weeks later the directors agreed to sell 150 shares to the Boston Manufacturing Company, at 10 percent above the par value of $1,000. With all of the five original stockholders giving up some of their holdings, Moody's interest now dropped to thirty shares. Of course, these original five Merrimack investors were also Boston Manufacturing Company shareholders, so they were actually transferring stock to themselves and their Waltham associates. Through this procedure, after giving up thirty shares, Moody received ten shares of Merrimack stock, five of which he immediately sold to a new shareholder. He must have transferred other shares as well, for a recapitulation of stock ownership as of February 27, 1822, shows Moody with twenty-one shares. While this is a significant drop from his original sixty, it undoubtedly matched the original plan for wider distribution. And it was just in time, since on that same day the directors made the first assessment of $500 per share, which meant Moody owed "only" $10,500 rather than $30,000 had he held all of his original shares.[16]

Although these transactions suggest that Moody was simply a placeholder until a wider stock distribution could be effected, there was one huge advantage to his being among the founders. Late in 1823, when the established and expanding Merrimack Company decided to increase its capital by issuing new stock, the directors voted to pay $15,000 to purchase the right that the original subscribers (Appleton, Jackson, the Boott brothers, and Moody) had written into the charter regarding future purchases of new shares. This amount was distributed in proportion to the original holdings, so by having subscribed for 10 percent of the original shares (on which he had paid no assessment), Moody received a windfall of $1,500. In this instance, the MMC did not grant Moody the special dispensation he had regarding his BMC stock, so he was obligated to pay his assessments in the same manner as other stockholders.[17]

In one further respect, Moody appeared to be among the wealthy capitalists who financed the expansion at Chelmsford. Just as the BMC had done, the

Merrimack Company often borrowed from its wealthy investors as an alternative to short-term bank loans. In December 1821, before the company had made any assessments on capital stock, the agent borrowed $16,500 from Nathan Appleton, $20,000 from P. T. Jackson, and $26,615 from John W. Boott. Moody contributed $4,700 which, although much smaller than the other loans, still represented two years' salary. When the company reimbursed him in April, he received $86.95 in interest—nearly what he had paid for a year's rent at Waltham. He also lent $1,900 at 6 percent interest to P. T. Jackson in August 1822, probably for company matters although it showed up in Jackson's personal account book.[18] While he was now at the point at which he could use his wealth as well as his labor to earn money, he was in other ways reminded that he was not among the elite investors. Despite his founder status, he was not a director of the Merrimack Company, which is consistent with the class basis of the Boston Associates' criteria for treasurer, agent, and directors. While he enjoyed a remarkable financial package, including insider stock benefits, he continued to be excluded from the top echelon of the corporation.

~

For some time the Merrimack Company directors had been concerned about Ezra Worthen's health. Although he was only forty-three years old in 1824, Ezra had suffered from heart disease for several years, and had been advised by his doctor to avoid overwork. Appleton had been in contact with Samuel Batchelder, an accomplished mill owner in his home town of New Ipswich, New Hampshire, regarding the possibility of his assuming the position of agent should a new company be formed in Chelmsford, while at the same time keeping Batchelder in mind for the position of superintendent of the Merrimack Company in the event of Worthen's disability.[19]

On June 18, while supervising workmen digging a building foundation, Ezra Worthen died. According to one account, he had become impatient with the inefficient digging of one of the workers and taking the shovel in hand, demonstrated how to use it efficiently. The exertion brought on the heart attack that killed him instantly. In another account he was merely "conversing with a person in the street," but in any event, "one of the most useful and inventive men that our country can boast of" was dead. He had served the company well in his two years at Chelmsford, was both respected and well liked by those who worked for him, and was remembered as "a most benevolent man [who] clothed the naked, fed the hungry, and was never more happy than when administering to the wants of the poor & distressed." His body was returned to his home town of Amesbury for burial.[20]

Moody's reaction to his friend's death is unrecorded, but given their long partnership and their having remained in touch during Paul's decade away at Waltham, it would be safe to assume that he and his family were greatly saddened, particularly as the families had just been reunited in Chelmsford. In addition to the impact on his family, Paul had to consider the death of a contemporary, two years younger, working in a high pressure environment under the unrelenting eye of Kirk Boott, certainly a sobering thought. Yet as a company man, Moody would have been proud of the Merrimack Company's efforts to ease the burden on Mary Worthen. A week after her husband's death the directors voted to award her $750, or one-half of Ezra's annual salary. Ezra also left ten shares of Merrimack stock, and Mary was allowed to subscribe for three shares in the second subscription of October 1824, and for six shares of the associated Locks and Canals Company, which she must have been able to afford on her own, since it is highly unlikely that the special arrangement to pay for the stock out of dividends would remain in effect after Ezra's death. We know little about Mary's life, but apparently there was enough money (or a benefactor) to send her son William, only three years old when his father died, to prep school in Boston. He graduated from Harvard in 1838, and began his long and distinguished career in hydraulic engineering working with Loammi Baldwin Jr. and the renowned James B. Francis at Lowell.[21]

Worthen's position needed to be filled as quickly as possible. Batchelder was still too much engaged at New Ipswich to answer the call, so the one employee who knew the most about superintending the construction of a Waltham-style mill was asked to fill in. Paul Moody took up where his good friend had left off, and carried on the work until Warren Colburn, who had been superintendent at Waltham, assumed the role in August. For about two months, Paul acted as the Merrimack superintendent while he simultaneously managed the new machine shop at Chelmsford, once again proving his worth to the Boston Associates.[22]

The East Chelmsford village that Moody came to in 1824 was beginning to resemble the industrial city envisioned by Francis Cabot Lowell, as implemented by Kirk Boott. The Merrimack Company owned four hundred acres of prime real estate and the primary water privilege, and as they constructed the first factories and expanded the canal system, they also considered the population that would work in the mills and, secondarily, the commercial, social, and religious organizations that would support them. The planners, Boott in particular, have come in for some criticism for accommodating the needs of the factories so well but allowing the town "to fit into the area left over," although the particular geography of East Chelmsford and the existing roads and bridges were significant impediments. Boott was the primary architect, and under his direction the workers' housing was constructed, in a hierarchical scale from four-to-a-room boarding houses for the machine operatives to more spacious duplexes for the skilled workers to single-family houses for executives such as Moody, and on to the imposing mansion of Boott himself.[23]

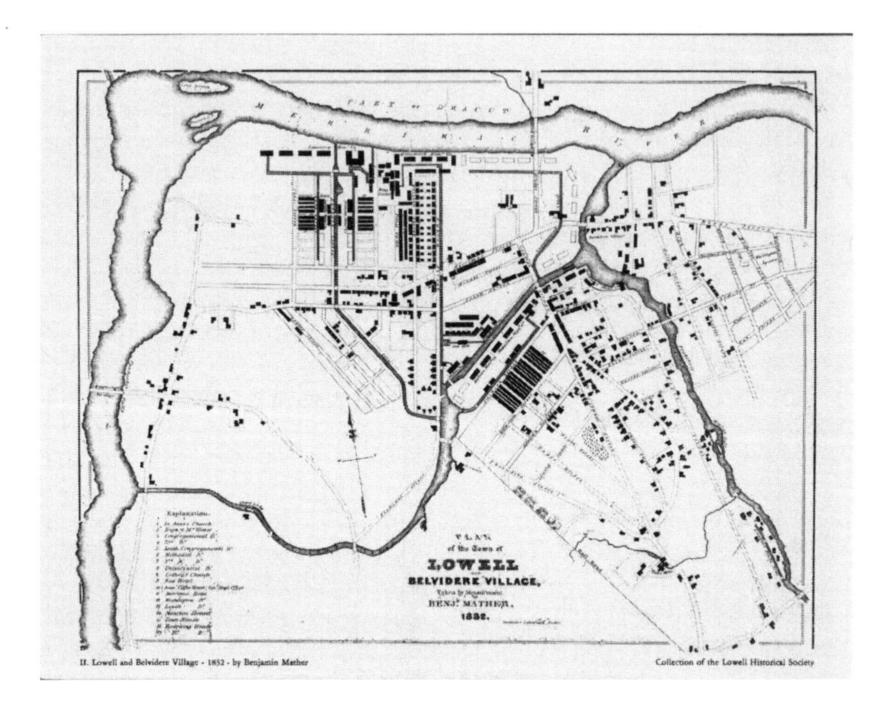

Figure 7.2
This map of Lowell in 1832, the year after Paul Moody's death, shows how the corporations dictated the development of the town. Moody played an important role in the extensive canal system that powered the textile mills.
Courtesy of the Lowell Historical Society.

At Waltham, the BMC's imposition of its professional and cultural organization over an existing town had resulted in a confused social structure, with conflict between the new industrialists and the older settlers during the period that the Moodys were there. In the new industrial village, it was very different. Although there had been a farming community with some business development before the Boston Associates "discovered" East Chelmsford, the company so dominated the planning and growth of the town that company position translated directly to social standing in the town. While the urbane merchant-investors remained in Boston, the companies' highest-ranking and best-paid employees, along with the new professionals, became the elite of the town. At the next layer of management below Boott, and with a large new house, ample salary, and dividends from company stock, Moody was in a very comfortable position.[24]

While the new town lacked the sophistication of Boston, a newspaper editor observed in 1825 that "the houses for the people . . . are handsomely and uniformly painted and are beautifully ornamented with flower gardens in front and separated by wide avenues. There is a beautiful Gothic stone church opposite the dwelling houses and a parsonage of stone is erecting. There is a post office, fine taverns, one of which is a superb stone edifice with out-buildings of the same material, and perhaps two hundred houses all fresh from the hands of the workmen. The ground is intersected with fine roads and good bridges. The whole seems like the work of enchantment." But another Lowell resident recollected, "In September, 1828, when I took up my abode there, Lowell was but a scattered and unsightly village."[25] Enchanted or unsightly depended on the bias of the beholder, but Lowell was certainly a work in progress throughout the 1820s.

The town's cultural amenities advanced rapidly. A local newspaper, the *Chelmsford Phenix* (established in 1825), advertised highbrow magazines such as the *US Literary Gazette* and the *Boston Monthly,* and a ladies magazine by a "Mrs. Hale," promising "to elevate and refine the female character." A new circulating library advertised the availability of James Fenimore Cooper's latest novel, *The Last of the Mohicans*. Several private schools—one taught by "Mr. Ralph W. Emerson"—opened their doors to the children of the wealthy. A wide variety of evening courses were available to the general public, some practical (algebra, penmanship, bookkeeping), but increasingly of a cultural nature, such as a dancing school to teach "the latest German and French cotillions, Fancy Dances and Waltzes." In February 1828, the Middlesex Mechanics Association began a series of science lectures, once a fortnight, for the reasonable price of $1.50 per year.[26]

As at Waltham, the Boston Associates had no company store at East Chelmsford, and the commercial life of the town was allowed to occupy the spaces left over from factory development and corporate housing. There had been a few stores before 1821, but within a short time, as the population rapidly expanded, doctors, watchmakers, and other professionals were setting up shop, or making regular visits by way of the Middlesex Canal packet boat from Boston. East Chelmsford got its own post office in April, 1824, with Susan Moody's brother Jonathan Morrill as the first postmaster, and in April 1826 there was daily stage service to Boston. A British visitor noted in 1827 that "several school-houses were pointed out to me, and no less than three churches; besides innumerable boarding-houses, taverns, newspaper offices, watch-makers, book-shops, hatters, comb-makers, and all the family of stores, every one of them as fresh and new as if the bricks had been in the mould but yesterday." The merchants and professionals who moved in had little doubt that their future depended on manufacturing success. "The place is properly called 'East Chelmsford,'" one observer noted, "which makes a very handsome and very City like appearance; but in common parlance it is the 'Corporation.'"[27]

In a town dominated by conservative corporate interests and predicated on moral strictures that would draw the right kind of employees to a safe environment and, at the same time, ensure their tractability through what an admirer had to admit amounted to "moral police," the life of the citizenry was circumscribed by work, church, and approved, well-chaperoned activities. In a real sense, citizens policed themselves, partly out of fear of blacklisting by the company, but also because the moral environment met their own needs. French visitor Michel Chevalier observed that Lowell was very straitlaced, and public opinion severe, but he considered it a reasonable trade-off when the alternative was the degrading social and economic conditions of cities like Manchester, England.[28] And the watchful eyes of company men such as Kirk Boott and Paul Moody—moralists in their own right—would help ensure that the town grew along the straight path laid out by the Boston Associates.

The Merrimack Company itself was a huge success, producing its first cloth in October 1823 and awarding its stockholders a dividend of $100 per share by early 1825 (Moody received $2,100, which may have been used to pay the capital assessments on his shares). By mid-1823 the directors received permission from the legislature for a capital stock increase to $1,200,000 in order to expand the operation. The method of expansion, it was decided in early 1825, was to revive the Locks and Canals Company—originally only a means of acquiring the water power of the Pawtucket Falls area—and transfer to it all of the real estate and water privileges that the Merrimack Company did not need for its own operations or future plans. The reconstituted Proprietors of Locks and Canals on Merrimack River (PL&C), a company owned and managed by the same men as the Merrimack and Boston Manufacturing companies, became at that point the dominant industrial organization in Chelmsford: it would develop sites for mills, sell land to new companies, and lease the water power of its expanding network of canals. There would also be a machine shop (transferred from the Merrimack company) capable of building all of the textile machinery for the new mills. This concept of a land and power company controlling the development of a large-scale, multi-corporation industrial complex would soon become the model for other capitalist ventures at places such as Lawrence, Massachusetts (funded by many of the Lowell investors) and Cohoes, New York (where David Wilkinson was among the founders). Charles S. Storrow, agent and treasurer of the Essex Company at Lawrence, explained the concept very simply: "We have created the power, and given value to the land. Our business now is to sell them both."[29]

The manufactories envisioned for this new industrial center would be companies started and capitalized by the Boston Associates and their growing circle of family, friends, and business acquaintances. Because of the interlocking directorates of these companies, the PL&C sold or leased their assets at cost or for a small profit, and the companies that were formed chose to manufacture products that would not directly compete with the other mills in which they had invested. Despite obvious conflicts of interest, this interrelated ownership was perfectly legal. It was also wildly successful, as evidenced by the formation of the Hamilton Manufacturing Company in 1825, the Lowell and Appleton Manufacturing Companies in 1828, and the Suffolk, Tremont, and Lawrence corporations in 1831; and by the shareholder dividends, which averaged above 10 percent up to the Panic of 1837.[30]

For Paul Moody, this organizational change meant the conveyance of his machine shop to the Locks and Canals company, although this amounted to a paper transfer since his location remained the same, as did his manager, Kirk Boott, who was both agent and treasurer of the PL&C. There are clear indications that Moody acted as agent of the PL&C during the first part of 1826: PL&C account entries list payments to "Paul Moody, Agent" and the amounts, one of $81,881 "for cash at sundry times," suggest the sort of cash outlays the agent would make to contractors and suppliers. By August, however, all references to the agent are to Kirk Boott.[31] Whether this is the result of Moody's inability to fill the role properly or if it had only been a temporary responsibility (like his filling in for Ezra Worthen at the Merrimack) is unknown. It would appear that his management of the machine shop would keep him sufficiently occupied, although if this had been an opportunity to move up in the company organization, it never materialized.

The relationship between Moody and Kirk Boott merits further exploration. At Waltham, Paul had been under the direct management of Patrick Tracy Jackson and the general guidance of Francis Cabot Lowell. The collaborative relationship between Moody and Lowell had inspired Moody to his most innovative and useful work. Jackson had been very much involved in the development of the power loom and knew firsthand the degree of Moody's contributions to the full range of machinery that had made the Boston Manufacturing Company a success. While Moody remained a step below the BMC founders, he was made to feel valued and was allowed to join the ranks of stockholders for his contributions. After the death of Lowell in 1817, Jackson managed the company in a style that was consistent with the ideals developed by the two merchant-investors and their talented machinist in the company's earliest days.

Kirk Boott was nothing like F. C. Lowell. He was a hard-driving, opinionated man, much appreciated by his fellow directors for carrying out their directives and protecting their financial interests, but widely disliked by the factory workers, who considered him "imperious" and told tales of how he whipped boys who did not get out of his way quickly enough as he drove his chaise through town. Born in Boston of English parents, Boott was educated at Rugby and other English schools before obtaining a commission in the British army, serving under Wellington in France and Spain. In 1818, he married Anne Haden, of a prominent and staunchly conservative Derby family, and returned to Boston to work in the family importing business. Through associations with the Lowell family, and with the influence of his brother John, a BMC director, he became agent of the Merrimack Company.[32]

Boott's British military bearing added to his unpopularity in Chelmsford. His friend and physician, Dr. John Green, wrote later than Boott had "a decided military air. . . . He spoke in an undertone, always in few words, directly to the point . . . he had a commanding manner." Even an admirer such as the historian William Bagnall wrote that Boott was "of decided, often vehement, expression," and "of strong, even impetuous will"; "His energy and perseverance made everything bend to them." Lowell's first, and decidedly pro-manufacturing historian, Henry A. Miles, related that once, in Boott's absence, "his workmen finding it difficult to make a current of water flow in a desired channel, it was proposed that Mr. Boott's hat and walking stick should be brought and laid on the bank, they feeling sure that then even the water would obey."[33] As these and many more examples indicate, Boott and Moody were polar opposites in style and temperament.

One of the earliest unpopular acts by the Merrimack Company, usually attributed to Boott's influence, was the creation of a company-supported church. There was a Congregational Church in Chelmsford Center, and although its parish extended to the area of new development, it was four miles distant and thus inconvenient for workers who lived in the factory village. Mindful of the need to provide a setting that would draw workers (in addition to good wages and attractive housing), the company voted on June 1, 1822, to authorize Boott and P. T. Jackson "to build a suitable church for the use of the Company at Chelmsford, and that a sum not exceeding five thousand dollars be appropriated for that purpose." Very little happened until early 1824 when the Merrimack Religious Society was formed and space was provided for worship in the company schoolhouse. This society, according to long-time member John O. Green, was "organized under the general statute, and had no distinctive Church feature in its structure," and therefore attracted Congregationalists, Baptists, Methodists, Presbyterians, Universalists, and Episcopalians. Yet for the choice of rector it was clear from the start that the company favored Theodore Edson, an Episcopalian who had been recommended to Boott by the Reverend J. S. J. Gardiner of Trinity Church in Boston and who performed the first service on March 6, 1824. In April, the directors again authorized the agent to build a church, this time specifying that it be built of stone and raising the company contribution to $9,000. At the same time, Boott wrote to Edson, asking him to become minister, for $800 per year and a house rent free.[34]

Apparently, Boott was the only person attending Edson's first service who knew the role of clerk, and few knew the liturgy. "How distinctly do I call to mind [Boott's] loud and full response, almost alone!" Dr. Green recollected. Aware that only the tiniest minority of the village population were Episcopalians, Boott had guaranteed Edson a year's salary, "in case the form of worship we have adopted should, contrary to my belief and expectations, be found so unpalatable to the majority of our people that the church is neglected and the Company should in consequence deem it prudent to substitute some other." Despite this concern, Edson immediately accepted the position, and remained rector for fifty-eight years. Edson's diary for 1824 indicates the degree to which he was in alien religious territory as he interviewed workers and boardinghouse owners and found many of them "not acquainted with the Church nor very partial to it," and he could only hope that "the boarders will be gradually reconciled to the Church." After a Sunday service in early May, Edson admitted that he "was mortified exceedingly this morning to see so few present." Yet while he often "met with a very cool reception," he was welcome at the Moodys' home: "Called at Mr. Worthen's, also called at Mr. Moody's where I saw Mrs. Morrill [Susan Moody's sister-in-law]. Mrs. Moody asked me to call and take tea any time—think I shall accept the invitation."[35]

Kirk Boott's defenders credit the Boston Associates directors with the unrepresentative choice of religion, while Boott simply carried out their wishes. Although several of the directors were Episcopalian, most were Unitarians. Why that religion was not chosen by the directors is perhaps explained by early Lowell historian Frederick W. Coburn, who wrote that the controversy splitting Trinitarians and Unitarians was at its height during this period, and the directors did not want to add to the bitterness by forcing Unitarian worship on a more orthodox (that is, Trinitarian) population. Still the evidence, especially the accounts of Reverend Edson's daughter and of Boott's physician Dr. Green, points to Boott as the driving force.[36]

The directors' selection of a high church religion over the competing evangelical religions of the period is particularly interesting. It was a time of great competition between the high-toned religions (Episcopal, Unitarian) and those considered by some to be "uncouth" (Methodist, Baptist, old-style Congregational). Even though the vast majority of workers had low church affiliations, the directors had decided that the town they were building would have one of the most "respectable" churches. Dr. Green spelled out the class basis of the decision: "The *better class,* to whom every inducement to settle here was desirable, could not be expected to be willing to forego their lifelong privileges, even for high wages. If they did, how long could they retain their superiority in intelligence and morals?" In other words, the Episcopal church would draw the best people and help them maintain their superior status. Former mill girl Harriet Hanson Robinson remembered being attracted as a child to Lowell's Episcopal church "because their little girls were not afraid of the devil, were allowed to dance, and had so much nicer books in their Sunday-school library."[37]

The church building itself, designed by Boott based on a church in his wife's home town of Derby, England, added to the genteel appeal of the religion. It was an early example of Gothic Revival architecture in America, a trend so powerful that by midcentury even the Methodists and Baptists were building huge and ornate churches across America. Even at this early stage, other religious societies could not ignore the impact of such beauty on the minds of local churchgoers. Shortly after the completion of St. Anne's, the new Baptist Society responded to the genteel competition of the Episcopalians by contracting for "an elegant and commodious church." Unitarians and Episcopalians set the standard for refinement in New England, and as Richard L. Bushman notes, the evangelical sects "had to protect themselves against high-toned religion, so that while pure and humble converts were coming in through one door the wealthy and refined would not be leaving through another."[38]

Had the directors created a religious society intended for themselves and a few others, the workers would have made their own choices and there would have been little resentment. But Merrimack employees were required to attend church and to pay 37½ cents per quarter for pew rent. (Until 1833, the state of Massachusetts required residents to pay for the support of their local Congregational church.) But with disestablishment in the air and Episcopalianism so low in the ranking of religious preferences among the growing village population, the Merrimack directors, Boott in particular, were criticized for their unrepresentative choice. Boott's naming the church St. Anne's—his wife's name—added to the irritation. This situation was of short duration, however. Boott's rule stipulated that "all persons are required to be constant in attendance on religious worship, *either at the church in this place or in some of the neighboring parishes,*" leaving open the option to attend alternative churches. Within a year, Baptist, Methodist, and Congregational societies were organized in the village, and taxes paid to the Merrimack Company were apportioned to whichever religious society each resident chose to join. As early as February 1826, the Baptist Society advertised that all prospective members should contact the church clerk, "otherwise they will be taxed in the societies to which they severally belong."[39] St. Anne's struggled during the flurry of new church foundings in the mid-1820s, but it managed to recover, partially owing to the care and open-mindedness of the Reverend Edson, and also because of its emphasis on gentility and respectability, qualities so prized by the up-and-coming middle class of the town.

As we know from his religious involvement at Waltham, Paul Moody had remained loyal to his ancestors' attachment to the Congregational church. But at Lowell he became an Episcopalian. Like former Quaker David Wilkinson at Pawtucket, this conversion took place in Paul's mid-forties, and while the age at which they converted may be a coincidence, the act itself is not. Both men were under the influence of powerful business leaders, Samuel Slater and Kirk Boott, who had been prime movers in the establishment of the Episcopal churches at Pawtucket and Lowell. Moody had the added burden of corporate loyalty: this was the company church and Moody was always a company man. At Waltham, he took the company's part in church controversies and still remained within the Congregational fold; at Lowell, he made a conscious choice to change affiliation. When the Merrimack Religious Society was first formed in February 1824, Moody was not directly involved, although his friends Ezra Worthen and John Dummer—and of course Boott—were among the signers of the application. Moody's Congregational background may have led him to take a low-key role in the founding of the society, but once it was established he joined, along with his son David, who was also a member of the Beethoven Musical Society, which performed at the church consecration on March 16, 1825. The rest of the family most likely joined as well, although the available records list only adult males.[40]

Once Moody converted he was an exemplar, always in his pew at Sunday services, and a generous contributor to the church. His devotion was more than a personal religious commitment. He took very seriously his self-defined role as the sober, moral, industrious—and prosperous—citizen that others might emulate. Certainly, he could have done this in a Congregational church, which would have had the advantage of long family tradition as well as being more representative of the local population. But St. Anne's was the company church, and while it is unlikely that any of the directors directly pressured him to join, he felt a duty to lend his support to their chosen institution. Moreover, St. Anne's soon became *his* institution, one that drew "his warm affections" as well as support.[41] His religious feeling was genuine, and it was all the better that it could be demonstrated in the most respectable church in town.

Moody also developed a strong friendship with St. Anne's rector, Theodore Edson. In addition to his religious duties, Edson was on the first school committee when the town of Lowell was incorporated in 1826. Like his friend, Moody "was a warm friend of education and favored the most liberal public expenditures for this purpose," which put him at odds with Kirk Boott, who later had a public showdown with Edson over the increase in corporate taxation if the committee's plan for school expansion were endorsed. (When Edson's plan was approved at town meeting in 1832, Boott responded by withdrawing from St. Anne's church.) In 1827, the Merrimack Company backed out of all obligations to the Episcopal Society by leasing the church and parsonage for fifteen years in exchange for the society's assumption of the minister's salary and all taxes. Edson seriously considered leaving Lowell, because he saw "no prospect of being successful as a minister of the gospel under existing circumstances," even though he was "willing to engage myself here for life even with a diminution of salary provided this congregation can be afforded equal facilities with the other denominations here." But Edson received crucial support from Moody and several other corporation managers who "remained attached to the church," and the rector stayed on and the church prospered.[42]

In addition to his steady example as a devout Christian, Paul Moody also took a public stand on temperance. Drinking had become a particularly worrisome problem in the early republic, not only for the disorder that it caused but because it was considered a barrier to social and economic progress. Lowell was certainly not a dry town: at least one local store sold a wide variety of "choice liquors" such as Champagne, Madeira, brandy, gin, and whiskey, and by March 1827 the Lowell Brewery was in full operation and ready to deliver beer and ale to the growing population. General Benjamin Butler, who moved to Lowell as a boy of ten in 1828, remembered the Lowell Brewery as "a prime necessity, because where there are Englishmen there must be beer."[43]

Like most entrepreneurs of the 1820s, the Boston Associates saw the benefits of a sober labor force in their factories, not only out of economic self-interest, but also because they personally believed that sobriety was a critical component of national moral progress. The directors did little to explicitly control alcohol consumption, although by owning most of the real estate they could impose restrictions on the companies to whom they sold land. One such restriction was spelled out by the Proprietors of Locks and Canals in 1826: unless given explicit permission, no grantee was allowed to "keep, or permit to be kept, any tavern or other public house of entertainment, nor any livery stable, nor sell, nor permit to be sold any spirituous liquors of any kind in less quantity than one gallon in any shop, store, or building upon the granted premises." This emphasis on hard or "spirituous" liquor was very much in keeping with the prevailing view among temperance advocates that moderate drinking, especially of wine or beer, was not a threat to public order. Even the stipulation of "quantity less than one gallon" was consistent with the current temperance effort to prevent the proliferation of dram shops where rum was sold by the shot.[44]

Many Lowell citizens agreed with these sentiments. Newspaper editorials put forth temperance as a reasonable response to the problem of excessive drinking, and temperance poems occasionally graced the front pages. At least by 1828, Lowell had a representative in the Massachusetts Society for the Suppression of Intemperance, as well as a local temperance society.[45] But there appears to have been little public discussion of drinking in the workplace, even though it was well known that the practice ranged from commonplace to rampant. At Waltham, a BMC agent remembered, "ardent spirits [were] bought at different times for use by the workmen, as was customary in the olden days." At the Cocheco Manufacturing Company in Dover, New Hampshire (controlled by the Boston Associates), it was common well into the 1830s for machinists and other male employees to take two rum breaks during the day.[46] According to Bagnall, "most mechanics were addicted to the daily use of ardent spirits, many of them to excess." Here Paul Moody exerted his considerable influence by prohibiting drinking in the Locks and Canals machine shop. This sort of reform was highly unusual at the time, having "secured the cooperation of comparatively few persons of prominence either in professional, mercantile, or mechanical pursuits." Moody's rules were quietly introduced and, with the support of his professional and personal example, the reform was successful. Like many men who saw the link between sobriety and their own success, Moody became a model of self-discipline; unlike most he was able to impose his own views directly on a large workforce of machinists and mechanics.[47]

It might seem inconsistent, then, that Paul Moody held stock in the Lowell Brewery. The Locks and Canals Treasurer's Journal for October 1827 lists "10 shares in the name of Paul Moody" ($500) and an equal number for Kirk Boott. It appears that these shares belonged to the company, because the total of $1,000 shows up on the Locks and Canals balance sheet in 1827, and in April 1830 the Treasurer's Journal notes "10 shares Lowell Brewery sold George Brownell and transferred by Paul Moody $500," and a similar notation for Boott's ten shares. While this suggests that Moody no longer held shares in the brewery, town records show that he was taxed on $250 worth of Lowell Brewery stock in 1829, 1830, and 1831, with his son David holding shares worth $125. Whatever the company involvement may have been, Paul was unquestionably a personal investor in the local brewery.[48]

The key to the apparent contradiction is the belief among many temperance moderates that beer was a healthy alternative to rum, and that a local brewery would reduce the consumption of ardent spirits. Basil Hall, a British traveler who recorded his impressions of Lowell in October 1827, wrote "I was much pleased to see a great brewery starting up like a Leviathan, amongst this small fry of buildings; and still more pleased when I learnt from my friend that there were hopes of being able to substitute malt liquor among the cotton-mill population, in place of the abominable ardent spirits so lamentably present elsewhere." Yet in that same year, the Massachusetts Society for the Suppression of Intemperance altered its moderate stance to one of "absolute abstinence." In a speech before the Lowell Temperance Society in 1830, Reverend Edson explained that "suppression of intemperance" had proved ineffective and only total abstinence might achieve "a tolerable degree of success." (Edson noted that "not less than fourteen hundred gallons of distilled spirits have probably been consumed in this town since we last met, a month ago, an astonishing amount" for Lowell's population, after subtracting known temperance men and "such respectable ladies and pious females, as we cannot suppose have consumed any considerable part of this quantity of rum.") The fact that Moody still held stock in a beer manufacturer into the 1830s indicates that he remained an old-style moderate on the temperance question. This is a bit surprising given his friend Reverend Edson's shift to the radical view, but perhaps less so considering that the influential Kirk Boott held on to his brewery shares as well.[49] Moody may have believed he could maintain more credibility with his workers by holding a moderate position on the issue.

While Moody's association with the brewery was limited to ownership of a few shares, he was much more involved with another new development in Lowell: banking. The Boston Associates had not used banks to a large degree, depending more on stock sales for most of their capital needs, and what banking they did was in Boston. As Lowell grew, it became clear that the various business interests in town required a bank to serve their borrowing needs, and the Lowell Bank was incorporated for that purpose. Among the eight incorporators were Kirk Boott and Paul Moody. Boott was also named to the board of directors, but Moody was not. While this is reminiscent of Moody's role in the Merrimack Company—a "founder" but not an active director—it should be noted that only four of the eight incorporators of the bank were named to the board. Furthermore, Moody had no banking experience, while Boott was treasurer of a major corporation. It soon became evident that the textile manufacturers needed a local bank for their specific interests, and in March 1831 Kirk Boott and four associates incorporated the Railroad Bank. This time, Moody was elected to the board, along with Boott and members of the Appleton, Cabot, and Lawrence families.[50]

Although banking was a relatively minor aspect of Moody's life, it could be seen as disproportionately symbolic. In a portrait that was apparently commissioned by the Locks and Canals company in the late 1820s, he looks much more like a banker than the manager of a machine shop. Dressed in a fancy coat and vest, with a high collar, he has a thoughtful, pleasant look, short hair combed straight back, thinning a bit at the temples, and long thick sideburns. His full face and stocky torso suggest a substantial, satisfied burgher. It is the portrait of a man one can imagine pulling up in his chaise to the banking room in the new building at the corner of Central and Hurd streets, certainly not flashy—not Boott—but nonetheless obviously one of the most influential people in town. This is not to suggest that Moody had become smug or self-righteous; but he had indeed become a wealthy man, one of the handful of most prominent business people in town, and a pillar of its highest-toned church—all important elements of the upwardly mobile middle-class goal of respectability.

As at Waltham, the Moodys did not own their own home, although they did pay real estate taxes on the property, apparently part of the agreement with the Merrimack and Locks and Canals companies.[51] Why would an upwardly mobile family like the Moodys, who had owned a house when they lived in Amesbury, opt to live in company housing, especially if they were paying taxes on the property? One obvious reason is the size and quality of the house that the company provided, and another is the fact that Boott's mansion was also company owned. But a more general explanation is that home and land ownership, which had traditionally been the basis of class distinctions, became less important in the early nineteenth century because status could be demonstrated through other displays of gentility, such as home furnishings, consumer goods, children in private schools, a respectable church, and servants. (The Moodys probably had servants, for whom there was plenty of space among their fourteen rooms.)[52] A tastefully furnished company house was perfectly in keeping with the emerging rules of respectability.

He led by example at work and at church, but Moody was by no means a public figure. There is no evidence that he joined any civic organizations, although the St. Anne's–affiliated Masons might have been a reasonable choice, as would the Middlesex Mechanics Association.[53] His high-ranking position in

Figure 7.3
This portrait of Paul Moody was probably commissioned by the Locks and Canals Company in the 1820s, when Moody was in his mid-40s. He looks more like a banker than a machinist, in keeping with his status as one of the most influential people in Lowell.
Courtesy of the Lowell Historical Society.

the Locks and Canals company might easily have led to political leadership, as it did for Warren Colburn on the school committee and Kirk Boott as town meeting moderator, town council member, and state legislator. Just as he had dreaded appearing in court for patent infringement cases during his Waltham years, Moody continued to avoid speaking roles except at work, where he was on firm and comfortable ground. This sober, industrious, successful church member considered it his duty to be a public example, but his reticent style was a poor match for formal civic leadership.[54]

In politics he was likely a National Republican—a Whig in the making, before the advocates of tariffs, industrialization, and internal improvements formally established the Whig party in 1834. While David Wilkinson clearly expressed his objection to the anti-tariff, anti-bank Democrats, we can only surmise that Moody would have shared his sentiments. Virtually all of the Boston Associates were anti-Jacksons—especially Boott, who warned the people of Lowell that if Andrew Jackson were elected, "the grass will grow in your streets, owls will build nests in the mills, and foxes burrow in your highways." It is improbable that any of the manufacturing men of Lowell would have supported the Antimasonic Party, despite the shared antipathy to Jackson. The Antimasons were not only too evangelical for the refined tastes of the local gentry, but they also opposed "privileged corporations." Lowell's business interests were well represented in the U. S. Congress by budding Whigs Edward Everett in the House and Daniel Webster (a Merrimack company stockholder) in the Senate. Nathan Appleton himself was elected to Congress in 1830 on the pro-tariff, anti-Jackson ticket.[55]

Avoiding open political involvement, as well as membership in local organizations, throughout the 1820s and into the 1830s, Paul Moody devoted himself to work, church, and family. The Moodys socialized with Susan's two brothers, with the Edsons, and most likely with other families of the supervisory class within the corporations as well as professionals in town such as the family physician Dr. Green. They went to concerts of the Beethoven Musical Society, not only because of its association with St. Anne's Church, but also because their son David was a member. With their horse and chaise they could drive to the main shopping area on Merrimack Street, or about the rolling countryside that surrounded Lowell, even to their home towns of Amesbury and Byfield, less than thirty miles away. Paul probably did not take the chaise to work, but rather walked, past the pretty pond across from his house, on to Dutton Street, and about a block to the machine shop.

There is no evidence of Paul and Susan Moody's socializing with Boott and his "lady," both of whom were "of highly genteel parentage," according to Reverend Edson. Alvan Clark, a Merrimack Company calico printer who knew Moody "pretty well," remembered him as "an ingenious and very approachable man, but unpolished."[56] Although Moody and Boott were both executives of the Locks and Canals, Boott was part of that Boston Associates elite that Moody had never been able—perhaps had never even tried—to penetrate. Boott's constant presence in Paul's life went far beyond their employee-manager relationship. Moody was always in Boott's shadow, not only professionally, but economically and culturally as well. Paul attended the church that Boott had mandated, lived in a house that Boott had designed, used Boott as his attorney for all company stock transactions, and made all his investment choices (the brewery and two banks) in line with Boott's. Of course, aligning one's investments with those of a shrewd and well-connected local leader was not necessarily a poor policy, so long as Moody did not mind being overshadowed by his more commanding colleague. Perhaps Moody simply knew and accepted his place, high in the second tier of Lowell society. He had wealth and respect, was by all accounts well liked, and had achieved much despite his mechanic's background and his reticent personality. "Moody lacked the vision of Lowell and the sparkle of Jackson," wrote George Gibb. "He was the workhorse of the enterprise—a nimble-fingered Yankee with a single-mindedness of purpose. So great was his value to the company that he could have bargained for a top position in management, yet he remained a mechanic to the day of his death." While not totally accurate, Gibb's assessment captures the essence of Moody's demeanor and public persona. Moody knew himself well enough to limit his own ambition and to enjoy with satisfaction the status, wealth, and respect that his devotion to the corporation had brought him.[57]

While Moody's job at Lowell was in many respects an extension of his work at Waltham, in other ways it was significantly different. At Waltham, he had concentrated on building, improving, and when necessary inventing textile machinery. He had been awarded six patents, and while several failed to stand up in patent infringement suits, Moody's innovations had been a critical factor in the technological edge of the Boston Manufacturing Company. At Lowell, the business plan was less reliant on innovative technology and more on scale and efficiency. The objective of the Proprietors of Locks and Canals was to sell land, lease water power, and produce fully equipped and operational textile factories as quickly as possible. Certainly, the Lowell mills took advantage of the latest machine improvements, but increasingly, new technology entered the system by way of other machine shops and the Locks and Canals company acted more as agents than as technology innovators. Thus the corporations were no longer dependent on Moody to invent, but rather to integrate and rationalize the processes in order to "package" efficient mills and machinery.[58]

With his comprehensive understanding of the full range of machines—from carders to spinning frames to power looms, and all the various intermediate processes—Moody was essential to the Locks and Canals' ability to estimate the kind and number of machines, power requirements, labor, and other costs of producing a packaged mill. In early 1829, for example, Jackson received a sample of cloth from merchant-investor John Cushing, who wanted to know the cost and feasibility of producing the cloth in bulk. Jackson responded with an initial estimate of the number of spindles and looms required, then added, "Instead of the above, Mr. Moody says . . . ," and conveyed his engineer's suggestion of forty-eight spinning frames with 6,144 spindles, 160 looms, plus his estimates for the cost of day labor, warping, dressing, weaving, and bleaching.[59] While there is no indication whether this information was ever applied, it does provide a good idea of what Moody was doing at Lowell, which was to use his deep understanding of the machinery to work out estimates to be used by the various agents and directors to make sound business decisions. In some ways, this might have been formulaic and not particularly interesting work; on the other hand, it shows a thorough knowledge of the products of his machine shop, and his importance to the Locks and Canals company in making reliable estimates.

Only rarely now did Moody produce the kind of innovations that made him famous at Waltham. In 1828, the directors of the new Appleton Manufacturing Company made the uncharacteristic decision to produce heavy shirtings and sheetings from No. 14 yarn, in direct competition with the Boston Manufacturing Company. They did so to exploit Moody's recent speed improvements, which would give their product a significant edge in this market. This major innovation was the introduction of leather belts in place of metal gears and shafts to transfer power more efficiently from the waterwheel's main drum to the secondary shafts on each floor of the factories. Leather belts had been used to connect a secondary shaft to an individual machine, but now very long straps of stitched cow hides, pulled "almost as tight as fiddle strings," provided the main drive to each floor. This was not only more efficient, but could be repaired much more quickly than iron components, and Moody's improvement later became widely adopted in American factories.[60]

But Moody made few such innovations at Lowell. For the most part, cost estimation and overall management of the machine shop were his primary responsibilities, and the layers of management suggest how "corporate" his job had become. Moody was superintendent of the Locks and Canals machine shop; under him was assistant superintendent Thomas Borden; and under Borden was overseer George Brownell, a Moody protégé at Waltham. Moody was now far removed from hands-on management of the machinists. Locks and Canals company records show that Brownell gave the detailed instructions to the machinists and carpenters in the shop.[61]

While Moody's importance is obvious, it is remarkable how seldom he appears in the directors minutes of the various Boston Associates companies during these years. Aside from his brief role as a founding partner of the Merrimack Company, he was rarely on the important committees appointed by the directors or involved in policy decisions of the Merrimack or Locks and Canals companies. For example, in May 1827 the directors "voted that N. Appleton and Kirk Boott be a committee to determine what kind of cloth shall be made in the fifth Mill at Lowell, and to give the requisite orders to Mr. Moody." Certainly, he had free rein at the machine shop, where his word on all mechanical matters was final. But with no inventions during this period, his job had become one of making his previous work more efficient, managing more people and expenses, occasional consulting in Waltham, and making the observations and calculations that allowed the Locks and Canals company to make accurate estimates of the machine requirements for each new mill that arose in Lowell.[62]

~

Despite the apparent lack of attention to the Waltham mills during this period of explosive growth at Lowell, we must remember that Jackson, Appleton, Boott, Moody, and many of their associates were still the major stockholders of the Boston Manufacturing Company, and they continued to protect their investments. Late in 1829, a committee was formed to investigate serious power problems on the Charles River, and Moody traveled to Waltham to consult on the project. On October 6, the directors reported that "Mr. Moody thinks that it may be worthwhile to alter the Gearing of the large mill with a view to the saving of Power." But even with these changes the Waltham factories could not match the output of the Lowell mills, and during 1830 and early 1831, Moody put his mind and considerable experience to the problem. Along with the directors responsible for the evaluation, Moody recommended that part of the water power at the lower dam be sold, that the machinery in the lower factory be consolidated with the upper factories, and finally that the lower factory be turned into a bleachery or print works "to be carried by steam." Moody's opinion was that by enlarging the two upper factories only slightly, all additional machinery could be accommodated, and "that by such an arrangement the whole product of cloth would be increased."[63]

By the time these recommended changes were reported to the BMC directors in August 1831, Paul Moody was dead. On Monday, July 4, the citizens of Lowell had gathered for the Independence Day celebration, as yet unaware that former president James Monroe had died. The following morning, Paul went to work feeling slightly ill; he returned home in the early afternoon and retired to bed, and was in great pain throughout the night. On Wednesday the pain subsided, but he grew increasingly weaker, and "in spite of all the efforts that could be used to rally the energies of the system," he died at seven a.m. on Thursday, July 7, at the age of fifty-two. His death was completely unexpected. "He died in his full strength of body, in the very vigor of age and constitution," Reverend Edson told the congregation on the following Sunday. "But the last Sunday he was here in his accustomed place, and perhaps not a person in the whole congregation could have been selected with a fairer prospect of long life and vigorous health than he." "In the fullness of health and vigor . . . ," wrote the *Lowell Journal*, "Mr. Moody was struck down like lightning." No cause of death is given in any records, so we are left to wonder whether it was a virus or infection that eluded the diagnosis of Dr. Green. There is the inevitable comparison to the early death of his friend Ezra Worthen, although Worthen's heart condition was well known, and Moody had no apparent health problems. Many years later, Reverend Edson brought up the fact that Worthen, Moody, and later Warren Colburn had all died young while working directly for the hard-driving Kirk Boott, and mused whether they had been overworked into early graves.[64]

The eulogies poured in for the "ingenious machinist" who had "identified himself with the rise, growth, and prosperity of this flourishing village." The *Lowell Journal*'s long obituary was copied in full in the prestigious *New England Magazine* for August 1831. Moody was praised for his single-minded devotion to his work, for his ability to "arrange in his mind all the parts of a complicated machine, whether described by others or invented by himself, without the aid of a model, or of any sensible exhibition of it," and for his agency in the founding and development of Lowell. He was equally extolled for his personal qualities. "[W]hile the talents of Mr. Moody excited admiration and while from these his fame has been derived," the *Journal* continued, "among those who were near him, his moral qualities were more highly prized, and cause his loss to be most deeply felt." He was mild mannered, fair to his workers, and went about his business "without a particle of selfish anxiety for fame." Reverend Edson spoke of Moody's "extraordinary intellect," but stressed his generosity to the poor: "He was not wont to turn away from actual suffering without an effort to relieve it." Perhaps characteristic of the self-made man, Moody's charity manifested itself less in giving alms than by promoting the benefits of hard work. According to Edson, "No person more fully appreciated the superiority of that charity which provides for the destitute by encouraging their own laudable exertions and industry." "What he was as a friend, a brother, a father, a husband," the minister concluded, "has been involuntarily attested to by the deep, unaffected and irrepressible emotion which this truly mournful event has occasioned."[65]

The funeral was held July 8 at St. Anne's church, officiated by Paul's good friend Reverend Edson. He was buried in the family plot in the old village of Byfield where he had been born and raised. He had made his reputation as a highly innovative machinist at Waltham; and to his "business sagacity, ripe judgment and mechanical skill Lowell is more largely indebted perhaps than to any other, with a single exception, for its existence," wrote Benjamin Butler. But his earthly remains were laid to rest where it all began, where his curiosity about the operation of a hand loom started him on his path to technological prominence, wealth, and respectability.[66]

The Locks and Canals company responded in word and in deed. "The Directors, deeply impressed with the sense of the severe loss the Corporation have sustained in the death of their Agent Mr. Moody who expired in the midst of his labors on the 7th inst, after an illness of short duration, feel desirous to enter upon their records as a feeble tribute to his work the expression of their high admiration of his skill as a mechanic, as well as their unbound regard for his character as a man." While the style of nineteenth-century eulogies tends to mask any negative qualities of the deceased, it is interesting to note the directors' choice of words to describe Moody's character. "Unsparing of his own labor, he exacted & secured the same assiduity from others" might suggest a strict taskmaster; "he never had the weakness to indulge a favorite" might imply a cool distance from the workers under his direction. The *Lowell Journal* had written that Moody was "most sensitive of injury," but added that "his temper was not easily ruffled, and his feelings were habitually kept under perfect control." While some of this might suggest an anxious, somewhat rigid man trying to maintain control of his emotions and his leadership position in the company hierarchy, it is risky to mine the eulogies too deeply, especially since, in the directors' opinion, for those who worked with and for Moody, "his memory is cherished with affection and respect, & furnishes to those who survive him an invaluable model for imitation." The directors ended their tribute with a glowing assessment of their engineer's contribution to machine making and the success of their business:

> To mechanical talent of the very first order he united prudence and foresight in so eminent a degree, that his judgment in machinery was almost unerring, hence the use of few of his inventions have been superseded by more modern discoveries and they were so numerous & important that to no one are we more indebted for the advance & successful state of the Cotton Manufacture amongst us.[67]

More significant than the words of praise was the company's decision to allow Susan Moody and her children to continue to live in the Worthen Street house rent free for one year. Early in 1832, the directors authorized the agent "to let to Mrs. Moody the house she now occupies with a strip of land of 140 ft. front by about 212 ft. deep for a rent of $500 per ann; or to sell her the same for $16,000, with the usual restrictions as to occupation." She did not take the company up on its offer to purchase the house, but apparently agreed to the rental terms, since a notation in the company records refers to work being done on Worthen Street "north of Mrs. Moody's house," in September 1832, and in 1833 she was assessed for real estate that is consistent with the Worthen Street property. In 1834, however, the Locks and Canals company hired West Point engineer George Washington Whistler to manage the machine shop, and the Whistlers moved into the Moody house, where the artist James McNeill Whistler was born that year. Susan Moody bought a small house a few blocks away on Gorham Street, where she lived until 1846, when she purchased three acres of land and built a new home on Nesmith Street in the fashionable Belvedere section of Lowell. She remained a Lowell resident until her death at the age of eighty in 1861.[68]

If providing for one's family is a key measure of success, then Paul Moody was exceptionally successful. Susan, aged fifty-one at the time of Paul's death, and her children—David (28), Mary (24), William (19), Susan Harriet (15), and Hannah (8)—were the beneficiaries of the substantial stock shares that Moody owned in the Boston, Merrimack, Hamilton, and Locks and Canals companies. Over the years he had received thousands of dollars in dividends, some applied to his principle (at BMC) but mostly in cash distributions, and he also occasionally sold shares for cash. The records of his holdings at the time of his death are unambiguous only for the Boston Manufacturing Company and Locks and Canals, but these indicate that Susan and her children each held between two and five shares of each company.

As the children reached their majority, they made various decisions whether to sell their shares or hold them to collect the steady cash dividends. Susan sold two of her Locks and Canals shares in 1834 (along with her half ownership of the old Byfield mill that Paul had bought for $5,455 in 1826), probably to finance the house on Gorham Street. But she held on to three shares, as did Hannah, and the long-term payoff was astonishing. In addition to average dividends of 17 percent per year between 1831 and 1844, the Locks and Canals company paid special dividends in 1845 as it sold off some of its valuable land holdings before spinning off the Lowell Machine Shop as an independent company. The dividends that year totaled $800 per share, and the final stock buyback in November netted stockholders $782 per share. For the year 1845, Susan and Hannah each received $4,746 for having held on to stock that Paul Moody had been privileged to purchase twenty years earlier.[69]

David Moody not only benefited from his father's stock, but through Paul's influence also worked for the Merrimack Manufacturing Company, even before his parents moved to Chelmsford. From April 1, 1823, to May 1, 1824, he was paid at the rate of $400 per year, very respectable for a young man of twenty. Although the company records give no indication of the type of work he did, he explained in a letter written about 1880 that "In the year 1822, John Dummer and myself went up the Merrimack River, near Nashua, brought down a raft of logs, to the Stony Brook saw-mill, and there got out the lumber for the first two wheels of the Merrimack mill." Possibly he was a millwright, like Dummer, or perhaps a sawyer or carpenter. Later, between 1830 and 1834, he was employed by the Locks and Canals company as a provider of services such as teaming, smithing, and hay deliveries—a substantial contract with a monthly payroll of over $1,000.[70]

All of the Moody children married and had children of their own, and all but Susan outlived their mother. Mary (married April 25, 1832, to George H. Carlton) made two sad attempts to carry on the memory of her father: her first child, Paul Moody Carlton, was born in April 1833, but lived only eight months; her third, in April 1837, carried the same name, but died at the age of sixteen months. David married in 1832 and stayed in Lowell for only a few years before moving to Illinois, although in the 1840s he was active in Lowell politics and in the 1850s he and his family lived with his mother on Nesmith Street. Apparently more outgoing and active in civic affairs than his father, David was an assistant marshal during the ceremonies when Andrew Jackson visited in 1833, and served on the city council in 1846. His first child, born in October 1833, was christened Paul Moody.[71]

By any professional measure, Paul Moody's corporate career had been a remarkable success. Well before the Boston Associates came to prominence he had already taken part in the "cotton fever" expansion, but by choosing not to remain an entrepreneur in 1813, and instead hitch his wagon to the well-financed plans of some of the richest men in the commonwealth, he had minimized his personal risk while still participating fully in the textile revolution. There had been some family dislocation, first in the move to Waltham and then to Lowell, but this mobility was geographically limited to less than fifty miles from the towns where he and his wife were born. His socioeconomic mobility had been great, however. While he was by no means poor as a child, he ended up much wealthier than his parents or his siblings, and he had clearly demonstrated that there were alternate paths to respectability in a family of college-educated teachers and ministers. His upward mobility had been achieved along the new path of technological innovation, not as a lone inventor or owner of a small partnership, but in the service of highly capitalized corporations.

The respectability he achieved was more than that of wealth, although his position as one of the prosperous burghers of the new industrial town of Lowell was one of the important components. It was critically important to a man of Moody's character that he could look back on his career as one that emphasized moral and civic goodness, and his life is indeed a fine nineteenth-century example of republican virtue rewarded. He would have agreed that workers and entrepreneurs in Lowell were "one in interest, one in the loss, and one in the gain; one in prosperity, and one in adversity," as former mayor Frederick T. Greenhalge declared in 1886. The company was benevolent, morality was enforced, religion (especially the genteel church promoted by the corporation) was stressed, and industrial capitalism was good for all involved. One only had to look around at the well-dressed, well-behaved mill girls and the orderly growth according to Boott's plan to see that it was good. In retrospect, the Irish riots in Lowell in 1831 sounded a dissonant note, and the strikes of 1834 and 1836 showed what the Yankee mill girls thought of reduced wages and deteriorating conditions.[72] But during Moody's lifetime, it appeared to most observers that the town of Lowell was a model of industrial and social development, for which Moody could take his share of the credit.

And yet, his career at Lowell was marked by a striking lack of innovation. This is partly due to the fact that invention, as a business asset, had become much less critical than it had been at Waltham; the advances at Lowell were in scale and efficiency, turning the whole creation of a textile mill into a well-oiled machine.[73] At Lowell, in the professional (and cultural) shadow of Kirk Boott, he had reached his ceiling, an important employee, but no longer as vital as he had been at Waltham. He was solid, wealthy, and had achieved the respectability that was so important to the age. The corporate life had provided the means of this comfortable respectability, but perhaps after a time the corporate life was no longer the source of satisfaction in itself. Most likely, it was enough—a very good bargain.

The pressure of working under Boott may have taken its toll, as his friend Reverend Edson hinted, but since his move to Waltham in 1813 he had had no financial worries, and he left his family well off when he died. But the technology by which he had made his name was changing dramatically in the 1830s, as clearly indicated by the coincidence of Moody's death and the initial plans to construct a railroad linking Lowell and Boston, a project that would soon transform Moody's machine shop into a locomotive factory. Moody was certainly aware of these changes that would become the province of younger, more scientifically trained engineers.[74] As he settled into middle age, a decade after his agency in the founding of Lowell, he may have longed for the days when the mathematician-industrialist Francis Cabot Lowell would suggest an innovation and the young ingenious machinist Paul Moody would turn it into a marvelous reality.

8

"We All Broke Down"

David Wilkinson, 1829–1852

> David Wilkinson has gone down the falls. His failure is a serious one, and it affects my mind and body seriously, and purse too for the present.
>
> —Samuel Slater, 1829

In June 1829, the finishing touches were being put on St. John's Church in Wilkinsonville in preparation for the dedication. David Wilkinson had donated the land and $1,000 toward construction of this Greek Revival building, with its Gothic-arched doors, windows, and belfry, overlooking the common. For four years, the religious services had been held in the hotel that David built across the street, but now the picture was complete—his chosen Episcopal church, in his planned village, supported by his factory of 2,500 spindles and 108 looms, along with grain and saw mills, a tavern, store, bank, and twelve houses for employees.[1] But as the dedication was taking place on Wednesday, June 3, and Wilkinsonville was finally about to match the vision of its founder, the mill village was already slipping from his grasp.

Just the previous summer, business prospects appeared to be very good. The *Niles Weekly Register* declared that "[t]he cotton manufacture is increasing at a wonderful rate in the United States. Many of the old mills are worked to their utmost production; and new ones are building . . . in all parts of our country. The more the better." David was doing his part in Sutton by expanding his Centre Falls mill at Wilkinsonville, effectively doubling its capacity. It was also in 1828 that a petition to incorporate the Sutton Bank was granted, with a group of local businessmen and farmers, plus David's brother-in-law Hezekiah

Howe, as directors. David was not a director, probably because he would not be able to attend the weekly meetings, but he was the leading investor. Howe, the next largest investor, was elected president at the first board of directors meeting in September.[2]

David Wilkinson was at his entrepreneurial peak in 1828, with his industrial base in Pawtucket and Providence, his own mill village in Sutton, and other more speculative investments in Massachusetts, Connecticut, South Carolina, and Cohoes, New York. As we have seen, Paul Moody was also at the peak of his career at this time, securely settled near the top of the corporate hierarchy of the huge and successful Lowell industrial complex. But the paths of these two ingenious machinists had diverged widely. Moody had risen within the corporate ranks, well paid and protected but with a distinct ceiling on his ambition, which perhaps suited his risk-averse nature. Wilkinson, who had always been entrepreneurial, had become increasingly speculative, with less regard for risk as time went on. While his investments showed a fair amount of diversification—machine shop, textile mills, foundry, hotels, banking—they were still largely associated with the textile industry. And as the financial downturns in 1816, 1819, and 1825 had demonstrated, textiles could be a financially uncertain business.[3]

Hints of impending trouble were starting to spread in January 1829, as one Pawtucket newspaper reported on "the circulation of rumors affecting the credit of monied institutions, firms, or individuals," although readers were reassured that few, if any, of the allegations were true. By late February there were a few small failures and more disquieting rumors. But more factual news intruded: due to textile overproduction, prices on world markets had declined to the point at which cloth costing eleven cents to manufacture would fetch only eight or nine cents at market.[4]

One prominent New England manufacturer had an inkling of the extent of the looming crisis. In a letter of January 7, 1829, Samuel Slater noted that "it is rather a pinching time here for money" and that there were factory owners "whose chins are barely above water." Referring to Lowell woolen mill owner Thomas Hurd, Slater wrote that "since the failure of Mr. Hurd, money jobbers and anti-tariff folks have propounded almost every one who has seen, or at least touched of late, a cotton or woolen factory, that he must go down stream." He feared that antimanufacturing zealots would use the general downturn, the glut of cotton products, and a few business failures to drum up support for the reining in of manufacturing expansion and tariff preference—which was indeed occurring. The letter's more specific intent was to counter any rumors his correspondent might have heard that he had insufficient assets to cover his outstanding notes. On the contrary, Slater declared, "I think I can boldly say, after the whole company debts are paid . . . there will be left from 800,000 to 1,000,000 of dollars to all concerned." He was not bluffing—there were in fact sufficient assets to keep the Slater enterprises afloat. But, he admitted, "I am on two neighbours' paper," which he downplayed by adding "but am partially secure, and hope in a day or two to be fully secured against an eventual loss, providing Mount Etna should not extend its lava much beyond the usual limits."[5]

Being "on two neighbours' paper" meant that Slater had endorsed bank loans for two borrowers. In early-nineteenth-century banking, a loan was less often secured by putting up collateral—real estate, for example—than by obtaining the signature of one or more financially secure individuals. Thus, the loan was backed not only by the borrower, who presumably was creditworthy, but by the full resources of the endorser as well. Slater's involvement in the finances of his relatives and friends was therefore standard practice, really nothing more than an extension of the kinship networks that had provided credit since colonial times, now adapted to more formal banking. What was unusual, however, was the amount, a total of $300,000, which a conservative estimate would put at seven million in today's dollars.[6]

One "neighbour" was John Kennedy, a close friend who owned a weaving mill in nearby Central Falls and had frequently invested in industrial ventures with the Wilkinsons. Slater was unaware of the total indebtedness of his friend. "Kennedy's debts amount to $115,000, which greatly surprised me and every other person," he wrote. "It is about double what I expected." Slater's other weighty borrower was David Wilkinson. A document from this period lists loans totaling $16,000 for which Slater had supplied surety for David, but also notes "various other notes, drafts & obligations" that raise the total Slater debt by an additional $30,000. It is likely that Slater did not know the full extent of his brother-in-law's other loans and endorsements, for he stated in March that he "contemplates continuing to be the endorser or surety for the said David Wilkinson for his accommodation in the course of his business."[7]

While Slater was shoring up David's finances, the affairs of Abraham and Isaac Wilkinson were unraveling. In addition to their iron works at Pawtucket, they also owned the Valley Falls Company just upriver in Central Falls and the Albion Company in Lincoln, and had financial stakes in the Fall River Iron Works, the Providence Furnace Company, and the Fox Point Union Company. They also controlled the Farmers and Mechanics Bank, which was part of the problem: not only did the bank disproportionately provide credit to the textile and iron industries that were currently undergoing contraction, but it had awarded $150,000 in loans to Abraham and Isaac Wilkinson—nearly 50 percent of the total loans of the bank.[8]

In March the twin brothers began selling their interest in some of these companies, and in early June they advertised an extensive list of their properties—mills, land, houses, stores—for private sale or public auction. This only intensified the sense of panic in Pawtucket and surrounding areas. The Farmers and Mechanics Bank was forced to suspend specie redemption in June. The bank explained that "the suspension of specie payments has been rendered unavoidable by the uncommon pecuniary embarrassments which press so heavily on this community, and the failure of some of our heaviest manufacturers, most of whom were largely connected with this Institution." Although there were brave public statements of confidence in the bank's solvency, the Rhode Island legislature felt compelled to appoint a commission to manage the bank's affairs.[9]

Samuel Slater noted the "dreadful storm in and about Pawtucket," particularly the assignment of property that marked the early stages of bankruptcy. (Rather than resorting to state insolvency proceedings, debtors and creditors often preferred voluntary assignments, which tended to be quicker, less expensive, and more amicable.) "I believe on Friday last," Slater wrote on June 15, 1829, "Samuel B. Harris made an assignment of his property without even consulting his endorsers, A. & I. W[ilkinson]. On Saturday A. & I. W. made an assignment of their property, and as a great amount of paper [outstanding loans] was lying over, both of their own and that which they had endorsed for W. Harris and S. B. Harris, as soon as the alarm was given in Providence, the Providence people, with their lawyers and sheriffs, were busy enough here until midnight on Saturday night, but the conjecture is, they were too late." Three days after Slater's letter relating Abraham and Isaac's woes came the failures of Timothy Greene & Sons and S. & D. Greene & Co. Timothy Greene was the husband of David's sister Lucy, and Samuel and Daniel Greene were his sons. Thus the interrelated misfortunes of the Wilkinson clan continued to spread.

On July 21, Pawtucket manufacturer Barney Merry, a state Masonic leader and member of David's Union Lodge, assigned his property to David Wilkinson, as did John Kennedy the following day. Kennedy's assignment suggests that David's financial position was strong enough to withstand the pressure from creditors, but a more fundamental reason is that David had endorsed several of Kennedy's loans. Within days, David Wilkinson & Co. had collapsed, along with the nail manufactory and the Orleans Manufacturing Company. "D. W. has gone down the falls," Slater wrote on July 29. "His failure is a serious one, and it affects my mind and body seriously, and purse too for the present."[10]

Although David was generally overextended, his most severe financial woes were related to his Wilkinsonville holdings. When the Sutton Bank had begun approving loans in December 1828, he had been the first recipient, for $21,000, and Hezekiah Howe the second, for $10,400, and they continued to borrow throughout the first half of 1829. In every case they were the endorsers of each other's loans. As his situation grew worse in March, David mortgaged the Centre Falls property to Samuel Slater for $100,000. Although he had held a mortgage on this property two years prior to these events, Slater had no intention of owning the Wilkinsonville factories, and appeared confident that David's debts would be paid and this second mortgage voided. But even this substantial infusion of cash did not provide the liquidity Wilkinson required, nor did a mortgage of the smaller Lower Falls Estate to the Sutton Bank on June 1. Implausible as it may seem, the bank continued to lend to David and Hezekiah in early June, totaling over $20,000, again secured by each other's endorsement.

(Equally strange, on June 1, just as things were falling apart, Slater took out a $1,250 loan from the Sutton Bank—endorsed by David Wilkinson.) Then, on July 24, in a loud echo of his brothers' bankruptcy in Pawtucket, came David's own official failure, as he assigned all of his Sutton area property—factories, dams, machinery, tools, cloth on hand, even cattle—to Rhode Island lawyer John Whipple. A week later he also assigned his 385 shares in the Sutton Bank to Whipple, who in turn transferred them to the bank on August 30. In a public demonstration of Wilkinson's failure, the shares in the bank he had started were sold at an auction held at the hotel he had built in the center of Wilkinsonville. Howe's shares were sold as well, as his connection with the bank deteriorated further. Although still president in name, Hezekiah had not attended a board meeting since July 8, and at the annual meeting in October he was replaced by Joshua Leland.[11]

Now that control of the bank had shifted to local shareholders and directors, they used every means to shore up the capital of the institution. On July 27, the Worcester County Sheriff was instructed "to attach the goods and Estate of David Wilkinson of North Providence . . . to the value of Thirty Thousand Dollars, and for want thereof to take the body of the said David, if he may be found in your precinct, and him safely keep . . . to answer unto the President Directors and Company of the Sutton Bank." The bank expected $30,000, plus damages, by the end of August. With the bank suing its founder, the dream of the mill village had become a nightmare.[12]

As David's endorser and mortgage holder, Slater now acted to protect his own interests by assuming Wilkinson's share of the Providence Steam Cotton Mill. Then, on September 14, he foreclosed on the primary Wilkinsonville operation, the Centre Falls Estate, "for the purpose of managing said estate so as to receive the rents and profits thereof in part satisfaction of the debt due from the said Wilkinson to the said Slater." Attorney John Whipple was present as the assignee, and gave over "quiet and peaceable possession of the premises." David estimated that he had spent $150,000 on Wilkinsonville, and now it was completely beyond his control.[13]

After the foreclosure, Slater made every effort to protect his new investment. Keeping the Centre Falls factory operational was no easy matter, since the textile business continued to be depressed. At his Providence Steam Cotton Mill, for example, Slater's agent told their distributor that "[w]e rely on your best exertions to get for us all [the goods] are worth—we dare not ask for all they cost." At Wilkinsonville, David's son John was helping in the struggle to meet the payroll. The company clerk wrote John at the end of November that "Amasa [Roberts] is in want of about 600 $ to pay his help the last fortnight. there is in the bank about 100 $ [and] in store 20 $. he wishes you to equip yourself with the [illegible] so that he can pay them off on Wednesday. he thinks if you get 425 there that we can get along." Young John apparently never resided at Wilkinsonville but, along with the other Wilkinson and Howe children, he had been a small shareholder in the bank, a stake they would all soon forfeit. Now, not yet twenty, John did what he could to alleviate the distress of his father's failure.[14]

Early in 1830, the last vestige of David Wilkinson's Sutton holdings, the Lower Falls Estate, was sold at auction to an agent for John Slater (Samuel's brother) and John Slater 2nd (Samuel's son) for $11,515. Since David had mortgaged this smaller factory to the Sutton Bank in June, the proceeds went to the bank. David's mortgages of his Wilkinsonville properties proved to be fortunate, because it forced the Slaters to take an interest in the continued operation of the factories, which kept Sutton's industrial economy afloat. The Wilkinsonville mills now became known as the Sutton Manufacturing Company, which, as part of the network of Slater companies in Massachusetts, Rhode Island, Connecticut, and New Hampshire, carried on a successful business throughout the nineteenth century. The Sutton Bank also survived, because the directors were able to retain their capital by selling the shares originally belonging to Wilkinson and Howe (about two-thirds of the bank's capital) to other shareholders who were local to the Sutton area and not overextended in textiles. Needless to say, they were considerably more cautious in their lending practices.[15]

In Pawtucket, the story was very different: the economic and social losses were staggering. The mainstays of the iron business—David Wilkinson & Co., A. & I. Wilkinson, Stephen Jenks & Sons—went out of business and their assets were sold or auctioned. The symbols of the textile industry that had catalyzed Pawtucket's growth—the Stone Mill (A. & I. Wilkinson), the Green Mill (brother-in-law Timothy Greene), and the historic Old Mill (Slater)—had either changed hands or were in bankruptcy proceedings. The newspapers were packed with notices of assignment of business and personal property: eight notices were prominently displayed on the front page of the June 29 *Manufacturers and Farmers Journal*. David's usual newspaper advertisement for iron goods and machinery was replaced with one headlined "Machinery For Sale . . . sold low to close a concern."[16]

The extensive list of auction items indicates the impressive scale of David's iron business. There was a ton of cast steel and various castings for carding machines, looms, and spinning frames. There were also a great many finished machines, including thirty carders, eight spinning frames, two mules, and thirty-four of the power looms that he had perfected. But the list includes only one grinder and one screw machine—a hint that he kept his lathes and other machine tools for possible future work, an allowance specified in Rhode Island's recently revised Act for the Relief of Insolvent Debtors.[17]

The Wilkinsons and Slater had been very active in Pawtucket real estate, and now it was all on the auction block. One newspaper notice placed by the assignees of Abraham and Isaac listed fifteen houses, as well as numerous parcels of land, several water privileges, and the old Anchor Shop on Sargent's Trench. Samuel Slater placed an ad offering seven house lots, seventy acres of woodland,

and "the Brick House which the subscriber now lives in." Advertisements for David's property listed forty-six house lots in Pawtucket and twenty-five acres known as the Great Meadow on the Moshassuck River in Smithfield. Hezekiah Howe also assigned all of his property, and David's nephews were forced to auction land that their grandfather Oziel had bequeathed in his will.[18]

Another measure of the personal loss sustained by the affected families is the assignment or sale of pews at St. Paul's Episcopal church, one of the symbols of status in Pawtucket village. Pews that had originally cost more than $250 in 1817 were trading for $150 in the summer of 1829. In September 1830, Slater advertised six pews for sale, and the following month David announced the sale of his six and a half pews. One of David's pews went through several owners before it was repurchased in 1833 by Edward S. Wilkinson, son of David's late brother and partner Daniel, for seventy-five dollars, an indication not only of the dislocation of the once stable Pawtucket elite, but also of the shrinking value of church "stock" in the wake of the financial crisis. A related victim of the crash was the newly chartered First Universalist Society, which had just completed the auction of their pews when the crisis occurred, leaving so many members unable to meet their obligations that the church building was sold to the Baptists and the society disbanded. This mix of religion and market capitalism only added to the sense of depression in the village.[19]

Of course it was not only the elite who suffered. Local shop owners who sold jewelry, hats, clocks, and watches to the wealthy were hurt by the loss of business. The Mozart Society, which had been putting on very popular concerts since 1826, saw a severe drop in attendance after 1829, because fewer people could afford the admission price of twenty-five cents. More seriously affected were the factory workers who now faced increased job insecurity, and risked expulsion from town by residents who refused to pay for their welfare. Ironically, given his role in banking for the benefit of the manufacturing elite, David had been working on a commendable project that would have brought a savings bank to the workers of the village. In 1827, he and Samuel Slater had become charter members of the Pawtucket Institution for Savings, but the crash delayed the opening of the bank until 1836, by which time Slater was dead and David had left town.[20]

Adding to the gloom was the death of Sam Patch, a local folk hero whose daring rooftop leaps into the Blackstone River had provided popular entertainment for Pawtucket's working people, especially those who, like Patch, labored all day in the cotton factories. "I have seen boys, and even men, jump from the bridge and the peak of the Yellow Mill," David Benedict recalled. "They would go down feet foremost, and, like divers, remain out of sight till the spectators began to fear for their safety, when out they would shoot like a sturgeon, in an erect position, quite above the surface, and swim off, and climb up the rocks for another jump." When a citizens' group put an end to this dangerous, and to some minds indecent, entertainment, Sam embarked on a career as a celebrated jumper, thrilling crowds at Passaic, Niagara Falls, and elsewhere. On Friday November 13, 1829, in a jump at Genesee Falls, Sam's luck ran out.[21] Pawtucket seemed to have lost its financial, iron, textile, tool-making, and popular heroes all at once.

Amid this general atmosphere of personal loss, anxiety, and shattered pride came a fundamental shift in the management of Pawtucket's commercial affairs. Abraham and Isaac Wilkinson, now in their early sixties, simply retired from business and lived on what they managed to salvage from the crash. David's brother and partner Daniel had died in 1826, and thus was spared these painful proceedings, although his son Edward, along with Abraham's son George, struggled to recover some parts of the older generation's business. Slater sold out of Pawtucket completely and focused most of his attention on his mills in Massachusetts. Reverend David Benedict, a keen observer of Pawtucket affairs since settling there in 1804, lamented many years later: "Indeed, from the time of the great breakdown in 1829, when a large number of heavy failures took place among the large owners of property of the village . . . an unfavorable state of things has existed. A large amount of the property has been in the hands of non-residents, and the business has been done by agents. In this state of things there has, to all appearances, been a want of calculation for, and of an interest in, the prosperity of the place, any further from their rents and profits have been concerned."[22]

Slater's abandonment of Pawtucket was a serious blow to the village's business prospects. Aside from the endorsements, he had managed his business affairs conservatively, and his $1 million in personal assets assured his survival. But he paid a price: to cover the $300,000 debt for David Wilkinson, John Kennedy, and others, he was forced to take out loans and to sell much of his property. Slater was staggered emotionally as well. Not only did his long-time partner William Almy refuse to give him a loan, but Almy took advantage of Slater's vulnerable position to acquire full control of Slatersville and the Old Mill in Pawtucket. (Slater had a special fondness for the "Old Factory," which was "old and decrepit like myself." He later repurchased Slatersville but never again did business in Pawtucket village where it all started.) Although his old friend Moses Brown saw to it that he could continue his manufacturing operations while he restructured his affairs, Slater's faith in his kinship and business network was shattered, contributing to the poor health that plagued him until his death in 1835.[23]

The only mistake Slater made in this affair had been to acquiesce in the normal kinship practice of endorsing loans. Yet, except for his surprise at the extent of Kennedy's debts, he never directly expressed his opinion of the business acumen of the relatives and friends who nearly brought down his empire. There may be a clue to his feelings from his friend and biographer George White, who noticed that in the margin of one of his papers from this period Slater had jotted (from Jeremiah 17:11): "As the partridge sitteth on eggs, and hatches them not, so he that getteth riches, and not by right, shall leave them in the midst of his days, and at his end shall be a fool." Perhaps more revealing of his judgment is an unpublished letter to a Rhode Islander who held a Slater-endorsed $850 note from the now-bankrupt Pawtucket manufacturer Jabel Ingraham. While agreeing to pay, Slater asked for leniency since "this demand did not arise from money lost either at a Horse Race or at the billiard table, but by being taken in by another set of jockeys." The plural suggests that Ingraham was not the only "jockey" that had disappointed him.[24]

~

The 1829 depression was a watershed event in Pawtucket history, and while the Wilkinsons were at the center of events, there are factors to be considered in their defense. Neither the courts, nor the press, nor public opinion judged them guilty of illegal behavior. The insider lending at their banks was in fact the norm of accommodation banking of the period.[25] The fundamental causes of the downturn—the decline in the prices of cotton goods and the overexpansion of capacity—were beyond their control, and these problems extended far beyond New England, as British manufacturers dumped textiles on world markets. The contraction of credit, remarked one Philadelphian, "was so sudden and abrupt, that it has caught even prudent men unawares." The Wilkinsons were also disadvantaged by the lack of corporate structure and the relatively low capitalization of Rhode Island businesses, although a look at Smith Wilkinson's continued existence is instructive. His prudent management of the Pomfret factory (a partnership) ensured its survival in 1829, as well as through the much more difficult trial of the Panic of 1837. It appears that Smith, who had been educated from the age of ten in the textile business, stuck more cautiously with his core competency and avoided the overexpansion that brought down his brothers.[26]

Having survived previous downturns in 1815, 1819, and 1825, the Wilkinsons might honestly have believed they could ride out this one as well. Yet in this tight credit situation, what characterized their actions was an irresponsible extension of their businesses, as if, as one critic put it, they possessed "an injudicious and overweening confidence in the power and stability of manufacturing corporations." Compelled to extend and then to protect their beleaguered businesses, yet lacking the cash to do so, they looked to the easy credit available from the banks that they had founded for this very purpose.[27]

Access to credit aggravated rather than eased their situation because of the extent of their borrowing. John Kennedy's $115,000 liability surprised everyone. David's loans and mortgage that had been secured by Samuel Slater amounted to an equally astonishing $140,000, and if we include the money he owed the Sutton Bank, Millbury Bank, and Manufacturers Bank, and his endorsements of other borrowers, the total approaches $200,000.[28] This level of financial extension might have been salvageable by someone with Slater's wealth (and conservative business practices), but very few New England businessmen, apart from the Boston Associates, were in this league. Another reason is that, despite years of involvement in banking, the Wilkinsons were not professional bankers. Rather, to use Naomi Lamoreaux's phrase, they were leaders of "investment clubs" created for the purpose of supplying credit to their metals and textile enterprises. Their need to expand or protect their already overextended businesses overrode the safeguards that more professional or impartial bankers would have insisted on, and thus they exploited their insider lending privileges far beyond the limits of safety.[29]

Exacerbating the credit problem was the fact that the capital resources of these banks were, in the words of one economic historian, "largely fictitious." The Wilkinson kin had paid for their Sutton Bank shares with borrowed money—that is, they contributed money for the purchase of the bank stock then borrowed it back with the stock itself put up as security for the loans. According to a congressional report, the bank even went so far as to borrow $50,000 in specie from the City Bank of Boston for one day in order to be certified by the state commissioners that the bank had met its requirements of incorporation.

Even with fictitious assets at startup, other banks survived because, as a bank's stock increased in value over time, insiders would sell some of their shares and "real" money would represent an increasing percentage of the bank's capital stock. Having opened its doors only a few months before trouble started, the Sutton Bank faced a crisis when it was most vulnerable. But responsibility must be directed at Wilkinson and Hezekiah Howe for their evasion of specie requirements and mismanagement of the bank's loans as well as for the overextension of their businesses that drove them to seek such risky levels of credit in the first place.[30]

Had there been substantial stock ownership by investors other than Wilkinsons, there might have been better diversification of the capital base of their banks. Instead, the bulk of the stock was held by one extended family, all engaged in related businesses that were under pressure, and the founders and directors loaned nearly all of the capital back to themselves. An astonishing 88 percent of the Sutton Bank's capital available for loans went to Wilkinson family members and their Rhode Island associates. Worse, the circular endorsements, such as David and Hezekiah providing surety for each other's loans, provided too narrow a base over which to spread the credit risk.[31]

While the *Pawtucket Chronicle* opined that "the conduct of our own monied institutions during these pressing times has been such as to deserve the *serious attention,* if not the indignation of the public," bankers generally encountered only mild public censure. The fact that there was no finding of fraud (which would have made the directors liable for the losses) and that neither the industry-friendly *Manufacturers and Farmers Journal* nor the Jacksonian *Republican Herald* sought to blame the Wilkinsons for the Farmers and Mechanics failure indicates the degree to which credit banking was viewed as a private matter. A Newport acquaintance told Abraham Wilkinson that "the extensive mischiefs attendant on your failure were by the best men in society attributed to errors of judgment and not of intentions." In the public mind, banks incorporated for lending were expected to be tied up in the business affairs of their founders. As Nathan Appleton observed in 1831, "The public have a deep interest in the solidity and good management of a bank of circulation; whilst they have comparatively none in the management of a bank employing their own funds, in making discounts [loans] only, or in buying and selling bills of exchange."[32]

Although banking was sufficiently implicated in the depression for the Rhode Island legislature to deny charters to new banks until 1831, the "great smash up of 1829" was not primarily a banking crisis. It would be more accurate to describe it as a downturn in the dominant manufacturing sector whose too intimate association with a few banks triggered a panic throughout the financial and industrial markets of the region. Its effects spread far beyond the Wilkinson holdings: one of every seven Rhode Island companies went out of business and many textile manufacturers who survived were forced to retrench. Even Patrick Tracy Jackson, speaking of the heavily capitalized Lowell factories, complained in early 1830 of "the present distressed state of our business, both as machine builders and manufacturers."[33] In the long view of nineteenth-century history, this downturn fits the pattern of frequent and poorly understood boom and bust cycles of the period. What transformed an "ordinary" contraction into a southern New England crisis was the connection between the Wilkinson-controlled banks and the suffering textile industry, the fact that the Wilkinsons were so highly concentrated in that one sector, the degree of their overextension of credit, and the particular mismanagement of the banks with which they were associated.[34]

If the public did not question the integrity of bank directors, there was considerable resentment directed toward manufacturers—many of the same people, of course—for their heedless expansion of their businesses. One proponent of manufacturing defended the industry as a whole, but blamed the crisis on "the reckless and indiscreet [who] have chosen to throw themselves into the current, without chart, pilot, or compass, and without knowing their own strength, or considering their resources." The most bitter condemnation came from the editor of the *Pawtucket Chronicle,* toward the end of Summer 1829. He warned his readers of the growing "tyranny" of the mill owners, whose rule was "founded upon riches."

> Riches are dissipated by extravagance, or lost by imprudence, or taken away by a concurrence of unforeseen events leaving their former possessors in want of the same necessaries and privileges which they have withheld from others. Is this not an every day occurrence? Need we look twice, in the circle around us, for distress and poverty among those who have lorded it, with a high hand, over their poorer neighbours?

The writer saw some justice in the fall of the mighty: "the same All-Wise Providence that created the bane has also provided the antidote."[35] David Wilkinson, his brothers, Samuel Slater, and other Pawtucket manufacturers had, in this view, received their divine retribution.

In the aftermath of the crisis, it was a time to reflect, and to amend one's life if it were perceived to have been in error. Those who saw these sad events as simply a problem of business diversification might agree with a letter in the *Pawtucket Chronicle* suggesting that it was a good opportunity for manufacturers to develop a new market producing "Negro cloth," a coarse fabric considered fit for slaves. Others, more sensitive to the larger issues, might concur with a very different editorial, entitled "Farmers." Its ending was appropriate, for those who were listening: "The late distressing times will be a source of much good, and a means of bringing folks to their senses in this particular, and lead many to leave the crowded and uneven walks of speculation for a life of usefulness and contentment."[36]

Losing Wilkinsonville was not the most difficult part of David's ordeal. Despite his conception and funding of this mill village, he was an absentee owner who, he admitted, "resided at a distance of about 30 miles from the Centre Falls Estate—was there but seldom, perhaps not more than once a month," and thus had no deep social ties to the community. The bank's activities had been curtailed, but few locals would have been affected, since it had been created for the benefit of its expansion-minded directors rather than to circulate money in the local economy. In fact, as the Rhode Islanders sold their Sutton Bank stock, the shares were purchased by local businessmen. Moreover, the factory stayed in business under the ownership of Samuel Slater and later his sons. If the village economy would survive, perhaps the factory workers and local farmers felt no great loss at the departure of the village founder.[37]

If David could have retreated to his home town to recover from the financial loss and wounded pride of Wilkinsonville, it all might have been tolerable. But in Pawtucket his failure was complete, especially the mill that he had shared with his father and where he had done his most innovative tool and machine making, including the sturdy, low-cost power looms that were installed in factories throughout the eastern United States. This machine shop had been his love and his legacy and his source of greatest pride. Now his factories were being examined by potential purchasers, creditors had attached his landholdings, and his personal property was for sale at auction. In his insolvency petition to the state Supreme Court, he estimated his total loss at $289,280. The damage extended well beyond Pawtucket and Wilkinsonville, to other locations in Rhode Island, Bristol County in Massachusetts, Killingly and Stafford, Connecticut, and as far as South Carolina, where he had textile and steamboat interests. The effects of his personal disaster were widespread.[38]

David's laconic version of the crash was: "In 1829 we all broke down." There is no mention in his reminiscences of what went wrong, in fact no mention of Wilkinsonville at all. He and other disgraced manufacturers were not forced to leave Pawtucket. Abraham and Isaac retired there, Timothy Greene and his sons remained, and although Slater moved to Webster, he and his wife maintained a residence in the village. As the mills began to operate again under new ownership, there was a need for Wilkinson expertise. David's nephew Edward found work at a factory once belonging to the family in the late summer and early fall of 1829, and Abraham's son George was able to repurchase A. & I. Wilkinson's Stone Mill toward the end of 1830.[39]

For the remainder of 1829 and throughout 1830, David settled his affairs in Pawtucket as best he could, but the psychological strain of his unqualified failure resulted in what he described as a "severe fit of sickness." He had sorely strained his relationship with Samuel Slater, and must have felt even worse at the loss of buildings and land that had once been his father's. He had let down the entire kinship network with what, in retrospect, can only be seen as reckless overexpansion and dubious banking practices. While Americans no longer tended to equate financial failure with moral failure, as they had in colonial times, insolvency still had complex social costs, and public disapprobation might call into question a man's independence. Despite his embarrassment, however, David wanted very much to stay, as a letter from a prospective buyer of the Wilkinson Mill makes clear. "After you left here I was called on by David Wilkinson, who had seen us looking at his property in Pawtucket, to enquire whether we had any idea of purchasing," Samuel Arnold wrote in November 1830 to his nephew (and David's fellow machinist-inventor) Aza Arnold. "He informed me that he was making arrangements to try to get hold of that property again, and was very anxious to succeed, as it appears to be the only opening for him to do anything in Pawtucket, and that he was very loth to quit the place."[40]

But he did not stay. As he later recalled, "Although I was sixty years of age, and in very bad health, I thought I would move away, and see if I could not earn my own living." He had lost his means of support, and was too ill—and perhaps too proud—to work for someone else. Moreover, his chances of getting the credit necessary to get back into business were slim, a common consequence of insolvency in the antebellum period. Even if legally freed from debt, bankrupts often lost access to capital for entrepreneurial ventures.[41] Not only would banks shun him, but his network of endorsers was shattered. Fortunately, Wilkinson had an alternative. When remaining in Pawtucket was no longer a viable option, he had a place to go where his prospects looked brighter.

That place was Cohoes, New York, where he had been one of the founders of the Cohoes Company in 1826. Apparently, while he was losing everything he owned in New England, he managed to hold on to his shares in the New York company, or at least to stay on good terms with the owners. Very little had happened at Cohoes since David's first involvement in1826, but about the time that the Wilkinson empire was starting to crumble, Hugh White—the brother of Erie Canal engineer and Cohoes Company founder Canvass White—was planning his move to the village to begin implementing the plan for exploiting the immense water power of the Cohoes Falls.

Canvass White had patented his "Water Lime Cement" for use in canal building in 1820, and Hugh, after being admitted to the bar, joined his older brother in the waterproof cement business. Cement sales slowed after the Erie Canal was completed in 1825, and Canvass focused his energies on harnessing the water power at Cohoes, and was elected president when he, Wilkinson, Peter Remsen, and others founded the Cohoes Company in 1826. Due to his brother's other business activities and later ill health, Hugh White became the supervisor of the works at Cohoes. In late 1829, Hugh had prepared all the lumber for a new house, and had it shipped by canal boat to the new location, where the house was nearly completed by the time he arrived with his family in April 1830. Cohoes was no more than an area of scattered farms, one small manufacturing company, and a canal boat landing at this point, and his task was a difficult and lonely one. "I should advise you to have nothing to do in any [shape?] with the old man at the Cohoes bridge or any of that class living about there," his brother Canvass warned. "They are a worthless troublesome sort to have any dealings with or even conversations on business." With his brother otherwise engaged, Hugh White needed the assistance of an expert in canals, water power, and machinery, and he found his man in David Wilkinson, whose background included the creation of his own industrial village. It was sometime in late 1830 or early 1831 that "urgent solicitations and liberal offers" from the company directors convinced David to leave Pawtucket.[42]

This was not the kind of voluntary mobility that Wilkinson had once engaged in, the curiosity-satisfying sort of travel available to him with a secure family and economic base in Pawtucket. Nor was it like his father's moving the family to Pawtucket when David was twelve, since that was only a few miles distant, and Oziel remained within the Quaker network. When Paul Moody and his family moved from Waltham to Lowell, it was a corporate transfer that was not only orchestrated and paid for by the corporation, but actually placed the Moodys closer to their original home. David's was a wrenching move that uprooted the family to an unfamiliar location with uncertain financial prospects. Mobility was less an option than it was a last resort.

"I moved with my family to Cohoes Falls," he wrote, "and there fixed my new home." His wife Martha, then fifty-four years of age, left no record of her thoughts about quitting the relative luxury of Pawtucket and long-established ties on both sides of the family, but surely the primitive and lonely life in Cohoes was taxing. The move, in April 1831, was made much more bearable by the fact that their children, Albert (26), John (20), and Ardelia (19) came with them, as did a few friends from Pawtucket. The following month, David's youngest sister Lydia and her husband, Hezekiah Howe—like David, disgraced at Wilkinsonville—also began a new life at Cohoes with their four children. There is no record of the Wilkinsons' journey, except that they arrived by canal boat. Most likely they departed from Providence on one of the steamships that left for New York two or three times per week, heading down Narragansett Bay, then west along the Rhode Island and Connecticut coasts to New York City, where they would have boarded another boat to make their way up the Hudson River to the Erie Canal, and then by canal boat to Cohoes.[43]

The accommodations in the village at this time were very limited. The Howe family stayed at the Richard Heamstreet Tavern for a short time, then moved into a house that had been built for employees of the Cohoes Manufacturing Company. The Wilkinsons settled in what was known as the Whiting house, close to the Mohawk River. There were at most twenty-five buildings in the area. The nearest town of any size, Troy, was two hours away by canal boat. One early historian noted that "it was almost impossible to obtain the commonest necessities of life; groceries, and those of an inferior description, could only be procured at the canal stores, at either extremity of the village, and fresh meat was a luxury only to be found occasionally at the junction."[44] How far the Wilkinsons had traveled from fine hat and watch shops and Mozart Society concerts!

Figure 8.1

This postcard depicts Cohoes Village and Falls, a few years after David Wilkinson's death. The town had developed considerably since his pioneering efforts there in the 1830s.

Courtesy of the Waterford Historical Museum and Cultural Center, Waterford, New York.

They did what they could to make the area habitable. The very day after the Howes arrived, David and Hezekiah organized St. John's Episcopal Church, and with the Reverend Orange Clark of nearby Waterford officiating, services were held the following Sunday in the schoolhouse on Oneida Street. David and Hugh White were church wardens; Hezekiah and David's son Albert were vestrymen. Taking charge of Sunday school were David's daughter Ardelia and her cousin Maria Howe. The church—a small wooden structure, thirty-eight by forty-eight feet, with a very plain interior—was built the following year by Joshua R. Clarke, the Pawtucket carpenter who arrived with the Wilkinsons. The church bell was a gift from David Wilkinson, and he paid the minister's salary, although how a recent bankrupt could afford this generosity remains a mystery. The total cost of the church was under $1,500, of which the Cohoes Company contributed $500. The company also supplied the land for the church, which David had insisted upon as a condition of his coming to Cohoes. Just west of the church a new brick house was built for Hugh White, and at the

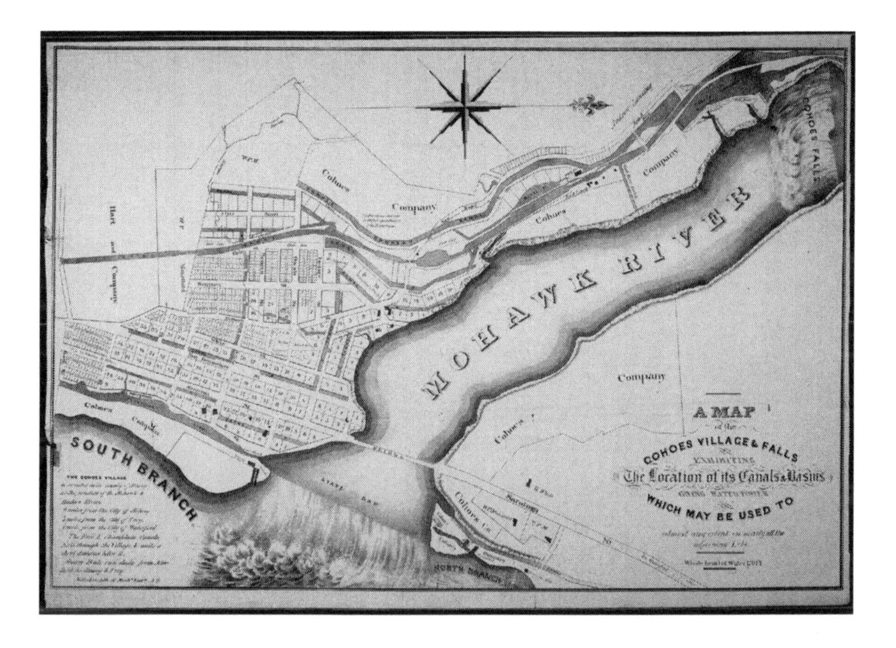

Figure 8.2
This map of Cohoes Village c. 1835 shows the Cohoes Company's extensive canals, David Wilkinson's industrial space (lots 6 and 7), and Wilkinson's house at the corner of Mohawk and Oneida, described as "the most imposing residence the village had yet seen."
Courtesy of the New York State Library, Manuscripts and Special Collections, Albany, New York.

corner of Oneida and Mohawk streets was the Wilkinsons' new home, "the most imposing residence the village had yet seen."[45] Given David's recent financial problems, it seems likely that his house was owned by the Cohoes Company.

The business plan for the Cohoes Company was similar to the development managed by the Proprietors of Locks and Canals at Lowell. The Cohoes Company would not engage directly in manufacturing but rather would build the industrial infrastructure of power canals and mill sites, and invite capitalists to lease the facilities. It looked promising, given the tremendous potential of the Cohoes Falls—which was capable of producing considerably more power than Lowell—plus it had the transportation network afforded by the Erie and Champlain canals. The initial effort was the construction of a wooden dam and the grid of power canals that diverted water from the Erie Canal to the industrial area, and the laying out of lots for the potential mills and machine shops. David would get an industrial site for his own use, as Canvass explained to Hugh early in 1831: "I will make a square basin next to the canal and place Mr. Wilkinson's lot next to it—and then extend the [illegible] lots along the bank towards the machine shop lots."[46]

By the summer of 1831, the Wilkinson machine shop was in operation. Water from the Erie Canal was channeled through a waste gate into a small ditch to provide power for David's equipment. (The absence of machine tools in his inventory of assets for his bankruptcy proceedings suggests that he salvaged lathes and other machine tools from his shops to employ at Cohoes.) As at Pawtucket, he concentrated on the construction of textile machinery, but because the potential customers in Cohoes had not yet materialized, some of the machinery he built was shipped to a factory in Seneca Falls. Also during this initial period, Hezekiah Howe set up the village's first general store, located in a new building at Three Locks and run by his elder son. Howe also used the store as a post office when he was appointed postmaster in 1833.[47] It is interesting to note that the brothers-in-law did not propose a village bank.

By mid-1832 much of the infrastructure had been built, including the rebuilding of the original wooden dam, which had been destroyed by ice in January, and the completion of the first two power canals. But only a few of the anticipated capitalists had arrived, and the Whites were clearly worried. "My spirits have been kept up by the anticipation of soon realizing some advantage from the Cohoes property, but if Miller and Wilkinson leave it will be hard to reinstate confidence," Canvass wrote to Hugh in May. E. L. Miller had moved from Charleston, South Carolina, with the intention of engaging in cotton manufacture, and built a large residence on Mohawk Street. His mill was completely furnished with machinery by David Wilkinson. But no sooner were his home and factory completed than Miller fell ill, "became dissatisfied with all his investments here, abandoned his idea of engaging in business, and went to New York, leaving his property to be disposed of for what it would bring." All the machinery that David had built for Miller's factory was removed and sent to New Jersey to be sold. Another promising development, the satinet manufactory of John Tillinghast, who had arrived with the Wilkinsons in the spring of 1831, did not work out as expected and was closed.[48]

Despite the gloom, there were bright spots, such as Egberts and Bailey's mechanized knitting operation, which took up part of the abandoned cotton factory building in 1832. Knitting is the business that eventually made Cohoes famous, but it started slowly. Moreover, the knitting looms were made by Bailey—not by Wilkinson—and because the yarn was at first imported from elsewhere, there would be no spinning equipment purchased from David's shop. Whether the later expansion to include yarn production resulted in sales of carding and spinning machinery from Wilkinson's machine shop is unknown. But the Cohoes Company investors remained optimistic, and in 1833–34 there was a major expansion of the power canal system, especially the construction of the one and three-quarter–mile-long upper canal that even the Lowell engineers might envy.[49]

The Cohoes Company founders' plan for another Lowell was actually becoming a reality, but perhaps too slowly to realize at the time. The 1836 edition of Thomas F. Gordon's *Gazetteer of New York* extolled the formidable industrial benefits of the Cohoes Company—the 120-foot head of water furnished in six levels of power canals, the minimum flow of one thousand cubic feet of water per minute, capable of driving three to four million spindles—and concluded that "the advantages of this position for manufactures are unquestionably the greatest in the state." But it was still about *potential.* Ten years after the founding of the company, Cohoes village had a mere sixty dwellings, and the only businesses it could claim were the Wilkinsons' machine shop and foundry, the knitting mill, and two small factories, one producing carpets and the other axes and edge tools.[50] Lowell at this point was just becoming incorporated as a *city,* with eleven huge multifactory corporations and 17,633 inhabitants.

There are a number of reasons for the failure of the founders' dream to materialize in the first ten years. They had started slowly, with little progress on the physical plant between 1826 and 1831, and slight population growth. It is possible that the nearby city of Troy, already an industrial success, drew capital away from Cohoes. A few promising customers, like Mr. Miller, had experienced a change of heart and moved away. An outbreak of Asiatic cholera in 1832 frightened off several businessmen who "took it for granted that the race would soon become extinct, and that it would be useless to make any business arrangements." To David, however, the failure was largely political. "The prospects at Cohoes were flattering for a time," he wrote in 1846. "But Nullification, Loco-focory, Jacksonianism, Free trade, and such abominations, killed the new village just born." In particular, foreign investors who had counted on tariff protection now considered Cohoes less advantageous. As David explained, "Europeans who were applying for water power at Cohoes, at this time, went away, saying, now we were going to have free trade; they could do our work cheaper at "ome' than they could in this Country, and they would build their factories there."[51]

This outburst of partisan sentiment not only helps explain part of the reason for Cohoes' slow development, but more importantly gives us some insight into Wilkinson's view of American political culture. It is not surprising that he would object to free trade, given that most manufacturers supported tariff protection. The *Manufacturers and Farmers Journal,* the newspaper that David had helped launch in 1820, had a strong pro-tariff policy.[52] His disdain for Jackson is clear, and probably predated the growth problems at Cohoes (Pawtucket voters had overwhelmingly preferred John Quincy Adams to Jackson in 1828). David's calling specific attention to the radical Democrats known as Loco-Focos indicates his strong opposition to their platform of free trade and abolition of monopoly privileges. Clearly David's political sentiments were with the Whigs, the anti-Jackson party whose platform promoted the banking, internal improvements, and industrial development that matched his own views. Given his staunch support for the Masons, David probably would have seen the current mix of Jacksonianism and antimasonry as anathema. This political sentiment was not isolated to New York, as a Democratic/Antimasonic coalition had come to power in Rhode Island in 1836—and passed banking reform legislation. Perhaps that allayed his longing for his home state.[53]

But he apparently could no longer remain in Cohoes to wait for the expected development to occur. He turned over the management of the machine shop to his son John, who also ran the Cohoes Iron Foundry, and rented the upper story of the machine shop to the partnership of Hawes and Goodwin, producers of wood veneers. "We were compelled, now, to get our living where we could," David explained, "to go abroad, if we could not get work at home." So, just as he had done years ago when he was investigating lathes or steam engines, David resumed his peripatetic ways, but now he traveled for financial survival in the wake of an economic disaster (partly of his own making) and the sluggish progress of his plan for recovery. It was hard and lonely work, far from his wife and children. The direction of his travels was north to Canada, west to Ohio, and south to Virginia—never eastward to the familiar ground of Pawtucket and the Blackstone Valley. This mobility was involuntary and arduous. On the positive side, David demonstrated that he was resourceful and undaunted by physically demanding work, traits that he developed early and that now helped him manage the economic problems that beset him. Perhaps invigorated by this outdoor work and the opportunity to be productive, he "recovered [his] health wonderfully."[54]

When Wilkinson later listed the locations where he found work during this period, the first named was the Delaware and Raritan Canal. Designed as a freight route across New Jersey linking Philadelphia to New York, the canal was begun in 1830 under the direction of chief engineer Canvass White, and completed in 1834, the same year that White died of consumption just after moving to Florida. White's work on the Erie Canal had caught the attention of internal improvements advocates such as Henry Clay, and it is likely that David's acquaintance with the now famous canal engineer provided the work opportunity at the Delaware & Raritan. (There is credible evidence that David met Henry Clay, probably through Canvass White.) These work opportunities were not simply a matter of who he knew; David's experience constructing the iron wheels and gates for the Middlesex Canal locks and casting the draw for the Charles River Bridge in the 1790s made him a valuable contributor to the work on the canal.[55]

After his employment in New Jersey, Wilkinson went to work on "the St. Lawrence improvements, in Canada." Largely in response to the success of the Erie Canal, Canadian commercial and government interests had been working on an engineering project to improve navigation on the St. Lawrence River in order to create a deep shipping channel from the Great Lakes to the Atlantic Ocean by way of Montreal. While there had been much work done on regional canals in Canada before this period, it was during the mid-1830s that significant progress began to be made on the national plan.[56] How Wilkinson became connected to these events in Canada, and why he would work on a transportation system that competed with the interests of American internal improvements, are matters worth a closer look.

The connection appears to have been Benjamin Wright, chief engineer of the Erie Canal project, and close associate of David's partners Canvass and Hugh White. It is possible that David met Wright when the latter surveyed the Blackstone Canal in 1822. Wright was engaged as a planner of the St. Lawrence improvements, and it is likely that he involved David in the project. We know little about the work he did there, only that it was in the years 1835 and 1836, that at least part of the time was spent in Kingston (where the St. Lawrence River meets Lake Ontario), and that his son John, now about twenty-five, also worked on the project. This last point raises the question of what happened to the Wilkinsons' business interests in Cohoes. Ownership of the iron foundry was transferred, probably in the 1830s, to David's son-in-law Charles A. Olmsted. It appears that the machine shop had over time been transformed into industrial rental space. Most references to the "Wilkinson Machine Shop" in Cohoes after the mid-1830s are related to the dozen or so businesses that occupied parts of the building over the years rather than to a business owned and operated by David or his son. The building stayed in the family; when it was destroyed by fire in 1858, the owner was listed as "Mrs. C. A. Olmsted"—David's daughter Ardelia.[57]

Why the Wilkinsons would be working in Canada on a commercially competitive engineering project is somewhat less clear, though not inexplicable. First, Kingston, Ontario, is only about 150 miles northwest of Cohoes, not very far for a man with David's inclination for travel. It is also obvious that he needed work, and that the location was secondary. "Wherever I could find anything to do, I went," he explained.[58] Finally, it appears that even though he was a firm promoter of internal improvements in the United States, that did not mean he would refuse to lend his talents to a project across the border, especially a large undertaking that pushed the boundaries of current engineering.

David's restrained memoirs contain an uncharacteristically long and odd anecdote from this time in Canada:

> In 1835–6 while engaged on the St. Lawrence river, I met a gentleman at Kingston, who advised me to go back of the Rideau Lake, to get what I wanted, about seventy miles north of Kingston, to a village named Perth, which was given to the officers and soldiers who served in the late war with the United States. At the hotel in Perth, the landlord showed me a silver clasp, which was taken from the leg of a large eagle, which was shot in the village. The plate, or clasp, was . . . directed to Henry Clay. It was after the war, and the bearer of the express probably thought he might safely take a circuitous route through the British provinces. But these Canadians didn't like the name of Henry Clay; his policies had too anti-British a tendency to suit them, so they took the poor express eagle as a spy, I suppose, and refused to sell the clasp, at any price. Perhaps, they wanted to have the story to tell, that our American eagle had been struck to them, at least.[59]

While his precise meaning is difficult to interpret, perhaps this was his tongue-in-cheek way of saying that Henry Clay–hating eagle shooters were just a minor and amusing obstacle to doing business in Canada.

Wilkinson was noted for his physical strength; his friend George Taft wrote that "[h]e was physically educated; every muscle was developed, every nerve braced up, and his whole frame energized by manual labor." This outdoor work apparently suited him. "It is wonderful how I endured exposure to wet and cold, as I did," David wrote of his travels during this period. But he also continued to learn, think, and invent. In August 1835, he patented a canal lock gate improvement that featured a new "mode of adjusting the friction Roller." He improved upon it with another patent issued in April 1838. This sort of work was a continuation of the canal lock machinery he had built for the Middlesex Canal in the mid-1790s, but also showed that he had benefited from his association with Canvass White, who had become one of the nation's experts in the design of canal locks and their associated machinery. Drawing on his experience with water-powered machinery, David did an evaluation of the waterpower potential from Lake George with William J. McAlpine, a civil engineer for the state of New York and later chief engineer for the construction of the state capitol at Albany and the Washington Bridge. Together they wrote "Description of the Hydraulic Power at the Outlet of Lake George" (1839).[60]

Between projects, David returned to Cohoes to live with Martha and their daughter Ardelia, until she married Charles Olmsted in January 1835. If he was home for the wedding he most likely was there when twenty-year-old Hezekiah Junior died in March. He also had to deal with the deaths of Samuel Slater in April and his sister Lydia, Hezekiah's wife, at age fifty-three, the following year. David remained involved in church and civic affairs in the village, including financial support in 1834 or 1835 for the town's first fire engine, "a small rotary hand engine called the Excelsior No. 1," which provided good service in its day. His involvement was limited, however; he needed to work, and the opportunities were elsewhere. Yet at his age, mid-sixties now, he would not have been drawn away if he had perceived opportunities at home. Although slow to develop, the long-anticipated growth was beginning to show some promise in the creation of the Harmony Manufacturing Company in 1836. Wilkinson's Cohoes Company co-founders Peter Remsen, Stephen van Rensselaer, and Hugh White all became Harmony stockholders, but not David. (Joshua Clarke, who had come from Pawtucket with the Wilkinsons, was the builder of Harmony's first mill, and went on to play an important role in the economic and political life of Cohoes.) We can only speculate why David did not participate in the new enterprise. He may have been traveling far from Cohoes at the critical time, and most likely had little capital to invest anyway. Perhaps after his experience at Pawtucket and Wilkinsonville he had lost his appetite for speculation, and now put his trust in the simple value of hard work in his area of expertise, in ventures funded with someone else's money.[61]

By the late 1830s, the Harmony Company was still struggling, perhaps justifying David's pessimistic view of prospects at Cohoes. Once again he went on the road, this time to Ohio to work on the Sandy and Beaver Canal which connected the canal systems of Ohio and Pennsylvania. This was an ambitious undertaking, covering seventy-three miles, with ninety locks and two tunnels, one of which was more than a half-mile long. The civil engineering was so complicated that the middle section of the canal never worked properly, as the tunnels were considered unsafe. The canal company was incorporated in 1828, construction began in 1834, and then stopped during the national financial panic of 1837 and was not completed until 1848. We do not know the connections that brought Wilkinson to Ohio (this was not a Benjamin Wright project) or exactly when he was there. It was after 1836, and most likely during the first phase of the Sandy and Beaver construction that ended during the Panic of 1837, since work on the canal did not resume until 1845.[62]

His next engineering project can be more specifically dated to the early 1840s. Again with his son John, he returned to Canada to work on "the new Wire bridge, on the Ottawa river, at Bytown," as the city of Ottawa was originally called. Construction of Canada's first wire suspension bridge was begun in 1840 and completed in September 1844. How long David was there is unknown. All we really know from this time is that John met and married an Englishwoman, Elizabeth Ward, and decided to remain in Canada.[63]

The final project that David listed was simply "Virginia," and was most likely the James River and Kanawha Canal, which was begun in the mid-1830s and continued throughout the 1840s. At various times in the canal's long construction Benjamin Wright was the chief engineer, which gives us a plausible link to David. Wright died in 1842, ending a long association that had helped the Wilkinsons financially for a decade.[64]

Back in Cohoes in 1846, David appeared contented with his lot. "At this moment, being about seventy-six years old," he wrote, "I am hearty and well—enjoy my food as well as any one, and can bear a good deal of fatigue and exposure. Few men of my age enjoy their faculties and health better than I do." But he was clearly getting too old for long-distance travel and the rigors of canal and bridge building, and he now put his energy into local affairs, such as the establishment of a Masonic lodge, Cohoes Lodge No. 116, which he helped organize in the latter part of 1846. While Hezekiah kept up some links to Pawtucket—he was still paying taxes on two pews at St. Paul's Church in 1842—David appears to have maintained few connections.[65] He did write a long letter to his old friend, Reverend George Taft of Pawtucket, on December 1, 1846, in which he described his role in the industrial development of Rhode Island. Taft astutely kept the letter until 1861, at which time he passed it on to the Rhode Island Society for the Encouragement of Domestic Industry, who published it as "David Wilkinson's Reminiscences" in their *Transactions* for that year. "These are the recollections of an old man," David wrote to Taft, "and you will please take them for what they are worth. If they are worth anything to any one, I shall be glad. To yourself, I believe, they will be valuable, and be the means of recalling many pleasant incidents of olden times, and of an old friend."[66]

Despite his financial setbacks, David considered himself fortunate. "Have I not much to be thankful for?" he asked Reverend Taft. "I have, and I am most sincerely thankful to a merciful God, for the many and great blessings." But, perhaps like a good (albeit former) Quaker who believed that a merciful God would help those who helped themselves, or perhaps a Whig who believed in the power of the central government to reward those who had played a role in the internal improvements of the nation, David turned to the United States Congress for financial aid in his declining years. In late 1847, he petitioned for a delayed reward for his lifelong contributions to the country, specifically his invention of the slide lathe in 1798, which he had failed to exploit financially. In his letter to George Taft in 1846, he had taken a philosophical view. "I was always too much engaged in various business to look after and make profit out of my inventions," he wrote. "Other people, I hope, gained something by them." At the same time, he lamented that he had invented the lathe at a time when machine making "was only in its infancy," and his patent would expire before the lathe would see widespread adoption. "It certainly did run out without my deriving that benefit from the invention I was so justly entitled to. One solitary ten dollar note is surely but small recompense for an improvement that is worth all the other tools in use, in any workshop in the world, for finishing brass and iron work."[67]

With no prospects in Cohoes, no investments, and no longer able to make his living by traveling to remote civil engineering sites, he certainly needed a source of income. Writing his short reminiscences in 1846 may have gotten him thinking about his undervalued contribution to American tool and machine making, for the language of the Senate report on his petition closely resembles his letter to George Taft. The first mention of a "petition for the relief of David Wilkinson" in the congressional records is the presentation of the petition by Senator Edward A. Hannegan on January 18, 1848. Hannegan was a Democrat from Indiana, with no known direct link to Wilkinson, but his position as chairman of the Senate Committee on Roads and Canals is a likely connection. The petition, "praying compensation for the benefits which the government has derived from [Wilkinson's] inventions, for which he has received no pecuniary return," was referred to the Committee on Military Affairs. In parallel House activity, Representative John Quincy Adams sponsored a bill to compensate Wilkinson which was "laid on the Clerk's table" on January 25. Two possible connections link Wilkinson to the former president. One is Adams's previous support for a petition from Jeptha Avery Wilkinson, the inventive nephew of the nail and card maker Jeremiah from Cumberland. Another is that as president and later as a congressman, Adams had been a tireless proponent of the "American System" of internal improvements and tariff protection of domestic industries. Whatever the specific motivation, he now, at eighty years of age, took time out from his fulminations against President Polk's conduct of the Mexican War to present David Wilkinson's petition, although he died one month later and never saw its outcome.[68]

In July, the House version, H. R. 244, was referred to the Committee on Patents, which "reported the same back without amendment" on July 25. Most of the action was in the Senate, where bill S. 187 had been referred to the Committee on Military Affairs, made up of five Democrats, Thomas Jefferson Rusk of Texas, Jefferson Davis of Mississippi, Lewis Cass of Michigan, John Adams Dix of New York, and Thomas Hart Benton of Missouri. In their report to the full Senate on March 28, 1848, they focused on Wilkinson's notable contribution of the "gauge or slide lathe" and "perfecting the power loom." The committee expressed no doubt that his 1798 patent would have been extended, and they attributed his failure to renew it to "the inattention to matters of detail which too often characterize men of genius." Wilkinson's mistake, "if any blame can be attached to him, has been that he cared more for extending the field of human knowledge, and thus benefiting mankind, than for the comparatively secondary consideration of enriching himself."[69]

Of course, we know that David's interest in enriching himself is one of the reasons why he failed to exploit his patent. Moreover, the committee's reasons for supporting his petition emphasized aspects of his work that were in fact relatively minor—for example, that he had been distracted partly because he was occupied "in the manufacture of cannon for the navy." The committee did justly emphasize that Wilkinson's lathe was indispensable "in turning and forming the various portions of fire-arms of different descriptions" and "was made use of in all of the arsenals and armories of the United States." These military uses may seem inappropriately applied to a man who was a Quaker during the period in question, but this was, after all, the Committee on Military Affairs, and wartime defense made a good case. The other anomalous aspect of the report is the ranking of Wilkinson among those brilliant machinists from "what are termed the working classes." Viewed from the perspective of his post-1830 career, spent mostly in the Cohoes machine shop or at far-flung engineering works, David was of the working class; but his three preceding decades had been dominated by the investment of capital and acquisition of credit that gained him membership in the class of elite business leaders of the period—hardly the working-class machinist-hero suggested by the Senate committee.[70]

However, the goal of the petition was not literal accuracy, but rather to make the best case for a well-deserved reward, and the approach was successful. The bill, stipulating that David Wilkinson be paid $10,000 for the "public service" derived from his lathe invention, passed the Senate in June and the House of Representatives in August 1848. That sum of money, worth well over $200,000 today, was a welcome relief to David and Martha Wilkinson, and was probably sufficient to fund their retirement.

Their last years were marked by domestic events. In November 1850, Ardelia gave birth to her sixth child and named him David Wilkinson Olmsted. (Her first, born in 1837, had been named for Martha.) In January of the following year, Albert, at the age of forty-six, married Abby Howell of Cohoes. The marriage notice in the *Cohoes Cataract* listed Albert's home as Caledonia Springs, Canada—where David and Martha had gone to live in their final years.[71]

Caledonia Springs was a spa village located forty-five miles east of Ottawa, where David and his son John had worked on the suspension bridge, and where John had met his wife. The spa was a popular resort for wealthy Canadians and Americans to take the water cure and enjoy the luxurious accommodations. John had bought the Canada House Hotel in 1847. Apparently, as the aged couple became less able to care for themselves they went to live at their son's small hotel, and at least for a time, Albert was staying there with them. Why they did not move in with Ardelia in Cohoes can perhaps be explained by her inability to look after her parents when she had a newborn plus other children aged three to thirteen to care for.[72]

David and Martha died within two days of each other in 1852. After Martha passed away at five o'clock in the afternoon on February 1, David was not told. The next day he reportedly said to his family "I want to see the sun set for the last time," and he died at three o'clock in the morning on February 3. She was seventy-five, he was eighty-one. Their remains were transported to Cohoes, and a funeral was held at St. John's Church on February 11. The newspaper announcement expressed the standard platitudes: "They lived to a good old age, blessed themselves in being the means of blessing to those around them." But there was an odd detachment, as if David had already been mostly forgotten. What interested the newspaper was the unfortunate dispute that arose during the funeral. Several local Masonic chapters had expected to perform the rites of Masonic burial, but were thwarted by "discourteous and ungentlemanly" behavior on the part of the officiating clergymen. The Cohoes Lodge claimed that a Masonic burial was David's "oft expressed wish" and challenged one clergyman's assertion "that he was authorized by the friends of the deceased to protest against the performance of the funeral rites" of the fraternity. Thus whatever vague tributes had been paid to the Wilkinsons were greatly overshadowed by the apparently more interesting controversy between the local organizations that had been the two pillars of David's social and religious life.[73]

This unpleasant incident is not the reason that David and Martha were not buried in Cohoes. Their daughter Joanna had been laid to rest in Pawtucket in 1815, and it appears that David had made plans to be buried there long before he left his home town. A look at the last two decades of their lives suggests the rightness of this decision. Cohoes would grow enormously in the coming years and boast one of the largest cotton mill complexes in the United States. For many it was a place of success and satisfaction. David's friend and business associate Hugh White, for example, was able to retire comfortably on the fortune from his Cohoes investments. But that was certainly not the case for David. Despite his acknowledged contributions to the early development of Cohoes, he would be a relatively minor figure in the town's history. Other important figures from the early years—Canvass and Hugh White, Remsen, Rensselaer, even David's son-in-law Charles Olmsted—were remembered in the city's street names, but the Wilkinson name is absent.[74] Better that he was returned to Pawtucket, where he had grown up, married, raised a family, and for a good span of years had been happy and successful.

Immediately after the controversial funeral in Cohoes, there was a final journey to Pawtucket, home to David's greatest triumphs and ultimate failure. The Pawtucket and Providence newspapers that had once carried so many notices of David's achievements and advertisements for his innovative and useful products now offered only muted praise. "As a man of mechanical genius, and of enterprise and energy, he has seldom been equaled," was all the *Manufacturers and Farmers Journal* had to say, a weak tribute for a founder of the newspaper. More lines were devoted to the place and time of the funeral than to the eulogy. The *Pawtucket Gazette and Chronicle* of February 20 offered a frustrating excuse for its brevity: "Mr. and Mrs. Wilkinson were too well known in this community to require eulogium." Martha received the standard nineteenth-century platitudes: she was "beloved and respected" and "a model of female excellence." In the style of the era, she was reduced to her role as wife: "She verified the inspired maxim, that 'a virtuous woman is a crown to her husband.' " Yet the *Gazette and Chronicle* did mention that Wilkinson had built the town's first fire engine, and was generous in its appraisal of his overall contribution: "It would be difficult to mention any undertaking for the moral, social or pecuniary benefit of the village . . . that was not promoted by his valuable counsel, and liberally aided by his money when necessary."[75]

The Pawtucket funeral was held at St. Paul's Church on the afternoon of Friday February 13, with a procession from Masonic Hall in honor of a found-

Figure 8.3

After David and Martha Wilkinson died in Canada, there were funerals in Cohoes, New York and Pawtucket, Rhode Island. They are buried in a family plot in Mineral Spring Cemetery in Pawtucket.

Photo by author.

ing member who had "discharged with uprightness and fidelity his trust as a man and a mason." David and Martha were buried together, with their daughter Joanna, at Mineral Spring Cemetery, a once-peaceful spot at the western edge of Pawtucket village, but by the 1850s surrounded by the sprawl of the industrial city. There, many of the architects and builders of that industrialization—Timothy Greene, Barney Merry, and dozens of Jenkses—were laid to rest. His twin brothers Abraham and Isaac were already there, although in a separate plot, as well as his sister Lucy and her husband Timothy Greene, and his sister Hannah, Samuel Slater's first wife. Buried with Hannah Wilkinson Slater are six of her children, five of whom died before she did. Samuel Slater's second wife, Esther, would later be buried next to Hannah, although not Slater himself, who apparently had no intention of *ever* returning to Pawtucket.[76]

For years, Reverend David Benedict had lamented the loss of cohesion that began to disintegrate during the Sargent's Trench dispute and the social changes of the 1820s, and that culminated in the crisis of 1829, which drove away many of Pawtucket's finest minds and enterprising men. "And to complete the downward march in the retrograde state of things," he wrote the year after David's death, "in almost all respects, the great smash up of 1829 operated much like one on a railroad train, the passengers scattered in every direction, and but few of them have come together since."[77] David Wilkinson was perhaps foremost among these displaced native sons, and it is both fitting that he was returned to the Pawtucket village of his youth and active, productive adulthood, and poignant that his posthumous homecoming took place after so long a period of self-imposed banishment, wandering, and unfulfilled expectations.

Epilogue

Ingenious Machinists

> There is an untold, probably an unimagined, amount of human talent, of high mental power, locked up among the wheels and springs of the machinist; a force of intellect of the loftiest character.
>
> —Edward Everett, 1837

It is almost certain that David Wilkinson and Paul Moody never met, but just as certain that they were well aware of each other's work. Moody's Boston Manufacturing Company managers, F. C. Lowell and Nathan Appleton, visited Wilkinson at his machine shop in 1816; and Moody's partner and mentor Jacob Perkins knew of David's screw lathe and even stopped by his home in Pawtucket to learn more about it. There were patent suits involving the power loom and other machines of common interest which both inventors followed closely. Moody's Merrimack Company bought equipment from the Wilkinsonville Manufacturing Company in 1825, and the Boston Manufacturing Company journals indicate that Moody made at least two trips to Providence, for unspecified reasons, in 1814 and 1815.[1] It would be satisfying and fitting if these two prominent machinists had met face to face, and while that is possible, there is no record that they did.

Only a few years apart in age, Wilkinson and Moody lived at a time of boundless opportunity as experimental industrial capitalism became rooted in the American economy, and these two men developed into leading actors in the creation of the textile and machine tool industries that came to dominate New England's economy in the first half of the nineteenth century. They are two of the best examples of the "ingenious machinists" of the age, and because they were very different in background, temperament, and the way they responded to the opportunities of industrialization, the linking of their lives provides a richer view of the ways in which the textile revolution developed, the risks and rewards of participating in the new industrial economy, and some sense of the quality of the lives of those who rode this wave of economic and social change.

Their paths to wealth and respectability were not predetermined. A combination of factors, including large trends such as British technology transfer and America's drive for economic independence, as well as individual matters like timing and native skill and interest, presented opportunities and decision points that led these two individuals to prominence. Many men with comparable talents were similarly affected during this expansive period. Machinists held some of the best-paying jobs in the factories that increasingly dotted the rural landscape, while some of the most brilliant, the inventors, usually lacked the capital and legal resources to exploit and protect their patents, and their risk taking often ended in failure. There were unlimited possibilities and alternate routes in the "cotton fever" era.

Given the paths these men took, it is interesting to consider alternatives for Moody and Wilkinson. Had the Boston Manufacturing Company opportunity never occurred, Moody most likely would have been successful in small businesses such as the textile factory partnership with Ezra Worthen at Amesbury, but it is doubtful that he would have made such an impact on American machine making or attained a comparable level of wealth and status. The corporate path he chose was exceptionally successful, and working in a large structured organization suited his reserved, risk-averse style. There, he was encouraged to be innovative, most brilliantly at Waltham, although he was burdened by more planning and management responsibilities in his forties and fifties. Always aware of the corporate ceiling, Moody nevertheless became very wealthy and, especially at Lowell, was able to afford a highly respectable style of living. Private schools, a large new house, his roles as bank director, pillar of the Episcopal Church, and temperance advocate all combined to ensure his social status. He had taken fewer risks than Wilkinson, but his comparatively structured corporate life paid off handsomely. His collaboration with Francis Cabot Lowell was stimulating and deservedly made his reputation. His work life was generally satisfying, despite questions about his last years under the management and influence of Kirk Boott. Furthermore, the corporations offered a stable life for his family, with modest demands for mobility, plenty of corporate support when a move was required, and considerable assets that provided for his family after his death. Since the Moody family had been socially respectable in Newbury for generations, Paul Moody's story is not one of rags to riches. But his position in the corporation and the attendant wealth raised his status to a level that far exceeded the predominantly land- and education-based status of his family. Moody's story corresponds nicely with the new measures of respectability emerging in the 1820s. It is, in fact, difficult to imagine a scenario that plays out better for Moody, except one in which he lived longer.[2]

David Wilkinson's story, on the other hand, has a great many "what-if" decision points in his varied career. One question is unavoidable: What if he had chosen to remain in Rhode Island after the debacle of 1829? It was clear to at least one Pawtucket observer that the loss of Wilkinson and other talented men had hurt the town's economic prospects. "Our town committed one suicidal act nearly forty years ago," wrote Massena Goodrich in 1865. "In the severe business revulsion of 1829, David Wilkinson and other enterprising mechanics were allowed to leave the place. The capitalists of the neighborhood should have prohibited it. A few words of encouragement, and, in due time, seasonable pecuniary aid had kept them here."[3] After the crash, David's business interests in Pawtucket survived in the hands of others. A former employee of his machine shop, Clark Tompkins, bought Wilkinson's tools and patterns and was soon advertising the latest power looms for sale, and Thomas LeFavour took over the Wilkinson Mill and made profitable use of it as a textile factory. While much of the tool-making business moved away from Pawtucket after 1829, it thrived in Providence under the leadership of men such as Thomas J. Hill, James Brown, and Aza Arnold—some of whom had been David's protégés. Finally, one of the Slater-Wilkinson partnerships, the Providence Steam Cotton Company, was very successful after 1830, producing, Slater had been told, "the best goods in the country." Steam-powered businesses in general came to the fore in the 1830s, proving the viability of a technology that David Wilkinson had helped pioneer in the state.[4]

Had he stayed, he might well have prospered along with these other Rhode Island machinists. But the fact remains that Wilkinson left New England and the success of the Cohoes enterprise did not occur soon enough to benefit him. This gloomy ending to a brilliant career contrasts sharply with the safer corporate path of Paul Moody, and their interwoven stories both enrich the individual chronicles and give us a fuller picture of the textile revolution of the early nineteenth century. This comparison broadens the context and geographical range, allowing more side roads to be explored, including Moody's pursuit of temperance reform and Wilkinson's disastrous foray into banking. Together, these stories yield fresh insights into matters such as mobility—both as opportunity and as necessity—and financial risk taking in the uncertain economic environment of the early nineteenth century, exemplified by the shattering effect of Wilkinson's insolvency on his family compared to the dividends that Moody's stock continued to pay throughout his widow's long lifetime.

While my focus has been on the lives and careers of these two individuals, their stories make full sense only within the context of such broad issues as social class, capitalism, technological innovation, and the costs of industrial development. While neither man was poor to start, each bettered his lot significantly by moving up from artisan to senior manager, in Moody's case, or to mill village entrepreneur in Wilkinson's, at a time when industrialization was just beginning to exacerbate relations between master artisans and poorer workers in manufacturing towns. Here, the particulars of their income, stock ownership, religious and political affiliation, and pursuit of refinement mesh with the larger picture of social mobility and respectability in the early national period. Similarly, the knotty question of capitalism can be explored through these men, both of whom had considerable access to capital. Needing additional funds to expand his operations, Wilkinson created his own bank, although bad timing and mismanagement turned this into a liability. Moody became a capitalist by means of his inventive work for a well-financed corporation. As a large stockholder, he became wealthy enough to provide loans at interest to the new Merrimack Company, and later became a bank director and investor in a local brewery. While he had been a small-scale capitalist in his early business venture, it was through the auspices of the Boston Associates that he became a wealthy investor, and this wealth was a primary component of his status and respectability in Lowell.

This is not simply a story of social mobility, of wealth maintained or squandered. It is also about men who enjoyed and took great pride in their work, at a time when technological achievement had taken on civic and even moral qualities. Their crafting of highly functional tools and machinery was for the good of American independence, to sustain republican ideals. They possessed the rare and special quality of inventiveness, at a time when transatlantic technology transfer provided opportunities for important, commercially viable achievements in the mechanic arts. Their success was all the more remarkable because it occurred in an era of rudimentary engineering conditions, with no established standards of construction or ability to measure fine machine tolerances. Moreover, their success was attained without benefit of formal training. Both men had only brief classroom education, yet Paul outshone his college-educated brothers, and an admirer of David could say that "I have met with men more book-learned than he was, but I have never met with, nor do I ever expect to meet, a *wiser* man than David Wilkinson." A later generation of engineers would be formally trained in mathematics and science, yet Moody and Wilkinson's "rule of thumb" methods, based on trial and error and experimentation, produced remarkably precise, innovative, and fundamentally useful mills, machines, and tools.[5]

The results of their innovations had a harsh side as well. The labor-saving machinery that they specialized in and built their careers on initially matched the needs of the labor-starved American economy and helped the young nation achieve economic independence, but eventually these increasingly sophisticated machines put people out of work. Over time, artisanship became less important in the manufacture of textiles and other products, and workers increasingly became "operatives," although certain occupations such as mule spinning continued to require special expertise. Machinists were less subject to replacement than machine operators because machine making and repair required considerable artisanal skill. Certainly, Moody, as manager of a large machine shop, and Wilkinson, mentor of so many talented machinists, dwelt on the skilled jobs they created rather than the employment their machines took away.

The larger picture of industrial decline must also be considered. After years of expansion, the American textile industry suffered a severe setback in the 1837 financial crisis, and the Lowell corporations were forced to look for ways to continue paying healthy dividends to shareholders. The alternative was to exploit the workers, which they did by cutting wages, increasing machine speed, and forcing each worker to tend more machines. Heavy Irish immigration, especially during the potato famine of the 1840s, introduced a new labor force to be exploited, and the paternalistic system came to an end. As Caroline Ware put it, "The last years of the [antebellum] period witnessed a tendency toward the depression of wages, the extension of hours, the continuance, where profitable, of child labor, and the maintenance of the same unhealthy conditions of life and work. The retention of earlier standards left the mills, which had once been in the vanguard of social progress, behind the social conscience of the community."[6] This declension forms a postscript to our story: only the first clues were apparent during Moody's lifetime or Wilkinson's active engagement in manufacturing.

It is interesting to consider how these two pioneers have been remembered over time. Wilkinson's obituaries were fairly muted, perhaps because he missed the economic wave at Cohoes and was no longer relevant in Pawtucket after living away for twenty years. Cohoes's historian gave him a better obituary in 1877 than the Rhode Island newspapers had in 1852. The efforts of the Rhode Island Society for the Encouragement of Domestic Industry (RISEDI) placed renewed emphasis on the state's textile pioneers and restored Wilkinson's place. His reminiscences were published in the RISEDI *Transactions* of 1861, and were reprinted in two consecutive issues of *Scientific American* in 1862. In 1870, the *Providence Journal,* in its fiftieth anniversary issue, finally atoned for its poor coverage of Wilkinson's death in 1852. More recently, the American Society of Mechanical Engineers designated the Wilkinson Mill a National Historic Mechanical Engineering Landmark.[7]

Moody received substantial accolades after his death in 1831, at a time when industrial leaders could still point to the (mostly) benign effects of their entrepreneurial ventures. Lowell's historians continued to laud Moody throughout the nineteenth century; even when Kirk Boott's stock was low, Moody's remained steady, if unspectacular. The creation of the Old Residents Historical Association (the forerunner of the Lowell Historical Society) in 1868 rediscovered the founding generation, producing biographical sketches of "mechanics" such as Moody, Ezra Worthen, and John Dummer alongside the more entrepreneurial P. T. Jackson, Kirk Boott, and F. C. Lowell. In one of these articles, Ezra Worthen's son William, by then a well-known civil engineer, wrote that at the time of Paul Moody's death, his machine shop's "reputation for good designs and work was the best in the United States." In 1890, the *New England Magazine,* which had reprinted a long and glowing obituary of Moody in 1831, included him among the greatest industrial leaders in the nation's history: "Moses Brown and Slater and Lowell and Lawrence and Appleton and Boott and Anthony and Paul Moody and Patrick Jackson certainly constituted one of the most remarkable groups of 'captains of industry' that has ever been seen in America."[8]

In the second quarter of the twentieth century, the *Dictionary of American Biography* included moderate-length accounts of both Wilkinson and Moody, but by the end of the century the *American National Biography* (1999) had eliminated Wilkinson. Reminders of Wilkinson are rare: there are no streets or monuments in his home town or in Cohoes that bear his name, and Pawtucket's Wilkinson Park is named for the man who donated the land, his father, Oziel. Moody, on the other hand, is remembered in eponymous streets in Waltham and Lowell, as well as a Lowell school.[9]

Fortunately we can still visit the stone 1810 Wilkinson Mill in Pawtucket, see the reconstructed waterwheel and fly-ball governor in motion, and observe a working machine shop (albeit with later nineteenth-century machinery). As part of the Slater Mill Historic Site it keeps the names of David and Oziel Wilkinson in memory, and a full-page story in the Providence *Journal* covered the bicentennial of the Wilkinson Mill in 2010.[10] The Wilkinsonville mill village is still a distinct section of Sutton, Massachusetts, although all that remains of David's dream is St. John's Episcopal Church, the houses he built for the minister and the bank cashier, and an apartment building that was once the Wilkinsonville Hotel. The Cohoes Company sold its land, buildings, and water rights to a hydroelectric company in 1910, and most of the power canals were abandoned to fill up with silt and debris. The massive Harmony Mills went bankrupt in the Great Depression. David Wilkinson's house has been torn down, and while there are monuments to several of the founders, there is none for David.[11] In Lowell, we can tour the house built for Paul Moody in 1823–24, and get some sense of how he lived, even though his life there has been eclipsed by James McNeill Whistler's birth in that house. And we can stroll down Moody Street in Waltham—still the city's most lively area, with a theater, shops, and a wide array of good restaurants. The Moody Street bridge crosses the Charles River at the dam that once powered the original BMC factory, which still survives, as a museum, senior housing, and a computer resource center. But few, if any, of the people walking down Moody Street on a busy Saturday would know anything about the clever machinist for whom the street is named.

In our postindustrial age, perhaps we no longer care about the agents of industrial growth, associating it as we do with urban blight and labor strife. Waltham, Lowell, Pawtucket, and Cohoes have all experienced difficult times. But at one time the prospect of respectable jobs, economic independence, republican virtue, clean and safe urban spaces, and technological advancement were bright, and these manufacturing towns had their long day in the sun. The brilliant inventiveness of David Wilkinson and Paul Moody helped to turn that promise into reality, even if it proved to be ephemeral. Out of wood and iron, with flashes of insight and tireless experimentation, these two ingenious machinists, and many who learned from them, forged the American Industrial Revolution.

Notes

Abbreviations

BMC	Boston Manufacturing Company
CORHA	Contributions of the Old Residents Historical Association
HBS	Harvard Business School
MHS	Massachusetts Historical Society
MMC	Merrimack Manufacturing Company
PL&C	Proprietors of Locks and Canals [on Merrimack River]
RIHS	Rhode Island Historical Society
RISEDI	Rhode Island Society for the Encouragement of Domestic Industries

Introduction

1. Brooke Hindle, *Emulation and Invention* (New York: New York University Press, 1981), 9; Fay H. Martin, *Transactions of the New England Cotton Manufacturers Association*, no. 72 (Waltham: Press of E. L. Berry, 1902), 204. The term *Industrial Revolution* may falsely suggest an abrupt modernization when in reality the change was more evolutionary, part of a process that developed irregularly and with no uniform pattern. This process has a particular association with the rise of cotton manufacturing: as British historian Eric Hobsbawm noted, "Whoever says Industrial Revolution says cotton." For our purposes, the Industrial Revolution encompasses the advances in ironwork, tools, machines, and textile factories beginning in the late eighteenth and continuing through the nineteenth centuries. Walter Licht, *Industrializing America* (Baltimore: Johns Hopkins University Press, 1995), xv; Eric Hobsbawm, *Industry and Empire: The Birth of the Industrial Revolution* (London: Penguin, 1999), 34.

2. Drew R. McCoy, *The Elusive Republic: Political Economy in Jeffersonian America* (Chapel Hill: University of North Carolina Press, 1980), 7.

3. John F. Kasson, *Civilizing the Machine: Technology and Republican Values in America, 1776–1900* (New York: Hill and Wang, 1999 [1976]), 9–17; McCoy, *The Elusive Republic,* 247–48.

4. A clear explanation of the stages of spinning and weaving can be found in Steve Dunwell, *The Run of the Mill* (Boston: David R. Godine, 1978), 6–11.

5. Chris Aspin, *The First Industrial Society: Lancashire, 1750–1850* (Preston, UK: Carnegie, 1995), 2; Samuel Batchelder, *Introduction and Early Progress of the Cotton Manufacture in the United States* (Boston: Little, Brown, 1863 [reprint 1969]), 106–107.

6. David J. Jeremy, "Damming the Flood: British Government Efforts to Check the Outflow of Technicians and Machinery, 1780–1843," *Business History Review* LI, no. 1 (Spring 1977): 1–34; Anthony F. C. Wallace and David J. Jeremy, "William Pollard and the Arkwright Patents," *William and Mary Quarterly*, Third Series, 34, issue 3 (July 1977): 404–409.

7. Anthony F. C. Wallace, *Rockdale: The Growth of an American Village in the Early Industrial Revolution* (New York: Alfred A. Knopf, 1978); Philip Scranton, *Proprietary Capitalism: The Textile Manufacture at Philadelphia, 1800–1885* (New York: Cambridge University Press, 1984); Cynthia J. Shelton, *The Mills of Manayunk: Industrialization and Social Conflict in the Philadelphia Region, 1787–1837* (Baltimore: Johns Hopkins University Press, 1986).

Chapter 1. Industrial Glimmerings

1. Howard Harris, "The Transformation of Ideology in the Early Industrial Revolution: Paterson, New Jersey, 1820–1840," unpublished doctoral dissertation, City University of New York, 1985, 7–12; Stanley Elkins and Eric McKitrick, *The Age of Federalism* (New York: Oxford University Press, 1993), 263, 278–79.

2. Albert Bushnell Hart, ed., *Commonwealth History of Massachusetts,* Vol. 2, (New York: States History Company, 1928), 408–409; William R. Bagnall, *The Textile Industries of the United States* (New York: Augustus M. Kelley, 1971 [1893]), 33, 42, 45–50; Arthur H. Cole, *American Wool Manufacture,* Vol. 1 (New York: Harper and Row, 1969 [1926]), 63.

3. *Pennsylvania Gazette,* March 22, 1775; Walter Licht, *Industrializing America* (Baltimore: Johns Hopkins University Press, 1995), 13.

4. Margaret Morris Haviland, "Beyond Women's Sphere: Young Quaker Women and the Veil of Charity in Philadelphia, 1790–1810," *William and Mary Quarterly*, Third Series 51, no. 3 (July 1994): 428.

5. Shelton, *The Mills of Manayunk,* 26.

6. Joseph and Frances Gies, *The Ingenious Yankees* (New York: Thomas Y. Crowell, 1976), 38; Neil L. York, "Oliver Evans," in *American National Biography*, vol. 7, edited by John A. Garrity and Mark C. Carnes (New York: Oxford University Press, 1999), 617–18.

7. Carroll W. Pursell Jr., "Thomas Digges and William Pearce: An Example of the Transit of Technology," *William and Mary Quarterly,* Third Series 21, issue 4 (October 1964): 552.

8. Wallace and Jeremy, "William Pollard and the Arkwright Patents," 407–409.

9. Jacob E. Cooke, *Tench Coxe and the Early Republic* (Chapel Hill: University of North Carolina Press, 1978), 189; Wallace and Jeremy, "William Pollard and the Arkwright Patents," 409–10.

10. Leo Marx, *The Machine in the Garden: Technology and the Pastoral Ideal in America* (New York: Oxford University Press, 1964), 151.

11. Quoted in Samuel Batchelder, *Introduction and Early Progress of the Cotton Manufacture in the United States* (New York: Harper and Row, 1969 [1863]), 21.

12. George Rich, "The Cotton Industry in New England," *The New England Magazine* 9, issue 2 (October 1890): 168; Caroline F. Ware, *The Early New England Cotton Manufacture* (Boston: Houghton Mifflin, 1931), 21.

13. Orra L. Stone, *History of Massachusetts Industries* (Boston: S. J. Clarke, 1930), 51.

14. Bagnall, *Textile Industries,* 90; Henry Cabot Lodge, *Life and Letters of George Cabot* (Boston: Little, Brown, 1872), 14; Robert S. Rantoul, *The First Cotton Mill in America* (Salem, MA: The Salem Press, 1897), 15; Robert B. Gordon and Patrick M. Malone, *The Texture of Industry* (New York: Oxford University Press, 1994), 298.

15. Rantoul, *The First Cotton Mill in America,* 12–13; *Salem Mercury,* May 6, 1788.

16. George Washington, diary entry for October 30, 1789, *The Diaries of George Washington,* vol. 5, edited by Donald Jackson and Dorothy Twohig (Charlottesville: University Press of Virginia, 1979), 485–86.

17. Robert W. Lovett, "The Beverly Cotton Manufactory: Or Some New Light on an Early Cotton Mill," *Bulletin of the Business Historical Society* 26, no. 4 (December 1952): 221; Rich, "The Cotton Industry in New England," 169, 170.

18. George Cabot to Alexander Hamilton, September 6, 1791, Lodge, *George Cabot,* 45.

19. Moses Brown quoted in Daniel J. Hoisington, *Made in Beverly* (Beverly Historic District Commission, 1898), 11; Lovett, "The Beverly Cotton Manufactory," 228; George Cabot to Benjamin Goodhue, March 16, 1790, in Lodge, *George Cabot,* 34.

20. Rich, "The Cotton Industry in New England," 170.

21. George Cabot to Alexander Hamilton, September 6, 1791; Lodge, *George Cabot,* 44; Ware, *The Early New England Cotton Manufacture,* 20; Lovett, "The Beverly Cotton Manufactory," 234.

22. David J. Jeremy, *Transatlantic Industrial Revolution: The Diffusion of Textile Technologies Between Britain and America, 1790–1830s* (Cambridge: MIT Press, 1981), 15; Stone, *History of Massachusetts Industries,* 52. An interesting firsthand account from an employee of the Beverly factory is in Bagnall, *Textile Industries,* 98–99.

23. Stone, *History of Massachusetts Industries*, 54, 55; Charles G. Washburn, *Industrial Worcester* (Worcester: Davis Press, 1917), 17.

24. J. D. Van Slyck, in *Representatives of New England: Manufacturers* (Boston, Van Slyck and Company, 1879), 210; Paul E. Rivard, "Textile Experiments in Rhode Island, 1788–1789," *Rhode Island History* 33, no. 2 (May 1974): 37–38.

25. Brown & Almy to Pliny Earle, November 4, 1789, quoted in Washburn, *Manufacturing and Mechanical Industries in Worcester* (Philadelphia: J. W. Lewis, 1889), 19.

26. Quoted in Washburn, *Manufacturing in Worcester,* 19.

27. As cotton manufacturing became more geographically diverse and as specialty manufacturers emerged, the need for on-site installation or repair of machinery bought from a remote manufacturer increased significantly. Rhode Island's David Whitman (1799–1858), who began working as a mill-boy at the age of seven, became so adept at the design, machine installation, and operation of textile factories throughout New England that he was known as the "mill doctor." Van Slyck, *Representatives of New England,* 537–38, 211.

28. "Pliny Earle," in *Dictionary of American Biography,* vol. 3, edited by Allen Johnson and Dumas Malone (New York: Charles Scribner's Sons, 1958), 595–97.

Chapter 2. Revolutionary Technology

1. Smith was born in Medfield, Massachusetts, in 1755. He invented a machine that cut nails from cold iron, one for trimming straw braid, and another for ironing straw bonnets. But his most important contributions were a machine for making the teeth and another for piercing the leather of hand cards; however his idea for a machine to combine the two was stolen and patented by someone else, and he eventually died a pauper. Willard De Lue, *The Story of Walpole, 1724–1924* (Norwood, MA: Ambrose Press, 1925), 246; Jeremy, *Transatlantic Industrial Revolution,* 177–78.

2. David Wilkinson's Reminiscences, *Transactions of the Rhode Island Society for the Encouragement of Domestic Industry* (1861), 101.

3. Marvin Fisher, *Workshops in the Wilderness: The European Response to American Industrialization, 1830–1860* (New York: Oxford University Press, 1967), 46–47.

4. Edwin M. Betts, ed., *Thomas Jefferson's Farm Book* (Charlottesville: University Press of Virginia, 1987), 426–28, 369.

5. Robert B. Gordon, *American Iron, 1607–1900* (Baltimore: The Johns Hopkins University Press, 1996), 1.

6. Peter J. Coleman, *The Transformation of Rhode Island, 1790–1860* (Providence: Brown University Press, 1963), 73.

7. Rev. Israel Wilkinson, *Memoirs of the Wilkinson Family in America* (Jacksonville, IL: Davis and Penniman, 1869), 313–24.

8. Rev. Israel Wilkinson, *Memoirs of the Wilkinson Family*, 402, 104. The family biographer Reverend Israel Wilkinson was the great-grandson of the elder Israel. To avoid confusion, references to the biographer Israel Wilkinson will use the title *Reverend.*

9. James B. Hedges, *The Browns of Providence Plantations: Colonial Years* (Cambridge: Harvard University Press, 1952), 89–90. The original candle factory was started by Obadiah Brown. Upon his death in 1762, his four nephews—Nicholas, John, Joseph and Moses—took over the business, which became known as Nicholas Brown and Company.

10. Alexander Starbuck, *History of the American Whale Fishery* (New York: Argosy-Antiquarian, 1964 [1878]), 152–53; Richard C. Kugler, *The Whale Oil Trade, 1750–1775* (New Bedford: Old Dartmouth Historical Society, 1980), 14.

11. Hedges, *The Browns of Providence Plantations,* 11; Rev. Israel Wilkinson, *Memoirs of the Wilkinson Family,* 402.

12. Nicholas Brown and Company letter, October 9, 1763, quoted in Hedges, *The Browns of Providence Plantations,* 105.

13. R. J. Rivera to Nicholas Brown and Company, October 12, 1763, quoted in Hedges, *The Browns of Providence Plantations,* 106.

14. Israel Wilkinson to Benjamin and John Mifflin, October 18, 1763, quoted in Hedges, *The Browns of Providence Plantations,* 107.

15. Gordon, *American Iron,* 14. David B. Ingram, an expert in early New England furnaces, provided valuable insights in this area.

16. New England ore—from both bogs and mines—had been exploited since the earliest colonial days, most notably at the Hammersmith Ironworks at Lynn (now Saugus), Massachusetts, where a furnace, refining forge, and rolling and slitting mill produced a variety of iron products between 1647 and about 1670. Financial and political difficulties, rather than technical problems, caused its demise, and the technology was transferred to Taunton, Massachusetts, and New Haven, Connecticut, and (by way of the Jenks family) to Pawtucket, Rhode Island. See E. N. Hartley, *Ironworks on the Saugus* (Norman: University of Oklahoma Press, 1957), 208–10, 262, 272–305.

17. David Wilkinson's Reminiscences, 104. Reverend Manasseh Cutler's detailed description of the operation of the Cranston ore bed, and of the steam engine in particular, is in Hedges, *The Browns of Providence Plantations,* 278–79.

18. Rev. Israel Wilkinson, *Memoirs of the Wilkinson Family,* 403. Hope Furnace was most profitable in the Revolutionary War years, during which an estimated three thousand cannons were manufactured. Hedges, *The Browns of Providence Plantations,* 142–43.

19. Rev. Israel Wilkinson, *Memoirs of the Wilkinson Family,* 403.

20. Coleman, *The Transformation of Rhode Island,* 71ff.

21. Hedges, *The Browns of Providence Plantations,* 276; Augustine Jones, "Moses Brown," *New England Magazine* 6, issue 31 (June-July 1887): 37–38.

22. *Niles Weekly Register,* February 19, 1831; Rev. Israel Wilkinson, *Memoirs of the Wilkinson Family,* 410–13.

23. Rev. Israel Wilkinson, *Memoirs of the Wilkinson Family,* 411–12; *The Manufacturer and Builder* 1, issue 7 (July 1869); David Wilkinson's Reminiscences, 100–101. Wilkinson continues: "I think about 1820, I went to Cumberland, with Samuel Greene, my nephew, and purchased of Jeremiah Wilkinson, the old shears, with which he cut the first four nails. He was, I think, ninety years of age at the time. The shears were a pair of tailor's shears, with bows straightened out, and the blades cut off half the length. They were deposited with the Historical Society, in Providence, by Samuel Greene."

24. John F. Kasson, *Civilizing the Machine,* 3.

25. Charles Wetherill, *History of The Religious Society of Friends Called by Some The Free Quakers, in the City of Philadelphia* (Philadelphia: Society of Friends, 1894), 10–11, 23.

26. Cumberland was a hotbed of New Light religious enthusiasm. See William G. McLoughlin, "Free Love, Immortalism, and Perfectionsim in Cumberland, Rhode Island, 1748–1768," *Rhode Island History* 33 (1974).

27. Herbert A. Wisbey Jr., *Pioneer Prophetess: Jemima Wilkinson, The Publick Universal Friend* (Ithaca: Cornell University Press, 1964), 13. Three more of the Wilkinsons (sisters Marcy, Elizabeth, and Deborah) were eventually disowned by the Quakers for

following Jemima. See ibid., 15. This harsh treatment must be put into the context of the Quaker reform movement from about 1750 to the end of the Revolutionary War. Aberrant members reflected poorly on a society known for honesty and fair dealing, and during this period, Quaker meetings became more intent on ridding the Society of members who sullied its reputation. See Jack D. Marietta, *The Reformation of American Quakerism, 1748–1783* (Philadelphia: University of Pennsylvania Press, 1984), xiii, 3–10.

28. Wisbey, *Pioneer Prophetess,* 98, 111.

29. *Scientific American* 9, issue 14 (December 17, 1853): 106.

30. Rev. Israel Wilkinson, *Memoirs of the Wilkinson Family,* 469–70, 474.

31. Rev. Israel Wilkinson, *Memoirs of the Wilkinson Family,* 471, 472. See also Rev. Massena Goodrich, "Pawtucket and the Slater Centennial, *The New England Magazine* 3, no. 2 (October 1890): 140–41.

32. David Wilkinson's Reminiscences, 100.

33. Reverend George Taft, quoted in Rev. Israel Wilkinson, *Memoirs of the Wilkinson Family,* 515.

34. John Ross, "The Dark Day," *American Heritage* 58, no. 5 (Fall 2008). Newbury, Massachusetts, resident Sarah Emery wrote in her reminiscences, "Many families were in a perfect frenzy. 'The Judgment Day had come,' and amid tears and piteous lamentations and confessions, with prayer and Bible reading, the frightened creatures tremblingly passed the hours, momentarily expecting that the dread trump would sound. The darkness continued into the night, but the following morning the sun rose bright and the air had resumed its usual clearness." Sarah Emery, *Reminiscences of a Nonagenarian* (Newburyport: William H. Huse, 1789), 177. David Wilkinson's brother-in-law William Wilkinson left a short account of the event. "May 19, 1780, was the 'dark day.' When the darkness came on, I was reading Virgil in review. It soon became necessary to light candles. In the evening it was so dark that a light could not be seen across the street, & a friend of mine who made the experiment, having placed a lighted candle in the window got befuddled, & could not find his way back to the house." "Recollections of William Wilkinson, copied from the manuscript of E. M. Stone, Esq. Oct 29, 1849," Edwin M. Stone papers, Mss. 854, folder 8, Rhode Island Historical Society.

35. David Wilkinson's Reminiscences, 103. Taft quoted in Rev. Israel Wilkinson, *Memoirs of the Wilkinson Family,* 515.

36. Paul Rivard, "Textile Experiments in Rhode Island," 37; David Wilkinson's Reminiscences, 101; Robert S. Woodbury, *Studies in the History of Machine Tools* (Cambridge: MIT Press, 1972), 33. In centerless grinding, the piece to be ground is placed on a rest between two grinding wheels, one of which rotates the object while the other performs the grinding.

37. Mack Thompson, *Moses Brown, Reluctant Reformer* (Chapel Hill: University of North Carolina Press, 1962), 205–206.

38. George S. White, *Memoir of Samuel Slater* (New York: Augustus M. Kelley, 1967 [1836]), 65; David Wilkinson's Reminiscences, 101–102. William Anthony's letter (undated, but prior to 1836) is reprinted in White, *Samuel Slater,* 62–64.

39. David Wilkinson's Reminiscences, 102. The term *roping* is not commonly used, and refers to "ropes" of carded cotton that have been combined, stretched, and slightly

twisted. The several stages between carding and spinning are more often referred to as "roving."

40. "In 1788, Joseph Alexander and James McKerris, natives of Scotland, arrived in Providence, both being weavers, and understanding the use of the fly-shuttle; they were engaged to weave corduroy. Mr. Alexander to weave a piece in Providence, and Mr. McKerris went to East Greenwich to work there. A loom was accordingly built after the directions of Mr. Alexander, and put in operation in the market house chamber; this was the first fly-shuttle ever used in Rhode Island." William Anthony, quoted in White, *Samuel Slater,* 63.

41. David Wilkinson's Reminiscences, 102; Moses Brown to John Dexter, October 15, 1791, in *The Papers of Alexander Hamilton,* Volume IX, edited by Harold C. Syrett (New York: Columbia University Press, 1965), 434. Dexter was the supervisor of revenue for Rhode Island, and Brown's letter became a source for Hamilton's "Report on Manufactures." Brendan F. Gilbane, "A Social History of Samuel Slater's Pawtucket, 1790–1830" (PhD diss., Boston University, 1969), 105.

42. Rivard, "Textile Experiments in Rhode Island," 40.

43. On the penalties for emigrating, see David J. Jeremy, "Damming the Flood: British Government Efforts to Check the Outflow of Technicians and Machinery, 1780–1843," *Business History Review* LI, no. 1 (Spring 1977): 2. Strutt quoted in White, *Samuel Slater,* 34.

44. Moses Brown, the principal beneficiary of Slater's emigration, later thanked the state of Pennsylvania for "the publication of their grant to a certain person for a certain machine in this manufactory [which], reaching England, and coming to the attention of the workmen at Arkwright's mills, occasioned the young man, Slater, . . . privately coming to America." White, *Samuel Slater,* 36, 88.

45. Samuel Slater to Moses Brown, Dec 2, 1789, quoted in White, *Samuel Slater,* 72. The New York Manufacturing Society, incorporated in 1789 "for the purpose of establishing useful manufactures in the city of New-York, and furnishing employment for the honest industrious poor," included among its subscribers Alexander Hamilton and John Jay. By early 1790, more than one hundred spinners and weavers were employed, but the operation was never profitable and went out of business in January 1794. Joseph Stancliffe Davis, *Essays in the Earlier History of American Corporations* (New York: Russell and Russell, 1917 [Reprint 1965]), 275.

46. Gordon and Malone, *The Texture of Industry,* 38.

47. Rivard, "Textile Experiments in Rhode Island," 36.

48. For a thorough explanation of White's Slater-centric view, see James L. Conrad Jr., "The Making of a Hero: Samuel Slater and the Arkwright Frames," *Rhode Island History* 45, no. 1 (February 1986): 3–14.

49. White, *Samuel Slater,* 71; italics added; "The Cotton Manufacture," *North American Review* 52, issue 110 (January 1841): 48.

50. Gordon and Malone, *The Texture of Industry,* 41.

51. Gilbane, "A Social History of Pawtucket," 117; Smith Wilkinson to George White, May 30, 1835, in White, *Samuel Slater,* 76. In the same letter Smith described his first job as "laying the cotton . . . by hand, taking up a handful, and pulling it apart with both hands, and shifting it all into the right hand, to get the staple of the cotton

straight, and fix the handful, so as to hold it firm, and then applying it to the surface of the breaker, moving the hand horizontally across the card to and fro, until the cotton was fully prepared."

52. Rivard, "Textile Experiments in Rhode Island," 45; Moses Brown to John Dexter, October 15, 1791, *Papers of Alexander Hamilton*, Vol. 9, 435; White, *Samuel Slater,* 96–97.

53. Rivard, "Textile Experiments in Rhode Island," 44.

Chapter 3. The Progress of a Textile Machinist

1. *Massachusetts Soldiers and Sailors of the Revolutionary War,* Volume X (Boston: Wright and Potter, 1902), 899; William R. Bagnall, "Paul Moody," *Contributions of the Old Residents' Historical Association* (CORHA), Vol. 3, No. 1 (September 1884), 59; Rufus Emery, *The Descendants of Sergeant Caleb Moody of Newbury, Massachusetts* (1909), Special Collections, Haverhill Public Library.

2. Emery, *Descendants of Sergeant Caleb Moody.*

3. Moody family background in e-mail from Parker River historian David C. Mountain, October 6, 2001.

4. Bagnall, "Paul Moody," 59–60.

5. Charles C. P. Moody, *Biographical Sketches of the Moody Family* (Boston: Samuel C. Drake, 1847), 96. On Samuel Moody, see Samuel L. Knapp, *Biographical Sketches of Eminent Lawyers, Statesmen, and Men of Letters* (Boston: Richardson and Lord, 1821), 40. On Joseph Moody, see Brian D. Carroll, "'I indulged my desire too freely': Sexuality, Spirituality, and the Sin of Self-Pollution in the Diary of Joseph Moody, 1720–1724," *William and Mary Quarterly* LX, no. 1 (January 2003): 155–70.

6. Emery, *Descendants of Sergeant Caleb Moody,* 203; *Catalog of the Officers and Students of Dummer Academy* (Salem, MA: 1882), courtesy of Laurie DiModica, archivist at The Governor's Academy, October 2010.

7. Moody, *Biographical Sketches of the Moody Family,* 146; Bagnall, "Paul Moody," 61.

8. Herbert Gutman, "The Reality of the Rags to Riches Myth," in *Nineteenth-Century Cities,* edited by Stephan Thernstrom and Richard Sennett (New Haven: Yale University Press, 1969), 90–124.

9. John L. Ewell, *The Story of Byfield: A New England Parish* (Boston: George E. Littlefield, 1904), 61.

10. Emery, *Reminiscences of a Nonagenarian,* 89–91.

11. David C. Mountain, "The Mills of Byfield" (Byfield, MA: Parker River Clean Water Association, 1977), 4; Cole, *American Wool Manufacture,* 4, 10. Cole notes that about twenty families with clothmaking experience from Yorkshire settled in Rowley, in the Massachusetts Bay colony (the parish that became Byfield was originally part of Rowley). The gearing for the fulling mill was brought from England.

12. Cole, *American Wool Manufacture,* 12–13.

13. Emery, *Reminiscences,* 8.

14. Ewell, *The Story of Byfield,* 172.

15. Ewell, *The Story of Byfield,* 161–66; Emery, *Reminiscences,* 46; 1801–Chap 16,

Acts and Laws of the Commonwealth of Massachusetts (Boston: Wright and Potter, 1895), 447. This episode was part of a wider movement, active in Newbury since the 1770s, to allow citizens of the town to attend the church of their choice. In March 1795, the citizens of Newbury voted "that the inhabitants of this town have liberty to attend Publick Worship where they choose and be subject to the Rules and Regulations of the Society where they generally attend and be exempted from taxation elsewhere for the support of Publick Worship." Captain Paul Moody was one of the four committee members appointed to petition the state legislature to legalize Newbury's vote, but the attempt failed, and it was not until the Massachusetts Constitution was amended in 1833 that Newbury residents achieved the religious freedom they sought. John J. Currier, *History of Newbury, Massachusetts, 1635–1902* (Boston: Damrell and Upham, 1902), 290–91.

16. Bagnall, *Textile Industries,* 202–204; William T. Davis, "Byfield," in *History of Essex County, Massachusetts,* vol. 2, edited by D. Hamilton Hurd (Philadelphia: J. W. Lewis, 1888), 1729–30.

17. Davis, "Byfield," 1730.

18. Deed of sale from Paul Moody Senior to The Proprietors of the Newburyport Woolen Manufactory, March 1794. Southern Essex District Registry of Deeds, Book 157, Page 153; Mountain, "The Mills of Byfield," 11.

19. Southern Essex District Registry of Deeds, Book 25, Page 133; Ewell, *The Story of Byfield,* 161. One way to derive some sense of the value of £450 in 1794 is to compare it to the salary paid to Byfield's new minister in the late 1780s: £85 (plus 15 cords of wood) per year. Thus, Moody received about five times the annual salary of the minister for the land and water rights. My thanks to David C. Mountain for this very useful comparison, as well as for other valuable insights into the early history of Newbury.

20. Joseph S. Davis, *Essays in the Earlier History of American Corporations* (Cambridge: Harvard University Press, 1917), 277.

21. Emery, *Reminiscences,* 72; Hartley, *Ironworks on the Saugus,* 4.

22. Jeremy, *Transatlantic Industrial Revolution,* 121–22; Emery, *Reminiscences,* 72; Davis, *Earlier History of American Corporations,* 275; Joshua Coffin, *A Sketch of the History of Newbury, Newburyport, and West Newbury* (Boston: S. G. Drake, 1845 [Reprint Peter E. Randall, 1977]), 197, 213. The Byfield factory did create job opportunities for local artisans. One notable example is Paul Pillsbury, who was born in Newbury in 1780, and thus a close contemporary of Paul Moody. As a young man he began making shuttles and other textile machinery for the Byfield factory, before moving away to start his long career as an inventor. Davis, "Newbury," 1732–33; Ewell, *The Story of Byfield,* 168, 121, 188–90.

23. Harold Catling, *The Spinning Mule* (Newton Abbot, UK: David and Charles, 1970), 39. Hard times for British handloom weavers began in the early 1800s, even before they were displaced by the widespread adoption of power looms in the 1820s. Duncan Bythell, *The Handloom Weavers: A Study in the English Cotton Industry During the Industrial Revolution* (Cambridge: Cambridge University Press, 1969), 40–41. A visitor to the Byfield factory noted that "[i]n the Shearing House we saw many specimens of their Woolen Cloths, which appeared to be good. They weave 7 ¼ wide and use altogether the Spring shuttles." Rev. William Bentley, quoted in Mountain, "The Mills of Byfield," 12.

24. Moody, *Biographical Sketches of the Moody Family,* 146–47.

25. Bagnall, "Paul Moody," 61; *Essex Journal and New Hampshire Packet,* November 27, 1793; Greville Bathe and Dorothy Bathe, *Jacob Perkins: His Inventions, His Times, and His Contemporaries* (Philadelphia: Historical Society of Pennsylvania, 1943), 14. Perkins held dozens of patents, including pumps, waterwheel improvements, bank note engraving, and high-pressure steam boilers. "The Merits of Jacob Perkins," *The Manufacturer and Builder* 6, no. 5 (May 1874), 98.

26. *Newburyport Impartial Herald,* November 24, 1795, quoted in Currier, *History of Newbury,* 298.

27. Quoted in Mountain, "The Mills of Byfield," 11–12.

28. Emery, *Reminiscences,* 73; Cole, *American Wool Manufacture,* 70, 89.

29. In his classic study of the American woolen industry, Arthur H. Cole writes that the failure of the Byfield mill does not detract from the Scholfields' achievement. "The importance of the Scholfields . . . is not dependent upon the success or failure of a single industrial establishment. Their more significant role in the history of the American wool manufacture relates to the dissemination of the carding machine." On a wool-buying trip for the Byfield mill, John Scholfield had seen a promising mill site in Montville, Connecticut, and there the brothers set up shop when they left Byfield in 1799. In 1801, Arthur left for Pittsfield, Massachusetts; John later left Montville for Stonington, Connecticut. Their sons established carding operations in various locations in Massachusetts and Connecticut. By 1806, Arthur's wool-carding enterprise in Pittsfield was so successful that he sold the business and applied himself exclusively to the manufacture of carding machinery. Cole, *American Wool Manufacture,* 89–93; Davis, *Earlier History of American Corporations,* vol. 2, 277–78; Bagnall, *Textile Industries*, 209.

30. Emery, *Reminiscences,* 72.

31. Quoted in Bagnall, *Textile Industries,* 212. Although twelve years younger than Paul Moody, John Dummer was his "inseparable companion. All the wheel-work of Mr. Moody's mills was entrusted to John Dummer. He finished his wheels like cabinet work, so that one of them was a thing of beauty, and when a new one was completed the city flocked to see it." Ewell, *The Story of Byfield,* 199.

32. Cole, *American Wool Manufacture,* 93; Bagnall, *Textile Industries,* 209–12.

33. Joseph Merrill, *History of Amesbury* (Haverhill: Press of Franklin P. Stiles, 1880), 161; Currier, *History of Newbury,* 298.

34. Coffin, *History of Newbury, Newburyport, and West Newbury,* 262–63; Merrill, *History of Amesbury,* 335.

35. Amesbury Vital Records; Merrill, *History of Amesbury,* 338.

36. Bathe, *Jacob Perkins,* 22; 1802—Chapter 97 and 1804–Chapter 139, *Acts and Laws of the Commonwealth of Massachusetts* (Boston: Wright and Potter, 1895), 184, 221; *Newburyport Herald,* March 8, 1805, quoted in John J. Currier, *History of Newburyport, 1764–1905*, vol. 2 (Newburyport: By author, 1906–09), 365.

37. Merrill, *History of Amesbury,* 326; Bathe, *Jacob Perkins,* 21.

38. Essex County Registry of Deeds, Salem, Massachusetts, Book 221, Page 204. Moody children data is from Rufus Emery, *Descendants of Sergeant Caleb Moody,* 81.

39. William R. Bagnall, "Sketch of the Life of Ezra Worthen," *CORHA* 3, no. 1 (September 1884): 36.

40. Bagnall, "Paul Moody," 62; Mountain, "Mills of Byfield," 12.

41. Bagnall, "Ezra Worthen," 37; "Answer of the House [to Governor's speech]," *Resolves of the General Court of the Commonwealth of Massachusetts* (Boston: Adams, Rhodes, 1810), 33; Paul E. Rivard, *A New Order of Things: How the Textile Industry Transformed New England* (Hanover, NH: University Press of New Hampshire, 2002), 18; Cole, *American Wool Manufacture,* 95–97 (Gallatin quote, 95).

42. Bagnall, "Paul Moody," 64; Bagnall, "Ezra Worthen," 37–38. James Squires also passed on another bit of interesting information: "The name of the man who taught the operatives to weave was Schofield [*sic*]." This would likely be James Scholfield, the brother of Arthur and John, who stayed in the area when his brothers left for Connecticut. Bagnall believed that between the time that Scholfield gave up his business in North Andover and the time he became superintendent of a flannel mill in East Chelmsford, he was setting up the weaving department for Worthen and Moody's new company.

43. Bagnall, "Ezra Worthen," 39.

44. Hindle, *Emulation and Invention,* 23.

Chapter 4. Oziel's Son

1. Rivard, *A New Order of Things,* 34; *Windham Herald,* November 1811, quoted in Ellen D. Larned, *History of Windham County, Connecticut, 1760–1880* (Putnam, CT: Swordsmith Productions, 2000 [1880]), 331; Caroline F. Ware, *The Early New England Cotton Manufacture,* 37.

2. For useful discussions of the links connecting textiles, steam engines, and machine tools, see Hindle, *Emulation and Invention,* 3, and David R. Meyer, *Networked Machinists: High-Technology Industries in Antebellum America* (Baltimore: Johns Hopkins University Press, 2006), 274–78.

3. George Taft, quoted in Rev. Israel Wilkinson, *Memoirs of the Wilkinson Family,* 515.

4. Massena Goodrich, "Centennial Address," *Report of the Centennial Celebration on the Twenty-fourth of June, 1865 at Pawtucket* (Providence: 1865), 27; Brendan F. Gilbane, "Pawtucket Village Mechanics—Iron, Ingenuity, and the Cotton Revolution," *Rhode Island History* 34, no. 1 (February 1975): 6.

5. Gilbane, "Pawtucket Village Mechanics," 4, 6; Edward Wilkinson to Elisha Dyer, December 16, 1861, in *Transactions of the RISEDI* (1861), 12; Charles R. Morris, *The Dawn of Innovation: The First American Industrial Revolution* (New York: Public Affairs, 2012), 45.

6. Moses Brown to John Dexter, October 22, 1791, in *The Papers of Alexander Hamilton,* Vol. IX, edited by Harold C. Syrett (New York: Columbia University Press, 1965), 440. Blister steel was produced by covering iron bars with charcoal dust and heating them in a special cementation furnace for several days. Given the lack of knowledge of the chemistry of iron, eighteenth-century steel makers "considered cementation an obscure art and one that was difficult to execute." Gordon, *American Iron,* 175.

7. *U.S. Chronicle,* February 18, 1790, quoted in Gilbane, "Pawtucket Village Mechanics," 4.

8. David Wilkinson's Reminiscences, 104. The reverberatory process is explained in Gordon, *American Iron,* 16.

9. White, *Samuel Slater,* 102–103; Rev. Israel Wilkinson, *Memoirs of the Wilkinson Family,* 226. Although there is no definitive proof, there is evidence that Hannah Wilkinson Slater made her own contribution to industrial history. In 1793, she suggested that Slater make cotton thread as a substitute for the usual linen thread. He had shown her some very smooth, even yarn he had spun from long staple Surinam cotton, and Hannah and her sister spun it into thread on a hand spinning wheel. It proved to be stronger than linen thread. This is the earliest mention of cotton thread manufacture. Bagnall, *Textile Industries,* 161; Jonathan Prude, *The Coming of Industrial Order* (Amherst: University of Massachusetts Press, 1983), 49.

10. Gary Kulik and Julia C. Bonham, *Rhode Island: An Inventory of Historic Engineering and Industrial Sites* (Washington, DC: U.S. Department of the Interior, 1978), 143; Bagnall, *Textile Industries,* 159.

11. Barbara M. Tucker, *Samuel Slater and the Origins of the American Textile Industry, 1790–1860* (Ithaca: Cornell University Press, 1984), 57; Hedges, *The Browns of Providence Plantations* (Cambridge: Harvard University Press, 1952), 167; Smith Wilkinson to George S. White, no date, in White, *Samuel Slater,* 126.

12. Moses Brown biographer Mack Thompson points out that our attitudes about child labor result primarily from the "near servitude" that developed later in the nineteenth century. If Brown "lacked foresight in this instance, so did most of his contemporaries, for they too looked upon the child population in America to be utilized in developing domestic manufactures." Mack Thompson, *Moses Brown, Reluctant Reformer* (Chapel Hill: University of North Carolina Press, 1962), 234.

13. White, *Samuel Slater,* 108, 281; Bagnall, *Textile Industries,* 161; Hanna Josephson, *The Golden Threads* (New York: Duell, Sloan and Pearce, 1949), 23. For more on the religious paternalism of the early New England textile manufacturers, and the eventual divergence between the mill owners' "genteel style of religion" (Congregational or Episcopalian) and the more enthusiastic (Methodist and Baptist) inclinations of the factory workers, see Mark S. Schantz, *Piety in Providence: Class Dimensions of Religious Experience in Antebellum Rhode Island* (Ithaca: Cornell University Press, 2000), 44–53.

14. Gilbane, "Pawtucket Village Mechanics," 6.

15. Edward S. Wilkinson to Elisha Dyer, December 16, 1861, in *Transactions of the RISEDI,* 87.

16. George Rogers Clark, *The Transportation Revolution* (New York: Harper and Row, 1968 [1951]), 15–55; David Wilkinson's Reminiscences, 106; Ronald E. Shaw, *Canals for a Nation* (Lexington: University Press of Kentucky, 1990), 9, 12–15. Again, Wilkinson was not quite accurate—several shorter canals had been completed earlier, including one in western Massachusetts.

17. David Wilkinson's Reminiscences, 106; Coleman, *The Transformation of Rhode Island,* 102–103; Paul Israel, *From Machine Shop to Industrial Laboratory* (Baltimore: Johns Hopkins University Press, 1992), 17.

18. Edward Wilkinson letter in *Transactions of the RISEDI,* 90. "Swedge" can be a noun or a verb, and refers to "a mould through which the hot bar is pulled by the

smith, whilst it is hammered by the striker." *Oxford English Dictionary* (Oxford: Clarendon Press, 1978).

19. Jonathan Thayer Lincoln, "The Beginnings of the Machine Age in New England: David Wilkinson of Pawtucket," *New England Quarterly* 6, no. 4 (1933): 722.

20. David Wilkinson's Reminiscences, 104; John P. Johnson, "David Wilkinson: Father of the Machine Tool Industry" (MA thesis, Bridgewater State College, 1978), 14.

21. David Wilkinson's Reminiscences, 106; Edwin A. Battison, *Muskets to Mass Production* (Windsor, VT: American Precision Museum, 1976), 16–17.

22. Woodbury, *Machine Tools,* 90–92; Morris, *Dawn of Innovation,* 54.

23. David Wilkinson's Reminiscences, 107.

24. Kenneth L. Cope, *American Lathe Builders, 1810–1910* (Mendham, NJ: Astragal Press, 2001), 186; Woodbury, *Machine Tools,* 67, 92; Lincoln, "Beginnings of the Machine Age," 722, 727.

25. David Wilkinson's Reminiscences, 107, 108.

26. David Wilkinson's Reminiscences, 108; Hedges, *The Browns of Providence Plantations,* 251. For more on Slater's caution in adopting the power loom, see James L. Conrad Jr., "'Drive That Branch': Samuel Slater, the Power Loom, and the Writing of America's Textile History," *Technology and Culture* 36, n. 1 (January 1995): 1–28, and Alfred D. Chandler and Richard S. Tedlow, *The Coming of Managerial Capitalism* (Homewood, IL: Richard D. Irwin, 1985), 157–58.

27. Bagnall, *Textile Industries,* 421–22; Larned, *History of Windham County,* 329–30.

28. David Wilkinson's Reminiscences, 108; Johnson, "David Wilkinson," 30–31. In some accounts, Sylvanus Brown is given credit for the lathe improvements usually attributed to David Wilkinson. The pattern-burning incident does suggest some competition. By any standard, Brown was a gifted millwright and pattern maker, and certainly had talent as a machine maker—which he passed on to his son James S. Brown, who had an exceptionally successful career as an inventor and machine tool business leader in Rhode Island. James also worked in David Wilkinson's shop in 1817, which may indicate that David and Sylvanus had amicably settled whatever their problem had been in 1805. Bagnall, *Textile Industries,* 156, 390.

29. Gary Kulik and Patrick M. Malone, *The Wilkinson Mill* (American Society of Mechanical Engineers, 1977), 3; Zachariah Allen, "Historical, Theoretical, and Practical Account of Cotton Manufacture," in Gary Kulik, Roger N. Parks, and Theodore Z. Penn, *The New England Mill Village 1790–1860* (Cambridge: MIT Press, 1982), 149.

30. David Wilkinson's Reminiscences, 109.

31. David Wilkinson's Reminiscences, 108, 109; Richard Anthony quoted in Rivard, "Textile Experiments in Rhode Island," 44.

32. Rev. Israel Wilkinson, *Memoirs of the Wilkinson Family,* 507; David Wilkinson's Reminiscences, 109.

33. The basic principle of the Newcomen engine was a raised piston in a cylinder that was filled with steam from a boiler. When the cylinder was full, a spray of cold water condensed the steam, and the sudden vacuum caused the atmospheric pressure to push the piston downward. A counterweight then raised the piston, and the cycle

was repeated. The typical use, as at Cranston, was to pump water from mines. Because deep mines were uncommon in America, there was little need to invest in such huge, temperamental, and expensive engines. Apparently, only two Newcomen engines were built in America before Brown's: one at a copper mine in Belleville, New Jersey, in 1753 and another for the New York City waterworks in 1775. See Hindle, *Emulation and Invention,* 10; Hedges, *The Browns of Providence Plantations,* I, 278–79; Carroll W. Pursell Jr., *Early Stationary Steam Engines in America* (Washington: Smithsonian Institution Press, 1969), 3–4.

34. David Wilkinson's Reminiscences, 104. The "cap" refers to Boulton and Watt's innovation of a separate chamber to condense the steam, which kept the main cylinder from being cooled then reheated at each cycle, thus saving fuel.

35. David Wilkinson's Reminiscences, 104; Philip D. Borden, *Steamboating on Narragansett Bay* (Steamship Historical Society of America, Publication Number 7, December 1957 [1925]), 5; Captain John H. Ormsbee, quoted in Rev. Israel Wilkinson, *Memoirs of the Wilkinson Family,* 510; John Ormsbee to Zachariah Allen, February 14, 1832, Zachariah Allen Papers, Box 1, Folder 3, Rhode Island Historical Society.

36. Captain John Ormsbee, in *Memoirs of the Wilkinson Family,* 510. See, 82.

37. Ormsbee, in *Memoirs of the Wilkinson Family,* 510; Goodrich, "Centennial Address," 35.

38. David Wilkinson's Reminiscences, 104; Goodrich, "Centennial Address," 35.

39. David Wilkinson's Reminiscences, 104–106; "Aaron Ogden," in *Dictionary of American Biography,* vol. 7, 636–37; Fred Erving Dayton, *Steamboat Days* (New York: Frederick A. Stokes, 1925), 26–27.

40. David Wilkinson's Reminiscences, 105; Kirkpatrick Sale, *The Fire of His Genius: Robert Fulton and the American Dream* (New York: The Free Press, 2001), 169.

41. David Wilkinson's Reminiscences, 104–105. Their assessment of Fulton is close to the mark. Robert H. Thurston, a noted Rhode Island steam engineer and author of an 1891 biography of Fulton, wrote that Fulton was a prophet for seeing the future of steam navigation and a statesman for his role in promoting internal improvements; "but he has been recognized neither as prophet nor as statesman, both of which he was, but as the inventor of the steamboat—which he was not." Robert H. Thurston, *Robert Fulton: His Life and Its Results* (New York: Dodd, Mead, 1891), 49.

42. According to Pursell, *Early Stationary Steam Engines,* 24, Elijah Ormsbee later built a steam engine to power a pump at a Providence distillery, but it performed poorly and was abandoned. The papers of Daniel French at the Indiana Historical Society contain no reference to French's direct connection to Fulton.

43. Oliver Evans, *The Abortion of the Young Steam Engineer's Guide* (Wallingford, PA: Oliver Evans Press, 1990 [1805]), 1.

44. Kulik and Bonham, *Inventory,* 149; Pursell, *Early Stationary Steam Engines,* 84; Edward Wilkinson to Elisha Dyer, *Transactions of the RISEDI* (1861), 88. This landmark in industrial and economic history has gone relatively unnoticed. In Rhode Island histories, credit for the first steam-powered textile factory is usually attributed to the Providence Woollen Manufacturing Company, incorporated in 1812. In fact the Wilkinsons were first.

45. Pursell, *Early Stationary Steam Engines,* 84. When Samuel Slater opened his first steam-powered cotton mill in 1827, it too was powered by an Oliver Evans engine, purchased from Rush and Muhlenberg, Evans's successors.

46. Meyer, *Networked Machinists,* 128; Pursell, *Early Stationary Steam Engines,* 85.

47. Bagnall, *Textile Industries,* 504; Lincoln, "Beginnings of the Machine Age," 718, 724–25.

48. E-mail, Patrick Malone to author, April 30, 2013.

49. Lincoln, "Beginnings of the Machine Age," 722.

50. Bagnall, *Textile Industries,* 159, 251–55, 420.

51. Massena Goodrich, "Pawtucket and the Slater Centennial," *New England Magazine* III, no. 2 (October 1890), 147–48; Rev. Israel Wilkinson, *Memoirs of the Wilkinson Family,* 220; Bagnall, *Textile Industries,* 251, 253.

52. Smith Wilkinson to George White [no date] in White, in *Samuel Slater,* 127; mill agent quote in Dunwell, *Run of the Mill,* 128.

53. Bagnall, *Textile Industries,* 254–55.

54. Richard M. Bayles, *History of Providence County, Rhode Island* (New York: W. W. Preston, 1891), 298; *Manufacturers and Farmers Journal*, December 22, 1825.

55. Gilbane, "A Social History of Samuel Slater's Pawtucket," 461–63.

56. Larned, *History of Windham County,* 355; Rev. Israel Wilkinson, *Memoirs of the Wilkinson Family,* 228.

57. Rev. Israel Wilkinson, *Memoirs of the Wilkinson Family,* 474, 224.

58. Ibid., 279–80.

59. David Benedict, "History of Pawtucket," No. 45, in *History of Pawtucket, Rhode Island: Reminiscences and New Series of Reverend David Benedict,* compiled by Elizabeth J. Johnson and James L. Wheaton IV (Pawtucket: Spaulding House Publications, 1986), 224. Regarding the White Mill, Bagnall writes that from 1810 to 1815 the owners "were engaged with success and profit." *Textile Industries,* 254. Similarly, "the financial affairs of the [Pomfret] Company were very flourishing." Larned, *History of Windham County,* 365.

Chapter 5. Company Man

1. However, Israel Thorndike, one of the Beverly investors, bought $10,000 of Boston Manufacturing Company shares, as did his son. George S. Gibb, *The Saco-Lowell Shops* (Cambridge: Harvard University Press, 1950), 9. Francis Cabot Lowell's mother, Susanna Cabot, was the sister of George Cabot, the main force behind the Beverly Cotton Manufactory. Hannah Josephson, *Golden Threads,* 15.

2. On New England merchant capital investment in textiles in the early nineteenth century, see Lance Edwin Davis, "Stock Ownership in the Early New England Textile Industry," *Business History Review* 32, no. 2 (Summer 1958): 209.

3. Thomas Jefferson, *Notes on Virginia*, in *The Life and Selected Writings of Thomas Jefferson,* edited by Adrienne Koch and William Peden (New York: Modern Library, 1998), 259; Jefferson to Benjamin Austin, January 9, 1816, *The Papers of Thomas Jefferson: Retirement Series*, edited by J. Jefferson Looney (Princeton: Princeton University Press, 2013), 335.

4. Zachariah Allen, *The Practical Tourist,* excerpted in Michael B. Folsom and Steven D. Lubar, eds., *The Philosophy of Manufactures* (Cambridge: MIT Press, 1982), 342.

5. Quoted in Thomas Bender, *Toward an Urban Vision: Ideas and Institutions in Nineteenth Century America* (Baltimore: Johns Hopkins University Press, 1975), 19.

6. *Connecticut Courant,* April 6, 1808, quoted in Bradford Perkins, *Prologue to War: England and the United States, 1805–1812* (Berkeley: University of California Press, 1970), 96; Tench Coxe, quoted in Marx, *The Machine in the Garden,* 157.

7. Bender, *Urban Vision,* 21. McCoy, *The Elusive Republic,* 147–49, 242–46.

8. "Massachusetts Yeoman," *Columbian Centinel,* August 21, 1811, in William F. Hartford, *Money, Morals, and Politics: Massachusetts in the Age of the Boston Associates* (Boston: Northeastern University Press, 2001), 44.

9. Kasson, *Civilizing the Machine,* 29–30, 32.

10. Folsom and Lubar, *Philosophy of Manufactures,* xxiii.

11. Carl Siracusa, *A Mechanical People: Perceptions of the Industrial Order in Massachusetts, 1815–1880* (Middletown: Wesleyan University Press, 1979), 16–18; "Review of *Tench Coxe, A Statement of the Arts and Manufactures of the United States, for the Year 1810,*" *The North American Review* 1, issue 2 (July 1815): 237.

12. Folsom and Lubar, *Philosophy of Manufactures,* xxiii–xxiv; Benjamin Rush, "Speech to the United Company of Philadelphia for Promoting American Manufactures," in Folsom and Lubar, *Philosophy of Manufactures,* 3–9.

13. Quoted in Siracusa, *A Mechanical People,* 2.

14. Bagnall, *Textile Industries,* 178–84. Despite its initial failure, the Society for the Encouragement of Useful Manufactures maintained control of the water power at Paterson, which later developed into an important manufacturing center.

15. Cole, *American Wool Manufacture,* 110–13; Edward H. Knight, "The First Century of the Republic," *Harper's New Monthly Magazine*, January 1875, 90.

16. Rivard, *A New Order of Things,* 44. For background on social and economic conditions in Britain in the early nineteenth century, and specifically the riots over the introduction of power looms, see Aspin, *The First Industrial Society*.

17. Gibb, *The Saco-Lowell Shops,* 7–12.

18. Dane Morrison, "Patrick Tracy Jackson," in *American National Biography,* vol. 11, edited by John A. Garraty and Mark C. Carnes (New York: Oxford University Press, 1999), 760–61; Nathan Appleton, *Introduction of the Power Loom and Origin of Lowell* (New York: Harper and Row, 1969 [1858]), 8; Gibb, *The Saco-Lowell Shops,* 11.

19. Directors Minutes, October 20, 1813, Boston Manufacturing Company Papers, Mss. 442, Vol. 2, Baker Library, Harvard Business School; Bagnall, "Paul Moody," 64; and "Waste B," November 22, 1813, Vol. 26, Patrick Tracy Jackson Papers, Massachusetts Historical Society.

20. Moody contract, November 1, 1813, BMC records, Box 2-A, Folder 2, Baker Library, HBS; Directors Minutes, October 20, 1813, BMC records, Vol. 2, Baker Library; Bagnall, "Paul Moody," 65; Steven D. Lubar, "Corporate and Urban Contexts of Textile Technology in Nineteenth-Century Lowell, Massachusetts: A Study of the Social Nature of Technological Knowledge" (PhD diss., University of Chicago, 1983), 43.

21. Jackson to John Borden, March 7, 1814, quoted in Mailloux, "The Boston Manufacturing Company," *The Textile History Review* (January 1964): 7. There was still a need for British machinists who knew the latest machinery, although David Jeremy's research has shown that "the majority of textile immigrants to the United States possessed obsolete skills, predominantly hand loom weaving." Jeremy, *Transatlantic Industrial Revolution,* 160.

22. In June 1813, Perkins received a patent for "improvements in water mills by relieving the tail race of excess water." The key feature was a separate water chute at a steep angle, which sent a high velocity stream of water into the tail race to clear any "dead water" under the wheel. In 1815, Perkins placed an advertisement in the Newburyport *Herald* describing how his design "has been tried during the whole of the winter on a large scale, at the new and extensive Cotton Factory in Waltham, near Boston." Quoted in Bathe, *Jacob Perkins,* 44–45. After noting the advertised advantages of Perkins's waterwheel, industrial historian Patrick M. Malone concludes that "Perkins's machine joined the long list of clever ideas that did not work well in practice." Patrick M. Malone, *Waterpower in Lowell: Engineering and Industry in Nineteenth-Century America* (Baltimore: Johns Hopkins University Press, 2009), 17.

23. Richard M. Candee, "Architecture and Corporate Planning in the Early Waltham System," *Essays from the Lowell Conference on Industrial History, 1982 and 1983,* edited by Robert Weible (North Andover, MA: Museum of American Textile History, 1985), 24; James Montgomery, *A Practical Detail of the Cotton Manufacture of the United States of America, and the State of the Cotton Manufacture of That Country Contrasted and Compared with That of Great Britain* (Glasgow: John Niven, 1840 [reprint: Augustus M. Kelley, 1969]), 13–17; David Jeremy, "Innovation in American Textile Technology during the Early 19th Century," *Technology and Culture* 14, no. 1 (January 1973): 52.

24. Boston *Gazette*, March 20, 1815, quoted in Mailloux, "The Boston Manufacturing Company," 10; Jeremy, *Transatlantic Industrial Revolution,* 191; Gibb, *The Saco-Lowell Shops,* 25. The throstle frame, an adaptation of Arkwright's water frame, was so named because the sound of its tin roller resembled the song of the throstle, or thrush. The mule was a hybrid (hence the name) of the Arkwright water frame and the moving carriage of Hargreaves's spinning jenny. It was capable of making fine uniform yarn, but required a highly skilled (and well-paid) mule spinner.

26. Gibb, *The Saco-Lowell Shops,* 25.

27. Ibid., 26.

28. Ibid., 739.

29. Jackson to Lowell, January 30, 1814, Francis Cabot Lowell Papers, Box 7, Folder 14, MHS.

30. Quoted in Mailloux, "The Boston Manufacturing Company," 3.

31. Appleton, *Power Loom,* 9.

32. Ibid., 11–12; Gregory, *Nathan Appleton,* 164–65; Gibb, *The Saco-Lowell Shops,* 27.

33. There is a possibility that his friend and former business partner Ezra Worthen, whose later experience at the Middlesex Corporation in Lowell suggests a solid background in mill, canal, and waterwheel construction, helped him in the early phase at Waltham. Harry C. Dinmore, "Proprietors of Locks and Canals: The Founding of Lowell," in *When Cotton Was King,* edited by Arthur Eno Jr. (Lowell Historical Society, 1978), 72.

34. Gregory, *Nathan Appleton,* 159. Moody's rent is noted in Directors Minutes, December 31, 1814 and September 30, 1815, BMC Papers, Vol. 2, Baker Library, HBS; Waltham employee earnings, May 3-August 30, 1817, are in Jeremy, *Transatlantic Industrial Revolution,* 199.

35. The term *Boston Associates* was coined by historian Vera Shlakman in *Economic History of a Factory Town, A Study of Chicopee, Massachusetts* (1935). Boston Associates

quote in Josephson, *Golden Threads,* 103; Agreement between Paul Moody and BMC regarding payment for stock, December 1, 1817, Boston Manufacturing Company Papers, Mss. 442, Box 2-A, folder 1, Baker Library, HBS.

36. It also appears that Moody did most calculations in his head, "with but little use of pen and paper," according to family biographer Charles C. P. Moody, *Biographical Sketches of the Moody Family,* 149. While the reference is uncorroborated, it does fit the model of the visual and tactile, nonverbal thinker.

37. Eugene S. Ferguson, "The Mind's Eye: Nonverbal Thought in Technology," *Science* 197, no. 4306 (August 1977): 827 (Galton quote p. 834).

38. Wallace, *Rockdale,* especially "Thinking about Machinery," 237–39. Lowell's Harvard tutor wrote, "He has a happy genius for mathematics. I presume few if any of his class equal him in mathematics and astronomical attainments." Quoted in Josephson, *Golden Threads,* 15.

39. Gibb, *The Saco-Lowell Shops,* 13; Hindle, *Emulation and Invention,* 12–13, 22; Bagnall, "Paul Moody," 65.

40. Gibb, *The Saco-Lowell Shops,* 14; Jeremy, *Transatlantic Industrial Revolution,* 93; P. T. Jackson to F. C. Lowell, February 14, 1815 [more likely 1814], in Josephson, *Golden Threads,* 21.

41. John A. Lowell, "Sketch of Patrick T. Jackson," *CORHA* 3 (August 1877): 195.

42. Kristen A. Peterson and Thomas J. Murphy, *Waltham Rediscovered* (Portsmouth, NH: Peter E. Randall, 1988), xxiii, 79, 15.

43. Hartford, *Money, Morals, and Politics,* 19–20.

44. Seven of the mills were saw, grist, and fulling mills; the others produced chocolate, dyes, nails, paper, screws, snuff, and wire, as well as textiles. Theodore Steinberg, *Nature Incorporated: Industrialization and the Waters of New England* (Cambridge: Cambridge University Press, 1991), 21; Peterson and Murphy, *Waltham Rediscovered,* 88–89; Edmund L. Sanderson, *Waltham as a Precinct of Watertown and as a Town, 1630–1884* (Waltham: Waltham Historical Society, 1936), 58.

45. [Samuel Ripley], "Topographical and Historical Description of Waltham," *Collections of the Massachusetts Historical Society,* vol. 3, Second Series (Boston: Freeman and Bolles, 1815), 155; Peterson and Murphy, *Waltham Rediscovered,* 15, 89; Sanderson, *Waltham,* 58.

46. Howard M. Gitelman, *Workingmen of Waltham: Mobility in American Urban Industrial Development, 1850–1890* (Baltimore: Johns Hopkins University Press, 1974), 6; Ripley, "Description of Waltham," 262, 264, 270.

47. Ripley, "Description of Waltham," 270; Sanderson, *Waltham,* 65; Candee, "Architecture and Corporate Planning," 19.

48. Candee, "Architecture and Corporate Planning," 25–26.

49. Journal, June 30, 1814, Vol. 10 and Directors Minutes, February 7, 1814, Vol. 2, BMC Papers, Baker Library, HBS. Paul managed to direct BMC business to other family members. On June 30, 1814, the company "Paid Sewall Moody for a pair of Bay Horses." This would have to be Paul's older brother Sewall, a farmer in Byfield. Journal, May 2, 1814, BMC Papers, Vol. 10, Baker Library, HBS.

50. Stockholders Records, October 30, 1820, BMC Papers, Vol. 1, Baker Library, HBS; C. C. Chase, "Lives of Postmasters," *CORHA* 4, no. 2 (August 1889): 129; James S. Russell, "Biography of John Dummer," *CORHA* 2: 97.

51. Josephson, *Golden Threads,* 34; Gitelman, *Workingmen of Waltham,* 3. These conditions remained true into the 1830s, when Harriet Martineau visited and commented positively on what she saw of the mill girls' living conditions, and the neat homes some of them had managed to buy. Yet there were important indications of discontent whenever conditions or pay rates deteriorated, such as the strike that took place in 1819 (described later). The Boston Manufacturing Company's willingness to pay for worker contentment ended in the late 1830s with the influx of Irish laborers. Gitelman, *Workingmen of Waltham,* 5.

52. Gitelman, *Workingmen of Waltham,* 4; Dalzell, *Enterprising Elite,* 34–35.

53. Jackson's family was not resident in Waltham during the early years of the BMC, leaving the Moodys as the highest ranking corporate family. John A. Lowell, "Patrick T. Jackson," 200.

54. There is documentation that at least two of the Moody children, Mary and William, attended Bradford Academy in 1821, and most likely well before that date. "A Fragment, written in 1843, by Theodore Edson," *CORHA* 3 (August 1877): 250.

55. The BMC's contributions to the town were typically a mix of philanthropy and practicality. For example, a $500 fire engine was for general town use, but given the danger of whale-oil lamps in lint-filled mills, the fire engine was a necessity for the factory. The volunteer fire department was made up of BMC employees. Mailloux, "The Boston Manufacturing Company: The Factory and the Town," *Textile History Review* (July 1964): 116. Paul Moody was not among the members of the volunteer fire department, according to "A paper read by Mr. A. M. Goodale, Agent of the Boston Manufacturing Company, at a recent meeting of the Citizens' Club," 1891, Massachusetts Historical Society. The Manufacturer's Library, established in 1815, was the forerunner of the Rumford Institute (1827), which eventually became the Waltham Public Library. The BMC built Rumford Hall, where the public could attend lectures by such luminaries as Edward Everett, Ralph Waldo Emerson, Charles Sumner, Horace Mann, Horace Greeley, Louis Agassiz, and George Bancroft. Peterson and Murphy, *Waltham Rediscovered,* 16–17.

56. Peterson and Murphy, *Waltham Rediscovered,* 18–20; Joan W. Goodwin, *The Remarkable Mrs. Ripley* (Boston: Northeastern University Press, 1968), 75. In addition to being the son of the well-known Concord minister, Samuel Ripley was also the uncle of Ralph Waldo Emerson, who was a tutor at Ripley's Waltham school while a student at Harvard. Goodwin, *Mrs. Ripley,* 88.

57. Goodwin, *Mrs. Ripley,* 75, 99.

58. Peterson and Murphy, *Waltham Rediscovered,* 19.

59. Elizabeth D. Castner, *Tercentennial History of the First Parish in Waltham, Massachusetts, 1696–1996* (Waltham: The First Parish of Waltham, 1998), 26–30.

60. The tariff of 1816, for which F. C. Lowell lobbied before Congress, was moderate overall, but it placed a minimum value on imported cloth, so that the cheapest Indian sheeting would cost more than the same article woven at Waltham: Indian cotton worth 9 cents was thus raised to 31¼ cents per yard, well above Waltham's price of

25–30 cents per yard. Jeremy, *Transatlantic Industrial Revolution,* 184; Josephson, *Golden Threads,* 30. The effectiveness of the tariff is demonstrated by the fact that from 1816 to 1817 imports from India declined in value by nearly two-thirds. Joshua L. Rosenbloom, "Path Dependence and the Origins of Cotton Textile Manufacturing in New England," in *The Fibre that Changed the World,* edited by Douglas A. Farnie and David J. Jeremy (London: Oxford University Press, 2004), 383.

61. Appleton, *Power Loom,* 13–14.

62. Zachariah Allen, "History of Cotton Manufacture in America," in Kulik, Parks, and Penn, *New England Mill Village,* 148–49; Gibb, *The Saco-Lowell Shops,* 26.

63. Kenneth Mailloux, "Boston Manufacturing Company: Its Origins," *The Textile History Review* IV (October 1963): 159. Nor was Jacob Perkins a co-patentee. His significant help became an issue in 1818, the year after Lowell's death, when Perkins made a claim for $5,974.39 against Lowell's estate. The BMC directors made a generous grant of $20,000 to Lowell's heirs for his exceptional contribution, and thus Perkins's claim was satisfied. Gregory, *Nathan Appleton,* 156.

64. Mailloux, "The Boston Manufacturing Company," 13.

65. Ware, *The Early New England Cotton Manufacture,* 262; Jeremy, *Transatlantic Industrial Revolution,* 185.

66. Appleton, *Power Loom,* 10. Before 1816, yarn had to be unwound from the bobbins of the spinning frame and then wound by means of a hand wheel onto the "quills" of the loom shuttles. The Shepard and Thorp winder was a significant time saver. Jeremy, "Innovation in American Textile Technology," 54. No accounts mention the date for the visit to Shepard's shop, although it likely occurred between the date of Shepard and Thorp's patent for their winder (October 1816) and Lowell's death (August 1817).

67. Samuel Batchelder, *Introduction and Early Progress of the Cotton Manufacture in the United States* (Boston, Little, Brown, 1863) [Reprint 1969], 67; Bagnall, "Paul Moody," 66–67. It is likely that Lowell and Moody took only a minor risk by walking away from Shepard's offer. The BMC was using winding machines patented in 1815 by Worcester native Ebenezer Stowell. Moody thought Shepard's winder would be preferable, but he had the Stowell winder as a backup. Bagnall, "Paul Moody," 66.

68. Patrick M. Malone, "Little Kinks and Devices," *Industrial Archaeology* 14, no. 1 (1988): 59–76; See Jeremy, *Transatlantic Industrial Revolution*, 191–98, on how the BMC used both tariff and patent protection to secure early success.

69. Quoted in Jeremy, *Transatlantic Industrial Revolution,* 191.

70. Rosenbloom, "Path Dependence," 379.

71. Montgomery, *A Practical Detail of the Cotton Manufacture,* 89–90. It could be argued that the Moody warper was in fact simply a copy, and that the only significant difference was the stop motion, which was Perkins's work. Yet in Montgomery's second edition of *A Practical Detail* he gave Moody full credit. Montgomery's overall assessment is that "this warping machine in its general operations differs very little from those used in Great Britain. In every respect it is equally as simple, efficient, and easily attended—besides having the advantage of the stop motion." Montgomery, 86. See also David J. Jeremy, *Artisans, Entrepreneurs, and Machines* (Aldershot, UK: Ashgate, 1998), 22–23, and Jeremy, *Transatlantic Industrial Revolution,* 195. Credit to Jacob Perkins for the stop motion for Moody's warper is in Samuel Webber, *Manual of Power for Machines,*

Shafts, and Belts, with the History of Cotton Manufacture in the United States (New York: D. Appleton and Company, 1891), 30.

72. Ware, *Early New England Cotton Manufacture,* 73; Jeremy, "Innovation in American Textile Technology," 60–61; Montgomery, *A Practical Detail of the Cotton Manufacture,* 91, 98. Moody quoted in Jeremy, *Transatlantic Industrial Revolution,* 99–101.

73. Batchelder, *Early Progress of the Cotton Manufacture,* 67–68. It was George Gibb's opinion that Moody's dresser, with its soapstone rollers, "was a far greater mechanical success than the loom, and surpassed in efficiency the English model from which it was adapted. Unlike the Waltham loom, it continued in use without substantial change at least until the 1850's." Gibb, *The Saco-Lowell Shops,* 35.

74. For the specifics of this principle applied to yarn, see Jeremy, "Innovation in American Textile Technology," 57–58. Elsewhere, Jeremy explains that this roving machine was called a double speeder "because two of its movements, bobbin rotation and spindle rail traverse, underwent a change of speed during winding." *Transatlantic Industrial Revolution,* 287.

75. John A. Lowell, "Patrick T. Jackson," *CORHA* 3 (August 1877): 197. The mathematical complexity of the double speeder calculations is discussed in Lubar, "Corporate and Urban Contexts of Textile Technology," 256–57.

76. Henry Clay, *The Speeches of Henry Clay* (A. S. Barnes, 1857), 234.

77. Edmund L. Sanderson, *Waltham Industries* (Waltham: Waltham Historical Society, 1957), 121; Bagnall, "Paul Moody," 67–68.

78. Brooke Hindle and Steven Lubar, *Engines of Change: The American Industrial Revolution, 1790–1860* (Washington, DC: Smithsonian Institution Press, 1986), 75–77; P. T. Jackson's affidavit, July 25, 1821, in Jeremy, *Transatlantic Industrial Revolution,* 195.

79. John W. Lozier, *Taunton and Mason: Cotton Machinery and Locomotive Manufacture in Taunton, Massachusetts, 1811–1861* (New York: Garland, 1986), 70,76; Neil L. York, "Oliver Evans," in *American National Biography,* vol. 7, 617–618; Thomas R. Gold to Nathan Appleton, April 10, 1816, Appleton Family Papers, box 3, folder 3, Massachusetts Historical Society. For more on the unfortunate career of John Thorp, see Charles H. Clark, "John Thorp—Inventor of Ring Spinning," *Transactions of the National Association of Cotton Manufacturers* (1928), 72–95.

80. Jeremy, *Transatlantic Industrial Revolution,* 185, 193.

81. Ibid., 185–86. In his original patent Moody had made the mistake of bundling improvements for two different machines. B. Zorina Khan, "Property Rights and Patent Litigation in Early Nineteenth-Century America," *Journal of Economic History* 55, no. 1 (1995): 81.

82. Arnold wrote "I put the [differential] speeders in operation in 1822 and my patent was issued in Jan. 1823 and a notable prejudice was kept up by Waltham and Lowell manufacturers: the Waltham speeder was exclusively used at Waltham and Lowell until I had constructed the Great Falls factory at Somersworth N.H. which actually produced 30 per cent more goods per week than the Lowell or the Waltham factories. . . . This brought down the directors of the Lowell corporations to our place. . . . It brought also Mr. Moody, their engineer . . . [and] the celebrated mathematician, Mr. Warren Colburn to see if our calculation was right . . . and the result was that Mr. Colburn told Moody that it was mathematically correct." The speeders at Waltham and Lowell were soon

converted to the differential type. See *Transactions of the RISEDI* (1861), 80–85. Arnold's brilliant innovation—now commonly used in the drive axle of automobiles—suffered the common fate, stolen by the British in this case, and Arnold spent considerable time and money in the futile attempt to protect his patent. Batchelder, *Early Progress of the Cotton Manufacture,* 81–83; *Dictionary of American Biography,* vol. 1, 361–62.

83. Sanderson, *Waltham Industries,* 124, 121.

84. Siracusa, *A Mechanical People,* 19; Jack Beatty, ed., *Colossus: How the Corporation Changed America* (New York: Broadway Books, 2001), xv, 4; Folsom and Lubar, *Philosophy of Manufactures,* xxvi–xxvii. The downside of incorporation was that with legislative approval came state oversight, which reduced the corporation's flexibility. States began to express their regulatory power more explicitly after the 1819 Dartmouth College case ruled that a corporate charter was an inviolable contract. Naomi R. Lamoreaux, "The Partnership Form of Organization: Its Popularity in Early-Nineteenth-Century Boston," in Beatty, *Colossus,* 51.

85. The Amesbury Wool and Cotton Factory was capitalized at only $46,000 compared to the BMC's $400,000, leaving little in liquid assets to be used for expansion or to ride out hard times. Bagnall, "Paul Moody," 64.

86. Stockholders Meeting, October 4, 1814, BMC Papers, Mss. 442, Vol. 1, Baker Library, HBS. Moody's salary records can be traced through Journal entries, BMC Papers, Vol. 14.

87. Stockholders Meeting Minutes, October 3 and October 17, 1815, BMC Papers, Vol. 1, Baker Library, HBS; Dalzell, *Enterprising Elite,* 29–30.

88. Directors Minutes, September 22, 1818, BMC Papers, Vol. 2, Baker Library, HBS.

89. Gibb, *The Saco-Lowell Shops,* 738, based on BMC directors' records; Stockholders Records, May 7, 1817, BMC Papers, Vol. 1, Baker Library, HBS; Dalzell, *Enterprising Elite,* 30.

90. Essex County Registry of Deeds, Salem, MA, Book 221, Page 204.

91. Isaac E. Markham to his brother, May 30, 1831, BMC papers, Box 5, Baker Library, HBS; Peterson and Murphy, *Waltham Rediscovered,* 91–92; Dalzell, *Enterprising Elite,* 33–34. New England Workingmen's Association firebrand Seth Luther derided Henry Clay for a speech Clay delivered in the Senate about the joys of factory work. Luther wrote: "While on a visit to that pink of perfection, Waltham, I remarked that the females moved with a very light step, and well they might, for the bell rung for them to return to the mill from their homes in 19 minutes after it had rung for them to go to breakfast." Quoted in Josephson, *Golden Threads,* 223.

92. Mailloux, "The Boston Manufacturing Company: The Factory and the Town," 117.

93. Jeremy, *Transatlantic Industrial Revolution,* 186. Industrial historian George S. Gibb makes the valuable point that Moody should not be judged simply on his known patents, which "represent at best only the small climactic part of his total work." His technical and business acumen were very valuable even when he no longer made patentable inventions. Gibb goes on to say, "Moody stands out as the foremost innovator and inventor of the 1814–1824 period, and these ten years . . . possibly constitute the most dynamic period in the entire history of the American cotton machinery industry. From 1814 to 1824 Moody's inventions and adaptations of English inventions were the

most dominant development in the American textile industry. Almost single-handed he produced sweeping changes in manufacturing techniques—changes which primarily benefited the Boston Manufacturing Company, but which came to be shared by all cotton mills." Gibb, *The Saco-Lowell Shops,* 38.

94. Emery, "Descendants of Sergeant Caleb Moody."

95. Quoted in Thomas B. Lawson, "Lowell and Newburyport," *CORHA* 3 (1877): 221.

Chapter 6. Toward Wilkinsonville

1. An example of Wilkinson family civic involvement is the formation of a fire department in 1801, with Oziel as president of the village fire ward. The first fire engine, called the "Flower Pot," was built by Abraham, Isaac, and David Wilkinson. Hoag & Wade, *History of Rhode Island,* 243.

2. H. J. Habakkuk, *American and British Technology in the Nineteenth Century: The Search for Labour-Saving Inventions* (Cambridge: Cambridge University Press, 1962), 113–14; Alexander Hamilton, "Report on Manufactures," in *The Papers of Alexander Hamilton,* vol. 10, edited by Harold C. Syrett et al. (New York: Columbia University Press, 1966), 252.

3. Thomas Dublin, "The Boston Manufacturing Company," in Beatty, *Colossus,* 68; Peter J. Coleman, "Rhode Island Cotton Manufacturing: A Study in Economic Conservatism," *Rhode Island History* 23, no. 3 (July 1964): 65; Smith Wilkinson to George S. White, May 30, 1835, in White, *Samuel Slater,* 126; Editha Hadcock, "Labor Problems in Rhode Island Cotton Mills, 1790–1940," *Rhode Island History* 14, no. 3 (July 1955): 83.

4. Hadcock, "Labor Problems," 84, 89–90; Rivard, *A New Order of Things,* 95–98. Despite a few work stoppages, such as the strike in Pawtucket in 1824 related to wage cuts and long hours, Rhode Island mill workers did not unite in any sort of labor movement prior to 1840. Gary Kulik, "Pawtucket Village and the Strike of 1824," in *Material Life in America,* edited by Robert Blair St. George (Boston: Northeastern University Press, 1987), 400–401.

5. Gilbane, "Social History of Pawtucket," 11, 27, 34–35, 70, 80.

6. "Edward S. Wilkinson Reminiscences," *Pawtucket Gazette and Chronicle,* February 21, 1873; Gilbane, "A Social History of Pawtucket," 21–25, 501; Gary Kulik, "Dams, Fish, and Farmers: The Defense of Public Rights in Eighteenth-Century Rhode Island," in *The New England Working Class and the New Labor History,* edited by Herbert G. Gutman and Donald H. Bell (Champaign: University of Illinois Press, 1986), 204–206. A contemporary account of the Sargent's Trench law suit, *Ebenezer Tyler v. Abraham Wilkinson,* is in *Niles Weekly Register,* September 1, 1827.

7. Coleman, *The Transformation of Rhode Island,* 96; Coleman, "Economic Conservatism," 77, 66; Slater to Jeremiah Brown (undated, but 1816), in White, *Samuel Slater,* 215.

8. Rev. Israel Wilkinson, *Memoirs of the Wilkinson Family,* 476, 506.

9. Hadcock, "Labor Problems," 82–83. On how it suited Appleton's purposes to portray F. C. Lowell as "the informing soul" of a great and valuable industry, and the Rhode Islanders as less visionary, see Conrad, "Drive That Branch," 4–5.

10. Bagnall, *Textile Industries,* 289–90. Williams's loom, patented July 3, 1813, was designed for narrow products such as saddle girths and suspenders.

11. Lozier, *Taunton and Mason,* 65–67. The importance of smash protection is demonstrated in the following anecdote related by Rhode Island manufacturing pioneer Zachariah Allen in 1861: "To lessen the risk of this occurrence of a 'smash,' the shuttle was thrown with great velocity, which cause it frequently to fly out of the loom, and to become a somewhat dangerous missile. It is narrated that a neighboring farmer, after selling his load of wood at Mr. Franklin's mill in Olneyville, where some power looms were used in 1813, indulged his curiosity to see them operate, by stepping into the Weaving room. Whilst he stood gazing with wonder at the novel spectacle before him, the shuttle suddenly flew out and hit him in the head causing him to drop his whip in his haste to escape out the door. Fearful of again entering into the room, he begged one of the weavers to hand [the whip] out to him as he said he was not used to power weaving." Allen, "Historical, Theoretical, and Practical Account," 145.

12. The Waltham mill owners were well aware of Shepard and Thorp's 1816 loom. Appleton recalled that after their June 1816 visit to Pawtucket and Providence, they "returned by the way of Taunton. We saw, at the factory of Mr. Shepherd, an attempt to establish a vertical power loom, which did not promise success." Appleton, *Power Loom,* 14.

13. Gail Fowler Mohanty, "'All Other Inventions Were Thrown into the Shade': The Power Loom in Rhode Island, 1810–1830," in *Working in the Blackstone River Valley: Exploring the Heritage of Industrialization,* edited by Douglas M. Reynolds and Marjory Myers (Woonsocket, RI: Rhode Island Labor History Society, 1991), 77; Allen, "Historical, Theoretical, and Practical Account," 144; Conrad, "Drive That Branch," 5–6, 15. While there is no reason to doubt the very knowledgeable and usually reliable Allen, we must note that he was reacting to Appleton's *Introduction of the Power Loom and the Origin of Lowell* (1858), as the defenders of the Waltham-Lowell system and the Rhode Island system squared off on various issues of early manufacturing in America. Allen was irritated that on his visit to Rhode Island in 1816, Appleton had "traveled out of his way to sneer at the less fortunate position of Mr. Wilkinson and of his poorer fellow manufacturers of Rhode Island, and to depict them all as lacking sagacity to appreciate the advantages of improved machinery and the energy to help themselves." Allen, "Historical, Theoretical, and Practical Account," 146. Paul E. Rivard, former Curator of Technology at the American Textile History Museum in Lowell, lists Hines, Arnold, and Company, Job Manchester, John Thorp, Silas Sheperd, and T. A. Williams as makers of early power looms in Rhode Island and southeastern Massachusetts prior to 1817. In Rivard's opinion, "the Boston Associates did not build the first or even the best power loom of the era, but their loom was an outstanding commercial success." Rivard, *A New Order of Things,* 46.

14. Although Gilmore was Scottish, the loom he introduced was the invention of an Englishman, William Horrocks, who had patented his original power loom in 1803, with improvements patented in 1805 and 1813. Bagnall, *Textile Industries,* 547.

15. Conrad, "Drive that Branch," 16, 19; Henry B. Lyman to Elisha Dyer, May 28, 1861, in *Transactions of the RISEDI* (1861): 77–78.

16. Lyman to Dyer, *Transactions of the RISEDI,* 77–78; Massena Goodrich, "Centennial Address," *A Report of the Centennial Celebration at Pawtucket, North Providence, of the One Hundredth Anniversary of the Incorporation of the Town* (Providence: 1865), 39; Rivard, *A New Order of Things,* 46–47.

17. Allen, quoted in Kulik, *Mill Village,* 149; Jeremy, *Transatlantic Industrial Revolution,* 102–103. Gilmore's loom, based on Horricks's 1813 patented improvements, was considerably more advanced than the Waltham loom, based on Miller's 1796 wiper loom. Horricks's crank, a means of converting rotary motion to reciprocating (back and forth) motion, proved more effective than the cam (or "wiper") used to drive the moving parts of the Miller loom. Conrad, "Drive That Branch," 15–16; Jeremy, *Transatlantic Industrial Revolution,* 99.

18. Henry B. Lyman to Elisha Dyer, May 28, 1861, in *Transactions of the RISEDI* (1861): 78; Bagnall, *Textile Industries,* 550; "Statement of Peleg Wilbur, of Coventry," *Transactions of the RISEDI* (1861), in Kulik, Parks, and Penn, *New England Mill Village,* 140. Gilmore's renown and financial reward did not assure his future. According to James Montgomery, "Gilmour was a man of great mechanical genius, but neglected to turn his talents and opportunities to the advantage of his family, and, consequently, on his death, they were left in poor circumstances." Montgomery, *A Practical Detail of the Cotton Manufacture,* 155. David Fales came to Providence in early 1818, well after Gilmore was established. Their looms were very similar. See Job Manchester to Elisha Dyer, November 19, 1864, in *Transactions of the RISEDI* (1864): 71.

19. Job Manchester to Elisha Dyer, November 19, 1864, in *Transactions of the RISEDI* (1864): 70.

20. Providence Iron Foundry records, Slater Collection, Mss. 442, Vol. 1, Baker Library, HBS; *Rhode Island American,* December 12, 1817; Conrad, "Drive That Branch," 21–23.

21. Jeremy, *Transatlantic Industrial Revolution,* 103; Meyer, *Networked Machinists,* 64–65; Conrad, "Drive That Branch," 22.

22. By vertical integration I mean a company's control of multiple stages in the same line of business, for example an automobile manufacturer buying a parts supplier.

23. Edward S. Wilkinson to Elisha Dyer, December 16, 1861, *Transactions of the RISEDI* (1861): 90; *Rhode Island American,* December 10, 1817; *Manufacturers and Farmers Journal,* September 16, 1824; Johnson, "David Wilkinson." 55.

24. Malone, *Waterpower in Lowell,* 16; Stephan Tripp to David Wilkinson, October 25, 1821, Blackstone Mfg. Co. Records, RIHS. I am grateful to archivist Harold Kemble for finding this order, and to Pat Malone for bringing it and related information to my attention.

25. Robert Grieve, *Illustrated History of Pawtucket* (Providence: Henry R. Caufield, 1897), 64, 87.

26. Bagnall, *Textile Industries,* 255–56; *Providence Journal,* August 25, 1825.

27. Rivard, *A New Order of Things,* 124–25; Providence Industrial Sites: Statewide Historical Preservation Report P-P-6 (Providence: Rhode Island Historical Preservation Commission, 1981), 5–6; William R. Bagnall, *Sketches of Manufacturing Establishments in New York City, and of Textile Establishments in the Eastern States,* unpublished typescript, edited by Victor S. Clark (1908), 1438–39, Baker Library, HBS.

28. Edward S. Wilkinson, *Transactions of the RISEDI* (1861): 12; *Manufacturers and Farmers Journal,* January 3, 1820.

29. Kulik and Malone, *Wilkinson Mill,* 4; Bagnall, *Sketches of Manufacturing Establishments,* 936. Wilkinson's attempt at worsted manufacture predated by twenty

years the successful launch of that industry in the United States. Cole, *American Wool Manufacture,* 324–30.

30. *Manufacturers and Farmers Journal,* January 3, 1820. In 1829, this newspaper became the *Providence Journal,* which is still the major Rhode Island daily.

31. William E. Richmond, the first editor of the *Manufacturers and Farmers Journal,* recalling the early history of the newspaper in the *Providence Journal,* January 3, 1870.

32. *Niles Weekly Register,* August 11, 1827. Hannah Josephson had a wry view of Webster's conversion. "Hitherto the young representative of the shipping magnates of New Hampshire had stoutly opposed all notion of protective tariffs; after meeting Lowell, his ardor for free trade cooled rapidly. Possibly at Lowell's suggestion, and armed with introductions from his new acquaintance, Webster moved his law office from Portsmouth to Boston, where Lowell's friends helped him build up one of the largest practices in the country in return for his most selfish devotion to their interests." Josephson, *Golden Threads,* 31.

33. Taft quote in Rev. Israel Wilkinson, *Memoirs of the Wilkinson Family,* 517. The Morgan incident ignited the confused combination of evangelical Christian opposition to freethinking Masonry, the long-standing distrust of secret societies, and—on a larger scale—the problems associated with the transition from a simple, agricultural, Christian society to one that was more industrial, secular, and diverse. Paul Goodman, *Towards a Christian Republic: Antimasonry and the Great Transition in New England 1826–1836* (New York: Oxford University Press, 1988), 234; Robert V. Remini, *Andrew Jackson and the Bank War* (New York: W. W. Norton, 1967), 88–92.

34. Gilbane, "Social History of Pawtucket," 460, 474; *Niles' Register,* October 8, 1831; Johnson, "David Wilkinson," 48; *Pawtucket Herald,* December 31, 1828; *Report of the Committee Appointed by the General Assembly of the State of Rhode Island to Investigate the Charges in Circulation Against Freemasonry and Masons* (Providence: 1832), 29.

35. Gilbane, "Social History of Pawtucket," 434–35, 453; Mark S. Schantz, *Piety in Providence: Class Dimensions of Religious Experience in Antebellum Rhode Island* (Ithaca: Cornell University Press, 2000), 46; *Manufacturers and Farmers Journal,* August 15, 1822.

36. Gilbane, "Social History of Pawtucket," 443; Rev. Israel Wilkinson, *Memoirs of the Wilkinson Family,* 224; Kulik, "Pawtucket Village and the Strike of 1824," 389, 393.

37. Gilbane, "Social History of Pawtucket," 435–36; Schantz *Piety in Providence,* 16–24.

38. Kulik, "Strike of 1824," 393; Gilbane, "Social History of Pawtucket," 446; Schantz, *Piety in Providence,* 48–49. Conversion to the Episcopalian religion for reasons of elite association had been going on for some time in Rhode Island. "By the middle of the eighteenth century, the communities ringing Narragansett Bay had begun that transformation from low-church simplicity to high-church formality that so often accompanies the rise of commercial civilization and the accumulation of wealth." Daniel P. Jones, *The Economic and Social Transformation of Rural Rhode Island, 1780–1850* (Boston: Northeastern University Press, 1992), 22.

39. Kulik, "Strike of 1824," 390–93. Arson was common in Pawtucket in the 1810s and 1820s, reaching a peak in May 1820 when three fires were set within five days. Kulik, 397.

40. Albert T. Klyberg, "'We Walk': The Struggle for Worker Rights in the Industrial Blackstone Valley," in *Landscape of Industry: An Industrial History of the Blackstone Valley* (Lebanon, NH: University Press of New England, 2009), 135; Johnson, "David Wilkinson," 39, 49.

41. Lincoln, "Beginnings of the Machine Age," 726; David Wilkinson's Reminiscences, 100–101.

42. Charles H. Clark, "John Thorp—Inventor of Ring Spinning," *Transactions of the National Association of Cotton Manufacturers* (1928), 72–95.

43. Kulik and Bonham, *Inventory,* 150; Cynthia J. Shelton, *The Mills of Manayunk: Industrialization and Social Conflict in the Philadelphia Region, 1787–1837* (Baltimore: Johns Hopkins University Press, 1986), 66; Jonathan Thayer Lincoln, "The Cotton Textile Machine Industry," *Harvard Business Review* 11, no. 1 (October 1932): 90–91; and Lincoln, "Beginnings of the Machine Age," 726–31. For various business connections between Aza Arnold and David Wilkinson regarding the royalty cost to build Arnold's differential speeder, see David Wilkinson & Co. to Aza Arnold, September 7, 1827 and Aza Arnold to David Wilkinson & Co., September 13, 1827, Aza Arnold Papers, Mss. 266, "Correspondence—1827" folder, Rhode Island Historical Society.

44. Coleman, *Transformation of Rhode Island,* 89–90.

45. *Manufacturers and Farmers Journal,* May 31, 1824; Kulik, "The Strike of 1824," 395–96. This was the first strike among textile workers in America, as well as the first to involve women. The strike lasted less than two weeks, with the owners moving toward settlement after attempted arson at one of the mills. Kulik considers this an indication that at this stage of Pawtucket's industrial development, manufacturers were not yet powerful enough to directly challenge the coalition of mill workers, artisans, and townspeople who opposed them. Kulik, 385, 398.

46. *Transactions of the RISEDI* (1859): 65. The cotton press patent number is 4282X. Although a patent drawing exists, there is no description.

47. Bagnall, *Textile Industries,* 393, 379–80.

48. Richard E. Greenwood, "Natural Run and Artificial Falls: Waterpower and the Blackstone Canal," *Rhode Island History* 49, no. 2 (May 1991): 51, 58; Coleman, *Transformation of Rhode Island,* 174.

49. Nora Pat Small, "National History in the Local Landscape: Industrial Revolution in Sutton, Massachusetts," Eastern Illinois University Research and Review Series, No. 7 (May 2000), 21, 28; David Wilkinson's Deposition, September 14, 1832, Slater vs. Sutton Bank, Sutton Bank records, Mss. 781, "Sutton Bank vs. Samuel Slater / Wilkinson repository," Baker Library, HBS; Brennan, *Social Conditions,* 9; and Rev. Israel Wilkinson, *Memoirs of the Wilkinson Family,* 518. On Wilkinson's contribution of $1,000 toward the church building, and other contributions, see Flora Holbrook Dudley, *History of St. John's Church* (Wilkinsonville, MA: 1950), 6.

50. The *-ville* ending was a post-Revolution phenomenon (*-burgh* was more popular before the war) and peaked before 1850. George R. Stewart, *Names on the Land* (New York: Random House, 1945), 102–103, 195, 289.

51. Coleman, *Transformation of Rhode Island,* 82; Bagnall, *Textile Industries,* 396–98; Richard M. Bayles, ed., *History of Providence County,* vol. II (New York: W. W. Preston, 1891), 401.

52. *Manufacturers and Farmers Journal,* March 15, 1821; David Wilkinson's Reminiscences, 109.

53. Richard Greenwood, "Zachariah Allen and the Architecture of Industrial Paternalism," *Rhode Island History* 46 (November 1988): 123.

54. Small, "Industrial Revolution in Sutton," 30; Hadcock, "Labor Problems in Rhode Island Cotton Mills," 84–85.

55. "Wilkinson Village Historical Area," Massachusetts Historical Commission, 1999; Greenwood, "Zachariah Allen," 127; Smith Wilkinson to George White, May 30, 1835, in White, *Samuel Slater,* 127–28; William A. Benedict and Hiram Tracy, *History of the Town of Sutton, Massachusetts from 1704–1876* (Worcester: Sanford and Company, 1878), 422–23.

56. Benedict and Tracy, *History of Sutton,* 423; Rev. Israel Wilkinson, *Memoirs of the Wilkinson Family,* 225–26; David Wilkinson Deposition, September 14, 1832, Sutton Bank Papers, "Sutton Bank vs. Samuel Slater / Wilkinson repository," Baker Library, HBS; Dudley, *History of St. John's Church,* 4–6; Greenwood, "Zachariah Allen," 126.

57. Massachusetts Historical Commission, "Wilkinsonville Village Historic Area: Architectural Description," 4; Coleman, *The Transformation of Rhode Island,* 196.

58. Eight new banks were established in Worcester County in the 1820s, typically in manufacturing towns like Sutton, where expansion had been hampered by poor access to credit from the big city banks. John R. Brooke, *The Heart of the Commonwealth: Society and Political Culture in Worcester County, Massachusetts, 1713–1861* (New York: Cambridge University Press, 1989), 305.

59. Naomi R. Lamoreaux, *Insider Lending: Banks, Personal Connections, and Economic Development in Industrial New England* (New York: Cambridge University Press, 1994), 15 (Honorable Benjamin Hazard quote, 18).

60. Johnson, "David Wilkinson," 67; *Pawtucket Chronicle,* November 18, 1826. Isaac Wilkinson had come into possession, through assignment, of the Ide Manufacturing Company on the Palmer River in Rehoboth in May, 1825, and two months later sold it to David Wilkinson & Company and a group of other investors who renamed it the Orleans Manufacturing Company and installed forty-eight power looms to weave fine calicoes. Bagnall, *Sketches of Manufacturing Establishments,* 1496.

61. Hoag and Wade, *History of Rhode Island,* 234; Benedict and Tracy, *History of Sutton,* 536; David Wilkinson's Insolvency Petition, Rhode Island Supreme Court records.

62. Bagnall, *Textile Industries,* 380; Alanson Borden, *Our County and Its People: A Descriptive and Biographical Record of Bristol County, Massachusetts* (Boston: The Boston History Company, 1899), 555–56. Other A. & I. Wilkinson properties were the Albion Company, Valley Falls Company, Providence Furnace Company, and the Fox Point Union Company. *Pawtucket Gazette and Chronicle,* January 9, 1874.

63. Rev. Israel Wilkinson, *Memoirs of the Wilkinson Family,* 174.

64. Arthur H. Masten, *The History of Cohoes, New York* (Albany: J. Munsell, 1877), 37–49.

65. Johnson, "David Wilkinson,"47; Gilbane, "Social History of Pawtucket," 451; Grieve, *Illustrated History of Pawtucket,* 183.

66. Frank Lambert, *The Founding Fathers and the Place of Religion in America* (Princeton: Princeton University Press, 2003), 8; John H. McKenna, *The Centenary Story of Old St. Mary's, Pawtucket, R.I., 1829–1929* (Providence: Providence Visitor Press, 1929), 12–15.

67. Gilbane, "Social History of Pawtucket," 272–73. The term *Village Aristocracy* was leveled at the Pawtucket industrial elite in the *Pawtucket Chronicle,* August 29, 1829.

68. Gilbane, "Social History of Pawtucket," 279, 282.

69. *Pawtucket Chronicle,* August 29, 1829.

Chapter 7. Respectable Company Man About Town

1. C. C. Chase, "Lives of Postmasters," *CORHA* 4, no. 2 (November 1891): 129.

2. Bagnall, *Sketches of Manufacturing Establishments,* 2132–34; Nathan Appleton to John A. Lowell, May 23, 1848, Nathan Appleton papers, box 7, folder 2, MHS.

3. Frances W. Gregory, *Nathan Appleton, Merchant and Entrepreneur, 1779–1861* (Charlottesville: University Press of Virginia, 1975), 175; Appleton, *Introduction of the Power Loom,* 17–19. John W. Boott, Kirk's older brother, had been a BMC director since 1820. Stockholders Minutes, March 30, 1820, Boston Manufacturing Company records, Vol. 1, Baker Library, HBS.

4. Edson, "A Fragment," *CORHA*: 249–51. The implication that the Pawtucket Falls and the canal company were secrets unlocked by Worthen and Moody is a persistent fiction inconsistent with the fact that many of the Boston Associates were from Newburyport, and very familiar with the navigability of the Merrimack River. See Thomas B. Lawson, "Lowell and Newburyport," *CORHA* 3 (August 1877): 212–28. Moreover, Francis Cabot Lowell's mother owned four shares in the Proprietors of Locks and Canals at the time of her death in November 1816, a full five years before the "discovery" of the Chelmsford site, and Patrick Tracy Jackson's father was the first president of the original Locks and Canals company. See Inventory of the Estate of Rebecca Lowell, November 1816, Francis Cabot Lowell Papers, box 8, folder 15, MHS. Appleton's memoir of early Lowell made no mention of Jackson's previous connection with the canal company, perhaps, as Robert Weible suggests, because Appleton wanted to embellish his own role in the founding by diminishing Jackson's. Even though Appleton remembered fewer than a dozen houses in East Chelmsford in 1821, there were actually more than fifty homes, several small factories, a new power canal, two schools, two inns, and three stores. Robert Weible, "'More of a place than represented to have been': East Chelmsford, 1775–1821," in *The Continuing Revolution,* edited by Weible (Lowell: Lowell Historical Society, 1991), 3–4, 23.

5. Nathan Appleton to John A. Lowell, May 23, 1848, Nathan Appleton Papers, MHS; Bagnall, *Sketches of Manufacturing Establishments,* 2152. Worthen's salary was originally higher, but he agreed to a reduction in order to receive the stock deal: "Voted, that in consequence of Mr. Worthen consenting to have his salary reduced to fifteen hundred dollars per an. he be allowed to subscribe for Ten additional shares, the assessments upon which are to be charged to the Co.; and that as soon as the dividends upon the same shall amount to the principle & interest a certificate of said Ten shares shall be issued to him." Directors Minutes, November 7, 1822, Merrimack Manufacturing

Company records, Vol. 1, Baker Library, HBS. When Worthen and Moody incorporated the Amesbury Wool and Cotton Factory in 1813, the capitalization was set at $46,000, compared to the Merrimack Manufacturing Company's initial capitalization of $600,000. Bagnall, *Sketches of Manufacturing Establishments,* 2153, 2085.

6. Patrick M. Malone, "Canals and Industry: Engineering at Lowell, 1821–1880," in Weible, ed., *The Continuing Revolution,* 139; Appleton, *Origin of Lowell,* 24; Bagnall, *Sketches of Manufacturing Establishments,* 2157. The Worthen quote is in Malone, *Waterpower in Lowell,* 32.

7. Malone, *Waterpower in Lowell,* 28, 55.

8. Ibid., 33–34.

9. Proprietors / Directors Minutes, Aug 9, 1823, MMC records, Vol. 72, Baker Library, HBS; Stockholders Minutes, August 9, 1823, BMC records, Vol. 1, and Directors Minutes, October 7, 1823, BMC records, Vol. 2, Baker Library, HBS. In the same communication Jackson indicates that the machine shop will be moved to Chelmsford over the course of the year. Despite the apparent deemphasis of the Waltham factories, the BMC declared a 15 percent dividend in 1825. The Waltham machine shop, however, was reduced to a repair and maintenance facility. Gibb, *The Saco-Lowell Shops,* 58.

10. Directors Minutes, May 3, 1824, MMC records, Vol. 1, Baker Library, HBS; Malone, *Waterpower in Lowell,* 43. According to various account books in the Boston Manufacturing Company collection, Moody's $1,500 salary had not been increased since his original contract in 1813, although the other components of his compensation had grown considerably.

11. Journal, January 23, April 24 and May, 1824, MMC records, Vol. 14, Baker Library, HBS. Moody's last payment as BMC "agent" was in February 1824, although part of his salary continued to be carried by the BMC. Gibb, *The Saco-Lowell Shops,* 53, 57.

12. The Locks and Canals book value of the Moody house was $5,000, second only to Boott's at $9,000. Machine Shop Ledger Book, Vol. FB-1, PL&C records, Baker Library, HBS. Mrs. Cyril French to Charles Cowley, February 24, 1876, in *Semi-Centennial of Lowell,* 127. Mrs. French went on to say that the pond "was spoiled soon after he died, by being filled up and covered with ten-foot buildings, the only place that has not been improved in looks." My description of this house is based on a personal visit, guided by Michael H. Lally, former executive director of the Whistler House Museum.

13. John Coolidge, *Mill and Mansion: A Study of Architecture and Society in Lowell, Massachusetts, 1820–1865* (Amherst: University of Massachusetts Press, 1993), 238; "General Butler's Oration," *Semi-Centennial of Lowell,* 38–41; A. B. Wright, "Lowell in 1826," *CORHA* 4: 407. The map, by Benjamin Mather, is at the Center for Lowell History. Examination of various maps indicates that the naming of Worthen Street occurred in 1830.

14. Coolidge, *Mill and Mansion,* 32–45; Frederick W. Coburn, *History of Lowell and Its People,* vol. 1 (New York: Lewis Historical Publishing Company, 1920), 171; Bagnall, *Sketches of Manufacturing Establishments,* 2154; Malone, *Waterpower in Lowell,* 34.

15. "The first piece of cotton cloth produced by the Merrimack Manufacturing Company was woven by Miss Deborah Skinner. She commenced work for the company on the 8th day of October, 1823, having come to East Chelmsford to instruct girls in weaving." Z. E. Stone, "Before the Power Loom," *CORHA* 6: 71.

16. Proprietors / Directors Minutes, December 1 and December 22, 1821, Merrimack Manufacturing Company Papers, Mss. 442, Vol. 72, and Stockholders Minutes, February 27, 1822, MMC records, Baker Library, HBS; Bagnall, *Sketches of Manufacturing Establishments,* 2139. As the Merrimack Company broadened its distribution of stock, two of its new members were Nathaniel Bowditch and Daniel Webster, both of whom had helped the Boston Manufacturing Company in legal matters.

17. Stockholders Minutes, December 31, 1823, and January 1, 1824, Vol. 2, and Journal, January, 1824, Vol. 14, MMC records, Baker Library, HBS.

18. Directors Minutes, February 27, 1822, and Journal, February and March, 1822, Vol. 14, MMC records, Baker Library, HBS; Journal, 1820–1838, August 31, 1822, Patrick Tracy Jackson Papers, Vol. 39, MHS.

19. [no author], *Samuel Batchelder, 1784–1879* (Lowell: Press of Morning Mail Co., 1885), 11.

20. Bagnall, "Ezra Worthen," 40; Diary of Squire Lowell Bagley, June 18, 1824, in Mary Beecher Longyear, *The History of a House (Built by Squire Bagley, in Amesbury, Massachusetts)* (Brookline, MA: Longyear Foundation, 1947). The inscription on Worthen's tombstone reads: "He was the first Superintendent of the great manufacturing establishment at Chelmsford, and in that capacity made full use of those great and rare talents with which his Maker endowed him. Distinguished by the power of his mind, and by uniform application to beneficial purposes, he was yet more eminent by the virtues of his heart. Prompt to conceive, and vigorous to execute plans of benevolence and usefullness [*sic*], he was greatly beloved in life and lamented in death." Bagnall, "Ezra Worthen," 41.

21. Directors Minutes, May 1 and June 26, 1824, MMC records, Baker Library, HBS. It seems likely that Worthen's special stock purchase arrangement with the MMC was similar to Moody's at the BMC, which stipulated that in the event of his death his heirs could either purchase any partially owned shares by paying the remaining assessment, or they could relinquish the shares for a refund of the paid-in amount. Stockholders minutes, October 7, 1817, Vol. 1, BMC records, Baker Library, HBS. William E. Worthen obituary, *The New York Times,* April 3, 1897.

22. Bagnall, *Sketches of Manufacturing Establishments,* 2168. Warren Colburn (1793–1833) was a machinist in his teens, trained at Pawtucket (but in the machine shop of John Fields, not David Wilkinson), then worked in machine shops in southeastern Massachusetts for several years before entering Harvard in 1816. Like Francis Cabot Lowell, he excelled in mathematics, and upon graduation taught in Boston and published his first textbook. In 1823, P. T. Jackson offered him the position of superintendent of the Boston Manufacturing Company, a role he held for just over a year when Worthen's death prompted Colburn's move to Chelmsford. He remained with the Merrimack Company, and played an important cultural role in Lowell (especially as a member of the school committee, and as a lecturer on natural history) until his death at the age of forty in 1833. Bagnall, *Sketches of Manufacturing Establishments,* 2166–68, 2181–82. Samuel Batchelder became agent of the new Hamilton Manufacturing Company in January 1825. *Samuel Batchelder,* 17.

23. Shepley Bulfinch Richardson and Abbott, "Lowell National Historical Park and Preservation District: Cultural Resources Inventory Report," *Digital Scholarship @ UMass Lowell*, accessed April 14, 2013, https://digitalscholarshipumasslowell.omeka.net/items/show/2638, p. 63; Coolidge, *Mill and Mansion,* 24–27, 33. An 1832 map of Lowell shows Boott's house, labeled "The Mansion."

24. For a realistic view of the village's development before 1822, see Weible, "East Chelmsford." Peter Ford has pointed out that supporters of the Waltham-Lowell system liked to believe that society in these towns was open, but in fact there was a predetermined social order, with agents and overseers at the top, local businessmen in the middle, factory workers on the next lower rung, and immigrant laborers at the bottom. The owners occupied the topmost position, but they lived in Boston. Peter A. Ford, " 'Father of the Whole Enterprise': Charles S. Storrow and the Making of Lawrence, Massachusetts, 1845–1860," *The Massachusetts Historical Review* 2 (2000): 88, 95.

25. The positive assessment is in "Reminiscences of Dr. John O. Green"; the negative is in Seth Ames to Charles Cowley, February 24, 1876, both in *Semi-Centennial of Lowell,* 67, 80.

26. *Chelmsford Phenix,* February 17 and February 24, 1826, and February 15, 1828; *Merrimack Journal,* March 24, December 15, and December 29, 1826, and February 15, 1828. Emerson began teaching at the Chelmsford Classical School in September 1825. *Chelmsford Phenix,* October 7, 1825.

27. *Chelmsford Courier,* October 15 and December 3, 1824; *Chelmsford Phenix,* April 14, 1826; Chase, "Lives of Postmasters," 129–30; Basil Hall, *Travels in North America in the Years 1827 and 1828* (Philadelphia: Carey, Lea and Carey, 1829), 288; *Chelmsford Courier,* October 29, 1824.

28. Henry A. Miles, *Lowell as It Was, and As It Is* (Lowell: Powers and Bagley, 1845), 128; Michel Chevalier, *Society, Manners, and Politics in the United States* (New York: Augustus M. Kelley, 1966 [1839]), 139.

29. Richard M. Candee, "New Towns in the Early Nineteenth Century: The Textile Industry and Community Development in New England," Old Sturbridge Village Research Paper (May 1976), 17; Directors Minutes, May 18, 1825, May 21, 1823, and February 28, 1825, MMC records, Vol. 72, Baker Library, HBS; Bagnall, *Sketches of Manufacturing Establishments,* 2162; Ford, "Father of the Whole Enterprise," 79.

30. Samuel Batchelder to Nathan Appleton, September 25, 1824, Proprietors Minutes, Hamilton Company records, Baker Library, HBS; Ford, "Father of the Whole Enterprise," 80; Robert F. Dalzell Jr., *Enterprising Elite: The Boston Associates and the World They Made* (New York: W. W. Norton, 1993), 51.

31. Treasurer's Journal, July 31 and August 1, 1826, PL&C records, Vol. GA-0, Baker Library, HBS.

32. Coburn, *Lowell and Its People,* vol. 1, 150; Brad Parker, *Kirk Boott: Master Spirit of Early Lowell* (Lowell: 1985), 26–40; Joseph W. Lipchitz, "The Golden Age," in *Cotton Was King,* 84–86.

33. John O. Green to Theodore Edson, February 11, 1875, *CORHA* 4: 111; Bagnall, *Sketches of Manufacturing Establishments,* 2191; Miles, *Lowell As It Was,* 230.

34. John O. Green, "Consecration of St. Anne's Church," *CORHA* 3 (1887): 160, 162; Proprietors minutes, June 1, 1822, MMC records, Vol. 72, Baker Library, HBS; Josephson, *Golden Threads,* 46; Edward Cowley, "Rev. Theodore Edson, S. T. D., a Centennial Tribute," *CORHA* 5, no. 2 (1894): 269; Directors Minutes, April 9 and April 15, 1824, MMC records, Baker Library, HBS.

35. Green, "Consecration of St. Anne's," 161; Josephson, *Golden Threads,* 46; Directors Minutes, April 9 and April 11, 1825, MMC records, Vol. 72, Baker Library, HBS; Theodore Edson Diary, May 4, 9, 12, and 15, 1824, Center for Lowell History.

36. Gregory, *Nathan Appleton,* 177; Josephson, *Golden Threads,* 46; Coburn, *History of Lowell,* vol. 1, 156–57; E. M. Edson, "Memoir of Theodore Edson, S. T. D., by his Daughter," *CORHA* 4, no. 3 (September 1890): 207.

37. Green, "Consecration of St. Anne's," 160. Harriet Robinson quoted in Richard L. Bushman, *The Refinement of America: Persons, Houses, Cities* (New York: Alfred A. Knopf, 1992), 477.

38. *Chelmsford Phenix,* February 10, 1826; Bushman, *The Refinement of America,* 328–29, 341. The Merrimack Company had nothing to do with the establishment of the Baptist church, the land being donated by independent manufacturer Thomas Hurd. However, the Locks and Canals Company did donate the land for the Congregational church in 1827. Cowley, *History of Lowell,* 87; Proprietors minutes, May 17, 1826, MMC records, Vol. 72, Baker Library, HBS.

39. Bagnall, *Sketches of Manufacturing Establishments,* 2161–62; italics added; *Chelmsford Phenix,* February 17, 1826. In typical Boott fashion, when East Chelmsford was incorporated and renamed Lowell, he had proposed that the new town be called Derby, the English home of his father, but Appleton and others felt strongly that the town that matched so well the vision of Francis Cabot Lowell deserved to be named in his honor. Appleton, *Origin of Lowell,* 33.

40. Green, "Consecration of St. Anne's Church," 164–66.

41. Bagnall, "Sketch of Paul Moody," *CORHA* 3, no. 1 (September 1884): 70. Moody was particularly supportive of the Sunday School, to which he "furnished both pupils and teachers from his own family." Moody, *Sketches of the Moody Family,* 154–55.

42. Bagnall, "Paul Moody," 70; Cowley, *History of Lowell,* 104–105; Directors Minutes, September 3, 1827, MMC records, Vol. 72, Baker Library, HBS; Edson Diary, February 14, 1827; Kirk Boott to Theodore Edson, November 20, 1827, in *Historical Sketch of Saint Anne's Church, Lowell, Massachusetts* (Lowell: Courier-Citizen, 1925), 34.

43. Bagnall, "Paul Moody," 70; Thomas R. Pegram, *Battling Demon Rum: The Struggle for a Dry America, 1800–1933* (Chicago: Ivan R. Dee, 1998), 3; *Chelmsford Phenix,* February 24, 1826; "Gen. Butler's Oration," *Semi-Centennial of Lowell,* 38.

44. Ian R. Tyrrell, *Sobering Up: From Temperance to Prohibition in Antebellum America, 1800–1860* (Westport, CT: Greenwood Press, 1979), 7; [Proprietors of Locks and Canals], *Proposals by the Proprietors of the Locks and Canals on Merrimack River, for the Sale of Their Mill Power and Land at Lowell* (Boston: Wells and Lilly, 1826), 10, MHS.

45. *Chelmsford Courier,* April 22, 1825; *Chelmsford Phoenix,* March 21, 1827 and October 16, 1829.

46. A. M. Goodale, "Boston Manufacturing Company," a paper read at the [Waltham] Citizens Club, printed in *Chat* 1, no. 7 (January 31, 1891), MHS; David A. Zonderman, *Aspirations and Anxieties: New England Workers and the Mechanized Factory System, 1815–1850* (New York: Oxford University Press, 1992), 146–47. The company docked the workers' pay for these two half-hour breaks, but did not prohibit the practice until 1834.

47. Bagnall, *Sketches of Manufacturing Establishments,* 2096–97; In 1827, a new Fall River mill overseer decided to end the practice of giving rum to the workers at 11 a.m. every day, saying he was "hired to oversee the carding room, not to pass out liquor." While this caused an uproar at Fall River, it appears that Moody's restrictions were accepted more peacefully. Zonderman, *Aspirations and Anxieties,* 148. Ian Tyrrell could easily be describing Paul Moody when he writes: "Those who joined the temperance

movement attributed their prosperity to personal sobriety and believed that abstinence could promote national as well as individual progress. From their own careers, they acquired an almost obsessive concern with self-discipline, which they translated into a simple formula for the solution of complex social ills." Tyrrell, *Sobering Up,* 7.

48. Treasurer's Journal, October 22, 1827, PL&C Records, Vol. GA-0, Baker Library, HBS; City of Lowell Valuation Book, 1829–1831, Center for Lowell History.

49. Basil Hall, *Travels in North America,* 288; Theodore Edson, *An Address Delivered before the Temperance Society in Lowell, Mass., April 4, 1830* (Lowell: Thomas Billings, 1830), 9–10. Boott's brewery shares are noted in the City of Lowell Valuation Book, 1831, Center for Lowell History.

50. Lance Edwin Davis, "Stock Ownership in the Early New England Textile Industry," *Business History Review* 32, no. 2 (Summer 1958): 217. Boarding houses were not considered safe for cash, so both the Merrimack and Hamilton corporations instituted rules and procedures for maintaining interest-bearing accounts for employees in 1827. Samuel Batchelder petitioned for state incorporation of a savings bank, which became the Lowell Institution for Savings in 1829. Frank P. Hill, *Lowell Illustrated* (Lowell: 1884), 72. The Railroad Bank was associated with the Boston & Lowell Railroad which had been formed in June 1830. Charles Hovey, "The Discount Banks of Lowell," *CORHA* 3 (1887): 258–61.

51. Moody was assessed a real estate tax on the land, house, and barn. His total taxes in 1826, the year Lowell was incorporated as a town, amounted to $41.77. City of Lowell Valuation Book (1826), microfilm, Center for Lowell History.

52. Stuart M. Blumin, *The Emergence of the Middle Class* (New York: Cambridge University Press, 1989), 158–63. The 1830 census shows that in addition to Paul and Susan and their five children, there was one female aged between twenty and twenty-nine and one male aged between twenty and twenty-nine living at the residence. Massachusetts Census, 1830, roll 67, page 143, Center for Lowell History.

53. The Middlesex Mechanics Association records, at the Center for Lowell History, show that Paul Moody was not a member, which is in keeping with the association's intended audience of rank-and-file workers rather than corporate executives. The early records of Lowell's Mt. Horeb Royal Arch Masons were destroyed by fire, according to chapter historian Max Ludwig (phone conversation January 13, 2005). The fact that Moody's obituaries made no mention of the Masons strongly suggests that he was not a member.

54. Parker, *Kirk Boott,* 57; C. C. Chase, "Brief Biographical Notices of the Prominent Citizens of the Town of Lowell, 1826–1836," *CORHA* 4: 296. It is noteworthy that in Chase's long article on civic leaders of early Chelmsford and Lowell, there is not a single mention of Paul Moody.

55. Michael F. Holt, *The Rise and Fall of the American Whig Party* (New York: Oxford University Press, 1999), 2, 13; Z. E. Stone, "General Jackson in Lowell," *CORHA* 2 (February 1876): 107; Ware, *The Early New England Cotton Manufacture,* 96.

56. Theodore Edson, "Kirk Boott," *CORHA* 2 (February 1876): 95. Edson went on to describe Boott as "a gentleman of courtly manners, a large knowledge of the world, an extensive acquaintance with mankind, [and] at home and at ease in the cultured circles." Alvan Clark quoted in William A. Richardson to Alfred Gilman, July 10, 1889,

in "Autobiography of Alvan Clark, with an Introductory Letter by Chief Justice William A. Richardson, formerly of Lowell," *CORHA* 4 (November 1891): 166.

57. Gibb, *The Saco-Lowell Shops,* 59; Paul E. Johnson, *A Shopkeeper's Millennium: Society and Revivals in Rochester, New York, 1815–1837* (New York: Hill and Wang, 1978), 22.

58. Jeremy, *Artisans, Entrepreneurs and Machines,* 72, 76.

59. "Memorandum book on textile manufacturing companies, Aug. 1828-19 Oct. 1829," Patrick Tracy Jackson Papers, Vol. 42, folder 16, MHS.

60. Bagnall, *Sketches of Manufacturing Establishments,* 2279; Theodore Z. Penn, "The Development of the Leather Belt Main Drive," *IA: The Journal of the Society for Industrial Archaeology* (1981): 6–7; Malone, *Waterpower in Lowell,* 56–57.

61. "Orders to Job Hands by George Brownell," PL&C records, Box S-1, Baker Library, HBS; Bagnall, *Sketches of Manufacturing Establishments,* 2106.

62. Directors Minutes, May 22, 1827, MMC records, Vol. 72, Baker Library, HBS.

63. Directors Minutes, October 6, 1829, and August 13, 1831, Vol. 2, BMC records, Baker Library, HBS.

64. Theodore Edson, sermon delivered July 10, 1831, quoted in Bagnall, "Paul Moody," 71; *Lowell Journal,* July 9, 1831; Edson, "Kirk Boott," 91. It would be convenient to blame Boott for Moody's early death, but if Moody was overworked it was mostly due to his own sense of dedication to the company. My overall impression of Kirk Boott is that he was neither the dictator that Hannah Josephson claimed, nor the misunderstood gentleman whose energy and military/social background made him seem more insensitive than he was, as Brad Parker and William Bagnall have portrayed him. My point is that his demanding and difficult style, his haughty manner, and his English pretensions made him nearly the antithesis of Paul Moody. He depended on Moody's technical expertise, but also appears to have been a dominating figure in Moody's life, especially in financial matters. Lowell has remembered its founders very fondly, yet Boott is the only one who was disliked by a substantial number of people, and it seems unlikely that he was simply misunderstood.

65. *Salem Mercury,* July 13, 1831; Edson's funeral sermon, quoted in Bagnall, "Paul Moody," 71; *New England Magazine* 1, no. 2 (August 1831): 180–81.

66. Moody, *Biographical Sketches of the Moody Family,* 157; Lowell Vital Records, Vol. 4, 214; "General Butler's Oration," *Semi-Centennial of Lowell,* 38–41. Butler's "single exception" was Kirk Boott.

67. Directors Minutes, July 22, 1831, PL&C records, Vol. EA-1, Baker Library, HBS. The full text of the directors' eulogy is: "The Directors, deeply impressed with the sense of the severe loss the Corporation have sustained in the death of their Agent Mr. Moody who expired in the midst of his labors on the 7th inst, after an illness of short duration, feel desirous to enter upon their records as a feeble tribute to his work the expression of their high admiration of his skill as a mechanic, as well as their unbound regard for his character as a man. To extreme fidelity & uprightness, Mr. Moody added an untiring zeal in the execution of his trust; diligent & unsparing of his own labor, he exacted & secured the same assiduity from others. Prompt to acknowledge every instance of merit in those he employed, he never had the weakness to indulge a favorite; quick to discern their feelings he possessed too much command over himself to be violent or hasty in

reproof; so that in the scene of his activity his memory is cherished with affection and respect, & furnishes to those who survive him an invaluable model for imitation. To mechanical talent of the very first order he united prudence and foresight in so eminent a degree, that his judgment in machinery was almost unerring, hence the use of few of his inventions have been superseded by more modern discoveries and they were so numerous & important that to no one are we more indebted for the advance & successful state of the Cotton Manufacture amongst us." Directors Minutes, July 22, 1831, PL&C records, Vol. EA-1, Baker Library, HBS.

68. Directors minutes, July 22, 1831, Jan 14 and September 3, 1832, PL&C records, Vol. EA-1, Baker Library, HBS; City of Lowell Valuation Book, 1833, 1834, 1846; Deaths Registered in the City of Lowell, Vol. 148, Center for Lowell History; James S. Russell, "Residences on Nesmith Street," *CORHA* 4: 357.

69. Bagnall, *Textile Industries,* 209–10; Dividends, 1827–1845, PL&C records, Vol. EB-3A, Baker Library, HBS; Charles F. Carroll and Pauline A. Carroll, "Empirical Technology and the Early Industrial Development of Lowell," in *The Continuing Revolution: A History of Lowell, Massachusetts,* edited by Robert Weible (Lowell: Lowell Historical Society, 1991), 165.

70. James S. Russell, "Biography of John Dummer," *CORHA* 2: 97; David J. Moody Accounts, 1830–1834, PL&C records, Vol. A-14, Baker Library, HBS.

71. *Vital Records of Lowell, Massachusetts to the End of the Year 1849.* Vol. 2 (Salem: The Essex Institute, 1930), 126. David married Harriet Boyd of Hallowell, Maine, February 19, 1832 (Vol. 3, 80); William married Martha Brickett, July 21, 1833 (Vol. 3, 81); Susan H. married James Dana of Charlestown, June 1, 1837 (Vol. 2, 219); and Hannah married the Rev. Daniel Gordon Estes of Amesbury, Oct 14, 1846 (Vol. 3, 80). Rufus Emery, "The Descendants of Sergeant Caleb Moody of Newbury, Mass.," (1909), Haverhill Public Library; Lowell City Directory, various years; Z. E. Stone, "Gen. Jackson in Lowell," 118; *Semi-Centennial,* Appendix, 8.

72. Frederick T. Greenhalge, quoted in "Mr. Malloy's Oration," *Centennial Observance,* 51; Thomas Dublin, "Women, Work, and Protest in the Early Lowell Mills," in *The Continuing Revolution,* 78. The riot of May 31, 1831, in which the Irish fought drunken Yankees who were attempting to damage the nearly completed St. Patrick's Church, took place just five weeks before Moody's death, and only a few hundred yards from his house on Worthen Street. Peter F. Blewett, "The New People: An Introduction to the Ethnic History of Lowell," in *The Continuing Revolution,* 212.

73. Lubar, "Corporate and Urban Contexts of Textile Technology," 197; Dalzell, *Enterprising Elite,* 49.

74. Directors Minutes, July 28, 1831, MMC records, Vol. 1, Baker Library, HBS; Lipchitz, "The Golden Age," 87–88; Carroll and Carroll, "Empirical Technology," 160–61.

Chapter 8. "We All Broke Down"

1. Wilkinson sold the land to St. John's Church for one dollar on September 24, 1829. Sutton Manufacturing Company Records, Mss. 442, Vol. 45; Centre Falls Estate Mortgage, March 27, 1829, Sutton Bank records, Mss. 781, Box 1, Folder "Sutton Bank / Deeds," Baker Library, HBS.

2. *Niles Weekly Register,* June 28, 1828; Board of Directors Minutes, September 25, 1828, Sutton Bank records, Mss. 781, Vol. 1, Baker Library, HBS.

3. Coleman, *The Transformation of Rhode Island,* 92.

4. Bagnall, *Textile Industries,* 379–80; *Pawtucket Chronicle,* January 24, 1829; Fiftieth anniversary issue of the *Providence Journal,* January 3, 1870.

5. Slater to [unknown], January 7, 1829, in White, *Samuel Slater*, 246. For examples of the manufacturers' defensiveness in the face of anti-tariff criticism, see the *Pawtucket Chronicle*, May 16 and July 11, 1829, and Hon. Tristam Burges to Zachariah Allen, April 26, 1828, Zachariah Allen Papers, Mss. 254, Rhode Island Historical Society (RIHS).

6. Naomi R. Lamoreaux, "The Partnership Form of Organization: Its Popularity in Early-Nineteenth-Century Boston," in *Colossus: How the Corporations Changed America*, edited by Jack Beatty (New York: Broadway Books, 2001), 52–53; White, *Samuel Slater,* 247. The $7 million estimate was calculated using the Web site Measuring Worth, at www.measuringworth.com; accessed May 12, 2013.

7. *Central Falls, Rhode Island: Statewide Preservation Report,* Rhode Island Historical Preservation Commission (1978), 9; *Pawtucket Chronicle,* January 17, 1829; Slater to [unknown], July 29, 1829, in White, *Samuel Slater,* 247; Deed of mortgage of David Wilkinson's Centre Falls Estate property to Samuel Slater, March 27, 1829, and Deed of Assignment, July 24, 1829, Sutton Bank records, Mss. 781, Box 1, "Sutton Bank / Deeds" folder, Baker Library, HBS.

8. *Pawtucket Gazette and Chronicle,* Jan 9, 1874; Borden, *Our County and Its People,* 556; Kulik and Bonham, *Inventory,* 48, 100; Naomi R. Lamoreaux, *Insider Lending: Banks, Personal Connections, and Economic Development in Industrial New England* (New York: Cambridge University Press, 1994), 32.

9. *Pawtucket Chronicle,* June 20, June 27, October 1, and December 5, 1829; Gilbane, "Social History of Pawtucket," 483–84; and *Rhode Island Acts and Resolves,* June and October 1829.

10. Slater to [unknown], June 15 and July 29, 1829, in White, *Samuel Slater,* 247; Peter J. Coleman, *Debtors and Creditors in America: Insolvency, Imprisonment for Debt, and Bankruptcy, 1607–1900* (Madison: State Historical Society of Wisconsin, 1974), 51; Gilbane, "Social History of Pawtucket," 494. The various interests associated with David Wilkinson & Company were assigned to Thomas Burgess and Company of Providence on July 25, 1829. See Bagnall, *Sketches of Manufacturing Establishments,* 1499, Baker Library, HBS. David Wilkinson's endorsement for Kennedy is apparent from a newspaper notice: "All persons having claims against John Kennedy, for which David Wilkinson is bound as endorser . . ." *Pawtucket Chronicle,* September 24, 1830. For Wilkinson's endorsement of a $300 loan to Kennedy and a $500 loan to Barney Merry at the Sutton Bank, see Applications for Discounts, December 3, 1828 and January 28, 1829, Sutton Bank records, Mss. 781, Box 1, Baker Library, HBS.

11. Deed of mortgage of David Wilkinson's Centre Falls property to Samuel Slater, March 27, 1829, and Letter of assignment, July 24, 1829; Applications for Discounts, June 1 and June 3, 1829; Board of Directors Minutes, September 16 and October 5, 1829, Sutton Bank records, Mss. 781, Box 1, Baker Library, HBS.

12. Sutton Bank to Worcester County Sheriff, July 27, 1829, "Sutton Bank / Deeds, etc." folder, Baker Library, HBS.

13. The Providence Iron Foundry, of which David Wilkinson and Samuel Slater were founding members, merged into the Steam Cotton Manufacturing Company in 1827. The records of both companies are in the Slater Collection, Mss. 442, Vol. 1, Baker Library, HBS. On Slater's foreclosure see Addendum, September 14, 1829, to deed of mortgage, March 27, 1829, Sutton Bank records, "Sutton Bank/Deeds" folder, Baker Library, HBS. The total cost of Wilkinsonville comes from David Wilkinson's Insolvency Petition of September, 1829.

14. John H. Clark to Brown & Lewis, February 19, 1829, Slater Papers, Mss. 442, Steam Cotton Manufacturing Company Letterbook, Vol. 14, Baker Library, HBS; William Hovey to John Wilkinson, November 30, 1829, Sutton Bank records, Mss. 781, box 1, folder "Sutton Bank Letters 1828–," Baker Library, HBS. On January 1, 1830, the Sutton Bank directors voted to advertise the sale of seventy shares of bank stock belonging mostly to Wilkinson and Howe children. Directors' Minutes, Sutton Bank records, Vol. 1, Baker Library, HBS.

15. Miscellaneous note, January 12, 1830, "Sutton Bank/Deeds" folder, and Directors' Minutes, January 12, 1830, Sutton Bank records, Mss. 781, Vol. 1, Baker Library, HBS. In April 1836, the year following Samuel Slater's death, the Sutton Manufacturing Company was incorporated. The directors were Samuel's sons John, Horatio Nelson, and George, and two Providence-based partners. Sutton Manufacturing Company records, Slater Family Papers, Mss. 442, Baker Library, HBS; Tucker, *Samuel Slater,* 193–95. The Sutton Bank made enough of a turnaround under new management to reward its surviving shareholders with a 21 percent dividend in 1833, but appears to have closed soon thereafter. "Dividend Receipts" folder, Sutton Bank records.

16. *Manufacturers and Farmers Journal,* June 29, 1829; *Pawtucket Chronicle,* October 31, 1829.

17. Johnson, "David Wilkinson," 60–61; *Public Laws of the State of Rhode Island and Providence Plantations* (Providence: 1844), 210–19.

18. Slater's house at the corner of High and Main streets was sold to Dr. Johnson Gardner on November 4, 1830, for $3,250. Deed of Sale, Samuel Slater Papers, Mss. 719, folder 1, RIHS. *Pawtucket Chronicle,* October 15, 1830; Benedict, "History of Pawtucket," No. 10, 300.

19. *Pawtucket Chronicle,* September 10 and October 15, 1830; Gilbane, "Social History of Pawtucket," 450; Grieve, *Illustrated History of Pawtucket,* 183.

20. Gilbane, "Social History of Pawtucket," 488, 459, 492, 485.

21. Benedict, "Reminiscences of Pawtucket," No. 12, May 27, 1853, 65. For the colorful story of Sam Patch, see Paul E. Johnson, *Sam Patch, the Famous Jumper* (New York: Hill and Wang, 2003).

22. Bagnall, *Textile Industries,* 257; *Pawtucket Chronicle,* August 22, 1829; David Benedict, "Reminiscences of Pawtucket," No. 23, October 28, 1853, 121. Evidently the townspeople did not associate Edward with the financial disaster; he was town treasurer in 1831. Rhode Island *Acts and Resolves,* October 1831, 74.

23. White, *Samuel Slater,* 244–45; Gilbane, "Social History of Pawtucket," 494–96; E. H. Cameron, *Samuel Slater, Father of American Manufactures* (Freeport, ME: The Bond Wheelwright Co., 1960), 156. Jonathan Prude argues that despite losses, Slater took advantage of this opportunity to consolidate his holdings, which eventually paid off, as

well as to escape the financial and management control of Almy & Brown. Prude, *The Coming of Industrial Order,* 175.

24. White, *Samuel Slater,* 245; Slater to Samuel Smith, September 10, 1829, Samuel Slater Papers, Mss. 719, folder 1, RIHS.

25. Lamoreaux, *Insider Lending,* 9. Lamoreaux argues that when kept under control, insider lending was a useful and relatively safe method for funding industrial development in the early nineteenth century. However, few banks awarded 80 to 90 percent of their loans to their stockholders as the Wilkinson banks did.

26. *Pawtucket Gazette and Chronicle,* January 9, 1874; Philadelphian's quote in Donna J. Rilling, *Making Houses, Crafting Capitalism* (Philadelphia: University of Pennsylvania Press, 2001), 25. The limited liability of corporate charters would have offered manufacturers much better financial protection than the partnership form of their businesses. Rhode Islanders were certainly aware of the advantages of incorporation: David Wilkinson and Samuel Slater had applied for a corporate charter for the Providence Iron Foundry in 1827, a petition that stipulated that creditors must deplete corporate assets before suing individuals, but the state legislature postponed the bill and only after the crisis of 1829 was the petition formally dismissed. Coleman, *Transformation of Rhode Island,* 111–12. Incorporation—and high capitalization—certainly helped the Lowell companies. The Merrimack Manufacturing Company and Proprietors of Locks and Canals simply reduced their dividends in 1829 while operating at full production. Henry A. Miles, *Lowell As It Was,* 35; Directors' Minutes, November 29, 1829, MMC papers, Mss. 442, Vol. 1, and Directors' Minutes, August 22, 1829, PL&C papers, Mss. 393 1792–1947 P966, Vol. EA-1, Baker Library, HBS. On Smith Wilkinson, see Bagnall, *Textile Industries,* 421.

27. *Pawtucket Chronicle,* May 16, 1829.

28. The $140,000 figure is conservative, based on the mortgage of the Wilkinsonville property to Slater in March 1829. The deed lists $16,000 in endorsements, plus the $100,000 mortgage amount, but also mentions that there are "various other notes drafts & obligations" between them. Wilkinson's deed of assignment to John Whipple notes "a private debt of nine or ten thousand" to Slater plus another "of fifteen or twenty thousand." Deed of mortgage of David Wilkinson's Centre Falls Estate property to Samuel Slater, March 27, 1829, and Deed of Assignment, July 24, 1829, Sutton Bank records, Mss. 781, Box 1, "Sutton Bank / Deeds" folder, Baker Library, HBS.

29. An example of a impartial banker is Moses Brown who, along with his brother John, controlled the Providence Bank. Moses openly criticized the bank's high percentage of insider lending and the practice of allowing overdue debts of insiders to go unpaid, although John, as president, ignored his advice. Lamoreaux, *Insider Lending,* 12.

30. Lamoreaux, *Insider Lending,* 53; Document of transfer of 385 shares as collateral security by David Wilkinson to the Sutton Bank, June 18, 1829, Sutton Bank records, Mss. 781, Box 1, Baker Library, HBS. This method of securing loans was not unusual for New England banks at the time, given that "between 1800 and 1860 it is doubtful if more than one-third, and perhaps not one-fifth, of the nominal capital of the banks in Rhode Island was paid for in any other way than by stock notes." Edward Field, ed., *State of Rhode Island and Providence Plantations at the End of the Century: A History* (Boston: Mason Publishing Company, 1902), 296. The one-day loan of $50,000 is reported in Debates in Congress, Vol. 8, Part 2 (Washington, 1837), 151.

31. List of stockholders, May 13, 1828, Sutton Bank records, Box 1, Baker Library, HBS; Naomi Lamoreaux, "The Structure of Early Banks in Southeastern New England: Some Social and Economic Implications," *Business and Economic History,* Second Series, 13 (1984): 174, 176. When David Wilkinson took out his first Sutton loans he also endorsed loans for his son Albert and for Barney Merry, and a loan of $2,300 to Abraham and Isaac Wilkinson was endorsed by Hezekiah Howe. Application for Discount at Sutton Bank, December 3, 1828, and Bills Receivable, Sutton Bank records, Mss. 781, Box 1, Baker Library, HBS.

32. *Pawtucket Chronicle,* August 1, 1829; Lamoreaux, *Insider Lending,* 32; *Rhode Island Acts and Resolves,* January and May 1830; Providence *Republican Herald,* June 27, 1829; Richard K. Randolph to Abraham Wilkinson, July 4, 1829, in Alfred U. Collins Papers, Mss. 1065, box 2, folder 47, RIHS. Appleton quoted in Lamoreaux, *Insider Lending,* 36.

33. Gilbane, "Social History of Pawtucket," 479–80; Coleman, *Transformation of Rhode Island,* 183; Directors' Minutes, January 18, 1830, PL&C papers, Mss. 393, Vol. EA-1, Baker Library, HBS. It was David Benedict who referred to the crisis as "the great smash up of 1829," in "Reminiscences of Pawtucket," No. 23, October 28, 1853, 122.

34. Rhode Island economic historian Peter Coleman blames much of the crisis on Abraham and Isaac Wilkinson, whose bank was "managed with scandalous incompetence." Coleman, *Transformation of Rhode Island,* 196.

35. *Pawtucket Chronicle,* May 16 and August 29, 1829.

36. Ibid., November 7 and December 5, 1829. "Negro cloth" was a common name for various inexpensive cotton or wool fabrics, sold to Southern plantations for slave clothing. Rhode Island was a leading manufacturer of this material in the antebellum period. Myron O. Stachiw, "Negro Cloth: Northern Industry and Southern Slavery" (Merrimack Valley Textile Museum, 1981).

37. David Wilkinson's deposition, September 14, 1832, Slater vs. Sutton Bank, Sutton Bank records, Mss. 781, Box 1, and Meetings of Board of Directors, Sutton Bank Records, Mss. 781, Vol. 1, Baker Library, HBS.

38. David Wilkinson's Insolvency Petition. Aside from the petition's reference to "loss by steam boat work in Charleston, S.C.—$3,500," there appears to be no other indication of the nature or extent of his business affairs in South Carolina.

39. Bill for services, July 29-October 2, 1829, Edward S. Wilkinson Papers, RIHS; Bagnall, *Textile Industries,* 257.

40. David Wilkinson's deposition, September 14, 1832, Slater vs. Sutton Bank, Sutton Bank records, Mss. 781, folder "Sutton Bank vs. Samuel Slater / Wilkinson repository," Baker Library, HBS; Bruce H. Mann, *Republic of Debtors: Bankruptcy in the Age of American Independence* (Cambridge: Harvard University Press, 2002), 110; Samuel Arnold to Aza Arnold, November 10, 1830, "Correspondence—1830" folder, Aza Arnold Papers, Mss. 266, RIHS. The Wilkinson Mill was apparently under the control of the Manufacturers Bank at this point, as it was the cashier of that bank who placed a newspaper advertisement for the lease of a mill and water privilege, "being the same recently occupied by David Wilkinson & Co." *Pawtucket Chronicle,* September 17, 1830.

41. *Pawtucket Chronicle,* October 15, 1830; David Wilkinson's Reminiscences, 109; Edward J. Balleisen, *Navigating Failure: Bankruptcy and Commercial Society in Antebellum America* (Chapel Hill: University of North Carolina Press, 2001), 14.

42. Arthur H. Masten, *The History of Cohoes, New York* (Albany: J. Munsell, 1877), 284, 52–53; Canvass White to Hugh White, October 4, 1830, White Family Research Files, Waterford History Museum, Waterford, New York.

43. David Wilkinson's Reminiscences, 109; Masten, *History of Cohoes,* 53; Rev. Israel Wilkinson, *Memoirs of the Wilkinson Family,* 281. For typical steamship advertisements of the period, see *Manufacturers and Farmers Journal,* April 7, 1831. Masten lists the names of seven "friends of Messrs. Wilkinson and Howe" who arrived in Cohoes about the same time, although only two, Joshua R. Clark and John Tillinghast, can be directly linked to Pawtucket, as they show up in miscellaneous records of workers employed by Aza Arnold in 1821 and 1822. "Contracts, Agreements 1817–1846" folder, Aza Arnold Papers, Mss. 266, RIHS.

44. Masten, *History of Cohoes,* 53, 56.

45. Ibid., 56–57, 60; George Taft, "Memoir of David Wilkinson," *Transactions of the RISEDI* (1861): 40.

46. Thomas X. Grasso, Craig Williams, Duncan Hay, and Christopher H. Marston, "Canals at Cohoes: Navigation and Waterpower," *Canal History and Technology Proceedings* 26 (March 2007): 140; Canvass White to Hugh White, March 30, 1831, White Family Research Files, Waterford History Museum.

47. Masten, *History of Cohoes,* 57–58.

48. Canvass White to Hugh White, May 13, 1832, White Family History Files, Waterford History Museum; Masten, *History of Cohoes,* 59, 63; Bagnall, *Sketches of Manufacturing Establishments,* 1614.

49. Masten, *History of Cohoes,* 62–63.

50. Thomas F. Gordon, *Gazetteer of the State of New York* (Philadelphia: 1836), 348.

51. Grasso et al., "Canals at Cohoes," 140; Masten, *History of Cohoes,* 59; David Wilkinson's Reminiscences, 110.

52. As the first editor of the *Manufacturers and Farmers Journal* later recalled the newspaper's viewpoint, "through thick and thin, through faint-heartedness and compromise, through National Republicanism and Whigism, through Polk, Fillmore, Pierce, and Buchanan, it has been unwavering and effective in its support of legislative protection for home industry." *Providence Journal,* January 3, 1870.

53. Daniel Walker Howe, *What Hath God Wrought: The Transformation of America, 1815–1848* (New York: Oxford University Press, 2007), 546; Lamoreaux, *Insider Lending,* 43.

54. Masten, *History of Cohoes,* 64–65; David Wilkinson's Reminiscences, 110, 109.

55. Masten, *History of Cohoes,* 266–68; Taft, "Memoir of David Wilkinson," 115.

56. David Wilkinson's Reminiscences, 110; Donald Creighton, *The Empire of the St. Lawrence: A Study in Commerce and Politics* (Toronto: University of Toronto Press, 2002 [1937]), 231, 271.

57. Tom Kelleher, "The Blackstone Canal: Artery to the Heart of the Commonwealth," Old Sturbridge Village Research Paper (1997); Rev. Israel Wilkinson, *Memoirs of the Wilkinson Family,* 281; Masten, *History of Cohoes,* 64, 77, 83, 85, 137.

58. David Wilkinson's Reminiscences, 110.

59. Ibid.

60. Taft, "Memoir of David Wilkinson," 114. On Wilkinson's lock gate invention, see Letters Patent No. X9094, August 17, 1835, U. S. Patent Office; John H. Brown, ed., *The Cyclopaedia of American Biographies* (Whitefish, MT: Kessinger, 2006), 184.

61. *Pawtucket Chronicle,* August 5, 1836; Rev. Israel Wilkinson, *Memoirs of the Wilkinson Family,* 281; Elizabeth J. Johnson and James L. Wheaton IV, eds., *Pawtucket, Rhode Island and Vicinity: Marriages and Deaths from the Pawtucket Gazette & Chronicle,* vol. 2 (Pawtucket: Spaulding House, 1994), 5, 7; Masten, *History of Cohoes,* 96–97, 269; "Erie Canal Locks 37 and 38," *HAER NY-337* (Washington: National Park Service, 2011), 14. The Harmony Manufacturing Company lost money every year but one until 1850, when it was reorganized and renamed Harmony Mills, which became one of the largest and most successful cotton manufacturing companies in the United States. Daniel J. Walkowitz, *Worker City, Company Town: Iron and Cotton-Worker Protest in Troy and Cohoes, New York, 1855–84* (Urbana: University of Illinois Press, 1978), 48–51, 57.

62. Bagnall, *Sketches of Manufacturing Establishments,* 1619; W. H. Van Fossan, "Sandy and Beaver Canal," *Ohio History* 55, no. 2 (April-June 1946): 165–77; Shaw, *Canals for a Nation,* 132.

63. Rev. Israel Wilkinson, *Memoirs of the Wilkinson Family,* 281. On the Chaudiere wire bridge see *Transactions of the Canadian Society of Civil Engineers* 3 (Montreal: 1890): 333.

64. On the James River and Kanawha Canal see Emory L. Kemp, *The Great Kanawha Navigation* (Pittsburgh: University of Pittsburgh Press, 2000), 7. Loammi Baldwin is again a possible link to Wilkinson's working on this canal project. Baldwin had done a survey of the James and Kanawha rivers in 1817. Baldwin Papers finding aid, Baker Library, HBS.

65. David Wilkinson's Reminiscences, 109–10; Masten, *History of Cohoes,* 260, 269; Receipt for tax of $14.58 for pews 72 and 79, signed by Edward S. Wilkinson, October 1, 1842. Edward S. Wilkinson Papers, RIHS.

66. George Taft to Elisha Dyer, December 18, 1861, *Transactions of the RISEDI* (1861): 100; David Wilkinson's Reminiscences, 110–11.

67. David Wilkinson's Reminiscences, 109–10.

68. U.S. Patent Number 9525; *Journal of the House of Representatives of the United States (1839–1840),* July 3, 1840; Rev. Israel Wilkinson, *Memoirs of the Wilkinson Family,* 486–504; Leonard L. Richards, *The Life and Times of Congressman John Quincy Adams* (New York: Oxford University Press, 1986), 62–63, 202.

69. Bills and Resolutions of the House and Senate, S. 187, 30th Congress (1848); "Appreciation of David Wilkinson as an Inventor by Congress," *Transactions of the RISEDI* (1861): 111–12.

70. Lathes were indispensable to the fabrication of uniform parts required by the firearms industry during this period. Meyer, *Networked Machinists,* 232.

71. Rev. Israel Wilkinson, *Memoirs of the Wilkinson Family,* 281; *Cohoes Cataract,* January 18, 1851.

72. Michel Prévost, *La Belle Epoque de Caledonia Springs* (Hull, Quebec: Lettresplus, 1997), 15, 23; *Cohoes Cataract,* February 7, 1852; Reverend Israel Wilkinson, *Memoirs of the Wilkinson Family,* 281.

73. Johnson, "David Wilkinson," 82. *Cohoes Cataract,* February 7, February 14, and February 21, 1852.

74. Rev. Israel Wilkinson, *Memoirs of the Wilkinson Family,* 279; Samuel Rezneck, "Cohoes: The Historical Background, 1811–1918," in *A Report of the Mohawk-Hudson Area Survey,* edited by Robert M. Vogel (Washington, DC, 1973), 123–24; Masten, *History of Cohoes,* 285. Much of the phenomenal growth of Cohoes can be attributed to Robert Johnston, who took charge of cotton manufacturing just as David's life was coming to an end. Johnston was a mule spinner from England who had emigrated to Rhode Island and worked with Samuel Slater at the Steam Cotton Mill before moving to New York. Thus, a protégé of David's brother-in-law was achieving the dream of the Cohoes Company founders at the same time that David was leaving Cohoes. Walkowitz, *Worker City, Company Town,* 55–56; Bagnall, *Sketches of Manufacturing Establishments,* 1623–26.

75. *Manufacturers and Farmers Journal,* February 9 and February 12, 1852; *Pawtucket Gazette and Chronicle,* February 13 and 20, 1852.

76. *Pawtucket Gazette and Chronicle,* February 20, 1852; *Manufacturers and Farmers Journal,* February 12, 1852; Benedict Reminiscences, No. 6, *Pawtucket Gazette and Chronicle,* March 4, 1853. Sometime after David's interment, Isaac Wilkinson's remains were moved to the more fashionable Swan Point Cemetery. Rhode Island Cemetery database, RIHS.

77. Benedict Reminiscences, No. 23, *Pawtucket Gazette and Chronicle,* October 28, 1853.

Epilogue

1. Journal, October 31, 1825 and February 28, 1826, MMC records, Vol. 14, and Journal, May 31, 1814 and January 31, 1815, BMC records, Vol. 10, Baker Library, HBS.

2. Herbert Gutman, "The Reality of the Rags to Riches Myth," in *Nineteenth-Century Cities,* edited by Stephan Thernstrom and Richard Sennett (New Haven: Yale University Press, 1969).

3. Massena Goodrich, "Centennial Address," *Report of the Centennial Celebration on the Twenty-fourth of June, 1865 at Pawtucket* (Providence: 1865), 60. Goodrich misses the point that Wilkinson had been, in fact, one of the capitalists.

4. *Pawtucket Chronicle,* October 15, 1830 and March 25, 1831; Kulik and Bonham, *Inventory,* 149; Grieve, *Illustrated History of Pawtucket,* 138; Coleman, *Transformation of Rhode Island,* 150; J. Leander Bishop, *A History of American Manufactures from 1608 to 1860,* vol. 3 (Philadelphia: Edward Young, 1868), 397; "Aza Arnold," in *Dictionary of American Biography,* vol. 1, edited by Allen Johnson (New York: Charles Scribner's Sons, 1957), 361–62; Frederick L. Lewton, *Samuel Slater and the Oldest Cotton Machinery in America* (New York: S. Slater and Sons, 1936), 7.

5. Reverend George Taft, quoted in Israel Wilkinson, *Memoirs of the Wilkinson Family,* 516. Describing Moody, and by inference Wilkinson, as "empirical technologists," Charles F. Carroll and Pauline A. Carroll write: "These designers and craftsmen, working with stone, wood, and iron, were able to picture and mentally manipulate wheels, watercourses, and gearing in imaginary three-dimensional space. By coordinating their vivid spatial thinking with the operations of eye and hand, they were able to transform components of the physical world into effective forces of production. They accomplished this goal without resort to the abstract strictures of science or the abstruse theories of higher mathematics." Carroll and Carroll, "Empirical Technology," 158.

6. Joseph W. Lipchitz, "The Golden Age," 94; Ware, *The Early New England Cotton Manufacture,* 269.

7. *Transactions of the RISEDI* (1861); *Scientific American,* New Series, July 26, 1862, 59, and August 2, 1862, 75–76; *Providence Journal,* January 3, 1870; Kulik and Malone, *The Wilkinson Mill.* Samuel Slater had received mixed treatment when he died in 1835, but was practically deified in the cotton centennial of 1890. Massena Goodrich, "Pawtucket and the Slater Centennial," *New England Magazine*, October 1890, 141–48, 153–56.

8. William E. Worthen, "Life and Works of James B. Francis," *CORHA* 5: 230; "Editor's Table," *New England Magazine* November 1890, 402.

9. *Dictionary of American Biography,* vol. 8, 106–107 and vol. 10, 222; Gail Fowler Mohanty, "Paul Moody," *American National Biography,* vol. 15, 724–25. When a bridge was built over the Charles River near the BMC factories in 1847, the new road was named Moody Street. Edmund L. Sanderson, *Waltham Industries* (Waltham: Waltham Historical Society, 1957), 124; James S. Russell, "Deacon Seth Pooler," *CORHA* 6: 150.

10. John Hill, "The 'Other' Mill Marks 200th Anniversary," *Providence Journal,* September 23, 2010.

11. Grasso et al., "Canals at Cohoes," 149.

Glossary of Textile and Machine Tool Terms

Arkwright spinning frame A powered spinning machine that continuously stretches carded cotton by means of sets of rollers operating at different speeds, while imparting a twist to strengthen the yarn. Also called the water frame, it was patented by Richard Arkwright in 1769.

Calendering A textile finishing process in which fabric is passed through rollers under pressure and heat to impart smoothness and sheen.

Cam An irregularly shaped wheel mounted on a rotating shaft to convert rotary motion to reciprocating (back and forth or up and down) motion, for opening and closing valves, for example.

Carding The process of brushing cotton to align the fibers in preparation for spinning into yarn. Early mechanized carding typically involved two machines: a breaker and a finisher.

Centerless grinding A form of abrasive cutting in which the piece to be shaped is guided between two wheels, one of which grinds the work piece along its length.

Double speeder (differential speeder) A roving machine (see *Roving*) that controls two precise and coordinated movements: slowing bobbin rotation speed as the bobbin is filled with yarn, and adjusting the vertical position of the traverse rail that determines where on the bobbin the yarn will be wound.

Dresser A machine for applying sizing (a starch solution for strengthening the yarn) to the warp yarns of a loom.

Fly ball governor A device consisting of balls at the ends of two arms connected by pivots to a rotating shaft; as the shaft speed increases, centrifugal force spreads the arms, which raise a connecting link that in turn adjusts a valve or gate, for example, to control the volume of water to a waterwheel.

Fly shuttle loom An adaptation of the hand loom that propels the shuttle between the warp threads by pulling a cord, rather than passing the shuttle through by hand. This significant advancement in handloom weaving was introduced by John Kay in Britain in 1733.

Fulling The process by which woolen cloth is immersed in soapy water and pounded by wooden mallets in order to clean and shrink the cloth. Fulling was the first textile process to be water powered in America.

Jenny A hand-powered, multispool improvement to the traditional spinning wheel invented by James Hargreaves in 1764.

Lathe A machine for shaping a piece of wood or metal by rotating it rapidly along its axis while pressing a fixed cutting tool against it. A screw-cutting lathe (as patented by David Wilkinson) uses a "lead screw" to precisely move a carriage that holds the cutting tool, which cuts corresponding screw threads in the work piece.

Mule A spinning machine that combined the rollers of the Arkwright spinning frame with the moving carriage of the jenny. Called a mule because of its hybrid nature, it was capable of producing the highest quality yarns.

Mule spinner The highly skilled and highly paid operator of a spinning mule.

Power loom A machine, powered by water or other external source, that replicates the main actions of the handloom: forcing the filling yarn (held in a shuttle) through the warp threads; alternately separating the two sets of warp threads; and beating the filling yarn against the working edge of the cloth. Invented in Britain by Edmund Cartwright in 1785, the power loom was introduced with significant improvements (Miller's wiper loom and Gilmore's crank loom) in America in the 1810s.

Roving The process in which carded cotton is slightly twisted to strengthen it in preparation for spinning into yarn. The machine that imparts the twist is called a *Roving Frame*.

Satinet Typically a fabric woven with a cotton warp and wool filling.

Shirtings Plain woven cotton fabric suitable for shirts.

Sheetings Sturdy plain woven cotton fabric wide enough for bed sheets.

Sizing A starch solution applied to the warp yarns of a loom to strengthen the yarn for the strain of power loom weaving.

Throstle frame An early variant of the Arkwright water frame. The name stems from the sound of the machine, which resembled the song of a throstle (thrush).

Warp The yarn or threads running lengthwise in a piece of woven cloth.

Warper A machine for lining up the warp (lengthwise) yarns on a loom, and winding the yarn on a beam in preparation for weaving.

Weft The filling yarn that is forced between the warp threads of a loom.

Wiper See *Cam*.

Worsted A long-fibered wool that is combed rather than carded, and spun into a smooth yarn.

Most of the textile terms are derived from David J. Jeremy, *Transatlantic Industrial Revolution: The Diffusion of Textile Technologies between Britain and America, 1790–1830s* (Cambridge: MIT Press, 1981).

Essay on Sources

Primary Sources

Few of the participants in the early phase of the American Industrial Revolution—particularly the artisans—left a record of their lives through diaries or letters. These men are known by their work, their inventions, what their contemporaries or descendants wrote about them, and through the historical, technological, and business context of the period in which they lived. Fortunately, David Wilkinson wrote a short reminiscence, which was published in two successive issues of *Scientific American,* July 26 and August 2, 1862 and in the *Transactions* of the Rhode Island Society for the Encouragement of Domestic Industry (RISEDI) for 1861. A valuable genealogical source is Reverend Israel Wilkinson's *Memoirs of the Wilkinson Family in America* (Jacksonville, IL: Davis and Penniman, 1869). David Wilkinson's Insolvency Petition (1828), at the Rhode Island Supreme Court Judicial Records Center in Pawtucket, itemized the ruinous losses of his bankruptcy. Although not a primary source, John Johnson's "David Wilkinson: Father of the Machine Tool Industry" (MA Thesis, Bridgewater State College, 1978) was particularly helpful. While there is no known memoir written by Paul Moody, he is well represented in two family histories: Charles C. P. Moody, *Biographical Sketches of the Moody Family* (Boston: Samuel G. Drake, 1847); and Rufus Emery, *The Descendants of Sergeant Caleb Moody of Newbury, Massachusetts* (1909) in the Special Collections, Newbury Town Library, Newbury, MA.

Other primary sources include works by nineteenth-century writers who themselves participated in the dramatic industrial growth of the period, and knew either Moody or Wilkinson. These include two works by Zachariah Allen, "Historical, Theoretical, and Practical Account of Cotton Manufacture," in the Zachariah Allen Papers, Rhode Island Historical Society, and *The Practical Tourist* (Providence: A. S. Beckwith, 1832). Both are excerpted in *The New England Mill Village, 1790–1860*, edited by Gary Kulik, Roger N. Parks, and Theodore Z. Penn (Cambridge: MIT Press, 1982). Nathan Appleton's account of the development of Waltham and Lowell, *Introduction of the Power Loom and Origin of Lowell* (New York: Harper and Row, 1858; reprint 1969), is particularly valuable for his close association with Moody and Francis Cabot Lowell, but has a tendency to embellish his own role and is particularly dismissive of Slater, Wilkinson, and the "Rhode Island system." More reliable is Samuel Batchelder's *Introduction and Early Progress of the Cotton Manufacture in the United States* (New York: Harper and Row, 1863; reprint 1969).

The Rhode Island Society for the Encouragement of Domestic Industry, in Appendix D of its *Transactions* for 1861, published a trove of letters, statements, and memoirs by the state's early machine makers and their business colleagues. The entire collection on early Rhode Island industry is worth reading, but the most relevant are by David Wilkinson (Reminiscences); George Taft (Reminiscence of David Wilkinson); Edward S. Wilkinson (early family history); Peleg Wilbur, Job Manchester, and Henry B. Lyman (early power looms); Aza Arnold (differential speeder); Elijah Ormsbee (steamboat); and "Appreciation of David Wilkinson as an Inventor by Congress." Some of the same primary material, and much more, has been collected in the previously cited *New England Mill Village*.

The Old Residents Historical Association, the nineteenth-century forerunner of the Lowell Historical Society, published a great many valuable reminiscences of early Lowell in the *Contributions of the Old Residents Historical Association*. Among the most relevant are William Bagnall, "Paul Moody" and "Sketch of the Life of Ezra Worthen," both in Vol. 3, No. 1 (1884); Alfred Gilman, "Francis Cabot Lowell," Vol. 1, No. 2 (1876); John A. Lowell, "Sketch of Patrick T. Jackson," Vol. 1, No. 3 (1877); A. B. Wright, "Lowell in 1826" Vol. 3, No. 4 (1884); John O. Green, "Consecration of St. Anne's Church." Vol. 3 (1887); and two by Reverend Theodore Edson, "Kirk Boott," Vol. 1, No. 2 (1876) and "A Fragment, written in 1843, by Theodore Edson," Vol. 1, No. 3 (1877).

Sarah Smith Emery, who lived in Newbury during the period of Paul Moody's residence there, left a detailed and lively reminiscence of her childhood, *Reminiscences of a Nonagenarian* (Newburyport: William H. Huse, 1879). An interesting source from Paul Moody's time in Waltham is Reverend Samuel Ripley, "Topographical and Historical Description of Waltham," *Collections of the Massachusetts Historical Society,* Vol. 3, Second Series (Boston: Freeman and Bolles, 1815).

Several collections of business records at Baker Library are the richest source of the history of the various enterprises of this era. The most relevant to Moody are the Boston Manufacturing Company, Merrimack Manufacturing

Company, and Proprietors of the Locks and Canals on Merrimack River (parts of the PL&C collection are at the Lowell National Park and the Center for Lowell History). The most relevant to Wilkinson are the Samuel Slater Papers, the Sutton Manufacturing Company records (after Slater took over the Wilkinsonville properties), and the records of the Sutton Bank. There is additional business history (and a replica of Lowell and Moody's first power loom) at the Charles River Museum of Industry & Innovation (Waltham), information on the development of Cohoes at the Waterford Historical Museum (Waterford, N.Y.), and a full range of textile history at the American Museum of Textile History (Lowell). The Center for Lowell History is a gold mine of primary sources, tax and census records, and maps. A particularly important explanation of the business model for the industrial development of Lowell is *Proposals by the Proprietors of the Locks and Canals on Merrimack River, for the Sale of Their Mill Power and Land at Lowell* (Boston: Wells and Lilly, 1826).

The Industrial Revolution and Early Manufacturing

Paul Moody and David Wilkinson participated in a technological modernization, typically called the Industrial Revolution, which has a long history and a particular association with the rise of cotton manufacturing: as British historian Eric Hobsbawm noted, "Whoever says Industrial Revolution says cotton." The advances in ironwork, tools, machines, and textile factories beginning in the late eighteenth and continuing through the nineteenth century, have been covered in many volumes. Among the most useful are Walter Licht, *Industrializing America* (Baltimore: Johns Hopkins University Press, 1995); Eric Hobsbawm, *Industry and Empire: The Birth of the Industrial Revolution* (London: Penguin, 1999); and Robert B. Gordon, *American Iron* (Baltimore: Johns Hopkins University Press, 1996). An old but reliable and comprehensive study is J. Leander Bishop, *A History of American Manufactures from 1608 to 1860,* originally published in 1868, but reprinted by Nabu Press in 2010. A worthwhile collection of essays on various aspects of early industrialization is *The Industrial Revolution in America* (Boston: Houghton Mifflin, 1998), edited by Gary J. Kornblith, who provides a concise introduction. An insightful book from the perspective of industrial archaeology is Robert B. Gordon and Patrick M. Malone, *The Texture of Industry* (New York: Oxford University Press, 1994).

More specific to the textile machinists of New England in this early period is George S. Gibb, *The Saco-Lowell Shops: Textile Machinery Building in New England, 1813–1949* (Cambridge: Harvard University Press, 1950), which was key to my initial understanding of the influence of early machinists like Paul Moody. Two very important older sources by the incomparable William R. Bagnall are *The Textile Industries of the United States* (originally published in 1893, and reprinted in 1971 by Augustus M. Kelley), and *Sketches of Manufacturing Establishments in New York City, and of Textile Establishments in the Eastern States,* edited by Victor S. Clark (1908), unfortunately still an unpublished typescript at Baker Library, Harvard Business School. Caroline F. Ware, *The Early New England Cotton Manufacture* (Boston: Houghton Mifflin, 1931) and Arthur H. Cole, *The American Wool Manufacture* (New York: Harper and Row, 1926; reprint 1969) are still valuable. John W. Lozier, *Taunton and Mason: Cotton Machinery and Locomotive Manufacture in Taunton, Massachusetts, 1811–1861* (New York: Garland, 1986) connects the industrial developers of Taunton to both Moody and Wilkinson. Two very good sources on early Rhode Island machine development are Gail Fowler Mohanty, " 'All Other Inventions Were Thrown into the Shade': The Power Loom in Rhode Island, 1810–1830," in *Working in the Blackstone River Valley: Exploring the Heritage of Industrialization,* edited by Douglas M. Reynolds and Marjory Myers (Woonsocket, RI: Rhode Island Labor History Society, 1991); Jonathan Thayer Lincoln, "The Beginnings of the Machine Age in New England: David Wilkinson of Pawtucket," *New England Quarterly,* Vol. 6, No. 4 (1933); and Paul E. Rivard, "Textile Experiments in Rhode Island, 1788–1789," *Rhode Island History*, Vol. 33, No. 2 (May 1974). Rivard has also written a clear and nicely illustrated book on textile history, *A New Order of Things: How the Textile Industry Transformed New England* (Hanover, NH: University Press of New England, 2002).

For background on industrial development in Great Britain, an old but still useful classic from 1840 is James Montgomery, *A Practical Detail of the Cotton Manufacture of the United States of America, and the State of the Cotton Manufacture of That Country Contrasted and Compared with That of Great Britain* (New York: Augustus M. Kelley, 1969). For the socioeconomic conditions in Britain in the early nineteenth century, and specifically the riots against power looms, see Chris Aspin, *Lancashire: The First Industrial Society* (Preston, UK: Carnegie Publishing, 1995). Also helpful are Harold Catling, *The Spinning Mule* (Newton Abbot, UK: David & Charles, 1970) and Gilbert J. French, *Life and Times of Samuel Crompton* (Bath, UK: Adams & Dart, 1970). By far the best study of the British influence on American technological innovation is David J. Jeremy, *Transatlantic Industrial Revolution: The Diffusion of Textile Technologies between Britain and America, 1790–1830s* (Cambridge: MIT Press, 1981). Additional important contributions by the prolific David Jeremy are "Innovation in American Textile Technology during the Early 19th Century," *Technology and Culture,* Vol. 14, No. 1 (January 1973); "Damming the Flood: British Government Efforts to Check the Outflow of Technicians and Machinery, 1780–1843," *Business History Review,* Vol. LI, No. 1 (Spring 1977); and *Artisans, Entrepreneurs, and Machines* (Brookfield, VT: Ashgate, 1998).

Invention and Inventiveness

I have tried to show, through these two particularly inventive men, how machinists think and work. The most useful sources were Brooke Hindle,

Emulation and Invention (New York: New York University Press, 1981); Patrick M. Malone, "Little Kinks and Devices," *Industrial Archaeology,* Vol. 14, No. 1 (1988); and the "Thinking About Machinery" chapter of Anthony F. C. Wallace's *Rockdale: The Growth of an American Village in the Early Industrial Revolution* (New York: Alfred A. Knopf, 1978). David R. Meyer, *Networked Machinists: High-Technology Industries in Antebellum America* (Baltimore: Johns Hopkins University Press, 2006), traces the influence of early machinists throughout the eastern United States.

Places

The most important geographical locations in this work are Waltham, Lowell, and Sutton, Massachusetts; Pawtucket and Providence, Rhode Island; and Cohoes, New York. The history of Lowell—from paeans to the triumph of the founding industrialists to cautionary tales of industrial decline—has been told often. Here, the focus is on Paul Moody's career and residence there, the nature of his job and his relationship to the corporation, and, as far as the records will allow, his involvement in the economic, cultural, religious, and civic life of the emerging town. Useful histories of early Lowell include Henry A. Miles, *Lowell as It Was and as It Is* (Lowell: Powers and Bagley, 1845) and Charles Cowley, *Illustrated History of Lowell* (Lowell: B. C. Sargeant and Joshua Merrill, 1868), both pro-manufacturing; Frederick W. Coburn, *History of Lowell and Its People,* 3 vols. (New York: Lewis Historical Publishing Company, 1920) and William R. Bagnall, *Sketches of Manufacturing Establishments* (previously cited), both more balanced; and Hannah Josephson, *The Golden Threads: New England Mill Girls and Magnates* (New York: Duell, Sloan and Pearce, 1949) and Lawrence F. Gross, *The Course of Industrial Decline: The Boott Cotton Mills of Lowell, Massachusetts, 1835–1955* (Baltimore: Johns Hopkins University Press, 1993), both of which deal with the darker side of Lowell's industrialization. Patrick M. Malone's *Waterpower in Lowell: Engineering and Industry in Nineteenth-Century America* (Baltimore: Johns Hopkins University Press, 2009) is primarily about the post-Moody era, but provides concise background on Lowell's early development, and is particularly good in the explanation (and drawings) of the canal system—making a very complex system of hydraulic engineering comprehensible to the general reader.

Lowell's architectural development is covered in Shepley Bulfinch Richardson and Abbott, "Lowell National Historical Park and Preservation District: Cultural Resources Inventory Report," https://digitalscholarshipumasslowell.omeka.net/items/show/2638. A more provocative look at Lowell's architecture and its social implications is John Coolidge, *Mill and Mansion: A Study of Architecture and Society in Lowell, Massachusetts, 1820–1865* (Amherst: University of Massachusetts Press, 1993). Two indispensable collections of essays are Arthur L. Eno Jr., ed., *Cotton Was King: A History of Lowell, Massachusetts* (Lowell:

Lowell Historical Society, 1976) and Robert Weible, ed., *The Continuing Revolution* (Lowell: Lowell Historical Society, 1991), and two studies of industrialization and urban growth with valuable chapters on Lowell are Thomas Bender, *Toward an Urban Vision: Ideas and Institutions in Nineteenth Century America* (Baltimore: Johns Hopkins University Press, 1975) and John F. Kasson, *Civilizing the Machine: Technology and Republican Values in America, 1776–1900* (New York: Hill and Wang, 1976, revised 1999). British traveler Basil Hall offers contemporary observations of early Lowell in *Travels in North America in the Years 1827 and 1828* (Philadelphia: Carey, Lea and Carey, 1829).

General Waltham history is presented in two books by Edmund L. Sanderson, *Waltham as a Precinct of Watertown and as a Town, 1630–1884* (Waltham: Waltham Historical Society, 1936), and *Waltham Industries* (Waltham: Waltham Historical Society, 1957), and Kristen A. Peterson and Thomas J. Murphy, *Waltham Rediscovered* (Portsmouth, NH: Peter E. Randall, 1988). Richard M. Candee explains the physical impact of the Boston Manufacturing Company on the town in "Architecture and Corporate Planning in the Early Waltham System," *Essays from the Lowell Conference on Industrial History, 1982 and 1983,* edited by Robert Weible (North Andover, MA: Museum of American Textile History, 1985). Kenneth P. Mailloux's very useful three-part essay, "The Boston Manufacturing Company," was published in *Textile History Review* (October 1963, January 1964, and July 1964). The most thorough study of early manufacturing in Waltham is Robert F. Dalzell Jr., *Enterprising Elite: The Boston Associates and the World They Made* (New York: W. W. Norton, 1987).

Two helpful accounts of industrialization during Moody's pre-Waltham years are Robert S. Rantoul, *The First Cotton Mill in America* (Salem, MA: The Salem Press, 1897) and David C. Mountain, *The Mills of Byfield* (Byfield, MA: Parker River Clean Water Association, 1977).

Pawtucket's industrial history is covered well in Robert Grieve, *An Illustrated History of Pawtucket* (Providence: Henry R. Caufield, 1897). Better still is a collection by the perceptive nineteenth-century resident David Benedict, in Elizabeth J. Johnson and James L. Wheaton IV, eds., *History of Pawtucket, Rhode Island: Reminiscences and New Series of Reverend David Benedict* (Pawtucket: Spaulding House, 1986). Gary Kulik and Julia C. Bonham provide important technical details in *Rhode Island: An Inventory of Historic Engineering and Industrial Sites* (U. S. Department of the Interior, 1978). Kulik's HAER Report on the Old Slater Mill (RI-1) is very useful, and Kulik and Patrick M. Malone concisely describe the history of David and Oziel's mill in *The Wilkinson Mill* (American Society of Mechanical Engineers, 1977). While not generally available, Brendan F. Gilbane's "A Social History of Samuel Slater's Pawtucket, 1790–1830" (PhD diss., Boston University, 1969) is a gem. Gilbane's article "Pawtucket Village Mechanics—Iron, Ingenuity, and the Cotton Revolution," *Rhode Island History,* Vol. 34, No. 1 (February 1975) is also very useful. More general Rhode Island economic and industrial history is in Peter J. Coleman,

The Transformation of Rhode Island, 1790–1860 (Providence: Brown University Press, 1963) and "Rhode Island Cotton Manufacturing: A Study in Economic Conservatism," *Rhode Island History,* Vol. 23, No. 3 (July 1964). Two insightful articles by Richard E. Greenwood are "Natural Run and Artificial Falls: Waterpower and the Blackstone Canal," *Rhode Island History,* Vol. 49, No. 2 (May 1991) and "Zachariah Allen and the Architecture of Industrial Paternalism," *Rhode Island History,* Vol. 46 (November 1988).

David Wilkinson's mill village at Wilkinsonville, in the town of Sutton, Massachusetts, is described in Nora Pat Small, "National History in the Local Landscape: Industrial Revolution in Sutton, Massachusetts," Eastern Illinois University Research and Review Series, No. 7 (May 2000), and William A. Benedict and Hiram Tracy, *History of the Town of Sutton, Massachusetts from 1704–1876* (Worcester: Sanford and Company, 1878). An excellent source on mill villages throughout New England is Richard M. Candee, "New Towns in the Early Nineteenth Century: The Textile Industry and Community Development in New England," Old Sturbridge Village Research Paper (May 1976).

Cohoes's first historian, who appreciated David Wilkinson's contributions to the new town, is Arthur H. Masten, *The History of Cohoes, New York* (Albany: J. Munsell, 1877). More recent and technical is Samuel Rezneck, "Cohoes: The Historical Background, 1811–1918," in *A Report of the Mohawk-Hudson Area Survey*, edited by Robert M. Vogel (Washington, DC, 1973).

Valuable studies of Pennsylvania make it clear that the industrial impetus was evident far beyond New England in this early period. The most important are Anthony F. C. Wallace, *Rockdale* (previously noted); Philip Scranton, *Proprietary Capitalism: The Textile Manufacture at Philadelphia, 1800–1885* (New York: Cambridge University Press, 1984); and Cynthia J. Shelton, *The Mills of Manayunk: Industrialization and Social Conflict in the Philadelphia Region, 1787–1837* (Baltimore: Johns Hopkins University Press, 1986).

Political Economy and Economic History

Contemporary views on the philosophy of manufacturing, reactions to it, and the arguments over the maintenance of "republican" values, have been collected in *The Philosophy of Manufactures: Early Debates over Industrialization in the United States,* edited by Michael B. Folsom and Steven D. Lubar (Cambridge: MIT Press, 1982). John F. Kasson, *Civilizing the Machine* (previously mentioned) and Drew R. McCoy, *The Elusive Republic: Political Economy in Jeffersonian America* (Chapel Hill: University of North Carolina Press, 1980) explain the relationship between republicanism and manufacturing. Leo Marx's engaging *The Machine in the Garden: Technology and the Pastoral Ideal in America* (New York: Oxford University Press, 1964) addresses "the contradiction between rural myth and technological fact." Other relevant studies include Jennifer Clark, "The American Image of Technology from the Revolution to 1840," *American*

Quarterly, Vol. 39, No. 3 (Autumn 1987); Jonathan Prude, *The Coming of Industrial Order: Town and Factory Life in Rural Massachusetts, 1810–1860* (Amherst: University of Massachusetts Press, 1999); Carl Siracusa, *A Mechanical People: Perceptions of the Industrial Order in Massachusetts, 1850–1880* (Middletown: Wesleyan University Press, 1979); Theodore Steinberg, *Nature Incorporated: Industrialization and the Waters of New England* (New York: Cambridge University Press, 1991); and David A. Zonderman, *Aspirations and Anxieties: New England Workers and the Mechanized Factory System, 1815–1850* (New York: Oxford University Press, 1992).

Banking plays a large role in David Wilkinson's failure. Naomi R. Lamoreaux, *Insider Lending: Banks, Personal Connections, and Economic Development in Industrial New England* (New York: Cambridge University Press, 1994) is an interesting and informative book, with specific references to the Wilkinsons' risky banking practices. Other helpful studies are Peter J. Coleman, *Debtors and Creditors in America: Insolvency, Imprisonment for Debt, and Bankruptcy, 1607–1900* (Madison: State Historical Society of Wisconsin, 1974); and Bruce H. Mann, *Republic of Debtors: Bankruptcy in the Age of American Independence* (Cambridge: Harvard University Press, 2002).

Contemporaries

Several of the most important people in Paul Moody's development are covered in Frances W. Gregory, *Nathan Appleton, Merchant and Entrepreneur, 1779–1861* (Charlottesville: University Press of Virginia, 1975); Greville Bathe and Dorothy Bathe, *Jacob Perkins: His Inventions, His Times and His Contemporaries* (Philadelphia: Historical Society of Pennsylvania, 1943); and Brad Parker, *Kirk Boott: Master Spirit of Early Lowell* (Lowell: 1985). Robert Dalzell, *Enterprising Elite* (previously cited), covers Lowell's long visit to Britain in 1811–12, his industrial espionage, and his collaboration with Moody on the power loom at Waltham. Dalzell lucidly explains the workings of the interlocking directorates of investors that historians have dubbed the "Boston Associates" who controlled the industrial development of Waltham and Lowell.

Samuel Slater is an imposing figure in the Wilkinson story, but there is still no definitive biography. George S. White, a close personal friend, wrote *Memoir of Samuel Slater* (New York: Augustus M. Kelley, reprint 1967) in 1836, and it is useful for specific letters and dates, but too admiring to trust his analysis or matters of opinion. Barbara M. Tucker, *Samuel Slater and the Origins of the American Textile Industry, 1790–1860* (Ithaca: Cornell University Press, 1984) is the most extensive biography since White's, but is vague on Slater's construction of spinning equipment and provides little on his connection with the Wilkinsons. Gray Fitzsimons provides a concise up-to-date essay on Slater in the beautifully illustrated *Landscape of Industry: An Industrial History of the Blackstone Valley* (Lebanon, NH: University Press of New England, 2009). James

L. Conrad Jr.'s "'Drive That Branch': Samuel Slater, the Power Loom, and the Writing of America's Textile History," *Technology and Culture,* Vol. 36, No. 1 (January 1995) was particularly helpful on early power loom development, with an excellent discussion of Slater historiography. Conrad's earlier article, "The Making of a Hero: Samuel Slater and the Arkwright Frames," *Rhode Island History,* Vol. 45, No. 1 (February 1986), untangles the conflicting versions of Slater's first year in Rhode Island and counters the heroic story of the lone genius with a more accurate account that acknowledges other technical contributors. Jonathan Prude, *The Coming of Industrial Order* (Amherst: University of Massachusetts Press, 1999) concentrates more on Slater's later years in Massachusetts, but provides a good summary of his English background and first mills in Rhode Island. Moses Brown's influence on early manufacturing can be traced in James B. Hedges's two-volume study, *The Browns of Providence Plantations* (Cambridge: Harvard University Press, 1952; and Providence: Brown University Press, 1968).

Class and Religion

I have emphasized the growing refinement and self-controlled behavior exhibited by Moody, Wilkinson, and other members of the emerging middle class. The classic study of this phenomenon is Stuart M. Blumin, *The Emergence of the Middle Class* (New York: Cambridge University Press, 1989), although my observations were not based on Blumin's study—I simply let the behavior of Moody and Wilkinson demonstrate their growing middle-class taste and refinement. Richard L. Bushman, *The Refinement of America: Persons, Houses, Cities* (New York: Alfred A. Knopf, 1992) is a very useful source on social, architectural, and religious refinement among the emerging middle class in towns such as Lowell in the early nineteenth century. On temperance, Ian R. Tyrrell, *Sobering Up: From Temperance to Prohibition in Antebellum America, 1800–1860* (Westport, CT: Greenwood Press, 1979) and Thomas R. Pegram, *Battling Demon Rum: The Struggle for a Dry America, 1800–1933* (Chicago: Ivan R. Dee, 1998) are both worth reading. A relevant contemporary view from one of Moody's friends is Theodore Edson, *An Address Delivered before the Temperance Society in Lowell, Mass., April 4, 1830* (Lowell: Thomas Billings, 1830). Herbert G. Gutman's observations about the class origins of American machinists, in "The Reality of the Rags-To-Riches 'Myth': The Case of the Paterson, New Jersey, Locomotive, Iron, and Machinery Manufacturers, 1830–1880," in *Nineteenth-Century Cities,* edited by Stephan Thernstrom and Richard Sennett (New Haven: Yale University Press, 1969), held true for Moody and Wilkinson. Religion plays a part in this class development as well: Mark S. Schantz, *Piety in Providence: Class Dimensions of Religious Experience in Antebellum Rhode Island* (Ithaca: Cornell University Press, 2000) is particularly relevant.

Bibliography

Allen, Zachariah. "Historical, Theoretical, and Practical Account of Cotton Manufacture." In *The New England Mill Village, 1790–1860*, edited by Gary Kulik, Roger N. Parks, and Theodore Z. Penn. Cambridge: MIT Press, 1982.

———. *The Practical Tourist*. Providence: A. S. Beckwith, 1832.

———. "The Personal Roots of the First American Temperance Movement," *Proceedings of the American Philosophical Society* 141, no. 2. (June 1997).

Appleton, Nathan. *Introduction of the Power Loom and Origin of Lowell*. New York: Harper and Row, 1969.

Arlington Mills. *Tops, A New American Industry: A Study in the Development of the American Worsted Manufacture*. Cambridge: Riverside Press, 1898.

Aspin, Chris. *The First Industrial Society: Lancashire, 1750–1850*. Preston, UK: Carnegie, 1995.

Bagnall, William. "Paul Moody," *Contributions of the Old Residents' Historical Association* 3, no. 1 (September 1884).

———. "Sketch of the Life of Ezra Worthen," *Contributions of the Old Residents' Historical Association* 3, no. 1 (September 1884).

———. *Sketches of Manufacturing Establishments in New York City, and of Textile Establishments in the Eastern States* (1908). Typescript. Baker Library, Harvard Business School.

———. *The Textile Industries of the United States*. New York: Augustus M. Kelley, 1971 [1893].

Balleisen, Edward J. *Navigating Failure: Bankruptcy and Commercial Society in Antebellum America*. Chapel Hill: University of North Carolina Press, 2001.

Batchelder, Samuel. *Introduction and Early Progress of the Cotton Manufacture in the United States*. New York: Harper and Row, 1969 [1863].

Bathe, Greville, and Dorothy Bathe. *Jacob Perkins: His Inventions, His Times, and His Contemporaries*. Philadelphia: Historical Society of Pennsylvania, 1943.

Battison, Edwin A. *Muskets to Mass Production*. Windsor, VT: American Precision Museum, 1976.

Bayles, Richard M. *History of Providence County, Rhode Island*. New York: W. W. Preston, 1891.

Beatty, Jack, ed. *Colossus: How the Corporation Changed America*. New York: Broadway Books, 2001.

Bender, Thomas. *Toward an Urban Vision: Ideas and Institutions in Nineteenth-Century America*. Lexington: University Press of Kentucky, 1975.

Benedict, William A., and Hiram Tracy. *History of the Town of Sutton, Massachusetts from 1704–1876*. Worcester: Sanford, 1878.

Betts, Edwin M., ed. *Thomas Jefferson's Farm Book*. Charlottesville: University Press of Virginia, 1987.

Bezis-Selfa, John. *Forging America: Ironworkers, Adventurers, and the Industrious Revolution*. Ithaca: Cornell University Press, 2004.

Bishop, J. Leander. *A History of American Manufactures from 1608 to 1860*. Vol. 3. Philadelphia: Edward Young, 1868.

Blewett, Peter F. "The New People: An Introduction to the Ethnic History of Lowell." In *The Continuing Revolution: A History of Lowell, Massachusetts,* edited by Robert Weible. Lowell: Lowell Historical Society, 1991.

Blocker, Jack S. Jr. *American Temperance Movements: Cycles of Reform*. Boston: Twayne, 1989.

Blumin, Stuart M. *The Emergence of the Middle Class*. New York: Cambridge University Press, 1989.

Borden, Alanson. *Our County and Its People: A Descriptive and Biographical Record of Bristol County, Massachusetts*. Boston: Boston History Company, 1899.

Borden, Philip D. *Steamboating on Narragansett Bay*. Steamship Historical Society of America, 1957 [1925].

Bourne, Russell. *Invention in America*. Golden, CO: Fulcrum, 1996.

Briggs, Asa. *The Age of Improvement, 1783–1867*. New York: Longman, 1979.

Brinkley, Alan. *The Unfinished Nation*. Vol. 1. New York: McGraw-Hill, 1993.

Brooke, John R. *The Heart of the Commonwealth: Society and Political Culture in Worcester County, Massachusetts, 1713–1861*. New York: Cambridge University Press, 1989.

Bushman, Richard L. *The Refinement of America: Persons, Houses, Cities*. New York: Alfred A. Knopf, 1992.

Bythell, Duncan. *The Handloom Weavers: A Study in the English Cotton Industry During the Industrial Revolution*. Cambridge: Cambridge University Press, 1969.

Cameron, E. H. *Samuel Slater, Father of American Manufactures*. Freeport, ME: The Bond Wheelwright Co., 1960.

Candee, Richard M. "Architecture and Corporate Planning in the Early Waltham System." In *Essays from the Lowell Conference on Industrial History, 1982 and 1983,* edited by Robert Weible. North Andover, MA: Museum of American Textile History, 1985.

———. "New Towns in the Early Nineteenth Century: The Textile Industry and Community Development in New England," Old Sturbridge Village Research Paper. May 1976.

Carroll, Brian D. "'I indulged my desire too freely': Sexuality, Spirituality, and the Sin of Self-Pollution in the Diary of Joseph Moody, 1720–1724," *William and Mary Quarterly* LX, no. 1 (January 2003).

Carroll, Charles F., and Pauline A. Carroll. "Empirical Technology and the Early Industrial Development of Lowell," in *The Continuing Revolution: A History of Lowell, Massachusetts,* edited by Robert Weible. Lowell: Lowell Historical Society, 1991.

Carruthers, Bruce G. "Review of *Republic of Debtors: Bankruptcy in the Age of American Independence,* by Bruce H. Mann," *Business History Review* 78, no. 2 (Summer 2004).

Castner. Elizabeth D. *Tercentennial History of the First Parish in Waltham, Massachusetts, 1696–1996.* Waltham: The First Parish of Waltham, 1998.

Catling, Harold. *The Spinning Mule.* Newton Abbot, UK: David and Charles, 1970.

Chadwick, John White. "Leicester, Massachusetts," *New England Magazine,* New Series, 22, Issue 3 (May 1900).

Chandler, Alfred D., and Richard S. Tedlow. *The Coming of Managerial Capitalism.* Homewood, IL: Richard D. Irwin, 1985.

Chase, C. C. "Brief Biographical Notices of the Prominent Citizens of the Town of Lowell, 1826–1836," *Contributions of the Old Residents' Historical Association* 4.

———. "Lives of Postmasters," *Contributions of the Old Residents' Historical Association* 4, no. 2 (August 1889).

Chevalier, Michel. *Society, Manners, and Politics in the United States.* New York: Augustus M. Kelley, 1966 [1839].

Clark, Charles H. "John Thorp—Inventor of Ring Spinning," *Transactions of the National Association of Cotton Manufacturers* (1928).

Clark, George Rogers. *The Transportation Revolution.* New York: Harper and Row, 1968.

Clark, Jennifer. "The American Image of Technology from the Revolution to 1840," *American Quarterly* 39, no. 3 (Autumn 1987).

Coburn, Frederick W. *History of Lowell and Its People.* 3 vols. New York: Lewis Historical Publishing Company, 1920.

Cochran, Thomas C. *Frontiers of Change: Early Industrialism in America.* New York: Oxford University Press, 1981.

Coffin, Joshua. *A Sketch of the History Newbury, Newburyport, and West Newbury.* Boston: Peter E. Randall, 1977 [1845].

Cole, Arthur H. *The American Wool Manufacture.* New York: Harper and Row, 1969 [1926].

Coleman, Peter J. *Debtors and Creditors in America: Insolvency, Imprisonment for Debt, and Bankruptcy, 1607–1900.* Madison: State Historical Society of Wisconsin, 1974.

———. "Rhode Island Cotton Manufacturing: A Study in Economic Conservatism," *Rhode Island History* 23, no. 3 (July 1964).

———. *The Transformation of Rhode Island, 1790–1860.* Providence: Brown University Press, 1963.

Conrad, James L. Jr. "'Drive That Branch': Samuel Slater, the Power Loom, and the Writing of America's Textile History," *Technology and Culture* 36, no. 1 (January 1995).

Cooke, Jacob E. *Tench Coxe and the Early Republic.* Chapel Hill: University of North Carolina Press, 1978.

Coolidge, John P. *Mill and Mansion: A Study of Architecture and Society in Lowell, Massachusetts, 1820–1865.* New York: Russell and Russell, 1967.

Cope, Kenneth L. *American Lathe Builders, 1810–1910.* Mendham, NJ: Astragal Press, 2001.

Cowley, Charles. *Illustrated History of Lowell*. Lowell: B. C. Sargeant and Joshua Merrill, 1868.

Cowley, Edward. "Rev. Theodore Edson, S. T. D., a Centennial Tribute," *Contributions of the Old Residents Historical Association* 5, no. 2 (1894).

Creighton, Donald. *The Empire of the St. Lawrence: A Study in Commerce and Politics*. Toronto: University of Toronto Press, 2002 [1937].

Currier, John J. *History of Newbury, Massachusetts, 1635–1902*. Boston: Damrell and Upham, 1902.

———. *History of Newburyport, 1764–1905*. Vol. 2. Newburyport, MA: 1906–1909.

Dalzell, Robert F. Jr. *Enterprising Elite: The Boston Associates and the World They Made*. New York: W. W. Norton, 1993.

———. "The Rise of the Waltham-Lowell System and Some Thoughts on the Political Economy of Modernization in Antebellum Massachusetts," *Perspectives in American History* 9. Charles Warren Center, 1975.

Davis, Joseph Stancliffe. *Essays in the Earlier History of American Corporations*. New York: Russell and Russell, 1965 [1917].

Davis, Lance Edwin. "Stock Ownership in the Early New England textile Industry," *Business History Review* 32, no. 2 (Summer 1958).

Davis, William T. "Byfield." In *History of Essex County, Massachusetts,* edited by D. Hamilton Hurd. Philadelphia: J. W. Lewis, 1888.

Dayton, Fred Erving. *Steamboat Days*. New York: Frederick A. Stokes, 1925.

De Lue, Willard. *The Story of Walpole, 1724–1924*. Norwood, MA: Ambrose Press, 1925.

Deshler, Charles D. "How the Declaration Was Received in the Old Thirteen," *Harper's New Monthly Magazine* 85, no. 506 (July 1892).

de Vries, Jan. "The Industrial Revolution and the Industrious Revolution," *Journal of Economic History* 54 (1994).

Dinmore, Harry C. "Proprietors of Locks and Canals: The Founding of Lowell." In *When Cotton Was King,* edited by Arthur Eno Jr. Lowell: Lowell Historical Society, 1978.

Dublin, Thomas, "The Boston Manufacturing Company." In *Colossus: How the Corporations Changed America,* edited by Jack Beatty. New York: Broadway Books, 2001.

———. "Women, Work, and Protest in the Early Lowell Mills." In *The Continuing Revolution: A History of Lowell, Massachusetts,* edited by Robert Weible. Lowell: Lowell Historical Society, 1991.

Dudley, Flora Holbrook. *History of St. John's Church*. Wilkinsonville, MA: 1950.

Dunwell, Steve. *The Run of the Mill*. Boston: David R. Godine, 1978.

Edson, E. M. "Memoir of Theodore Edson, S. T. D., by his Daughter," *Contributions of the Old Residents' Historical Association* 4, no. 3 (September 1890).

Edson, Theodore. *An Address Delivered before the Temperance Society in Lowell, Mass., April 4, 1830*. Lowell: Thomas Billings, n.d.

———. "Kirk Boott," *Contributions of the Old Residents' Historical Association,* no. 2 (February 1876).

———. "A Fragment, written in 1843, by Theodore Edson," *Contributions of the Old Residents' Historical Association*, no. 3 (August 1877).

Elkins, Stanley, and Eric McKitrick. *The Age of Federalism*. New York: Oxford University Press, 1993.

Emery, Rufus. *The Descendants of Sergeant Caleb Moody of Newbury, Massachusetts.* (1909) Special Collections, Newbury Town Library, Newbury, MA.

Emery, Sarah Smith. *Reminiscences of a Nonagenarian.* Newburyport: William H. Huse, 1879.

Eno, Arthur L. Jr., ed. *Cotton Was King: A History of Lowell, Massachusetts.* Somersworth, NH: New Hampshire Publishing Company, 1976.

Evans, Oliver. *The Abortion of the Young Steam Engineer's Guide.* Wallingford, PA: Oliver Evans Press, 1990 [1805].

Everett, Edward. *Orations and Speeches on Various Occasions.* Boston: C. C. Little and J. Brown, 1850–68.

Ewell, John L. *The Story of Byfield: A New England Parish.* Boston: George E. Littlefield, 1904.

Ferguson, Eugene S. "The Mind's Eye: Nonverbal Thought in Technology," *Science* 197, no. 4306 (August 1977).

Field, Edward, ed. *State of Rhode Island and Providence Plantations at the End of the Century: A History.* Boston: Mason, 1902.

Fisher, Marvin. *Workshops in the Wilderness: The European Response to American Industrialization, 1830–1860.* New York: Oxford University Press, 1967.

Fitzsimons, Gray. "The Slaters of Rhode Island and the Rise and Fall of American Textiles." In *Landscape of Industry: An Industrial History of the Blackstone Valley.* Lebanon, NH: University Press of New England, 2009.

Folsom, Michael B., and Steven D. Lubar, eds. *The Philosophy of Manufactures.* Cambridge: MIT Press, 1982.

Forbes, J. D. *Israel Thorndike, Federalist Financier.* New York: Exposition Press, 1953.

Ford, Peter A. "'Father of the whole enterprise': Charles S. Storrow and the Making of Lawrence, Massachusetts, 1845–1860," *The Massachusetts Historical Review* 2 (2000).

French, Gilbert J. *Life and Times of Samuel Crompton.* Bath, UK: Adams and Dart, 1970.

Gervais, Pierre. "The Cotton 'Factory' in a Pre-industrial Political Economy: an Exploration of the Boston Manufacturing Company, 1815–1820." Charles Warren Center Seminar Paper, January 2003.

Gibb, George Sweet. *The Saco-Lowell Shops: Textile Machinery Building in New England, 1813–1949.* Cambridge: Harvard University Press, 1950.

Gies, Joseph, and Frances Gies. *The Ingenious Yankees.* New York: Thomas Y. Crowell, 1976.

Gilbane, Brendan F. "Pawtucket Village Mechanics—Iron, Ingenuity, and the Cotton Revolution," *Rhode Island History* 34, no. 1 (February 1975).

———. "A Social History of Samuel Slater's Pawtucket, 1790–1830." PhD diss., Boston University, 1969.

Gilman, Alfred, "Autobiography of Alvan Clark, with an Introductory Letter by Chief Justice William A. Richardson, formerly of Lowell," *Contributions of the Old Residents' Historical Association* 4 (November 1891).

Gitelman, Howard M. *Workingmen of Waltham: Mobility in American Urban Industrial Development, 1850–1890.* Baltimore: Johns Hopkins University Press, 1974.

Goodman, Paul. *Towards a Christian Republic: Antimasonry and the Great Transition in New England 1826–1836.* New York: Oxford University Press, 1988.

Goodrich, Massena. "Centennial Address," Report of the Centennial Celebration on the Twenty-fourth of June, 1865 at Pawtucket. Providence, 1865.

———. "Pawtucket and the Slater Centennial," *The New England Magazine* 3, no. 2 (October 1890).

Gordon, Robert B. *American Iron, 1607–1900.* Baltimore: Johns Hopkins University Press, 1996.

———, and Patrick M. Malone. *The Texture of Industry: an Archaeological View of the Industrialization of North America.* New York: Oxford University Press, 1994.

Grasso, Thomas X., Craig Williams, Duncan Hay, and Christopher H. Marston, "Canals at Cohoes: Navigation and Waterpower," *Canal History and Technology Proceedings* 26 (March 2007).

Green, John O. "Consecration of St. Anne's Church," *Contributions of the Old Residents' Historical Association* 3 (1887).

Greenwood, Richard E. "Natural Run and Artificial Falls: Waterpower and the Blackstone Canal," *Rhode Island History* 49, no. 2 (May 1991).

———. "Zachariah Allen and the Architecture of Industrial Paternalism," *Rhode Island History* 46 (November 1988).

Gregory, Frances W. *Nathan Appleton, Merchant and Entrepreneur, 1779–1861.* Charlottesville: University Press of Virginia, 1975.

Grieve, Robert. *An Illustrated History of Pawtucket.* Providence: Henry R. Caufield, 1897.

Gross, Laurence F. *The Course of Industrial Decline: The Boott Cotton Mills of Lowell, Massachusetts, 1835–1955.* Baltimore: Johns Hopkins University Press, 1993.

Gusfield, Joseph R. *Symbolic Crusade: Status Politics and the American Temperance Movement.* Urbana: University of Illinois Press, 1966.

Gutman, Herbert. "The Reality of the Rags to Riches Myth." In *Nineteenth-Century Cities,* edited by Stephan Thernstrom and Richard Sennett. New Haven: Yale University Press, 1969.

Habakkuk, H. J. *American and British Technology in the Nineteenth Century: The Search for Labour-Saving Inventions.* London: Cambridge University Press, 1962.

Hadcock, Editha. "Labor Problems in Rhode Island Cotton Mills, 1790–1940," *Rhode Island History* 14, no. 3 (July 1955).

Hall, Basil. *Travels in North America in the Years 1827 and 1828.* Philadelphia: Carey, Lea and Carey, 1829.

Harris, Howard. "The Transformation of Ideology in the Early Industrial Revolution: Paterson, New Jersey, 1820–1840." PhD diss., City University of New York, 1985.

Hart, Albert Bushnell, ed. *Commonwealth History of Massachusetts.* Vol. 2. New York: States History Company, 1928.

Hartford, William F. *Money, Morals, and Politics: Massachusetts in the Age of the Boston Associates.* Boston: Northeastern University Press, 2001.

Hartley, E. N. *Ironworks on the Saugus.* Norman: University of Oklahoma Press, 1957.

Haviland, Margaret Morris. "Beyond Women's Sphere: Young Quaker Women and the Veil of Charity in Philadelphia, 1790–1810," *William and Mary Quarterly*, Third Ser. 51, no. 3 (July 1994).

Hedges, James B. *The Browns of Providence Plantations.* 2 Vols. Cambridge: Harvard University Press, 1952, 1968.

Hill, Frank P. *Lowell Illustrated.* Lowell: 1884.

Hindle, Brooke. *Emulation and Invention.* New York: New York University Press, 1981.

———, and Steven Lubar. *Engines of Change: The American Industrial Revolution, 1790–1860.* Washington, DC: Smithsonian Institution Press, 1986.

Historical Sketch of Saint Anne's Church, Lowell, Massachusetts. Lowell: Courier-Citizen, 1925.

Hoisington, Daniel J. *Made in Beverly: A History of Beverly Industry.* Beverly Historic District Commission, 1898.

Holt, Michael F. *The Rise and Fall of the American Whig Party.* New York: Oxford University Press, 1999.

Hovey, Charles. "The Discount Banks of Lowell," *Contributions of the Old Residents' Historical Association* 3 (1887).

Howe, Daniel Walker. *What Hath God Wrought: The Transformation of America, 1815–1848.* New York: Oxford University Press, 2007.

Hurd, D. Hamilton. *History of Essex County, Massachusetts.* Philadelphia: J. W. Lewis, 1888.

Israel, Paul. *From Machine Shop to Industrial Laboratory.* Baltimore: John Hopkins University Press, 1992.

Jefferson, Thomas. *Notes on the State of Virginia.* In *The Life and Selected Writings of Thomas Jefferson,* edited by Adrienne Koch and William Peden. New York: Modern Library, 1944.

Jeremy, David J. *Artisans, Entrepreneurs, and Machines.* Brookfield, VT: Ashgate, 1998.

———. "Damming the Flood: British Government Efforts to Check the Outflow of Technicians and Machinery, 1780–1843," *Business History Review* LI, no. 1 (Spring 1977).

———. "Innovation in American Textile Technology during the Early 19th Century," *Technology and Culture* 14, no. 1 (January 1973).

———. *Transatlantic Industrial Revolution: The Diffusion of Textile Technologies between Britain and America, 1790–1830s.* Cambridge: MIT Press, 1981.

Johnson, Elizabeth J., and James L. Wheaton IV, eds. *History of Pawtucket, Rhode Island: Reminiscences and New Series of Reverend David Benedict.* Pawtucket: Spaulding House, 1986.

———. *Pawtucket, Rhode Island and Vicinity: Marriages and Deaths from the Pawtucket Gazette & Chronicle.* Vol. 2. Pawtucket: Spaulding House, 1994.

Johnson, John P. "David Wilkinson: Father of the Machine Tool Industry." MA Thesis, Bridgewater State College, 1978.

Johnson, Paul E. *Sam Patch, the Famous Jumper.* New York: Hill and Wang, 2003.

———. *A Shopkeeper's Millennium: Society and Revivals in Rochester, New York, 1815–1837.* New York: Hill and Wang, 1978.

Jones, Augustine. "Moses Brown," *New England Magazine* 6, Issue 31 (June–July 1887).

Jones, Daniel P. *The Economic and Social Transformation of Rural Rhode Island, 1780–1850.* Boston: Northeastern University Press, 1992.

Josephson, Hannah. *The Golden Threads: New England's Mill Girls and Magnates.* New York: Duell, Sloan, and Pearce, 1949.

Kasson, John F. *Civilizing the Machine: Technology and Republican Values in America, 1776–1900.* New York: Hill and Wang, 1999 [1976].

Kelleher, Tom. "The Blackstone Canal: Artery to the Heart of the Commonwealth." Old Sturbridge Village Research Paper (1997).

Kemp Emory L. *The Great Kanawha Navigation.* Pittsburgh: University of Pittsburgh Press, 2000.

Khan, Zorina. "Property Rights and Patent Litigation in Early Nineteenth-Century America," *Journal of Economic History* 55, no. 1 (1995).

Knapp, Samuel L. *Biographical Sketches of Eminent Lawyers, Statesmen, and Men of Letters.* Boston: Richardson and Lord, 1821.

Knight, Edward H. "The First Century of the Republic," *Harper's New Monthly Magazine* 50, Issue 296 (January 1875).

Kornblith, Gary J. "From Artisans to Businessmen: Master Mechanics in New England, 1789–1850." PhD diss., Princeton University, 1983.

———, ed. *The Industrial Revolution in America*. Boston: Houghton Mifflin, 1998.

Kugler, Richard C. *The Whale Oil Trade, 1750–1775*. New Bedford: Old Dartmouth Historical Society, 1980.

Kulik, Gary. Old Slater Mill, Historic American Engineering Record (HAER No. RI-1) (Washington, DC: 1983)

———. "Pawtucket Village and the Strike of 1824." In *Material Life in America,* edited by Robert Blair St. George. Boston: Northeastern University Press, 1987.

________. "Dams, Fish, and Farmers: The Defense of Public Rights in Eighteenth-Century Rhode Island." In *The New England Working Class and the New Labor History,* edited by Herbert G. Gutman and Donald H. Bell. Champaign: University of Illinois Press, 1986.

———, and Julia C. Bonham. *Rhode Island: An Inventory of Historic Engineering and Industrial Sites*. U. S. Department of the Interior, 1978.

———, and Patrick M. Malone. *The Wilkinson Mill*. American Society of Mechanical Engineers, 1977.

Lamoreaux, Naomi R. *Insider Lending: Banks, Personal Connections, and Economic Development in Industrial New England.* New York: Cambridge University Press, 1994.

———. "The Partnership Form of Organization: Its Popularity in Early-Nineteenth-Century Boston." In *Colossus: How the Corporation Changed America,* edited by Jack Beatty. New York: Broadway Books, 2001.

Larned, Ellen D. *History of Windham County, Connecticut, 1760–1880*. Putnam, CT: Swordsmith Productions, 2000 [1880].

Lawson, Thomas B. "Lowell and Newburyport," *Contributions of the Old Residents Historical Association*, no. 3 (1877).

Lewton, Frederick L. *Samuel Slater and the Oldest Cotton Machinery in America*. New York: S. Slater and Sons, 1936.

Licht, Walter. *Industrializing America: The Nineteenth Century*. Baltimore: Johns Hopkins University Press, 1995.

Lincoln, Jonathan Thayer. "The Beginnings of the Machine Age in New England: David Wilkinson of Pawtucket," *New England Quarterly* 6, no. 4 (1933).

———. "The Cotton Textile Machine Industry," *Harvard Business Review* 11, no. 1 (October 1932).

Lipchitz, Joseph W. "The Golden Age." In *Cotton Was King,* edited by Arthur L. Eno Jr. Lowell: Lowell Historical Society, 1976.

Lombard, Anne S. " 'The Woman Who Played the Man.' Review of *Masquerade: The Life and Times of Deborah Sampson, Continental Soldier* by Alfred F. Young," *Reviews in American History* 32, no. 4 (December 2004).

Longyear, Mary Beecher. *The History of a House (Built by Squire Bagley, in Amesbury, Massachusetts)*. Brookline, MA: Longyear Foundation, 1947.

Lovett, Robert W. "The Beverly Cotton Manufactory: Or Some New Light on an Early Cotton Mill," *Bulletin of the Business Historical Society* 26, no. 4 (December 1952).

Lowell, John A. "Sketch of Patrick T. Jackson," *Contributions of the Old Residents' Historical Association*, no. 3 (August 1877).

Lozier, John W. *Taunton and Mason: Cotton Machinery and Locomotive Manufacture in Taunton, Massachusetts, 1811–1861.* New York: Garland, 1986.

Lubar, Steven D. "Corporate and Urban Contexts of Textile Technology in Nineteenth-Century Lowell, Massachusetts: A Study of the Social Nature of Technological Knowledge." PhD diss., University of Chicago, 1983.

Mailloux, Kenneth P. "The Boston Manufacturing Company," *Textile History Review* (October 1963, January 1964, and July 1964).

Malone, Dumas. *Jefferson and the Ordeal of Liberty*. Boston: Little, Brown, 1962.

Malone, Patrick M. *Canals and Industry: Engineering in Lowell, 1821–1880.* Lowell: Lowell Museum, 1983.

———. "Little Kinks and Devices," *Industrial Archaeology* 14, no. 1 (1988).

Marietta, Jack D. *The Reformation of American Quakerism, 1748–1783*. Philadelphia: University of Pennsylvania Press, 1984.

Martin, Fay H. *Transactions of the New England Cotton Manufacturers Association,* no. 72. Waltham: Press of E. L. Berry, 1902.

Marx, Leo. *The Machine in the Garden: Technology and the Pastoral Ideal in America.* New York: Oxford University Press, 1964.

Massachusetts Soldiers and Sailors of the Revolutionary War. Vol. X. Boston: Wright and Potter, 1902.

Masten, Arthur H. *The History of Cohoes, New York*. Albany: J. Munsell, 1877.

Matson, Cathy D. "Capitalizing Hope: Economic Thought and the Early National Economy." In *Wages of Independence: Capitalism in the Early American Republic,* edited by Paul A. Gilje. Madison: Madison House 1997.

McCoy, Drew. *The Elusive Republic: Political Economy in Jeffersonian America*. Chapel Hill: University of North Carolina Press, 1980.

McDonald, Forrest. *Alexander Hamilton*. New York: W. W. Norton, 1982.

McGaw. Judith A. "In Memoriam—Brook Hindle," *Uncommon Sense*, no. 114 (Winter/Spring 2002).

———. *Most Wonderful Machine: Mechanization and Social Change in Berkshire Paper Making, 1801–1885.* Princeton: Princeton University Press, 1987.

McKenna, John H. *The Centenary Story of Old St. Mary's, Pawtucket, R.I., 1829–1929.* Providence: Providence Visitor Press, 1929.

McLoughlin, William G. "Free Love, Immortalism, and Perfectionsim in Cumberland, Rhode Island, 1748–1768," *Rhode Island History* 33 (1974).

———. *Rhode Island: A Bicentennial History*. New York: W. W. Norton, 1978.

Meier, Hugo A. "Technology and Democracy, 1800–1860," *The Mississippi Valley Historical Review* 43, Issue 4 (March 1957).

Merrill, Joseph. *History of Amesbury*. Haverhill: Press of Franklin P. Stiles, 1880.

Miles, Henry A. *Lowell, As It Was, and As It Is*. Lowell: Powers and Bagley, 1845.

Mohanty, Gail Fowler. "'All Other Inventions Were Thrown into the Shade': The Power Loom in Rhode Island, 1810–1830." In *Working in the Blackstone River Valley: Exploring the Heritage of Industrialization,* edited by Douglas M. Reynolds and Marjory Myers. Woonsocket, RI: Rhode Island Labor History Society, 1991.

Montgomery, James. *A Practical Detail of the Cotton Manufacture of the United States of America, and the State of the Cotton Manufacture of That Country Contrasted and Compared with That of Great Britain.* New York: Augustus M. Kelley, 1969 [1840].

Moody, Charles C. P. *Biographical Sketches of the Moody Family.* Boston: Samuel G. Drake, 1847.

Morris, Charles R. *The Dawn of Innovation: The First American Industrial Revolution.* New York: Public Affairs, 2012.

Mountain, David C. *The Mills of Byfield.* Byfield, MA: Parker River Clean Water Association, 1977.

Noll, Mark A. "Review of *The Founding Fathers and the Place of Religion in America*, by Frank Lambert," *Journal of the Early Republic* 23, no. 3 (Fall 2003).

Padover, Saul K., ed. *The Complete Jefferson.* New York: Duell, Sloan, and Pearce, 1943.

Parker, Brad. *Kirk Boott: Master Spirit of Early Lowell.* Lowell: 1985.

Pegram, Thomas R. *Battling Demon Rum: The Struggle for a Dry America, 1800–1933.* Chicago: Ivan R. Dee, 1998.

Penn, Theodore Z. "The Development of the Leather Belt Main Drive," *IA: The Journal of the Society for Industrial Archaeology* (1981).

Perkins, Bradford. *Prologue to War: England and the United States, 1805–1812.* Berkeley: University of California Press, 1970.

Peterson, Kristen A., and Thomas J. Murphy. *Waltham Rediscovered.* Portsmouth, NH: Peter E. Randall, 1988.

Peterson, Merrill. *Thomas Jefferson and the New Nation.* New York: Oxford University Press, 1970.

Potter, C. E. *The History of Manchester.* Manchester, NH: C. E. Potter, 1856.

Prévost, Michel. *La Belle Epoque de Caledonia Springs.* Hull, Quebec: Lettresplus, 1997.

Proposals by the Proprietors of the Locks and Canals on Merrimack River, for the Sale of Their Mill Power and Land at Lowell. Boston: Wells and Lilly, 1826.

Prude, Jonathan. *The Coming of Industrial Order: Town and Factory Life in Rural Massachusetts, 1810–1860.* Amherst: University of Massachusetts Press, 1999 [1983].

Pursell, Carroll W. Jr. *Early Stationary Steam Engines in America.* Washington: Smithsonian Institution Press, 1969.

———. "Thomas Digges and William Pearce: An Example of the Transit of Technology," *William and Mary Quarterly,* Third Series 21, Issue 4 (October 1964).

Rantoul, Robert S. *The First Cotton Mill in America.* Salem, MA: The Salem Press, 1897.

Ratner, Lorman. *Pre–Civil War Reform.* Englewood Cliffs: Prentice-Hall, 1967.

Remini, Robert V. *Andrew Jackson and the Bank War.* New York: W. W. Norton, 1967.

Rezneck, Samuel. "Cohoes: The Historical Background, 1811–1918." In *A Report of the Mohawk-Hudson Area Survey,* edited by Robert M. Vogel. Washington, DC: 1973.

Rhode Island Historical Preservation Commission. *Central Falls, Rhode Island: Statewide Preservation Report* (1978).

Rich, George. "The Cotton Industry in New England," *The New England Magazine* 9, Issue 2 (October 1890).

Richards, Leonard L. *The Life and Times of Congressman John Quincy Adams.* New York: Oxford University Press, 1986.

Rigal, Laura. *The American Manufactory: Art, Labor, and the World of Things in the Early Republic.* Princeton: Princeton University Press, 1998.

Rilling, Donna J. *Making Houses, Crafting Capitalism.* Philadelphia: University of Pennsylvania Press, 2001.

Ripley, Samuel. "Topographical and Historical Description of Waltham." In *Collections of the Massachusetts Historical Society*. Vol. 3, Second Series. Boston: Freeman and Bolles, 1815.

Rivard, Paul E. *A New Order of Things: How the Textile Industry Transformed New England*. Hanover, NH: University Press of New Hampshire, 2002.

———. "Textile Experiments in Rhode Island, 1788–1789," *Rhode Island History* 33, no. 2 (May 1974).

Rolt, L. T. C. *A Short History of Machine Tools*. Cambridge: MIT Press, 1965.

Rosenberg, Chaim M. *The Life and Times of Francis Cabot Lowell*. Lanham, MD: Lexington Books, 2010.

Russell, James S. "Biography of John Dummer," *Contributions of the Old Residents' Historical Association* 2.

———. "Deacon Seth Pooler," *Contributions of the Old Residents' Historical Association* 6.

———. "Residences on Nesmith Street," *Contributions of the Old Residents' Historical Association* 4.

Sale, Kirkpatrick. *The Fire of His Genius: Robert Fulton and the American Dream*. New York: The Free Press, 2001.

Sanderson, Edmund L. *Waltham as a Precinct of Watertown and as a Town, 1630–1884*. Waltham: Waltham Historical Society, 1936.

———. *Waltham Industries*. Waltham: Waltham Historical Society, 1957.

Schantz, Mark S. *Piety in Providence: Class Dimensions of Religious Experience in Antebellum Rhode Island*. Ithaca: Cornell University Press, 2000.

Scranton, Philip. *Proprietary Capitalism: The Textile Manufacture at Philadelphia, 1800–1885*. New York: Cambridge University Press, 1984.

Sellers, Charles. *The Market Revolution: Jacksonian America, 1815–1846*. New York: Oxford University Press, 1991.

Shaw, Ronald E. *Canals for a Nation*. Lexington: University Press of Kentucky, 1990.

Shelton, Cynthia J. *The Mills of Manayunk: Industrialization and Social Conflict in the Philadelphia Region, 1787–1837*. Baltimore: Johns Hopkins University Press, 1986.

Siracusa, Carl. *A Mechanical People: Perceptions of the Industrial Order in Massachusetts, 1850–1880*. Middletown: Wesleyan University Press, 1979.

Small, Nora Pat. "National History in the Local Landscape: Industrial Revolution in Sutton, Massachusetts." Eastern Illinois University Research and Review Series, no. 7 (May 2000).

Smith, James Morton, ed. *The Republic of Letters*. New York: W. W. Norton, 1995.

Stachiw, Myron O. "Negro Cloth: Northern Industry and Southern Slavery." Merrimack Valley Textile Museum, 1981.

Starbuck, Alexander. *History of the American Whale Fishery*. New York: Argosy-Antiquarian, 1964 [1878].

Steinberg, Theodore. *Nature Incorporated: Industrialization and the Waters of New England*. Cambridge: Cambridge University Press, 1991.

Stewart, George R. *Names on the Land*. New York: Random House, 1945.

Stone, Orra L. *History of Massachusetts Industries*. Boston: S. J. Clarke, 1930.

Stone, Z. E. "Before the Power Loom," *Contributions of the Old Residents' Historical Association* 6.

———. "General Jackson in Lowell," *Contributions of the Old Residents' Historical Association*, no. 2 (February 1876).

Stott, Richard. "Artisans and Capitalist Development." In *Wages of Independence: Capitalism in the Early American Republic,* edited by Paul A. Gilje. Madison: Madison House 1997.

Syrett, Harold C., ed. *The Papers of Alexander Hamilton*. Vol. IX. New York: Columbia University Press, 1965.

Thompson, Mack. *Moses Brown, Reluctant Reformer*. Chapel Hill: University of North Carolina Press, 1962.

Tucker, Barbara M. "Our Good Methodists: The Church, the Factory, and the Working Class in Antebellum Webster," *Maryland Historian* VIII (1977).

———. *Samuel Slater and the Origins of the American Textile Industry, 1790–1860.* Ithaca: Cornell University Press, 1984.

Tyrell, Ian R. *Sobering Up: From Temperance to Prohibition in Antebellum America, 1800–1860.* Westport, CT: Greenwood Press, 1979.

Van Fossan, W. H. "Sandy and Beaver Canal," *Ohio History* 55, no. 2 (April-June 1946).

Van Slyck, J. D. *Representatives of New England: Manufacturers*. Boston: Van Slyck, 1879.

Walkowitz, Daniel J. *Worker City, Company Town: Iron and Cotton-Worker Protest in Troy and Cohoes, New York, 1855–84.* Urbana: University of Illinois Press, 1978.

Wallace, Anthony F. C. *Rockdale: The Growth of an American Village in the Early Industrial Revolution.* New York: Alfred A. Knopf, 1978.

———, and David J. Jeremy. "William Pollard and the Arkwright Patents," *The William and Mary Quarterly* 34, no. 3 (July 1977).

Walters, Ronald G. *American Reformers, 1815–1860*. New York: Hill and Wang, 1978.

Ware, Caroline F. *The Early New England Cotton Manufacture*. Boston: Houghton Mifflin, 1931.

Washburn, Charles G. *Industrial Worcester*. Worcester: Davis Press, 1917.

———. *Manufacturing and Mechanical Industries in Worcester.* Philadelphia: J. W. Lewis, 1889.

Weible, Robert. "'More of a place than represented to have been:' East Chelmsford, 1775–1821." In *The Continuing Revolution: A History of Lowell, Massachusetts,* edited by Robert Weible. Lowell: Lowell Historical Society, 1991.

Wetherill, Charles. *History of The Religious Society of Friends Called by Some The Free Quakers, in the City of Philadelphia.* Philadelphia: Society of Friends, 1894.

White, George S. *Memoir of Samuel Slater*. New York: Augustus M. Kelley, 1967 [1836].

Wilentz, Sean. *Chants Democratic: New York City and the Rise of the American Working Class, 1788–1850.* New York: Oxford University Press, 1984.

Wilkinson, David. "David Wilkinson's Reminiscences," *Transactions of the Rhode Island Society for the Encouragement of Domestic Industry* (1861).

Wilkinson, Israel. *Memoirs of the Wilkinson Family in America*. Jacksonville, IL: Davis and Penniman, 1869.

Winthrop, Robert C. "Memoir of Hon. Nathan Appleton," *Proceedings of the Massachusetts Historical Society* (October 1861).

Wisbey, Herbert A. Jr. *Pioneer Prophetess: Jemima Wilkinson, The Publick Universal Friend.* Ithaca: Cornell University Press, 1964.

Woodbury, Robert S. *Studies in the History of Machine Tools*. Cambridge: MIT Press, 1972.

Worthen, William E. "Life and Works of James B. Francis," *Contributions of the Old Residents' Historical Association* 5 (March 1894).

Wright, A. B. "Lowell in 1826," *Contributions of the Old Residents' Historical Association* 4.
Young, Alfred F. "The Mechanics and the Jeffersonians," *Labor History* (Fall 1964).
Zonderman, David A. *Aspirations and Anxieties: New England Workers and the Mechanized Factory System, 1815–1850.* New York: Oxford University Press, 1992.

Index